## THE AUTHOR

ALLAN NEVINS, who recently retired as De Witt Clinton Professor of American History at Columbia University, to join the staff of the Huntington Library at San Marino, California, has written on nearly every aspect of American history, from John C. Frémont to Henry Ford. He is now completing *The Ordeal of the Union,* a comprehensive survey of American history from the Mexican War to Reconstruction. *The War for the Union,* Volume 5 of *The Ordeal of the Union,* covers the first year of the Civil War, and will be published in the fall of 1959.

# JOHN D. ROCKEFELLER

*Allan Nevins*

# JOHN D. ROCKEFELLER

*A ONE-VOLUME ABRIDGEMENT*

*by William Greenleaf*

*OF*

*Study in Power*

CHARLES SCRIBNER'S SONS

*New York*

41030

Printed in the United States of America

SBN 684-10422-9

Library of Congress Catalog Card Number 59-7202

# CONTENTS

# LIST OF ILLUSTRATIONS

*TO MARY RICHARDSON NEVINS*

# JOHN D. ROCKEFELLER

*CHAPTER I*

# VENTURE IN OIL

ALMOST from beginning to end, the career of John D. Rocke-feller was attended by heated controversy. Falling into two parts, the one the organization of a colossal industry, and the other the distribution of an enormous fortune, it aroused violent condemnation and abuse, and equally powerful defense and ad-miration. Yet to a singular degree it was a career dominated by logic and plan. Some of the most famous of American lives are full of the unpredictable, the fortuitous, and the illogical. Not so with Rockefeller. His nature, for all its strength, was simple; his intellect, never clouded by emotion, was direct and analytical; his will, fixed on a few large purposes, was unwavering. With no great personal magnetism or versatility or breadth, he accom-plished two epochal tasks: he set an original pattern in the ef-ficient organization of industry, and an equally original pattern in the efficient superintendence of benefactions. He was not a mere rearranger or manipulator of existing forces; he was a creator of new ideas and systems. By his clarity of thought, keen-ness of foresight, and strength of purpose, he made his life an important part of the nation's history.

It was a long career; it began on July 8, 1839, and closed May 23, 1937. His first distinct recollections were of the rough farm-ing country near the village of Moravia in western New York, where he lived from his fourth to his eleventh year; for in 1843 his father paid $3100 for a ninety-two acre tract in Moravia town-ship. Three children had been born on another small farm thirty miles away, at Richford in Tioga County: Lucy early in 1838, John in 1839, and William Avery Jr. in the spring of 1841. Three other children followed: Mary Ann, born the late summer of

1843, and twins, Frances (who soon died) and Franklin or Frank, in the summer of 1845.

Both parents possessed strong individuality. His mother, Eliza Davison, daughter of a prosperous farmer of Scottish stock who lived in Niles, Cayuga County, was a spirited young woman, slender, red-haired, and blue-eyed. Her education was rudimentary, but she possessed intelligence and strong common sense. She was devoutly religious, straitlaced in matters of conduct, a severe disciplinarian who spared not the rod, and a believer in hard work, thrift, and austerity. Her deep piety and strong will were accompanied by a remarkable serenity, which she transmitted to her son.

William Avery Rockefeller was at every point different. A young man of powerful physique—nearly six feet tall, deep-chested, muscular—he had an abounding energy and a daring adventurousness. He loved gaiety, song, talk, and general sociability; his temperament was jovial, exuberant, and ostentatious. Vibrant with health, full of the joy of life, and supremely self-confident, he took the center of every gathering, and made any circle merrier as soon as he appeared. But he also had stronger —and darker—traits. He did precisely as he pleased; his will brooked no opposition; he lacked moral scruple in certain relationships, and followed his impulses without proper thought of the consequences.

Although he owned farms first at Richford and later at Moravia, William Avery was no tiller of the soil. He was a trader, a businessman, and in a small way an entrepreneur. Thirty-four years old when the family removed to Moravia, he left the farm work chiefly to a hired hand. Legendary material, derived from neighbors, pictures him as sometimes going away on long mysterious trips, from which he returned with handsome horses, a spic-and-span wardrobe, and plenty of money. Perhaps at this time, and certainly at a later date, he peddled patent medicines and herbal remedies.

In July, 1850, he sold his Moravia farm and removed his family to Owego, New York. Here they stayed from the spring of 1850 to the summer of 1853. Then they went west to the vicinity of Cleveland, Ohio, settling first in Strongsville, later (1855), after an interval in the city, in Parma, and then again in Cleveland. The father was still frequently absent from home on his mysterious trips. For a time he advertised himself as "Dr. William A.

Rockefeller the Celebrated Cancer Specialist," selling "cancer treatments" and medicines; when he first appears in the Cleveland directory it is as an "herbal doctor."

John spent his fifteenth and sixteenth years, 1853–55, at the Cleveland high school. He took all his work seriously, giving little time to play. "I was very sedate and earnest, preparing to meet the responsibilities of life," he recalled later. The school failed to give him any considerable fund of general culture, and left his mind completely unawakened in various directions. But it did contribute to the development of his natural thoroughness, and to the habit of clear thinking which he revealed as soon as he entered the world.

Quite as important as school was John's training at home. It might seem commonplace to say that his mother taught all her children piety, neatness, industry, modesty of deportment, and strict avoidance of waste. Actually the rigor and assiduity with which she inculcated these virtues left a distinct imprint on the boy's character. As an old man, Rockefeller could still hear her voice echoing: "Willful waste makes woeful want."

Religion became more and more important in the boy's life. The attendance at church and Sunday School which had begun in Moravia was continued in Owego, where every week the mother and children filed into a pew of the First Baptist Church. In Cleveland John at once began attending the Erie Street Baptist Church. He was taken into full church membership by public baptism in the fall of 1854, and before long was clerk of the Erie Street church.

From an early age, meanwhile, John was taught to develop his innate gift for business. William Avery Rockefeller was as anxious as the mother that the children should grow up self-reliant, industrious, keen-witted, honest, and dependable. He insisted on concentration. He taught John to draw up notes and other simple business papers. Bills and rents were to be paid promptly and exactly; no error in accounts was to be tolerated; every engagement had to be met. The father knew that his sons were going out into a harshly competitive world, still largely governed by the David Harum maxim: "Do unto others as they would do unto you, and do it fust." Himself shrewd and alert, he very likely gave the lads those practical lessons in business wiles of which a Strongsville neighbor later spoke. This neighbor reported one of his boasts: "I trade with the boys and skin 'em

and I just beat 'em every time I can. I want to make 'em sharp."
More important, however, were his lessons in precision, prompt-
ness, and responsibility.

Inasmuch as William intended that his sons should be businessmen, he decidedly negatived the suggestion of a college education for any of them. John went instead to Folsom's Commercial
College, spending three months there in 1855. During this period
he mastered single-entry and double-entry bookkeeping; devoted
some time to "business computation"; and learned the rudiments
of mercantile practice, banking, and exchange. He had received
his high school diploma on July 16, 1855, when he was already
at work in the commercial school, and he finished his business
course in August.

Then he began to ransack Cleveland for a position. With characteristic acumen, he refused to think of a clerkship in any shop,
for he wanted a training that would lead to the establishment of
his own business. "I went to the railroads, to the banks, to the
wholesale merchants," he said later. "I did not go to any small
establishments." Already he had a high if vague ambition. "I
did not guess what it would be, but I was after something big."
The search went on for weeks.

Finally his persistence was rewarded. On September 26, he obtained a place as bookkeeper and clerk in the office of Hewitt &
Tuttle, commission merchants and produce shippers. Early that
afternoon he was shown the high desk where he was to labor, the
ledgers and letter-press, and the blotter on which the day's
transactions were noted. He hung up his coat and went to work.
Not a word was said about salary: "I cared very little about that,"
he has recorded. Later his wage was fixed at $3.50 a week, rising
to $25 a month, then to $500 a year, and then in 1858 to $600.
The best part of his pay came in experience. Feeling that he had
put his foot on the first rung of the business ladder, he was en-
chanted. The place "was delightful to me—all the method and
system of the office."

The little office Rockefeller entered at sixteen, and in which he
remained for three and a half years, was excellent as a business
training-ground. His principal employer, Isaac L. Hewitt (for
Tuttle retired in 1856), was kindly. The firm's activities were
sufficiently diversified to bring the bookkeeper-clerk into relationship with railroads, lake steamships, merchants, jobbers, and
primary producers. "My eyes were opened to the business of

transportation," he tells us, recalling transactions with five rail-roads reaching Cleveland in the fifties. The little city was growing rapidly—it had nearly 44,000 people by 1860; and the firm owned or managed dwellings, warehouses, and office-buildings, on which the youth collected rents. Going over the old books, Rockefeller soon mastered the business as done for years past. He profited from hearing his seniors discuss their problems and policies. After a time he was given responsibility for rather complicated deals.

It was inevitable that so able and ambitious a young man should soon grow discontented with the meagre salary and limited opportunities which Hewitt's office afforded him. In 1858 Rockefeller asked Hewitt for a salary of $800. But the firm offered him only $700, leaving the other hundred for future consideration; and early in 1859 he began looking for larger fields. He was anxious to strike into business for himself. An enterprising young Englishman of the city, Maurice B. Clark, was equally unhappy over his own situation; and the two decided to form a partnership as commission merchants in grain, hay, meats, and miscellaneous goods, each investing $2000. Clark had saved that amount. John had accumulated only about $900, but his father had promised each child $1000 at twenty-one, and John therefore proposed that the "doctor" advance him that sum at once, he paying interest for the sixteen months remaining before he came of age.

The young men took risks, but they had energy, experience, and optimism, while they knew that the hour was favorable. Emigration to the West was rising, production of grain and meats in Ohio, Michigan, and the prairie states was increasing, and eastern demand was strong. Traffic in Middle Western food-stuffs was steadily shifting from the old Mississippi River channel to the east-west lines, and particularly to the Great Lakes and the railroads parallelling them. On March 18, 1859, Clark & Rocke-feller opened their doors at 62 River Street and sent out circulars announcing their readiness to accept consignments. The venture of Clark & Rockefeller prospered. In their first year they did a gross business of about $450,000, on which they made a net profit of $4400. Clark & Rockefeller made the most of the Civil War boom. They dealt in salt, mess pork, breadstuffs, and other commodities needed by the Northern armies, in clover seed and timothy seed, in farm implements and minerals. As most of the

Clark & Rockefeller business was done on commission, their chief risks were in the advances made on consignments of goods, and the ever-rising price level kept these at a minimum.

Rockefeller gave most of his time to office management and to the firm's relations with bankers. He had developed great confidence and enterprise, and was ready to attack a banking house on short notice. But so careful was his management that he riveted the confidence of shippers, buyers, and credit agencies alike. "He was methodical to an extreme," Clark later testified, "careful as to details and exacting to a fraction. If there was a cent due us he wanted it. If there was a cent due a customer he wanted the customer to have it."

Although Rockefeller had sprung from a culturally barren environment and had met his full share of early hardships, he had received a training remarkably adapted to the career he was to follow. True, he was narrow; he knew nothing of art, letters, and science, and cared nothing for them; his passionate interest in business success struck many as purely materialistic. But he would never have made the success he did had he been less single-minded; and though criticism of his excessive materialism is valid, it must be qualified by acknowledgment of two of his strong traits, his interest in constructive achievement and his readiness to share what money he made with others.

Anxious as he had been at seventeen and eighteen to save capital for establishing himself in business, Rockefeller had not failed to give generously to church and charity. The most creditable chapter in the young man's life is that recorded in the pages of his first account book, the "Ledger A" which he began in 1855. Entries from December, 1855, to April, 1856, show that he had received less than $95 for four months' work. Out of this he had paid $1 for pew-rent in the Erie Street Church, a small sum for a religious paper, and $5.88 for various charitable objects. His gifts for the four months just about balanced the sum he spent for clothing, $9.09. This was a remarkable performance: on his meagre income, allowing himself almost nothing for amusements, and skimping on luncheons, he had approached a literal interpretation of the Biblical injunction respecting a tithe of a man's earnings.

And he gave more than money; he gave time and labor. The Erie Street Church was a poor man's conventicle, in a rapidly growing part of town populated mainly by clerks, artisans, and shopkeepers. It had a poor, uncarpeted, ill-lighted auditorium and a badly paid minister. Rockefeller served as clerk to the church, paying the costs for postage and stationery, and after a time as Sunday School teacher. When in 1859, $2000 had to be paid to save the church building, it was Rockefeller who took charge of an arduous but successful campaign to raise the fund. As soon as he was twenty-one he was elected one of the five trustees of the church, and in that capacity acting as auditor of the treasurer's accounts. Next to the minister, he was soon the most important member of the congregation.

As his income rose, so did his gifts; he made extra subscriptions to the church, which in time actually grew rather wealthy. His gifts at an early age were of a strikingly varied nature. In 1857 the recorded total of his donations was $28.37. By this time they included various outside churches, and the Y. M. C. A. In 1858 the recorded total grew to $43.85, and in 1859 to $72.22, which was certainly a full tenth of his income. One item this last year was a gift to help a Cincinnati Negro buy his slave wife. In 1860 his donations aggregated $107.35, and in 1861 they rose sharply to $259.97—again including a grant for the purchase of a slave. During the war, disregarding lines of faith, race, and nationality, he gave to a Catholic orphanage, a colored mute and blind society, an industrial school, and a Swedish mission in Illinois. In 1864 his gifts suddenly swelled to $671.86, and in 1865 went above the thousand-dollar mark. He had not waited to become rich before he became generous.

"Now you are in business—true," he said to himself. "It is an opportunity. But be careful. Pride goeth before a fall. Nothing in haste, nothing ill-done. Your future hangs on every day that passes." This earnest self-counseling was to become a habit. "These intimate conversations with myself," he wrote later, "had a great influence on my life. I was afraid I could not stand my prosperity, and tried to teach myself not to get puffed up with any foolish notions."

Business activities—the development of the resources of the half-explored country, the raising of the standard of life, the establishment of the material basis on which any ideal superstructure must rest—were already America's principal challenge to her young men. They offered the great main arena of endeavor. As energetic young Frenchmen in Froissart's time turned to war, as energetic young Englishmen in Elizabethan days turned to exploration, as energetic young Americans of 1800 turned to pioneering, so now energy and ambition turned to business. It was much more than the road to wealth; it was the field to which the majority of Americans looked for distinction, authority, and self-expression. A whole generation pushed into it partly for money, partly for the satisfaction of successful competitive effort, partly for eminence and power. With the raw country demanding development, with growing multitudes pressing upon its resources for food, clothing, and comfort, with wealth indispensable to create universities, museums, and a higher life, business was the great immediate necessity of the time. The next generation after Lincoln was to produce no great statesmen, few novelists and poets of stature, and but two or three artists of world eminence; but it produced more business genius than any country in the world had yet seen.

By the beginning of 1863 Clark & Rockefeller was a well-established firm, making large profits. Its two members had a substantial amount of capital saved. The firm were ready to consider new ventures. And one fertile field for ventures was at hand. On August 27, 1859, "Colonel" Edwin L. Drake had opened at Titusville, Pennsylvania, the nation's first commercial oil well. An immediate rush to the Oil Regions had ensued; in 1860 the production of Pennsylvania oil had reached an estimated total of 200,000 barrels; petroleum had been shipped into Cleveland in large quantities; and in 1860–62 a number of refineries had sprung up on the Cuyahoga, their scum discoloring the river that flowed past Clark & Rockefeller's door. Inevitably, Clark & Rockefeller had handled consignments of crude oil and kerosene, and inevitably, they had learned how high were the initial profits made in the business.

In 1859 Pennsylvania petroleum was romance, it was excitement, it was opportunity; even staid businessmen surrendered to it as to an enchantress. Rockefeller may or may not have made a trip to the Oil Regions some time before 1862. One fact is certain: everything he heard impressed him with the riskiness and waste of oil-production. Men paid high prices for land that proved barren as Sahara; they opened promising wells only to find the gush dwindling to a trickle; they barreled their crude just as a glut knocked the supports from the market.

It was also evident to Rockefeller that if production was highly speculative, refining offered greater certainties. The difference between crude oil prices in the Regions and refined oil prices in the cities was highly alluring. While petroleum was selling at the wells in the spring of 1862 at 35 to 50 cents a barrel, in seaboard markets refined oil was fetching 25 to 35 cents a gallon. Here obviously lay a glittering opportunity, for costs of refining were low. Some bold pioneers in the refinery business had made almost as much money as the first owners of gushers. In the refining industry, as in producing, capital already counted. Small refineries were likely to be ruined by the terrific unpredictable fluctuations in prices, and the alternations of glut and shortage; large refineries could breast these vicissitudes and make profits.

The petroleum industry, growing by spectacular spurts, was throwing branches far outside the Regions and attaining national scope. In New York the oil-export business was becoming more important every month. Every railroad president whose lines ran near the fields was eager to share in the new traffic; the Atlantic & Great Western, for example, was operating a line to Franklin in July, 1863, and the next month began building an extension to Oil City. Oil refineries went up in Buffalo and Pittsburgh, New York and Philadelphia, Boston and Baltimore. In August, 1863, twenty refineries were busy in or near Cleveland, which that month produced 103,691 gallons of refined oil, nearly one-fourth of it for export. The single Humboldt refinery in the heart of the Oil Regions still exceeded this entire Cleveland production. Nevertheless, the business seemed large to Clevelanders, and shrewd men could see that it would become far larger.

One of the first Cleveland men connected with refining was Samuel Andrews, an Englishman who had come to Cleveland in 1857. His friends Clark and Shurmer procured him a position in a lard-oil refinery owned by another Englishman, C. A. Dean, where he soon became a practical expert in oils, tallows, and candle-making. His employer was interested in new illuminants, and with the help of John Alexander, his foreman (also English), and Andrews, he began to make coal-oil from cannel coal in 1859. A year later, Dean ordered an initial shipment of ten barrels of petroleum, from which he, Alexander, and Andrews made the first oil kerosene in Cleveland. All three, and especially Andrews, foresaw that kerosene from petroleum would quickly supplant derivatives of coal or lard as an illuminant.

By 1862 Andrews was eager to launch into business for himself. He talked with Maurice Clark about an independent refining

business, for he knew that Clark had money; he talked also with
Rockefeller, for he and his wife were Baptists and attended the
Erie Street Church. Clark had two brothers, James and Richard,
who also were eager to engage in some paying business. The
refining firm of Andrews, Clark & Co. was organized in 1863.

A new railroad had suddenly placed Cleveland in a position
to compete with any other refining center. The Atlantic & Great
Western, a broad-gauge line projected long before Drake's discovery, ran its first trains into the city on November 3, 1863. Extending westward from Meadville and Corry, Pennsylvania, the
A. & G. W. gave Cleveland, by connection with the Erie Railroad,
a direct communication with New York City. It assured strong
competition to the New York Central-Lake Shore system when
that should be opened through northern Ohio. It also gave Cleveland a broad-gauge line into the heart of the Oil Regions, for
the Atlantic & Great Western had obtained a branch connection
from Corry to Titusville in the autumn of 1862, and another
from Meadville to Franklin the following summer.

This road at once became the principal oil-carrier of the nation.
In the two years 1863–64 it carried well over one and a half
million barrels of petroleum—evidence of the immense value of
oil freights. Most of this went to New York, but Cleveland had a
goodly share, approximately one-tenth of the whole. Refinery
after refinery sprang up in Cleveland along the Atlantic & Great
Western tracks. They were numerous but small, the owners having
little money, great enterprise, and exuberant hopes.

Andrews, Clark & Company built a refinery on the high south
bank of Kingsbury Run, the still-wooded tributary of the Cuyahoga, about a mile and a half southeast from the public square
of Cleveland. Lying near the point where the Run emptied
into the Cuyahoga, it had water transportation to the Lake, while
it abutted directly on the Atlantic & Great Western. At first they
leased three acres with an option, then bought it. It was one of
the best situations for a refinery in the city—perhaps, in its combination of water and rail facilities, the best. To this tract Rockefeller and his partners added rapidly; by 1870 its buildings and
yards (then in two groups, for another site at the head of the Run
had been acquired) covered sixty acres, and eventually they
spread over about one hundred. Sam Andrews had charge of
technical operations, with Richard Clark assisting him. The
process of refining was then cheap, simple, and clumsy. At this

time a barrel of Pennsylvania petroleum ordinarily yielded 60 or 65 per cent of illuminating oil, 10 per cent gasoline, and 5 to 10 per cent of benzol or naphtha, the remainder being tar and wastes. Five barrels of crude oil thus gave about three barrels of illuminant.

The year 1864 saw nation-shaking battles: Cold Harbor, and Spotsylvania, Farragut at Mobile and Sherman's March to the Sea. The war spirit rose high in the Western Reserve, and every private pursuit was carried on under the shadow of the conflict. Frank Rockefeller had gone to war in 1861. John felt restrained by nearer responsibilities. His commission firm had just got under thriving way, it had a number of employees, and his departure would mean its collapse. "I wanted to go in the army and do my part," he said later. "But it was simply out of the question. There was no one to take my place. We were in a new business, and if I had not stayed it must have stopped—and with so many dependent on it." Then, too, if his father's support of the mother and daughters failed, as it might at any time, John would have to step into the gap. He did contribute to the sending of substitutes, and made gifts to war funds, but assuredly not to the extent he later asserted.

Meanwhile, another interest had entered Rockefeller's life—an interest in Laura Celestia Spelman, an attractive girl of almost his own age. She and her sister Lucy were daughters of Harvey Buel Spelman, a prosperous Cleveland businessman who had been born in Granville, Massachusetts, in 1811, of Puritan stock, and Lucy Henry Spelman, also of Massachusetts birth. Cettie, after leaving high school, had attended Oread School at Worcester, Massachusetts, and had then taught in the Cleveland system. Their sustained acquaintance, according to Rockefeller, began about 1862. Laura Celestia had been twenty-four on September 9, 1863. Her photographs show her a girl of uncommon prettiness, and her friends have testified to her unusual poise and charm. She was a spirited girl, much more vivacious than John, better read and more widely traveled.

The two did not become engaged until March, 1864, and then said little to their friends about it. Both reached the decision to marry only after careful deliberation. Miss Spelman liked teaching and liked independence. Rockefeller had been deeply engrossed in his two businesses. But if both acted deliberately, they showed no lack of deep and happy feeling. All of Rockefeller's emotional relations were intensive rather than expansive, and this was the most intense of his life.

The marriage ceremony was performed in the Spelman residence at 58 Huron Street on September 8, 1864. The couple took a wedding trip to Niagara Falls, Montreal, and Quebec, and down through New England to New York City. Returning to Cleveland, they boarded for a time with Rockefeller's parents, and then moved into a house next door at 29 Cheshire Street.

By 1867 the William Avery Rockefeller family had struck firm roots into the soil of Cleveland and was expanding in numbers. William, just a month and a half before John's wedding, was married in Fairfield, Connecticut, to Almira Geraldine Goodsell —called "Mira"—who gave birth to their first son in 1865. John's first child, named Elizabeth and always called Bessie, was born August 23, 1866. Frank had come back from the war, attended business school, and in 1866–67 found employment as a bookkeeper. He and Mary Ann still lived with their mother at 33 Cheshire Street, but Frank was to marry Helen Scofield in the fall of 1870, and Mary Ann to marry William C. Rudd two years later. "Doctor" Rockefeller returned regularly, as in earlier years, from his long trips afield. John had already become the real head of the family.

The life of John and Laura Rockefeller, in the years just after their marriage, was busy and happy. Mrs. Rockefeller gave up her Congregational church and became a Baptist. Their social contacts were therefore chiefly with members of the Erie Street congregation. As president of the board of trustees, superintendent of the Sunday school, and principal donor, Rockefeller was becoming almost as influential in the affairs of the church as the minister himself.

In 1865, as we have noted, Rockefeller's gifts went above a thousand; they were $1012.35, to be exact. Then in 1866 he gave a total of $1320.43. In 1867, evidently a poor business year, the sum fell to $660.14; but in 1868 by way of amends he gave a total of $3675.39; and in 1869, doing still better, a total of $5489.62. Once more, we may emphasize the fact that he had not waited to grow rich before he began giving. It is to be noted that save for one year, his gifts constantly grew larger, and that by the later sixties he was giving some considerable lump sums—$558.42 to Denison University, for example. In his early giving, as later in life, he freely crossed lines of creed, nationality, and color.

His two companies both thrived and both had golden prospects. In the refining company, however, friction gradually appeared in the management. Rockefeller did not get on well with Maurice Clark's two brothers, who opposed rapid expansion. Even with the able, likable Maurice he had moments of difficulty, for his talents were not properly appreciated by the older man. It is evident that his force of intellect and character had made him by 1863 the dominant partner in the commission firm. In the oil company, however, the three Clarks now threatened to be too much for him. Even when Andrews, a steady, hard-headed young man, stood by him, the two were outvoted. As the tension grew Maurice sided with his brothers, while Andrews, who knew the value of Rockefeller's combination of vision in planning and precision in management, gave support to his masterful young associate.

Although at the outset the refinery had been a side venture, within a year it was the commission business which occupied the side track. Rockefeller soon fell under the fascination of the oil refining business. His quick insight saw that with proper capital and care it offered far richer possibilities than the produce commission business; that it was in a formative state and hence responsive to leadership; and that the future belonged not to the early plungers, but to men of energy, resourcefulness, and caution.

All refiners, groping in a new field and lacking expert techniques, were then wasteful in method and uncertain in result. Rockefeller abhorred waste, and believed that one secret of success was attention to details. He proposed to Andrews: "Let us hire a plumber by the month. Let's also buy our own pipes, joints, and other plumbing material." They saved at least half of their plumbing costs. Barrels soon became an urgent problem. Coopers charged excessive prices and made irregular deliveries. In 1864 Andrews, Clark & Co. built their own cooperage shop, in which they installed newly patented machinery; with the result that they were soon making excellent white-oak barrels, well-glued and painted blue, for ninety-six cents each. Rockefeller sometimes came to the shop at half-past six in the morning, and could be seen there, when help was needed, rolling barrels, piling hoops, or wheeling out shavings. The company soon bought tracts of white-oak timber. Instead of transporting the heavy green timber to the cooperage shop, as most manufacturers did, they dried it in kilns on the tract, and by carrying nothing but dried wood, saved materially on the cost of haulage. In a short time they acquired their own teams and wagons for hauling, a step which also reduced costs.

Meanwhile Andrews, with Rockefeller's encouragement, was making constant experiments in improving the refinery methods and utilizing by-products. Profits remained high. Later Rockefeller always emphasized the fact that this was an era of rich returns preceding an era of overcompetition and depression. Little by little Andrews, Clark & Co. gained a place among the largest Cleveland refiners. Meanwhile, by the end of the war Cleveland was outstripping Erie and the Oil Regions towns as a refining center and becoming a close second to Pittsburgh.

Finally the friction between Rockefeller and the Clarks became unendurable. The situation reached a crisis late one afternoon in January, 1865, when Rockefeller brought Maurice Clark some papers to sign and found him in a belligerent mood. Grumbling when he saw another note, Clark put down his name reluctantly.

"We have been asking too many loans in order to extend this oil business," he said. "And the commission business, too. Why, altogether we have borrowed a hundred thousand dollars."

Rockefeller defended his policy. "We should borrow whenever we can safely extend the business by doing so," he asserted. They discussed the matter, and finally Clark threatened a dissolution of the firm. But Rockefeller was undaunted; he knew that he had the support of Sam Andrews.

In conference with Andrews, Rockefeller arrived at a decision: he would accept the next offer of a dissolution, buy out the Clarks, and run the refinery to suit himself. Within a few weeks the partners again disagreed, and the Clarks once more threatened dissolution. At once, on February 2, 1865, he placed a dissolution notice in the Cleveland *Leader*. This took the Clarks aback. But the five partners held a formal meeting, the Clarks bringing a lawyer along; they agreed that the business should be sold to the highest bidder in the firm; and when somebody suggested that the auction be held forthwith, they all agreed. The lawyer served as auctioneer, and Maurice Clark, representing the brothers, bid against Rockefeller, representing himself and Andrews.

Maurice Clark began the bidding at $500, which Rockefeller raised to $1000. The price crept up to thirty thousand; to forty, fifty, and then to sixty thousand. Gradually, with neither side willing to yield, it reached $70,000.

"Seventy-two thousand," said Maurice Clark, desperately.

"Seventy-two thousand five hundred," replied the unhesitating Rockefeller.

Clark threw up his hands with the exclamation: "The business is yours!"

The first struggle was over; at twenty-six, Rockefeller was master of his own manufactory. A heavier struggle lay just ahead—to most business observers, oil then seemed a constant gamble. But he drew confidence from the knowledge that the prosperity the refinery had thus far attained was mainly his own work. Maurice Clark had arrogated to himself most of the credit for their progress, and Rockefeller knew that this was unjust.

All this was now past. In the Cleveland *Leader* for February 15 he inserted the following:

COPARTNERSHIP NOTICE.—The undersigned, having purchased the entire interest of Andrews, Clark & Co. in the "Excelsior Oil Works," and all stock of barrels, oil, etc., will continue the business of the late firm under the name of Rockefeller & Andrews.

John D. Rockefeller
Samuel Andrews

The same issue carried an advertisement by Rockefeller & Andrews of carbon oil, benzene, and lubricating oils. On March 2, 1865, a dissolution notice of Clark & Rockefeller, the grain commission firm, followed: "J. D. Rockefeller retiring." The young man was free from the restraint of plodding associates who lacked his penetration and resourcefulness.

"I ever point to the day when I separated myself from them," he declared in retrospect, "as the beginning of the success I have made in my life."

At first glance it seems astonishing that for the Clarks' share in a three-year-old refining company, Rockefeller should give not only his half of the grain commission business, but $72,500 in cash, a sum that in 1865 represented a substantial fortune. But actually there is nothing strange in this. The refinery was already the largest in Cleveland, and one of the largest in the world. By January 1, 1866, the Rockefeller & Andrews works had a capacity of 505 barrels a day, or more than twice that of any Cleveland competitor.

It is clear that Rockefeller took over the refinery because he had determined upon a swift and tremendous expansion, and was tired of the doubts and resistance of the Clarks. He turned back into the business nearly all its large profits. He borrowed as heavily as he could. He took decisive steps to strengthen all his departments. A tremendous confidence in the future of the Cleveland industry possessed him. Since Rockefeller did nothing without careful planning, the speed with which he enlarged his business indicates that he had mapped his course before he outbid the Clarks. He and Andrews retained the name of the Excelsior Oil Works, and the old employees and equipment. But he quietly took over Maurice Clark's share in the general business management, assuming charge of all selling and some of the buying.

Rockefeller also brought his own brother William into partnership, the two organizing William Rockefeller & Co. to build a second refinery, the Standard Works, at the head of Kingsbury Run. This was a firm, not a joint-stock corporation: "William was the head and Andrews and I were the company," said Rockefeller later. Before the end of 1866 another firm, Rockefeller & Co., was incorporated in New York to manage the export sale of oil. It had no president, consisted of the two Rockefellers and Andrews, and opened modest offices at 181 Pearl Street. The Cleveland offices of Rockefeller & Andrews were on the second floor of the new Sexton Block on the banks of the Cuyahoga.

The Cleveland *Leader* supplies us with a good account of the two refineries soon after Rockefeller took full command. It states that during September, October, and November, 1865, they had produced more than 375,000 gallons of "burning fluid" and nearly 10,000 gallons of "benzole." They stood on the bluff at Pittsburgh Street, near the tracks of the Atlantic & Great Western, which ran a spur to their doors:

The warehouse for crude, forty-five by eight-four feet, has doors for the unloading of eight cars now, and will be made to accommodate fifteen or sixteen when the switch is extended. There are two loaded warehouses on the premises—capable of holding about 6000 barrels— each about fifty by one hundred feet. The tankage for refined oil holds about 1500 barrels, for benzole 350 barrels, for crude oil 6700 barrels.

In the stillhouse there are ten boilers of various sizes, the daily capacity of which is 175 barrels. There is one agitator, holding from 130 to 140 barrels.

This refinery was established in 1863, and employs thirty-seven hands, at wages ranging from $45 to $58 per month. The capital invested in the business is in the neighborhood of $200,000. . . .

Directly on the other side, opposite the railroad track, is the new refinery of the above firm [William Rockefeller & Co.], which is made up in part from the firm of Rockefeller & Andrews—William Rockefeller, Esq., being of the late firm of Hughes, Davis, & Rockefeller. These works commenced running on the first of December last, and are now running only on half time, in consequence of the difficulty, at this season of the year, in procuring a sufficient and steady supply of crude oil. The establishment is not entirely completed. Tanks and a bonded warehouse will be built in the spring.

The stills are ten in number, of thirty barrels each, all new. The agitator holds 134 barrels. Capacity of the refinery, 330 barrels [a day].

Rockefeller now had two partners whose tastes and abilities he completely trusted. Andrews was the best superintending refiner in Cleveland; William Rockefeller soon proved one of the ablest export managers in America. No small part of Rockefeller's business genius consisted in the power to select gifted associates. The speculative boom which began in oil-producing in 1864 and continued through 1866 had spread to oil-refining, and there endured in 1867. Well owners could pay all expenses and make profits of $3 to $7 a barrel. Many of them rolled in wealth. Men were feverishly boring fresh wells in old areas, and prospecting and "wildcatting" new fields. Investors rushed to pour more money into speculative enterprises. Drilling rapidly extended up various "runs" emptying into Oil Creek and the Allegheny River, previously untouched but now worth exploration. In the summer of 1864 oil was struck in munificent quantities along Cherry Run, producing a quick new crop of millionaires, and in the first days of 1865 some diggers brought in a copious well on Pithole Creek. Great new rushes were the result, and the Federal Revenue Commission estimated in 1866 that more than $100,000,000 had been applied to the purchase and development of oil lands.

Methods of production had improved by 1866. Derricks were nearly twice as high as when the first wells were sunk around Colonel Drake's shaft. The drilling machinery was much larger and heavier. Improved appliances pumped out the water and pulverized rock from the drill hole more rapidly, and a greater depth could be reached more easily. The torpedo, patented by Colonel E. A. L. Roberts, became an indispensable part of well equipment. Transportation had also been strikingly improved. At first teamsters dominated the situation. In rainy periods their wheels churned the roads into bottomless swamps, and as water pumped from the oil wells swelled the downpour from the skies, the sloughs turned into veritable creeks.

The constant losses and delays made men take the obvious step required to meet the situation. In midwinter the creeks and rivers were choked with ice, in midsummer they were often too low for navigation; and then the teamsters, waxing arrogant, charged exorbitant sums. As early as March, 1863, the *Scientific American* suggested laying a pipe along Oil Creek so that the petroleum might flow underground like Croton water. The first pipe of any length, laid in 1863 from the Tarr Farm on Oil Creek to the Humboldt Refinery on Cherry Run, was only a partial success, for the oil had to be driven by steam power four hundred feet above the creek and no good pump was available. But it demonstrated what might be done, and the following year Henry Harley projected a longer line. In the spring of 1866 he put into operation two pipe lines, with a daily capacity of 1500 to 2000 barrels each, from Bennehoff Run to Shaffer on the Oil Creek Railroad.

Even earlier, in the summer of 1865, an oil buyer named Samuel Van Syckel ran a two-inch pipe, partly above ground and partly buried below ploughshare depth, from Pithole to Miller Farm on the Oil Creek Railroad. Two pumping stations swiftly carried the oil a distance of nearly five miles. A firm organized by Harley and W. H. Abbott soon took over the Van Syckel pipe, whose backers had fallen into financial difficulties, combined it with others, and formed the Allegheny Transportation Company, the first great pipe-line corporation. Various other enterprising individuals and firms entered the new field. By 1867 the lines were on the highroad to dominance of all transportation between oil well and railheads. The network of pipe lines cobwebbed the whole oil-producing district, tapping almost every well and converting a thousand streamlets of oil into a few great rivers and lakes of petroleum. The earliest pipe-line companies were merely common carriers and made no provision for storing oil, but as the boom increased, the production companies organized storage facilities with nests of tanks holding from five to twenty thousand barrels in a single place.

During these boom years Oildom seemed half a region of gilded romance, half of violent melodrama. "Almost everybody you meet," wrote the novelist J. T. Trowbridge in 1869, "has been suddenly enriched or suddenly ruined (perhaps both within a short space of time), or knows plenty of people who have." Yet even in the boom period the area of order was increasing. Trowbridge heard on every side "that the day of extravagant speculation is over; that the thing has settled down into something like a regular business. . . ."

It was inevitable that the boom in production should be accompanied by a boom in refining. The same factors of rising world demand, advancing gold values, and increased confidence in the future of the industry were at work. The speed with which the market for oil expanded astonished everybody. A commodity that had been a curiosity when Lincoln was nominated had become a necessity of civilization, the staple of a vast commerce, before he was murdered. The new industry had appeared when it was of peculiar economic value to the nation; when the Civil War swung the balance of trade against the United States, when gold was being exported, and when all the resources of the country were under a heavy strain. Oil exports quickly became a lucrative American resource. Nor was this all, for internal activity as well as foreign trade was benefited. Railways had a large new traffic, capital a rich field for investment, and labor an area in which it earned more than ordinary wages. Profits for the early comers were large. Men could double their capital in two years, sometimes in one.

It is not strange that the number of Cleveland refineries leaped to fifty by the end of 1866. As the plants grew in number they became more fiercely competitive. Many of them were tiny establishments. It required no prophet to foresee that the weaker firms would soon find the competitive pace too hot. Strong establishments like Rockefeller's two plants, Hussey, McBride & Company, and Alexander, Scofield would leave the rest behind to be devoured by the wolves of bankruptcy. So long as the boom lasted all was well—but how long would it last?

The sun of high prices brought out an equally lush growth of tender shoots in other cities. Western Long Island had an increasing number of refineries. Refineries had sprung up in Boston, New Haven, Jersey City, Baltimore, Buffalo, and Erie. The Regions, of course, contained many; William Wright, who carefully inspected them in the spring of 1865, found about thirty, and numerous others were soon added. The Downer works, covering half a dozen acres, employing nearly two hundred men, and capable of producing 1800 barrels a week, and the great Humboldt Refinery, were soon to have formidable peers.

Overproduction, overproduction!—this was to be the curse of both the well-owners and refiners for years to come. Among refiners one basic cause of overproduction was the smallness of the capital required to set up a plant. Most Americans later thought of the industry as involving heavy investments. But essentially the process was merely one of cooking combined with purification by a few chemicals; some vats, stills, and pipes sufficed. Any man with $10,000 could establish a small refinery, any one with $50,000 a large one. The bait in this boom period of rapid price fluctuations was the fact that a single lucky turn might double the capital of a small adventurer. This drew men by dozens into the business.

Already the refineries of the United States were falling into distinct groups, and regional rivalry accentuated the fierce competition of individual firms. The seaboard establishments of New York, Philadelphia, and Baltimore felt a powerful group interest; so did the Oil Regions refineries; so did the Pittsburgh refineries; and so did the Cleveland refineries. No economic reason existed for centralizing the industry at one point. With the requisite capital, skill, and care, a refinery could be run profitably at any place furnishing cheap fuel, cheap transportation, and a market. But reasons did exist why one district, the Cleveland area, was destined to draw ahead of the three main competitive groups and within a decade establish its primacy.

At the outset, the Oil Regions refineries had seemed to hold a clear advantage. Adjacent to the wells, they saved large sums upon transport of the crude oil, though this was partly offset by the high freights on machinery, coal, and chemicals from outside, and by the difficulties which many encountered in getting their refined oil to river or railroad. The owners could take immediate advantage of every turn of the market in purchasing crude oil. But they faced two tremendous handicaps. For one, costs of real estate, fuel, labor, and other necessities were half again as high, sometimes twice as high, as at other points. Until the oil boom ended and a more orderly regime obtained, these costs would continue exorbitant. For another, the centers of production in the Region shifted rapidly and unpredictably, tending to strand various refineries.

By 1865, Pittsburgh appeared to many the best point for refining and already boasted of receiving half of all the crude oil produced. Yet though few men saw it in 1866, Cleveland was not only a formidable competitor of the Regions and Pittsburgh, but possessed weapons that were destined to prove decisive. So far were some Clevelanders from seeing this that in the middle sixties they actually established refineries in the Regions. But Cleveland had more abundant labor and capital than Pittsburgh, for it was a larger, faster-growing city; it had cheap Mahoning Valley coal; being within one hundred and fifty miles of the first oil fields, it was less handicapped in obtaining crude-oil supplies than Philadelphia and New York. It was closer to the rich western market for refined oil than Pittsburgh. Cleveland soon had two trunk-line railroads and the Erie Canal, while Pittsburgh was left at the mercy of the grasping Pennsylvania Railroad. On this fact above all others turned the fate of the oil empire.

All too soon the great oil boom gave way to depression. Sheer overproduction resulted in 1866–67 in a calamitous price fall for crude oil. Hundreds of small wells were shut down, and drilling stopped on thousands more. Perhaps the word depression is misleading, and it would be more accurate to say that the Oil Regions were half-boom and half-broke. In some areas immense new floods of oil were pouring forth. Over other districts brooded a midnight gloom.

The depression swiftly spread to the refining industry. Small establishments, inefficiently managed, winked out all over the country. Rockefeller, ceaselessly busy, radiating vitality as he managed two great refineries with abundant resources and every appliance for economy, had more reason for confidence than most men. But even he was worried.

# CHAPTER II

# THE BIRTH OF STANDARD
# OIL

L ATE in 1865 or early in 1866 Rockefeller rented desk space
in his office on the second floor of the Sexton Building to a
commission merchant recently come to Cleveland. This was
Henry M. Flagler, who though only in his middle thirties already
possessed a world of practical business experience. The presence
of the dynamic Flagler quickened the pace of life in the quiet
offices of Rockefeller & Andrews. His enthusiasm for new ideas
contrasted with the thoughtful and deliberate ways of Rockefeller. In their diverse talents the two men complemented each
other; and in little more than a year they had formed one of the
notable alliances of American industrial history.

Flagler was no stranger to Rockefeller. As a thriving grain
merchant in Bellevue, Ohio, he had dealt during the war years
with Clark & Rockefeller. And they had other ties, for like
Rockefeller, Flagler had begun life in western New York (he
was born at Hopewell, near Canandaigua, on January 2, 1830),
had early been thrown upon his own resources, and had taken
rapid strides in business. In 1853 he married Mary Harkness,
niece of Stephen V. Harkness, a leading citizen of Bellevue.

Flagler had entered Rockefeller's orbit at a time when the
latter was seeking by every available means to enlarge his already
impressive business. In this undertaking the Cleveland banks
were willing to help him. Still, all the money that Rockefeller
could get from Cleveland banks, or from profits, was not
enough to develop his enterprises at a rate which satisfied him.
Where could he find money to speed the process of expansion?

Flagler had some, and his wife's uncle, Stephen Harkness, a great deal more. And what an asset Flagler would be as one of the company executives; what imagination he could bring to the problems of the firm! Little persuasion was needed to show Flagler that oil offered possibilities superior to those presented by grain or barrels. "Full of vim and push," as Rockefeller said later, he was soon able to convert his wife's uncle. A larger organization was planned, and in 1867 Rockefeller & Andrews became Rockefeller, Andrews & Flagler.

We do not know how much money Flagler brought into the new company. He probably did not possess more than $50,000. Harkness himself, while remaining a silent partner, put in from $60,000 to $90,000. But Flagler's money was not so important to the new firm as his abilities. Two ingenious, uninhibited minds pooling their imagination and energy can often do more than twice what either could accomplish alone; and this fact was to be abundantly illustrated by the partnership of Rockefeller and Flagler.

Rockefeller's association with Flagler, never quite to be paralleled with any other colleague, at once brought results. The new capital was poured into plant expansion. As additional refining facilities were provided in Cleveland, as tank cars were built for hauling oil, and as new depots were erected in the Oil Regions, Rockefeller, Andrews & Flagler became not only the strongest of Cleveland refiners, but also the strongest in the country and therefore in the world. From a production of about 500 barrels of refined oil a day in 1867, they leaped in 1869, according to Rockefeller and others, to 1500.

As an experienced shipper, Flagler knew many railway officials; and one of the first tasks which he undertook as a partner was the negotiation of lower freight rates on crude oil supplies. These rates were vitally important because, varying from railroad to railroad and from shipper to shipper, they could give the refiners who paid the lowest charges a decisive advantage over their rivals. By enlarging his company, Rockefeller had not only made possible economies in purchasing, manufacturing, and marketing; he had also laid a basis for obtaining the cheapest possible transportation.

When Flagler set out to negotiate lower rates, the moment was distinctly favorable. Three important railroads had taken steps to throw tracks into the Oil Regions, untouched by any line when Drake sank his first well. For a time the Atlantic & Great Western had enjoyed a practical monopoly.

Then the Pennsylvania Railroad entered the field. It controlled the Allegheny Valley Railroad, while it dominated another road in the northern part of the state, the Philadelphia & Erie, which by a tributary line shortly traversed the entire "valley of petroleum" from Corry on the north down through Titusville to Franklin. We may date the termination of the heavy advantage of the Atlantic & Great Western from the summer of 1866, when the completion of a small Regions line, the Warren & Franklin, to Oleopolis, permitted oil to flow in heavy volume over the Philadelphia & Erie to the seaboard.

Meanwhile, the Lake Shore Railroad had become interested in a short line which was being built from Jamestown, Pennsylvania, to Franklin and which was completed in 1867. The Lake Shore's lease of this road gave it a direct entrance into the Oil Regions and made it also an aggressive competitor.

Even by the summer of 1866 trunk-line competition for the rich oil traffic had become spirited, and the battle for its control had attracted national attention. The Atlantic & Great Western was forced to begin sharp rate-cutting. Its program of drastic reductions brought the average charge per ton on its line from $4.70 in 1865 to $2.87 in 1866, resulting (despite a marked expansion of traffic) in a severe decline in earnings. Again in 1867 the Pennsylvania-controlled Philadelphia & Erie and the Atlantic & Great Western renewed their competitive rate-cuts, until charges on crude oil fell to unprecedented levels. To swell the oil traffic on the Philadelphia & Erie, the Pennsylvania had helped organize in 1865 a fast-freight line called the Empire Transportation Company.

The Pennsylvania, already a powerful system, was presided over by J. Edgar Thomson, a shrewd organizer at whose right hand stood the brilliant vice-president, Thomas A. Scott, who had made so able a record as Assistant-Secretary of War under Lincoln. The New York Central was in the hands of Cornelius Vanderbilt, the dominant railway genius of the country, who had just completely integrated the lines connecting New York City and Buffalo. He looked forward to complete annexation of the Lake Shore, more than five hundred miles in length, as part of a through road from the Atlantic to Chicago. The early months of 1868 witnessed the spectacularly shocking "Erie War" between Vanderbilt and the Daniel Drew-Jay Gould forces for control of the Erie Railroad. Its upshot was that Vanderbilt and Drew quit the field, leaving the Erie in the hands of the unscrupulous Gould and the clownish "Jim" Fisk; and in the fall Gould was elected president. Within a few months he leased the Atlantic & Great Western as part of his trunk line, which thus reached Cleveland in January, 1869. The struggle first of two and then of three great systems over the rich quarry of the oil trade created a situation in which Cleveland refiners, including Rockefeller's firm, could reach out for high stakes in the industry.

Flagler in 1867 went first to the vice-president and general manager of the Lake Shore, General James H. Devereux, a young veteran of the recent war. The railroad was just entering the arena as a crude oil carrier; its heads were anxious to take a large share of the business away from the Atlantic & Great Western. Devereux and Flagler quickly reached an agreement. Crude oil had been carried from the Regions to Cleveland at a cent a gallon or 42 cents a barrel.

Though no record exists of the rebate given Rockefeller, Andrews & Flagler, it was apparently at least fifteen cents a barrel. The Atlantic & Great Western no doubt matched the Lake Shore's offer. Rockefeller records that from this time the two railroads, with the Erie and New York Central behind them, "regarded us as their allies in the freight competition." That is, they were allied with Rockefeller's firm against the Pennsylvania.

But what of the ethics of this special advantage which Rockefeller's firm had gained? How widespread was rebating, and how did businessmen of the time regard it? As all authorities on railroading agree, in the ceaseless business battle the grant of rebates and drawbacks to shippers for diverting traffic from one railroad to another had been employed for many years before 1867–68.* In fact, they had been almost universally employed. Tom Scott, vice-president of the Pennsylvania, testified in the fall of 1867 that his road had until recently allowed drawbacks, and that "a great many of its competitors" had done the same. American businessmen by tens of thousands sought rebates or special rates eagerly, and in the main took them without any sense of im-

---

* Rebating by the anthracite railroads of Pennsylvania had begun at least as early as 1856.

propriety. Rebating was a child of the intense railroad competition of the period, and was destined to continue flourishing until the Elkins Act of 1903, effectively enforced by President Theodore Roosevelt, extirpated it.

As railroads grew in length, rebates increased in importance. In 1869 the New York Central, gaining full control of the Lake Shore, furnished through service to Chicago; in the same year the Pennsylvania acquired the Pittsburgh, Fort Wayne & Chicago, thus offering parallel facilities; the Erie had already reached St. Louis through the Atlantic & Great Western and other connections; and the Baltimore & Ohio was extended to Chicago in 1874. The building up of these great competitive systems lifted rebating from a relatively local to a national status. Its effect upon business became nationwide and revolutionary; and in no field was it to be more revolutionary than in oil.

John D. Rockefeller always intimated that the competitive advantage his company obtained through rebates was negligible. Indeed, Rockefeller repeatedly expressed the belief that small shippers—taking the situation over long periods—obtained as good rebates as any; and that considering the advantages which the large manufacturers offered the roads, "the favored shippers were the small shippers." This was unfounded. What we know of the years 1867–70 indicates that Rockefeller, Andrews & Flagler vigorously pushed their opportunities for preferential treatments, and that they secured better rebates than many of their Cleveland competitors for the simple reason that they could bargain with greater power.

But they did have other sources of strength. Rockefeller could justly assert later that his partners and he were better organizers, administrators, and technicians than the other Cleveland refiners. They had ampler and better-planned facilities, commanded greater capital, and operated with more energy and precision than any other refinery in existence. With larger resources and production came increasing opportunities for economy, and increasing progress in efficiency.

The cooperage plant had developed in step with the company's growth. In 1867 or 1868 Rockefeller and his partners first began buying tracts of white-oak timber and seasoning part of their own staves. They bought their own hoop-iron, and installed machines for barrel-making. They thus cut the cost of the finished barrel from the $2.50–$3.50 rate usually charged to about half those figures; and the barrels, strongly hooped, tightly glued, and painted blue, were exceptionally good. They manufactured their own sulphuric acid, and devised means for recovering it after use. The refineries by 1868 possessed a complete drayage service—twenty wagons which did the hauling cheaply, and which in slack periods were even hired out to competitors. They had their own warehouses in New York and their own lighters on the Hudson and East Rivers. They were among the first to ship by tank cars and in this economical form of shipment kept ahead of other companies; in 1869 they owned 78 cars. They had facilities for storing both crude and refined oil in tanks, whereas small firms had to use barrels.

Month by month Rockefeller, Andrews & Flagler increased their profits from by-products of petroleum. The mere volume of oil which they now handled gave them a tremendous advantage in this field. A small company would have negligible amounts of by-product material, too trifling for use. Rockefeller's refineries, on the other hand, had ample quantities for manufacture or sale. They also commanded the trained workmen, the expensive equipment, and the marketing arrangements requisite to make a profit from the residual matter left after distilling kerosene, while small companies did not. Rockefeller, Andrews & Flagler never threw away gasoline, or anything else. They employed some of the residuum for fuel, and at a later date also for paving. They manufacted benzene, paraffin, and petrolatum (later called vaseline). They shipped naphtha to gas-plants and other consumers. They doubtless sold lubricating oil in 1867–68, for Rockefeller & Andrews had advertised some in 1865.

All this belonged to Rockefeller's policy of ceaseless enterprise, vigilance, and economy. He imposed his own precision and foresight upon his lieutenants and workmen. Several years later, when the Standard was buying out other firms, some competitors were amazed and wryly amused by the thoroughness of its methods. They found that nothing was guessed at, nothing left uncounted or unmeasured. The precision was a ritual, important in itself as well as in relation to profit and loss, just as discipline is a ritual in any superb army, fostered for itself as well as for winning battles. As yet most conservative manufacturers regarded refining as precarious, and many declared flatly that it had no future. Rockefeller was proving that system, method, and enterprise could divest it of speculative elements.

Nevertheless, the rebates were indispensable. In smooth times they added to profits. In periods of crisis they could be used against competitors, as we shall see, with absolutely crushing effect. It was the union of rebates with the advantages of economy, system, and foresight which explains the swift rise of Rockefeller's organization. Equally important was the judicious purchasing of crude oil, for a manufacturer could easily ruin himself by rash buying. No single element can be ignored.

It was Flagler who, next to Rockefeller, counted for most in Cleveland. Samuel Andrews, ruddy, portly, and genial, looking more and more like the John Bull he was, attended exclusively to the technical work. But Flagler and Rockefeller, lunching at the Union Club together, walking home together at night, agreed on every policy. That they labored so harmoniously can be explained by the fact that Flagler was always constructive. "His courage in acting up to his beliefs," wrote Rockefeller, "laid strong foundations for later years."

Steady progress in the petroleum industry, so new, so violently competitive, so heavily affected by crude-oil supply, changes in market-demand, and the caprice of railroads, demanded youthful optimism and courage. Rockefeller, Andrews & Flagler never lacked daring. As 1870 opened, they were about to undertake the most momentous step that Rockefeller had thus far made.

Rockefeller, now a part of the oil industry for seven years, had become increasingly prosperous. Few refiners had been so fortunate, and many had gone bankrupt. Producers, too, had suffered. The historian of the Oil Regions calls this period 1868–1873 "the years of depression," and they were just that for most oil men down to the panic of the latter year.

On February 1, 1869, a meeting of troubled well-owners at Oil City appointed an organizing committee, and twelve days later the Petroleum Producers' Association of Pennsylvania was born. Just what it could do was uncertain. It attacked a proposal for placing a state tax on crude oil, collected statistics, and conducted patent litigation. However, it did not dare face the real cause of depression—too many wells.

Refiners had been suffering from the depression even more than the producers. With the growth of the industry the margin in price between crude oil and refined steadily shrunk. The refiner thus found himself squeezed more and more tightly between costs and selling price. Large companies like Rockefeller's, able to effect many economies, operated more easily within the narrowing differential than the smaller, less competent firms. Yet even Rockefeller, Andrews & Flagler seem to have been worried. A further cause for worry to all refining firms lay in the immense growth of plant facilities as compared with actual market needs. In 1870 capacity was estimated at three times as much as the existing demand warranted.

For a few years after Drake's strike, the Oil Regions had seemed the best situation for refiners; then Pittsburgh had for a time taken first place. But in 1869 Cleveland slowly drew abreast, and at the end of that year took the lead. One of the chief reasons for Pittsburgh's loss of ground lay in the outright unfairness of the Pennsylvania Railroad to the city. While the Lake Shore and the Atlantic & Great Western were vying with each other to serve Cleveland refiners, Pittsburgh found herself standing still as her chief rival caught up and passed her. The Pennsylvania had the city at its mercy, and seemed to be completely indifferent to its welfare.

The struggle of the refining centers for preëminence had undoubtedly encouraged the growth of mushroom plants. By the end of 1869 some of the reckless ventures had failed, but many others were still complicating a difficult situation. The prospect was grim; only the big refineries could hope to make money, and they were troubled by the almost chaotic state of the industry. Great and frequent fluctuations took place in the price of crude. There was too much refining capacity. There were too many incompetent and desperate refiners, clinging to their fly-by-night plants, making low-grade oil, and recklessly slashing prices to make a market for their product.

The reputation of Rockefeller, Andrews & Flagler was high. Many business observers, confident that well-conducted ventures in oil refining would pay handsomely, liked the way in which the firm had ridden out the squalls that had wrecked some competitors. Not a few potential investors looked with longing eyes at the company. Two such men were Benjamin Brewster and O. B. Jennings of New York.

"These men had money," said Rockefeller later, "and we soon found ourselves able to raise a million dollars as more money was needed." However, the chief partners did not wish to welcome newcomers in a haphazard fashion, perhaps thereby jeopardizing their control of the company. They resolved to replace the firm of Rockefeller, Andrews & Flagler with a joint stock corporation. By this time the joint-stock corporation was as indispensable in manufacturing as in banking and transportation, though in many communities it was still an object of suspicion. Opponents of the device asserted that it gave a few men control of such large bodies of capital that it represented a long step toward monopoly. A more reasonable accusation was that corporation directors, representing numerous stockholders, were less conscientious in using their capital and more unsympathetic to labor than the old-fashioned firms of a few members. Meanwhile, the oil-producing industry, like western mining, was honeycombed with a special kind of corporate dishonesty—the fly-by-night companies selling vast quantities of worthless stock to gullible people.

But the corporation which Rockefeller and Flagler planned late in 1869, however fiercely it was to be assailed in the future as a grasping monopoly, was never once charged with unfairness toward investors. The small group which controlled it, and in which Rockfeller was always leader, acted resolutely for the benefit of the stockholders. This group did not intend to sell shares to the general public, or to employ the stock-manipulating methods of Jay Gould or the stock-watering devices of the elder Morgan. They intended to facilitate the entrance of new capital as desired, and at the same time maintain efficient control under the two Rockefellers and Flagler.

Incorporation took place January 10, 1870. On that day the five men—John and William Rockefeller, Flagler, Andrews, and Harkness—associated themselves under the laws of Ohio "for the purpose of forming a body corporate for manufacturing Petroleum and dealing in Petroleum and its products under the corporate name of The Standard Oil Company."

The stock consisted of 10,000 shares of $100 par value, the total capitalization thus being $1,000,000. John D. Rockefeller held 2667 shares; William Rockefeller, Flagler, and Andrews had 1333 each; Harkness 1334; the firm of Rockefeller, Andrews & Flagler 1000; and O. B. Jennings 1000. Brewster was not represented, but probably came in soon afterwards, for more stockholders were added as the corporation got under way. Amasa Stone, Jr., as early as February 12, 1870, according to the original minute book, held 500 shares.

The actual transfer of the old company's holdings took place two days after incorporation, with O. B. Jennings in the chair. The Standard Oil bought the "whole property" of Rockefeller, Andrews & Flagler for $450,000. A mortgage of $77,994 still existed on the real estate and for this the five incorporators made themselves responsible. The six stockholders were elected directors of the Corporation, and on the following day chose John D. Rockefeller as president and Flagler as secretary and treasurer. William Rockefeller was elected vice-president, and voted $35000 in addition to his salary to meet the higher cost of living in New York. Andrews was superintendent.

The Standard Oil represented one-tenth of the refining industry of the country. It owned 60 acres of land in Cleveland, and would soon buy more; it operated two great refineries, a huge barrel-making plant, shipping facilities for lake traffic, a fleet of tank cars, sidings and warehouses in the Oil Regions, timberlands for staves, warehouses and tanks in the New York area, and lighters in New York harbor. However, the important feature of the change was the new corporate form, which gave the Standard greater flexibility than its predecessor, and greater capacity to expand.

The most urgent problem facing the new Standard Oil Company was not one of supplies, processes, or markets—those were being efficiently handled—but the relation with the railroads. That relation was sufficient, in the chaotic rate situation of the day, to make or break any organization. It had been a source of recurrent anxiety to Rockefeller and Flagler ever since the latter made his rebating arrangements in 1867.

In 1869 a furious rate war had broken out among the trunk-line railroads whose tracks linked the Atlantic Coast with the Middle West. The Erie, the New York Central, and the Pennsylvania began fighting over western trade like three lions over a kill. The oil freights of western Pennsylvania were immediately involved. General Devereux of the Lake Shore later termed the contest one of the most desperate he had ever seen. "Such rates and arrangements were made by the Pennsylvania Railroad," he swore, "that it was publicly proclaimed in the public prints of Oil City, Titusville, and other places that Cleveland was to be wiped out as a refining center as with a sponge."

These threats were hardly surprising. Many refiners in the Regions hated Cleveland for its rapid progress, as did others in Pittsburgh and New York. Many thought of the western city, outside the state which produced oil and six hundred miles from the coast harbors and the export trade, as an intruder in the refining industry. Officers of the Pennsylvania, allied with many members of the Petroleum Producers' Association and with numerous Regions manufacturers, were actually ready to "wipe out" the Cleveland establishments.

Most Cleveland refiners were panic-stricken at the threat of destruction. They rushed to the Lake Shore and Atlantic & Great Western offices. They would give up business at once, or remove to the Regions! Such talk was largely a bluff, thrown out to win rate concessions. According to Devereux's testimony, Rockefeller, Andrews & Flagler alone kept a stiff upper lip. Obtaining the Lake Shore's pledge that it "could and would handle oil as cheaply as the Pennsylvania," they promptly "proposed to stand their ground at Cleveland and fight it out on that line." Naturally the Lake Shore was determined to keep its oil traffic; its directors included heavy investors in Cleveland refineries; and it met the Pennsylvania with such low rates that the panic subsided.

But in 1870 a new and fiercer rate war had opened among the same three roads, reaching its climax when Gould and Vanderbilt slashed freight rates by one-half to three-fourths. Oil was again involved, and the threat of the Pennsylvania and its Region allies to expunge Cleveland still stood. It was a season of general belt-tightening. Every manufacturer was reaching for what advantages he could get. Rockefeller and Flagler, with the increased facilities of their new million dollar corporation, were in a stronger position than any competitor.

Flagler went to Devereux with a proposal that was revolutionary. In previous years Rockefeller, Andrews & Flagler had made considerable shipments of refined oil by lake and canal during the five warm months. Flagler offered to stop this practice, ship entirely by rail, and furnish quantities that were astounding. "You want both regular trade and a large volume," he said in effect. "We shall give you both. We shall ship sixty carloads of oil by rail every day of the year." In return he demanded a large rebate.

All Cleveland refiners at this time paid a freight charge of forty cents a barrel on crude oil from the Regions; but most of the larger firms—and probably all—received some rebate or drawback from the official rate of $2 a barrel from Cleveland to

New York. Two besides the Standard Oil later admitted taking such rebates, indicating that the practice was general though secret. Flagler now asked for a total two-way rate of $1.65 instead of $2.40—that is, 35 cents on crude oil to Cleveland and $1.30 on refined oil to the seaboard. At least so Devereux later testified under oath.

The Lake Shore heads recognized that Flagler's proposal would be profitable to their road. Devereux explained later that until then the average round trip for cars from Cleveland to New York had taken thirty days. To move an average of 60 carloads of oil daily would therefore have required 1800 cars if shipments were mixed with other freight cars, as had been the practice. But with regular and uniform shipments daily, the round trip could be made in ten days, for there would be few or no stops for an all-oil train. Only 600 cars would be required. Thus ten-day round trips would demand an investment of but $300,000 in rolling stock, as against $900,000 for 1800 cars used for thirty days. The Lake Shore stood to save the interest on $600,000 for twenty days, together with handling costs, repair costs, and depreciation costs on 1200 cars—all through the factors of quantity and regularity. "The proposition of Mr. Flagler was therefore accepted, and in the affiant's judgment this was the turning point which secured to Cleveland a considerable portion of the export traffic." The Lake Shore's expectations of larger profits proved to be justified.

No sooner did competitors of the Standard Oil in Cleveland hear rumors of this coup than they hurried to the Lake Shore to demand similar concessions. Devereux was polite but firm. He smilingly promised to give precisely the same rebate to any other firm that could ship the same quantity. Discontent, apprehension, and resentment filled the breasts of the Standard's rivals in Cleveland.

What, once more, can be said of the ethics of railroad rebating in this period before the Interstate Commerce Act? When it favored Cleveland as against Pittsburgh, the citizens of the latter city denounced it as deeply immoral; when it favored one manufacturer, the Standard, against others, these rivals, although glad to get rebates themselves, proclaimed any special rate wicked. The giving of rebates continued on such a wide scale that some roads made scarcely a pretense of regular charges. It remained what Rockefeller termed "the railroads' way of doing business";

the Hepburn Committee later showed that half of the whole business of the New York Central was done at special rates.

General sentiment was slow to crystallize on the subject. The public was pleased by the rapid growth of railroads, and the merging of little lines into grandiose systems. Unhappily, egregious abuses accompanied the growth. New railroads pushing their way from city to city demanded heavy tribute from each community they touched. Promoters frequently lined their pockets at the expense of investors, devised predatory construction companies like the Crédit Mobilier, watered stock, and manipulated railroad credit. The roads entered politics, their agents often becoming impudently active in state capitals and in Washington. They poisoned the courts of justice. Above all, rate abuses became the object of protest by individual shippers, cities, and entire states.

For a number of years state regulation was the only action vigorously promoted or undertaken. Massachusetts led the way in systematic state supervision by her act of 1869 establishing a commission. This body had broad powers of investigation and recommendation, but depended upon public opinion for enforcement of its proposals. The Northwest showed a more militant spirit. After the Grange began its swift growth in 1867, the farmers gradually gained control of many legislatures. In Illinois and Minnesota they passed "Granger laws" fixing maximum freight rates and passenger fares, and forbidding discrimination, and Illinois established a commission to help enforce such statutes. Within a few years Wisconsin, Iowa, Missouri, Kansas, and Nebraska had their comparable statutes. Cases contesting the new laws were soon brought to the Supreme Court, which in 1876 fully upheld the right of states to regulate railroads or any other business affected with a public interest.

A public sentiment was rapidly arising that in 1887 would outlaw rebating, though at first ineffectually. Rockefeller himself never outgrew the feeling that in so far as a special rate compensated "eveners" of traffic and large-scale shippers it was right and proper. "So much of the clamor against rebates and drawbacks," he said in 1917, "came from people who knew nothing about business. Who can buy beef the cheapest—the housewife for her family, the steward for a club or hotel, or the commissary for an army? These people would make no difference between wholesale and retail. . . . Who is entitled to better rebates from a railroad, those who give it 5000 barrels a day, or those who give 500 barrels—or 50 barrels?" He was doubtless honest in this view; but under a long line of British and American court decisions, enforcing the principle that a common carrier, fostered and protected by the state, must treat all citizens alike, he was utterly wrong.

The year 1871 drew to a close amid gloomy conditions for all the oil industry. The producers felt as keenly as ever the effect of low prices. Refiners in general were in the same plight. The three railroads concerned were perhaps greater sufferers. The Erie, after losing $694,000 on the Atlantic & Great Western in the year 1870–71, sold the line on October 2 of that year to George B. McClellan and others. The Pennsylvania and New York Central trunk systems were unhappy about the showing of their oil-carrying branches.

The new Standard Oil Company was perhaps the only highly prosperous organization in the oil industry. Early in 1871 it declared a dividend of 40 per cent, and had a small surplus remaining. This was four times the dividend its minutes had modestly mentioned a year earlier. Yet even the Standard leaders were worried by the conditions they faced. The industry was unstable and unpredictable.

Rockefeller long remembered this menacing period. After a lapse of fifty years, in 1921, Rockefeller still recalled vividly the dropping prices, the vanishing margin of profit, the sickening fluctuations and dark uncertainty. The situation moved him to seek earnestly for a remedy, for he did not believe that the Standard Oil Company, despite its prosperous record, dared to let the existing situation continue.

According to orthodox economic theory, the situation was perfectly natural, and the overbalanced industry would soon right itself. Free competition was forcing prices below the cost of production. When they reached such a point, the most inefficient manufacturers would theoretically become discouraged and suspend operations. Supplies would then be reduced and prices would rise. While this process caused a great deal of human suffering, according to Manchester doctrine it made for enterprise, efficiency, and the welfare of the greatest number.

But Rockefeller knew that the theory no longer corresponded with realities, for it cost many units more to discontinue than to keep running. Rockefeller felt that such a destructive process must be prevented. By combination, the big establishments could prevent a ruinous imbalance between manufacturing capacity and market demand, with excess productive facilities a heavy deadweight on the economy of the industry. They could also achieve manifold economies. "We recognized," he testified in the Federal anti-trust suit long afterward, "that if we would succeed we must, if possible, increase the volume of our business with a given expense, and thus reduce the cost of the business in every department of manufacture and merchandizing."

The Standard Oil Company was the strongest in America, the most likely to survive a depression. Rockefeller had no anxiety for his personal future, for his holdings were varied and considerable. Yet he was convinced that he could not let the industry as a whole drift into deeper chaos. Some plan for unification and consequent control must be devised. In his hardheaded, far-seeing fashion, he discussed various possibilities with his partners. Meanwhile other men were also searching for a way out. The result was the emergence of two plans, the first that of a Pennsylvania group, the second that of Rockefeller and Flagler.

The idea of organizing to check overproduction and ruthless competition was not new in the oil industry. As early as the fall of 1866 producers in the Regions had discussed a combination "for the purpose of attempting to make better terms with the refiners in the price of the crude market." In 1869 the Petroleum Producers' Association appeared. Rockefeller thought some combination of refiners the more necessary because of the attitude of the producers.

Rockefeller's distrust of the Oil Regions men was almost as strong as his fear of uncontrolled competition. What if the producers formed a really effective alliance with Regions refiners, perhaps including New York as well? Such distrust intensified his desire for combination, for he saw that some attempt to achieve it was inevitable—and should not this be made from Cleveland rather than from Philadelphia or New York? The Standard, shipping more than 3000 barrels of oil a day—fifty or sixty carloads—was the greatest refining organization in the world, and could exert tremendous force. As Rockefeller discussed the matter with Flagler, his ideas crystallized. He soon made up his mind as to the necessary solution.

This called for the consolidation of nearly all oil-refining units into one great organization, which would eliminate excess capacity and stop price-cutting. Rockefeller was convinced that a mere association or even pool could not long hold together. But he felt that with the Standard as a nucleus, a powerful merger could be achieved. "The idea was mine," he said long afterward.

As Rockefeller did not commit his plan to paper, no documentary evidence of its existence in 1871 exists. Some writers have therefore assumed that he had no plan prior to the organization of the South Improvement Company, soon to appear. But Rockefeller and Flagler always denied any part in devising this company. "It was not our idea," the former categorically told W. O. Inglis. "We had an idea of our own." He described how the formation of the Refiners' Association led him and Flagler to discuss the problem of "protecting the industry," and how out of their talks emerged his own project. "We were gathering information which confirmed us in the idea that to enlarge our own Standard Oil of Ohio and actually take into partners with us the refining interest would accomplish the protection of the oil industry as a whole." In the federal anti-trust suit he testified respecting the founders of the South Improvement Company: "We did not share their views as to the plan. We so frankly stated to them, and more than once."

The origins of this scheme are of particular interest. By 1871 the railroads of the United States had done a good deal of experimenting with that form of combination called the pool. A group of roads serving the same district would agree to maintain rates at a fixed level, and divide the traffic or the revenues on a prearranged scale. In studying the difficult oil situation— and the frantic rate wars of 1870–71 had made railroad leaders study it—the managers of the oil-carrying roads, or some of them, saw that their problem had a close resemblance to that which President Franklin B. Gowen of the Reading and President Asa Packer of the Lehigh had faced in the anthracite field. In both instances the fates of the producers and carriers were related. In both there had been overproduction, price-cutting, and chaos. Of course, the railroads could not buy up the expanding oil fields or the hundreds of refineries. They might, however, encourage some control of production, perhaps through the chief refiners, while at the same time they could effect an agreement on freight rates. They complained that these rates, already less than a cent per ton-mile, were far below costs; that the irregularity of shipments, now a flood and now a trickle, burdened them with excess employees and rolling stock; and that bad shipping practices cost them heavily in train fires and explosions.

It was these facts and possibilities, together with certain other elements, which led to the South Improvement Company. What were the other elements? One was the growth of the Pennsylvania Railroad. By 1871 its tracks ran from New York to Chicago, opening prospects which excited J. Edgar Thomson, its president, and his energetic second in command, Tom Scott. Scott in particular was restless and ambitious. Already president of the Union Pacific, and soon to be elected head of the Texas & Pacific, he had dreams which covered the vast West and the reviving South. Wendell Phillips caustically remarked that as he trailed his garments across the country, the members of twenty legislatures rustled like leaves in a winter's wind behind him.

At this very time the Pennsylvania legislature, one of the twenty, was responding to pressure from Scott and others by chartering a number of corporations with extraordinary powers. As yet the holding company had virtually no existence in America. Some states, New York and Ohio among them, even forbade one corporation to hold the stock of another. But in 1868–72 the legislators at Harrisburg, by special enactments, gave more than forty corporations amazing charters, with powers including the right to hold the stock of other companies in or outside the state. One of them, the South Improvement Company, was chartered in the spring of 1870, with Tom Scott's private secretary and two of Scott's friends its incorporators. It was not created for any specific purpose, and was soon on sale to the highest bidder.

The promoters of the "new view" for controlling oil refining and transportation quietly bought the charter, completing the purchase January 2, 1872. They immediately sold a group of insiders 1100 shares at $100 a share. And who were these promoters? The idea that Rockefeller and Flagler were among them is quite baseless. The plan was primarily a railroad project. Tom Scott stood sponsor in the background. The 1100 shares sold on January 2 were taken by Peter H. Watson, of the Lake Shore–New York Central system, and a group of Philadelphia and Pittsburgh refiners. No Cleveland man was on the list.

Upon the origins of the South Improvement plan we have a considerable variety of testimony which overthrows the old view that Rockefeller or Flagler was responsible for the enterprise.

Actually, their subsequent denials were emphatic, and were never contradicted by those who knew the facts. Although they never apologized for their support of the scheme, they always asserted that their faith in it was limited. "We did not believe in it," Flagler declared. Both felt that their own plan was the only one likely to succeed.

Why, then, did the South Improvement idea begin to grow on Rockefeller? For one reason, the situation seemed desperate—refined oil in New York was selling at 22.33 cents a gallon, one of the lowest prices yet known. For another, a trial of the scheme seemed only good policy. Here were the Pennsylvania refiners and two railroads bringing a coöperative plan on a silver platter. Possibly it would work. Whatever the event, to antagonize its promoters would be bad policy, for the Standard might want their aid in the future.

An outline of the scheme will make clear both its strength and weakness. It was essentially a plan to unite the oil-carrying railroads in a pool; to unite the refiners in an association, the South Improvement Company; and to tie the two elements together by agreements which would stop destructive price-cutting and restore freight charges to a profitable level. The railroads were to divide the oil freights on a prearranged scale; the refiners were to act as *eveners,* insuring each road its quota of business; and in return the refiners were to get rate concessions which would wipe out all recalcitrant competitors. The authors had a hazy notion of bringing the producers into the combination.

The first refiners to join the South Improvement Company were Lockhart, Frew & Company in Pittsburgh, Warden, Frew & Co. in Philadelphia, the Atlantic Refining Co. in Philadelphia, Jabez A. Bostwick in New York, and the Standard Oil in Cleveland. Peter H. Watson was elected president, and William G. Warden secretary. No city held a controlling interest, and Watson's presidency would provide neutral leadership and protect the railroads.

At the first meeting on January 2, 1872, the stockholders agreed that no refiner who accepted their basic principles should be shut out. As Rockefeller said later, "the doors were open." Meanwhile, the final arrangements with the railroads were being made, and on January 18, 1872, the Pennsylvania signed its contract with the South Improvement Company. Scott and Watson helped to arrange for the signatures of William H.

Vanderbilt, vice-president of the New York Central; H. F. Clark, president of the Lake Shore; Jay Gould, president of the Erie; and George B. McClellan, head of the Atlantic & Great Western. The South Improvement Company agreed to ship 45 per cent of all its oil over the Pennsylvania, 27.5 per cent over the Erie, and 27.5 per cent over the New York Central system.

The Company also agreed to much higher rates for oil shipments. The freight charge on crude oil from the Regions to Cleveland was to be 80 cents a barrel, double the previous tariff. Pittsburgh would pay the same. The rate on refined from Cleveland or Pittsburgh to New York would be $2.00 a barrel (the existing rate). The open rate on crude oil from the Regions was fixed at $2.41 to Philadelphia, $2.56 to New York, and $2.71 to Boston. The Standard's own overall rate of $1.65 for transportation from the Regions to Cleveland and then from Cleveland to New York, procured by Flagler in 1870, would thus compare with a new cost of $2.80.

However, members of the South Improvement Company were not to pay the full public rate. All received rebates—from 40 to 50 per cent on crude, and from 25 to 50 per cent on refined. There was nevertheless a raise. The Standard, for example, would now pay $1.90 a barrel instead of $1.65. This was quite satisfactory to Flagler and Rockefeller, for any non-member competitors would pay 90 cents more.

Such an arrangement, effectively enforced, would have crushed all competition; but it was not the only provision in the agreement designed to do this. Another stipulated that on every barrel of oil shipped by competitors, members of the company should receive a drawback equal to their rebate. For instance, Bostwick of New York would not only receive a rebate of $1.06 on every barrel of oil which he brought from Titusville to New York; he would also get another $1.06 on every barrel which a New York competitor, paying the full rate of $2.56, brought from the Regions! The Standard would not only get the 40-cent rebate from the Regions; it would also get 40 cents a barrel on oil brought to Cleveland by a competitor (who always paid 80 cents). Of all devices for the extinction of competition, this was the cruelest and most deadly yet conceived by any group of American industrialists.

The contracts also provided that each railroad should make out waybills for all shipments of petroleum or its products, showing the shipper and consignee, the place of shipment and destination, and the amount and quality of the product shipped; and that all such waybills should be sent daily to the South Improvement Company. Thus members of the combination would get detailed information about their competitors' business. Moreover, the South Improvement Company was to have access to all railroad books. This was plainly a means of enforcing payment of rebates and drawbacks—of making doubly sure that no independent refiners could long survive.

The object of these drastic devices was to render it utterly impossible for any refiner to stay out of the South Improvement Company. Who could afford to? Indeed, the authors of the scheme could argue that a less drastic machinery for enforcing combination would leave the competing refiners hesitant. They would remain outside, the oil struggle would continue, and the chaos would be perpetuated. Thus the most ruthless course might well be the most merciful. The argument is specious, for it assumed that vicious means can be justified by the end. If the South Improvement group had made it clear that they would welcome all outsiders on a full equality, with identity and financial interests both protected, the plea would have had considerable force. No such conditions were set forth, however, and undoubtedly some members of the group wished to use the ruthless machinery mainly to enrich themselves.

Then, too, what of the producers? What treatment were they to receive from this powerful combination of railroads and refiners? Later the South Improvement Company asserted that it had meant to invite well-owners to participate. Such an intention had not been unanimously approved; Warden, testifying in 1872, said that there was hostility to any union with the well-owners, and confessed to such a feeling himself, "inasmuch as the interests of the producers were in one sense antagonistic to ours." But Tom Scott and Potts of the Empire Transportation Company argued that to exclude the producers would invite failure. "You can't succeed unless the producers are taken care of," Scott insisted. He and Potts carried their point, said Warden, who was supported in this evidence by Watson, producing for the House Committee a pencil draft of an agreement the refiners had intended to submit to the producers.

The proposed agreement was fair enough. It specified that the producers were to limit the flow of the wells, and in return the

South Improvement Company was to pay not less than a stated minimum price for crude oil, to be fixed each year by a joint committee.

But this draft agreement had not been shown to any producers when the Oil Regions first became aware of the South Improvement scheme. Company leaders testified that their first task was to organize the refiners, and that as soon as this was done they had meant to approach the producers. Watson and his associates should have moved to organize refiners and producers simultaneously, not successively. When the producers discovered the combination of railroads and refiners, their rage and excitement made them deaf to anything that the South Improvement group could say.

Though years later Rockefeller protested that he had gone into the South Improvement scheme as a second-best plan, his initial hesitation quickly gave way to energetic espousal. He threw himself into the enterprise with tremendous zeal. The first requisite for success was to make sure that all three railroads would accept the plan. To the end Rockefeller played a leading part in the negotiations. This was natural, for he was the leading refiner in the country.

During January and early February, 1872 many refiners were asked to throw in their fortunes with the South Improvement Company. All were bound by a written pledge to absolute secrecy. Two prominent refiners of the Regions, J. J. Vandergrift and John D. Archbold, were solicited and refused. So did H. H. Rogers of Charles Pratt & Company, of New York, and many others. But the leaders were not discouraged. They hoped that the crushing force of their contracts would soon reduce these men to a humbler attitude. By the end of January, with the last railroad contract signed, more than a score of people knew about the South Improvement contracts. The middle of February found sensational rumors floating about the Regions of a combination between the railroads and the leading refiners.

On February 25 the resentment of the Oil Regions burst in a terrific storm. That day an officer of the Jamestown & Franklin branch of the Lake Shore became confused, and put the new rates into effect on the oil-carrying business. Lombard, Ayres & Company in New York learned of them, and telegraphed their buyer in the Regions, Josiah Lombard: "Oil rate prohibitive. What is the matter?" Lombard was astounded to find that the charge for carrying crude from Warren to New York had shot up from 87 cents to $2.14. As he and others learned that rates on crude and refined oil between all points had similarly risen, they were aghast. Streets and hotel lobbies immediately filled with angry men. Refiners pledged to secrecy forgot their promises and told all they knew, so that within a few hours the most carefully guarded details were public property.

On the night of February 27 three thousand wrathful men from all over the Regions gathered in the Titusville Opera House. Well-owners, refiners, oil-brokers, shopkeepers, and bankers trooped in. They bore banners with defiant slogans: "No Compromise!" "Down With The Conspirators!" "Don't Give Up The Ship!" Leading refiners were wildly cheered as they described the oath of secrecy, the proposals made to them, and their indignant rejection of the conspiracy.

But this gathering was only the first wave of the fury that had seized the Regions. The meeting had more violence than effectiveness, for it did little but pass searing resolutions. The alarm of the Regions was indicated by the Titusville *Herald* of February 26, which asserted that the refiners of the outside-cities were planning to destroy those of the Regions, "the only natural refining point in the country."

On March 1 crowds moved in a black stream through the streets of Oil City to a gathering at Love's Opera House as passionate as that held in Titusville. The Petroleum Producers' Association was now given aggressive leadership by a new board of directors which included William M. Irish, John D. Archbold, and J. J. Vandergrift among the refiners, and H. T. Beers, William Hasson, and E. G. Patterson of the producers. Rousing speeches were delivered. Archbold made an eloquent appeal for union against the common enemy. He was followed by the resourceful Lewis Emery, Jr., destined to be a lifelong enemy of Rockefeller. Emery urged a union of Regions producers and refiners, and proposed three immediate steps: (1) all producers should shut off one-third their capacity; (2) no torpedoes or other artificial aids to production should be used; and (3) no new wells should be started for thirty days. All three proposals were immediately carried.

The revitalized Producers' Association now became the Petroleum Producers' Union, with the aim of covering the entire oil-bearing area. Members pledged themselves to start no new wells for two months, to stop work on Sundays, and above all, to sell no oil to any member of the South Improvement Company. Only Oil Regions refiners and opponents of the "combination" were to get oil. The Oil City *Derrick* published a "black list" and kept it in a box day after day. Before long 112 producers had signed the agreement to cut off one-third of production. Any producer who did business with Warden, Waring, Logan, Bostwick, or Rockefeller risked his property and even his skin.

The Petroleum Producers' Union thus prepared to fight monopoly with monopoly. If it could extend its sway over most wells in the Regions, it would control the supply of crude oil and starve the "anaconda" to death.

Seldom has an economic organization faced a wilder uproar of attack than that which now raged about the South Improvement Company. For weeks almost the whole body of producers surged from town to town denouncing the combination. Their attack was moral: the Company was "the Forty Thieves," "the Monster," "the Octopus," "the Ring"; its members were "conspirators" and "robbers." What then of Rockefeller and Flagler? How did they defend joining such an organization, and working so aggressively for it?

As we have seen, combinations to reduce or abolish destructive competition were no novelties in 1870, and were sometimes commended by public opinion. We have also seen that the use of rebates and drawbacks was no novelty. At least as old as 1856, it was common practice in 1872. As Rockefeller said later, the refiners who assailed rebates were usually those who had failed to get them.

It was therefore easy for Rockefeller and Flagler to defend combination at a time when overproduction and unrestricted competition were threatening the entire refining industry with disaster. They had as much reason to attempt combination as the leaders in salt manufacture and anthracite production. They had every reason to accept rebates, which were widely regarded as a "quantity discount" and were in general still approved by business sentiment. No large manufacturer could afford *not* to seek them, for his rivals would.

But the savage and destructive drawbacks specified in the South Improvement contracts are another matter. To give a large shipper a rebate was standard practice; but to pay him in addition part of the higher rate imposed upon his rivals was utterly indefensible. Rockefeller committed one of the great errors of his career when he hurriedly aligned himself with such an arrangement.

The rebate provisions of the contracts were brutal, unjust, and outside the pale of business ethics even in that loose period. They ran counter to the essential spirit of fair play and democracy in American enterprise. Indefensible was the verdict of impartial observers then; indefensible must be the verdict now. However, Rockefeller sincerely persuaded himself that the South Improvement scheme was just. The excitement of the Oil Regions did not move him, for he despised excitement. The idea expressed by the Regions men did not impress him, for he believed his own idea far superior. What he did not as yet realize was that behind this idea of free competition lay the massive and immovable convictions of the American people. But even if he had realized it, probably he would not have wavered. He had considered his steps in advance. It was in the spirit of this consideration, and not merely to rationalize his own conduct, that he exclaimed in 1917: "I had our plan clearly in mind. It was right. I knew it as a matter of conscience. It was right between me and my God. If I had to do it tomorrow I would do it again the same way—do it a hundred times."

# CHAPTER III

# ROCKEFELLER FINDS NEW ALLIES

THE conflict that had now developed between the South Improvement Company and the Regions was not merely one between two groups struggling for the profits of the petroleum industry, for the character of the contestants had introduced a note of modern complexity. As the oil industry had developed, refining had altered its originally simple character. It was now rapidly becoming an activity of big, well-organized units operating with highly technical equipment and heavy overhead costs to meet an ever-growing demand from all the continents. The instincts of the leaders, like those of the newer railroad executives, were for order. Excess plant capacity and chaotic price-slashing were basically repugnant to them. On the other hand, the producing branch of the industry was itself a field for adventurous men with moderate resources. Its spirit was individualistic. Its members were akin in temper to the Grangers of the Middle West.

It was inevitable that the two groups should clash. The leading refiners were ready to join the railroads in building a great pool; the producers, passionately insistent on industrial freedom (unless they could form a monopoly of their own), were ready to oppose such an effort, and did not hesitate to call on the state itself to preserve their competitive regime. A war had opened between two economic orders.

The conflict, however, must not be regarded as one between wealth and poverty, or between economic greed and economic justice. The producers have been pictured as an oppressed band

struggling disinterestedly for a great principle. Actually few
were poor, most were men of moderate property, and a number
were rich. As for principle, each side unquestionably felt that it
was battling for a fairer and better order.

Dominant among the producers was Captain William Hasson,
the new president of the Petroleum Producers' Association. With
Hasson stood John L. and Foster W. Mitchell and John Fertig—
all as wealthy as he—and Edwin E. Clapp, D. S. Criswell, B. B.
Campbell, and others. Allied with them were the Regions refiners. Particularly notable among them were Captain Jacob Jay
Vandergrift, famous as a steamboat captain and pipeline organizer, and John D. Archbold, widely popular as one who
combined youth, high spirits, and brilliant ability. Only twenty-
four, Archbold had instantly won over the great Oil City meeting as he told how he had rejected an invitation in New York
to help establish the monopoly. He repeated his words to Peter
Watson: "If you think the people of this region will quietly
submit to a tax of five million dollars a year from this or any
other corporation, you very much mistake their character!"

With producers and refiners stood the tradesmen and laborers
of the Regions, and the local press. Indeed, two editors ranked
almost as high among the leaders as did Hasson, Vandergrift, and
Archbold. N. M. Allen of the Titusville *Courier* was a refiner as
well as a journalist. More rugged and explosive in character was
C. E. Bishop of the Oil City *Derrick*. He was the originator of the
"blacklist" which his paper carried in a box, and prided himself
on a command of satire and sledgehammer invective.

For all these men of the Regions, the moral objectives were
actually subordinated to profit, and their war was essentially one
for power. Yet while they united to cut off the supply of crude
oil, and starve the "monster" to death by its own monopolistic
tactics, they laid great emphasis on the alleged righteousness of
their cause. Shrewdly aware of the force of public opinion, they
poured out their story to audiences and reporters alike. Furthermore, they hurried a committee to Harrisburg to demand that
the legislature annul the South Improvement charter, and dis-
patched another to Washington to request Congressional investigation. They took steps to prepare a history of their battle
with the "Anaconda," and to scatter 30,000 copies throughout
the nation, "to the end that enemies of freedom of trade may
be known and shunned by all honest men."

On March 11 a special committee from New York appeared in the Regions to lay plans for joint resistance. This delegation was led by a handsome young man destined to play no small role in Rockefeller's own career and in the history of American business. Henry H. Rogers, then only thirty-two, was no stranger in Pennsylvania. He had operated a refinery on Oil Creek before going to Long Island in 1868 to join Charles Pratt in the Pratt Manufacturing Company. His handsome features, careful dress, and magnetic personality made him a distinguished figure in drawing room and business conference alike. But his urbane exterior covered a gamester's recklessness and lack of scruple. Now a dominant figure in the ten-still refinery which was making "Pratt's Astral" famous throughout Europe, he assured the producers that Bostwick was weak compared with his New York rivals, and that a union of the Long Island refiners and the Regions would be invincible.

The crude oil blockade was now almost completely effective. The tanks of the Standard Oil and other members of the South Improvement Company would soon be running dry.

Rockefeller was chagrined as he watched the success of the producers' storming attack. Its swiftness had dismayed him. He and Flagler had both hoped that the pledges of secrecy would prove far more effective. From the outset Rockefeller barred his door to reporters. Flagler saw them, and pooh-poohed the first mass meeting at Titusville as the work of a few "soreheads." But with the later meetings and the stoppage of oil he could no longer pretend to any confidence, and soon ceased to talk at all.

Public opinion was now decidedly nervous about the darker possibilities of monopoly. The exposure of the Tweed Ring in New York, with which Jim Fisk and Jay Gould of the Erie were involved, and the Crédit Mobilier scandal, had caused many Americans to associate industrial combinations with political "rings." The South Improvement Company was an attractive mark. It seemed balefully comprehensive in scope; its rebate scheme looked like impudent robbery. Enemies in its own field had already brought the behemoth to its knees, and a thousand men hastened to pour arrows into its hide. The company became for millions of Americans a symbol of monopolistic aggression, happily destroyed.

Tom Scott, Warden, Flagler, Rockefeller, all failed to perceive at the time the depth of the passions they had aroused. Not until decades had passed and many books had dealt with the subject did Rockefeller see how he had misjudged the situation. But fifty years later he explained that throughout his early business career he had followed a fixed principle of reticence. "I determined that it was useless to waste energy on denials and disputes with jealous or disappointed people. I persuaded our partners to keep silence, too. The more we progressed yet kept on gaining success and keeping silent, the more we were abused." This policy had prevailed in 1872, but he saw now that it was a mistaken one. "I shall never cease to regret," he exclaimed, "that at that time we never called in the reporters."

By the middle of March the campaign against the South Improvement Company had shown such strength that many of its supporters were passing from a state of concern into one of alarm. The railroads had the most to fear from public antagonism and possible legislative action. When a committee of twelve "independents," three from New York and nine from the Regions, called upon Tom Scott in Philadelphia on March 18, and asked him to cancel the Pennsylvania's contract with the South Improvement Company, the great executive had already decided to abandon the ship he had helped to launch. He promptly admitted that the contract was unjust. Then came an amazing proposal: the Pennsylvania Railroad would make a similar contract with the producers. The Committee declined this extraordinary offer, and proposed to see the officials of the other two roads in New York.

In New York, the twelve committeemen first waited upon old Commodore Vanderbilt, who greeted them with profane "heartiness and affability": "Goddam you all, boys, how are you? Glad to see you damned oil boys. How is your damned old oil, anyhow?" He offered them cigars. As head of the New York Central, he professed a hatred of monopoly and blamed the contracts on his son. "I told Billy not to have anything to do with that scheme," one version quotes him as saying. Someone mentioned a pool. "What's that you say?—a pool?" exclaimed the old fox. "What in hell's name's that?" The committee furnished an explanation. "Oh, damn it all, and is that what you call a pool!" said Vanderbilt. "Why, Tom Scott's been talking that to me for ten years, damn him!" According to this account, the old Commodore also produced a letter from the South Improvement Company offering to compromise its differences with the Regions,

John Davison Rockefeller in the early 1880's.

Eliza Davison Rockefeller

and William Avery Rockefeller,
John D. Rockefeller's parents.

Laura Celestia Spelman

and John D. Rockefeller.

Photographs taken not long before they became engaged.

First Standard Oil Refinery in Cleveland.
From a photograph by Mather in 1869 or 1870.

and to coöperate with all producers and refiners there. The New
York Central would doubtless have been pleased with such an
arrangement. But the Committee told Vanderbilt that they would
never treat with the South Improvement Company or any
member of it. Vanderbilt said that they should talk with his son,
in any event. Billy would not favor a pool or any alliance with
Jay Gould.

The Committee did not meet the notorious Gould, but on
March 25 it came to the Erie offices to discuss the situation with
all the railroads concerned. The visitors were kept waiting
several hours before they were ushered into the Directors' room,
to be joined there by William H. Vanderbilt of the New York
Central; several Erie directors; H. F. Clark, President of the Lake
Shore, General George B. McClellan of the Atlantic & Great
Western; and Scott of the Pennsylvania. Clark acted as chairman
for the meeting.

A spokesman for the Committee, after outlining the producers'
grievances, predicted that "violent measures" might be taken by
groups in the Regions unless the railroads' contract with the
combine was annulled. He began to denounce the contract itself
as vicious and "disreputable." Here both Clark and Vanderbilt
interrupted, asserting that it would "result in nothing but good
to the producing interest." Watson, they revealed, was in the
next room, and they proposed to call him in and let him explain
matters.

The Committee refused to permit this. They would not recognize the South Improvement Company or confer with its officers.
About this time, Watson, with Rockefeller, knocked at the door
and attempted to enter. "We want nothing to do with you!"
shouted the producers. Clark, chewing his cigar vigorously and
getting red in the face, said angrily that Watson was his lifelong
personal friend and he would have him in. He gave orders, the
door opened, and Watson entered; but the Committee members
scrambled to their feet and started to leave the room. Watson
finally left without a hearing, red-faced and flustered. The newspapers reported that he and Rockefeller walked away looking
"pretty blue."

Inside the Directors' room, Scott acted as peace-maker. He
favored annulling the South Improvement Company contract,
and substituting one with the producers themselves. This would
assure the equitable distribution of oil, the chief object of the

roads. Clark responded to this appeal, and Scott rapidly drew up an agreement which was finally signed by both sides.

Under this document, all rates were to be public and equal. The text declared that "no rebates, drawbacks, or other arrangements of any [such] character shall be made or allowed." The railroads tried to get the producers to act as "eveners," but the latter refused. They regarded such a service as promoting a form of special privilege. Their whole fight had been against such practices; they would not be traitors to their own ideals.

The new contract seemed to put Cleveland and Pittsburgh at a disadvantage. They paid 50 cents to get their crude oil; the Regions paid nothing. As shipment to New York cost both the same, the advantage for the Regions was 50 cents a barrel. Similarly, New York refiners got their oil for $1.35; but for export, or for sale in eastern United States, Cleveland had to pay 50 cents to get the crude, and $1.35 or more to take the refined product to market. Here Long Island refiners had at least a 50-cent advantage.

The Pennsylvania legislature now executed a maneuver which also pleased the Regions. It passed the "free pipeline bill"; but this bill made condemnation of rights of way for pipelines permissible only in the eight oil-producing counties, thereby excluding Allegheny, in which Pittsburgh lies.

The grip of the producers on the oil supply meanwhile seemed to be tightening. They were operating by a specific plan. This provided for sixteen districts covering the entire Regions territory. Each district had a complete local organization. Each sent delegates to a General Council, which issued final orders as to policy. Trading with members of the South Improvement Company had been forbidden. No producer could sell oil except to buyers approved by his local committee. The producers were not selling oil to the members of the combine, and the members needed it.

But the situation, apparently so favorable to the producer diehards, was actually two-edged, or even three-edged. For the Lake Shore and the Atlantic & Great Western were aghast at what had occurred. In March, these two carriers got only $13\frac{1}{2}$ and $4\frac{1}{2}$ per cent respectively of a trickling oil traffic, the Pennsylvania taking 82 per cent. Even this road could not have viewed the situation complacently. Its traffic, although large in percentage of the total, was pitifully small in actual amount, and it faced the need for greatly increasing its supply of cars if the big Cleveland and Pittsburgh shippers were inactive and withdrew their rolling stock. There simply was not enough refining capacity in the Regions or among their allies to handle anything like a normal output of oil. The railroads were all profoundly dissatisfied, and to any perceptive observer it was clear that they would move to change the situation if it did not soon change itself.

Of course, the Regions refiners and their Eastern friends, given enough time, could have built up capacity to handle the oil. But time was the fatal weakness: the producers were unwilling to wait. While the March shipments of crude had fallen to 264,692 barrels, the lowest figure in three years, the stocks of oil in the Regions had increased by more than 40 per cent, despite the inactivity of many producers, who stayed their drills for the common cause. Knowing at last that the power of the combine had been broken, well-owners were becoming restive. Agents of the ostracized firms were offering them bonus prices. What was the point in starving the members of a pool that was now totally ineffective?

Early in April came the news that an Oil City firm had broken the ice, selling 20,000 or 25,000 barrels of oil to the Standard. The widest indignation was expressed, and the General Council called a mass-meeting. Then came another report of a sale of 5000 barrels to the Standard. A mob assembled and refused to let the cars move. But opinion was divided. When in a few days the mass-meeting was held to discipline the first offender, his friends flocked to his support and blocked action against him.

The culprit was a prominent member of the Union, a former officer, writes W. T. Scheide. "There could be but one result: if one man could sell to the enemy, all should"; and the officers decided to make this possible. They telegraphed the railroads demanding "official notice" that the South Improvement contracts had been cancelled. "Please answer at once; as we fear violence and destruction of property." A similar telegram was sent to John D. Rockefeller. He replied on April 8 that the Standard Oil "holds no contract with the railroad companies or any of them, or with the South Improvement Company." He added: "I state unqualifiedly that reports that this company, or any member of it, threatened to depress oil, are false." At a meeting of producers on April 10 the officers were therefore able to report a complete victory: the formal extinction of the combination. When they declared that the time had arrived for trading with all buyers on equal terms, their announcement was hailed with delight.

With this act the Producers' Union closed its effective career. The producers were both relieved and jubilant. Monopoly had been crushed—for a long time, they believed.

Rockefeller's feelings were naturally different. True, he believed that the attempt in which he had participated had been unfortunate. But he considered it to have been a commendable attempt—one not to crush, but to unify. Many years later he pointed out that the plan had never been tested. "There never was a shipment made or a rebate or drawback collected under this South Improvement plan."

Certain conclusions seem inescapable from any careful review of the dramatic history of this famous combination:

(1) Although assailants of the Standard Oil Company later pictured the oil industry of early 1872 as in a happy and prosperous state, actually it was overexpanded, disorganized, and in grave danger of collapse. (2) The railroads had suffered from the state of the oil industry. With their knowledge of pools and holding companies, it was they who developed the outline of the scheme which Watson of the Lake Shore took to Warden and Waring, and later to Flagler and Rockefeller. (3) From the railroad standpoint, it was a plan for a refiners' pool to "even" traffic; in 1875 the New York–Chicago trunk lines gave a similar reward to a Western group that "evened" livestock shipments. (4) From the standpoint of the Standard and other refiners associated with it in the scheme, the combination was a device to *compel* all refiners to enter one organization, but wholly for their own benefit. But from the standpoint of the producers and independent refiners, it was a scheme to force everyone to bow to a selfish ring of Cleveland, Pittsburgh, and Philadelphia monopolists. (5) From the standpoint of the general public, it was a plan to create a dangerous monopoly in what had become a necessity of life.

Rockefeller's adherence to the plan for tactical reasons can be understood; but his participation was highly unfortunate for his business reputation. In the Regions especially it left a black mark of discredit and suspicion against his name. He should have stayed entirely clear of so hasty, ill-organized, and potentially tyrannical an organization. His participation suggests—as do numerous episodes in his later career—that he had an inadequate understanding of popular psychology, and an inadequate appreciation of the fact that in the last analysis business must work within the rules imposed by public opinion.

But while this chapter of errors was drawing to a close, on a more important field Rockefeller had been winning a spectacular victory. Out of the ashes of one combination another—more formidable, and of a different type, a single, greatly enlarged company—was arising like a phoenix.

One December morning in 1871, Rockefeller sent an invitation to Colonel Oliver H. Payne to attend a conference that afternoon at a Cleveland bank. Payne was the chief stockholder in Clark, Payne & Co., the Standard's strongest Cleveland competitor. Maurice and James Clark had an interest in his firm, along with the wealthy Hussey family.

The Payne family was wealthy, highly respected, and influential. Oliver's father, Henry B. Payne, was an earnest, cultivated man, a graduate of Hamilton College, who had made a fortune as a lawyer and manufacturer, meanwhile turning to politics. He had run for governor in 1857, had become one of Stephen A. Douglas's principal lieutenants, was presently to enter Congress, and in 1880 was to be Samuel J. Tilden's choice for the Democratic Presidential nomination.

Young Oliver Payne was a patrician and knew it. He had left Cleveland for Phillips Andover and Yale, had risen to a colonelcy in the war, and was now active in the manufacture of iron and oil. If Rockefeller and Flagler began with small refiners, they would have initial successes, perhaps, and then increasing difficulty as they approached the stronger ones. With Payne won over, and an associate, their strength would be immensely increased, and persuading the others might be easy.

The plan proved to be sound. The astute Payne saw the situation clearly. As his firm had been losing money, he agreed with Rockefeller that the general situation was dark, and that a courageous program was demanded. When Rockefeller proposed that the Standard increase its capitalization, that the Clark, Payne plant be appraised, and that its partners be given stock in proportion to their property and good will, Payne was receptive. He did not object when Rockefeller suggested that although Payne should take an active part in Standard management, the Clarks should not!

Payne quickly convinced other stockholders in his company that the proposed merger was desirable. "Let us get the appraisers and see what the plant is worth," said Payne. This was quickly done. The impending increase in the capitalization of the Standard provided for 25,000 shares with a total par value of $2,500,000. Of the 15,000 new shares, the executive committee was authorized to use 11,000 "in paying for certain refining properties in Cleveland and elsewhere that had been offered to the company." Clark, Payne & Co. received 4000 shares of Standard stock, although not all of this represented plant value, which was estimated at $251,110; the additional $148,890 was an allowance made for good will and for Payne's experience and brains—which proved worth a very large sum indeed.

Even before the end of 1871 other properties were added. The Cleveland plant of Joseph Stanley, valued at $20,000, was purchased. Rockefeller executed a telling stroke when he brought into the new combination Jabez A. Bostwick, of New York, whose Long Island Oil Company owned a valuable refinery and terminal equipment at Hunter's Point on the East River. Bostwick had bought large quantities of refined oil from Cleveland and other points for sale abroad; he knew the vigor of the Standard organization; as a member of the South Improvement Company, he had lately seen much of Rockefeller. Evidently his properties were worth $70,000, for on January 1 he is put down for 700 shares of the new stock. Thus the Standard had strengthened its position in New York as well as Cleveland.

With these additions it was incomparably the largest refining corporation in the world, and this, we should note, fully six weeks before the public knew about the South Improvement Company. This organization could not have influenced Payne or Stanley. With the expansion, a few new stockholders joined the company, and some of the old ones increased their holdings, as the following list will show:

| *Stockholders, Jan. 1, 1872* | | *Disposition of 15,000 new Shares* | |
|---|---|---|---|
| John D. Rockefeller | 2,016 shares | Existing stockholders, | |
| William Rockefeller | 1,459 shares | pro rata | 4,000 |
| H. M. Flagler | 1,459 shares | Clark, Payne & Co. | 4,000 |
| Samuel Andrews | 1,458 shares | John D. Rockefeller | 3,000 |
| S. V. Harkness | 1,458 shares | H. M. Flagler | 1,400 |
| Amasa Stone, Jr. | 500 shares | John D. Rockefeller as | |
| Stillman Witt | 500 shares | agent for company | 1,200 |
| O. B. Jennings | 500 shares | Jabez A. Bostwick | 700 |
| T. P. Handy | 400 shares | J. Stanley | 200 |
| Benjamin Brewster | 250 shares | P. H. Watson | 500 |
| Total | 10,000 shares | Total | 15,000 |

Thus Rockefeller held a total of 5016 shares of company stock as personal property, an investment worth more than $500,000 at face value. The other 1200 shares he held as an agent, to be used in future merger negotiations. Despite the influx of new stockholders, the original Standard group—the two Rockefellers, Flagler, Andrews, and Harkness—retained a firm control of the organization.

Having acquired his most formidable Cleveland rival, Rockefeller turned confidently to deal with the others. The campaign resulted in the absorption of 34 rivals (including Bostwick and Clark, Payne), the essential unification of all Cleveland refining in one organization, and important acquisitions outside that city. The Standard by the end of 1872 controlled a capacity of at least 10,000 barrels of refined oil a day, enough to handle half of all the oil then being produced.

The campaign for consolidation in Cleveland had been pushed to the point of a major success by April, 1872, and mopping-up operations continued for the remainder of the year. Public attention was riveted during those three months on the South Improvement battle. Nobody but the Standard officials and some of their rivals recognized that what was happening in Cleveland was really more important than the sensational events in the Oil Regions.

Yet the result was decisive: an industrial giant had risen in Cleveland—a towering corporation that was soon employing 1600 men and handling a payroll of $20,000 a week. The new Standard Oil Company with its 10,000 barrels a day capacity was ready to refine more oil than all the Regions plants (with an estimated 9231 barrel capacity), or all those in the New York area (9790 barrels capacity), or those in Pittsburgh, Philadelphia, and Baltimore combined (9249 barrels).

Even yet, however, few observers believed that the great Cleveland combination would permanently succeed; it was too grandiose. Rockefeller's old employer, Hewitt, had warned him against attempting any such consolidation. "John, it can't be done," he had declared. "We've tried it on the lake shipping. They won't hold together. You'll find it a rope of sand." Hanna also predicted failure. "Don't touch it," he warned his younger partners. "It has no future. The organization will fall by its own weight." Such was the hope of the embittered James Clark, even though as a partner in Clark, Payne & Co., he had taken some of the 4000 shares that company had received. Clark was so disruptive an element in the company that Colonel Payne soon bought him out at $112.50 a share—a total of $110,000. He thought he had done remarkably well. But when before many years passed the value of these shares rose into millions, his hostility to Rockefeller grew deeper still.

But Rockefeller had no doubts about the future of the Standard. Boldly but surely he set about the task of re-organizing the larger company for its work. And quickly it responded to the incisive measures which he and his associates adopted.

The first of these was a demand for a new rate on refined oil from Cleveland to New York. We have seen that the agreement of March 25 between the railroads and producers left Cleveland in a disadvantageous position as compared with other refining centers. It paid 50 cents a barrel to get crude oil, and $1.50 to send refined to New York. New York paid $1.35 for crude, and for the East the cost of shipping refined to neighboring markets was little. The Standard, of course, had its regional advantage as to the Western trade, and the advantages of its remarkable economies of production. But it wanted cheaper access to the East. Flagler went to the Lake Shore and demanded a rate of $1.25 a barrel on refined oil shipped to New York. Despite the agreement of March 25, he got it.

The Lake Shore had merely acted in self-protection. It was to carry four thousand barrels of oil a day for the Standard, and in return gave the lower tariff to that company. This arrangement was to prevail for the next seven months. What was the road's alternative to granting the concession? The Standard might ship by water, cutting off a great source of profitable traffic for a large part of the year. A pipeline might be laid from the regions to Cleveland, bringing in crude for a fraction of the rail charge, and again cutting off a profitable source of revenue to the road. (The Ohio legislature hurriedly passed an act facilitating such a line.) These threats and the proclaimed resentment of Cleveland business men and the Cleveland press would probably have been sufficient to ease the Lake Shore's conscience with respect to the producers.

But quite as strong a consideration was the news that its rivals were slashing their rates. Blanchard of the Erie declared in 1879 that he had seen proof that the Pennsylvania had broken the agreement within two weeks by granting a large drawback to its great fast-freight subsidiary, the Empire Transportation Company. Blanchard confessed that the Erie quickly broke it, too. The Lake Shore could hardly afford not to follow suit.

Whatever the ethics involved, the producers were a bit naïve in expecting anything more. They had broken up a railroad-refiner agreement intended to produce order in the field of oil shipments. They themselves had done nothing to create an alternative plan for order. So the old war between the roads had been resumed, with refiners grabbing such advantages as they could. It was anything but a pretty picture, it was completely un-moral, if not immoral, but it was to be expected. The Standard itself was in no position to correct conditions; it made the best arrangements it could and went ahead with its own business.

That business demanded all the concentration that Rockefeller, Flagler, and Payne could give it. For the Standard the volume of production had been immensely increased. Dozens of questions confronted its leaders. Which refineries should be scrapped, which kept in production? What officials from these plants should be made Standard officials (for many new ones were needed)? What should be done with clerks, workmen? A new company was being forged, and prodigious activity was required of those at the top.

The period of integration seems to have lasted for about eighteen months. In acquiring the refineries which it took over in 1872 the company seems to have contemplated an increase in the number of its products as well as the volume of production. Up to this time it had concentrated on the production of kerosene and naphtha, selling the material for by-products to other companies. For example, it had not made lubricating oil, preferring to sell the base for this to such firms as the Fred M. Backus Company and Morehouse & Freeman. But among the plants it acquired in 1872 were six tar refineries, two acid-restoring plants, and one small lubricating oil manufactory. Some of the general refineries taken over had also manufactured by-products. Rockefeller now believed that the Standard should produce lubricants, candles, paraffin, dyes, paints, and other materials, and supply its own acid. The increase in the number of products manufactured was gradual; it was not until 1878, for example, that a final drive was made to dominate the production of lubricants. But the plan for diversity was made six years earlier. Capital for the new ventures was supplied mainly by members of the company.

For all phases of expansion, men were needed as managers and assistants. Payne, of course, had come in at the top, an executive with brains, energy, and social connections who became almost as important in the company as Flagler. Rockefeller and the chief partners selected other lieutenants from the personnel of the companies they acquired.

Rockefeller himself watched carefully all selections, even of minor personnel. He showed the same vigilance in the yards, too, with a remarkable memory for names and faces. A worker who was inspecting miscellaneous materials outside the cooperage shop recalled his saying with a smile as he passed: "That's right, eternal vigilance!" Thomas H. Wheeler later remembered that early in the seventies Rockfeller suggested lopping several inches off the overlap of the iron hoops that bound each oil barrel. Experiment proved that this would not weaken the barrels, for the overlap was four or five inches. The idea saved thousands of dollars every year in iron. On being reminded of this in 1918, Rockefeller exclaimed, "A fortune!"

This direct knowledge of the industry gave him an advantage over most of his partners; but it was never gained at the expense of perspective or vision. Into his manner had grown the precision and power of the business he had built, and a part of his strength lay in his philosophical grasp of the problems he faced. He never seemed aggressive, he was always serene; so quiet in manner, indeed, that to many he seemed sly. He *was* subtle; he was also cool, determined, and self-confident, and worked perhaps harder at analyzing and planning than he did at watching the activities of various departments.

Rockefeller had applied all his remarkable abilities to the task of bringing order into the refining industry. He was now launched on the execution of that task. He had considered it fully, and he had no doubt as to the course that should be followed. The Standard must dominate the refining activity. What had been done was only a beginning, for to control Cleveland was not enough; other areas must become a part of one great efficient organization. As W. T. Scheide, a trusted and intimate associate, wrote later, Rockefeller was always essentially a radical in his desire to pierce to the root problems of the oil industry. He was deeply antipathetic to the chaos of the Oil Regions, an Eldorado or Klondike peopled largely by speculative men— army veterans, drifting adventurers, newly-rich farmers—who did not expect the industry to endure permanently, and were intent on quick fortunes before the bottom dropped out. He was still more antipathetic to the chaos in the overcrowded refining industry. Determined to give the oil business a healthy direction, a permanent prosperity, he had resolved to organize the industry with adequate completeness. His motives were mixed, for he meant to enrich himself and his friends in the process; but a passion for order was part of his motivation. He was resolved to create a great coöperative federation dominating the manufacture and marketing of oil, and putting an end to disorderliness and uncertainty.

Although the Standard Oil in 1871–72 had taken possession of nearly all refining in Cleveland, a chaotic situation still obtained in the oil industry as a whole. After all, Cleveland was but one city. In the Regions, in Pittsburgh and Baltimore, in New York and Philadelphia, scores upon scores of other refiners plied their business. When the South Improvement scheme collapsed, its promoters had intimated that some similar plan would soon have to be brought forward. In no time at all various oil leaders stepped forward with a project for a pool of refiners to work in harmony with the united producers.

This program, called the "Pittsburgh Plan," was apparently devised by William G. Warden, Charles Lockhart, and other manufacturers of that city. It was being discussed by the beginning of April, 1872, when the Pittsburgh *Gazette* outlined the basis of the pool (limitation of output to increase prices), adding that something would have to be done, and at once. The tentative plan called for a loose but comprehensive organization of refiners under a central board having broad powers. The organization would operate in the open; the board would control the buying of crude oil, allot each member-refinery its just share, fix prices, and negotiate public uniform freight rates with the railroads; and each member would receive profits in proportion to the appraised value of his property. To guard against sudden secession, the board would devise a plan for leasing the member-refineries. During May outlines of the Pittsburgh Plan were widely published in the Eastern press. The scheme was frankly open to amendment. Though Rockefeller had little confidence in so loose and flimsy an association, he quickly saw that the attempt to make it work would have valuable educative benefits.

Hence it was that when early in May a special expedition of

refiners was organized to offer an olive branch to the lately embattled Oil Regions, Rockefeller and Flagler boarded a train for Pittsburgh. There they met Warden, Frew, and Waring, and the five refiners were soon journeying up the beautiful Allegheny Valley to Titusville. They stepped boldly into the principal business offices to explain that they had come to meet their recent opponents, to bury the knife, and to ask for a general union to stabilize prices. Many refiners and well-owners were ready to discuss the problems of the industry, for overproduction again menaced the Regions. Wells were being drilled by the hundred. The Producers' Union lacked power to control the output, and while Regions men felt a natural distrust of the old South Improvement leaders, they were ready to consider proposals that might help stabilize the industry.

At two tense public meetings held in Titusville on May 15–16 to discuss "the Pittsburgh plan," Archbold, Vandergrift, and several other leading refiners accordingly shocked many of the die-hards by boldly espousing the new scheme. Though they reiterated their hatred of the South Improvement Company, they deplored the chaos which faced both producers and refiners, and lauded the fair character of the current proposals. "I am willing to do anything which will be of benefit to the trade," declared Archbold. "In whatever is the best plan, I am willing to coöperate."

Inevitably there was fiery opposition to such sentiments. A majority feared that if the plan went through, the former South Improvement leaders would be dominant, and that the new combination would use rebates to stamp out competitors.

The promoters of the Pittsburgh Plan, however, meant to go forward; and indeed, their defeat had some aspects of a victory. They had won over the two ablest refiners in the Oil Regions, and, quite as important, the two leaders of the New York independents, Charles Pratt and H. H. Rogers. Rockefeller valued these gains highly. He and his associates proceeded to push their project by conference and correspondence. On August 5 the Pittsburgh *Gazette* reported that it "promises to be a success . . . All the refiners here, with the exception of two, have gone into it. . . . Cleveland, Philadelphia, and New York refiners are favorable to it." On the 26th the paper announced that the National Refiners' Association had been formed and would begin to operate on September 1. Actually, August 15, 1872, seems to have been the day of formation, and operation may have begun at once.

The first officers of the Petroleum Refiners' Association (usually called the National Refiners' Association) were John D. Rockefeller, president; J. J. Vandergrift, vice-president; and Charles Pratt, treasurer. Thus the dominating position and personality of the Standard's head were recognized, while the three officers represented the West, the Regions, and the East. This was a symbol of the progress made toward unification and control less than five months after the crushing South Improvement defeat. From its printed charter we learn the following facts about the Association:

1. It was open to any refiner who would sign the agreement.
2. It was a representative body, covering five districts: Cleveland, Pittsburgh, the Oil Regions, New York, and Philadelphia. Each was organized under a local board, with officers. National headquarters were in New York.
3. The local boards each designated one agent, who served on a Board of Agents for the whole association; they also elected three directors, who made up a fifteen-man Board of Directors responsible for the Association's general policy, including purchases and sales (which apparently included a control of prices). The Board of Agents, after getting instructions from the local boards, made allotments and carried out other assignments under the general supervision of the Board of Directors.
4. Officers were elected by the Board of Directors.
5. The districts were allotted crude oil for refining on the basis of a total production of 18,000 barrels a day, which was distributed by quota as follows: Cleveland, 26.82 per cent; Pittsburgh, 23.68 per cent; the Oil Regions, 16.75 per cent; New York, 18 per cent; and Philadelphia, 14.75 per cent. Local boards made allotments to individual refiners.
6. No member could purchase or sell except under his allotment, although he could sell portions of his oil to other refiners in the association under supervision of the Board of Directors. All members must report all purchases and sales to the association.
7. The Board of Directors was to receive complaints and arbitrate differences between members.
8. The agreement was for five years; but any member might withdraw on a year's notice, and any district by a two-thirds vote of its members on three months' notice.
9. Amendments to the charter could be made by a four to one favorable vote of the districts.

Obviously the pool represented a heavy dilution of the original Pittsburgh Plan, for it contained no leasing agreement or
other means of coercion. According to the Titusville correspond-
ent of the New York *World*, it aimed at reducing the refining
capacity of the country by one-half, planned a statistical service
on production, stocks, consumption and other vital matters, and
meant to attack the speculators. All these objects were unquestionably held by Rockefeller and his associates, although not
explicitly stated in the agreement. Speculation, for example, was
covered by the pledge.

This pledge reveals an effort to impress members with the
gravity of their task, and to inspire them with loyalty and vigilance. It defines the purpose of the Association as "the improvement and protection of the legitimate trade in refined oil." It
then imposes complete secrecy "concerning any business which
it [the Association] may undertake," and requires members to
forswear all speculation themselves, and "not by hint or suggestion" to give outsiders any opportunity to speculate. Finally,
all are sworn to report any violation of the pledge by any member. While the stipulation that secrecy must be observed was not
wholly harmonious with the proclaimed public character of the
organization, in order to keep information out of irresponsible
hands it was perhaps necessary.

Meanwhile, the torrent of oil pouring from Clarion County
and other new fields had pushed the price of crude down. Each
day saw more wells being sunk, until by August 24 the drills
were biting into nearly 350 new shafts. Production for the Regions rose from 12,000 barrels a day to 15,000, to 16,000, to 17,000.
In August the average price paid for crude fell to $3.47½, almost
a dollar less than a year earlier. Unable to find cars for their
product, some desperate producers were running in into the
river. Yet men were feverishly bidding for fresh sites, drills were
thudding down at new spots every morning, fresh gushers were
swelling the tide of "black gold." What could be done? "Organize," came the cry. Only a few months before an association
had clamped an embargo on oil to the South Improvement
monopolists; now another must limit the supply for the world!

To carry out the intention, late in August a new Petroleum
Producers' Association was formed. The new organization did
not represent any hostility to the Petroleum Refiners Association.

In a burst of crusading spirit, the oil men elected Captain William Hasson, successful head of the Petroleum Producers' Union, president of the Association. Members were resolved to forge a body strong enough to protect producers for years to come. They would enlist every oil man in the Regions, even those pumping only ten barrels a day. The buoyant Hasson and his deputies took the pledge to the fields: signers would drill no shaft and lease no land for drilling for six months beginning September 1, 1872. The theory was that with no new wells coming in, production would decrease by from 3000 to 5000 barrels a day as the old wells fell off. The pledge was expected to prevent the sinking of about 500 new wells.

With public feeling and the press strongly behind him, Hasson found rich and poor operators willing to sign up. Each agreed to forfeit $2,000 for every well he drilled, the money to be collectable like any other debt. Each agreed to use all honorable means to prevent others from boring. Only in one area did the field agents encounter difficulty—in Clarion County. Here many of the landowners were Pennsylvania-German farmers, greedy, narrow-minded, and stubborn. And was it not natural that the holders of promising sites in a new field should object to sealing up their possible wealth while the existing producers could go on working their properties, smugly watching the rise in prices bought at the expense of others? Speculators who had bought lands or options insisted on working the properties which, if left undeveloped, would quickly break them.

With Clarion County (which had most need of regulation) left uncontrolled, and the stop-drilling argument neither fair nor effective, the Producers' Association began to close existing wells. It was forced into this step, for during August and early September production topped 18,000 barrels a day and went on soaring. Titusville prices dropped in mid-September to $2.75 a barrel. Experts estimated, probably with some exaggeration, that the district was then losing a dollar a barrel, or more than $500,000 a month. The movement for a thirty-day shutdown rapidly gained ground, and unanimous action was finally taken at an Oil City meeting. By midnight of September 28 three-fourths of the wells in the older producing areas had been stopped.

Average daily production for September was cut to 16,561 barrels, as against 18,816 the month previous. In October it fell to

14,308 barrels. Then on October 28 the embargo was removed; and the next month production soared to a new record of 23,275 barrels! It remained above 22,000 barrels in December, while prices naturally sagged once more.

Clearly only a comprehensive, highly centralized, permanent organization could control the output. Hasson and his associates therefore began maturing a new plan. Suggestions, some wild, some helpful, poured in on the leaders. Finally, late in October, 1872, Hasson presented a revised scheme.

He proposed a corporation, the Petroleum Producers' Agency, with a capitalization of $1,000,000, its stock to be held only by actual producers or men for whom they vouched. It would purchase all available oil from the Producers' Association, paying not less than $5 a barrel. If the price could be maintained at $5 or more, the full amount would be paid at once; if not, the Agency would store the oil in tanks which it meant to build, paying partly in cash, partly in tank certificates. Whenever the Board of Directors deemed it advisable, they could establish refineries and take other steps to maintain a high price. They were also to determine the line at which production should be restrained, and when necessary were to adopt measures to stop drilling. Meanwhile, they would constantly collect statistics as to wells, drilling, oil-production, and stocks on hand. In this way the committee hoped to control output and prices with an iron grip, to restrain the fast-growing body of speculators, and to offer a defiant front to the refiners. The Agency was to oppose all monopolies valiantly—all save its own!

For a time the scheme promised success. Bankers of the Region gave it their support and by October 24 about $200,000 in stock had been subscribed. Hasson urged oil men to back it without reservation. At a new producers' convention on November 6 in Oil City, confidence and unanimity prevailed. Next day the press announced: "Agency plan an entire success—over $1,000,000 subscribed to capital stock." Trustees and officers were elected.

Consumers now began to take notice, for $5 a barrel was a high charge, and if the agency could establish a monopoly, it might keep the price of oil there. Yet actually the Producers' Agency was a giant with feet of clay. Supported fervidly by most of the large, well-established producers, it was regarded by the small owners and new investors with a jaundiced eye.

The owners of little wells—men throughout the Allegheny

Valley whose engines lifted from five to twenty barrels a day, or like that Tipperary farmer's cow, gave just enough for a living—dreaded a monopoly by their wealthy and powerful brethren. If the big fellows could organize to raise or depress prices, they might extinguish men with small resources by one unexpected drop in oil quotations. The little men feared the fate of the small anthracite operators in the neighboring counties whose holdings had been swallowed up by a few powerful corporations. As for the recent investors, they felt it bitterly unfair that they should be deprived of the chances their predecessors had so blithely seized.

Moreover, the number of wells was increasing too rapidly for effective restraint. When it grew evident in December that production in Clarion, Butler, and Venango fields was breaking all records, the $5 price became preposterous, and the movement faced a certainty of failure. But while the scheme still looked promising, the Agency had received a remarkable offer of support from the refiners who welcomed the stabilizing influence of the agency. Rockefeller himself favored a strong association of refiners, a strong association of producers, and some working agreement between the two.

No sooner had the Agency obtained its capital of a million dollars than he ordered an Oil City agent of the Standard to buy 6000 barrels of crude from it at $4.75 a barrel, at the same time expressing the warmest good will. "It has been represented to us," he telegraphed, apparently on November 10, 1872, "that if we would buy of the producers' agent at Oil City and pay $4.75 a barrel, they would maintain the price. We are willing to go further and buy only of the producers' agent . . . See Hasson and others and let there be a fair understanding on this point. We will do all in our power to maintain prices, and continue to buy, provided our position is fully understood. We do this to convince producers of our sincerity, and to assist in establishing the market. The Titusville *Courier* next day announced heavy purchases by the Standard.

As a matter of fact, the Refiners' Association had made overtures to the producers even before this telegram was sent. Rockefeller as its president telegraphed Hasson on October 23, 1872: "We would be pleased to have your Council appoint a Committee to meet a committee from our association to consult in regard to our mutual interest and see if an arrangement could be made beneficial to both. If Committee is appointed, please name time and place of meeting." Hasson at once acknowledged the telegram, promising, "Will present to Council tomorrow morning." On October 24 he sent another telegram: "The Council would be pleased to confer with Refiners at any time with reference to the general interest of both but cannot entertain propositions looking to the exclusion of competition for crude oil." Rockefeller wired the same day: "Despatch received— Members of our Association will meet your Council at Oil City tomorrow morning." To this Hasson responded, still on the 24th: "Council adjourned at noon. Will not reassemble until twelfth November."

However, Hasson and others, while glad to sell oil at a good price, opposed any combination with recent members of the South Improvement Company. Hasson declared against "foreign entanglements" until the Agency had tested itself. But the moderates won; for committees from the refiners and producers met, and on December 19, 1872, at the Fifth Avenue Hotel in New York, a contract between them was signed. This was approved on December 23, at Titusville, by the Producers' Council. Hasson opposed it to the end, and he and the *Derrick* predicted that the "Treaty of Titusville" would fail and bring disaster to the Regions. Their dark prophecies sowed dissension among the producers, and fed a defeatist spirit.

The "Treaty of Titusville" as able an agreement as the producers could have expected to negotiate, provided that the Petroleum Producers' Association and the Petroleum Refiners' Association should appoint committees to meet together weekly, or as often as necessary. They were to "see that the provisions of this Agreement are executed in good faith," and each agency had the right to examine the books of the other. Both would admit to equal membership all refiners and producers respectively who wished to join. Producers were bound to sell oil only through their association, while refiners agreed to buy from the Producers' Association "daily such quantities of Crude Oil as the Markets of the World may take of them," the exact amount to be determined by the two committees. The price of oil was to be $5 a barrel, "conditionally." That is, $4 a barrel was to be paid in cash (though the committees could, if necessary, reduce this amount); while if refined oil were sold in New York at 26 cents per gallon, no further amount would be paid, but for each cent advance, an additional 25 cents per barrel was to be added, until the price reached $5. Either association might discontinue the agreement on ten days' notice.

It was further agreed, although this was not a part of the compact, that the producers should keep their output at or near 15,000 barrels a day, while the refiners pledged themselves not to negotiate rebates with the railroads. Apparently they considered the rate-changes made by the three trunk lines since March 25 to be open and general reductions.

"It now remains to be seen," remarked the New York *World* on December 24, "whether this new expedient—an alliance between the producers and refiners for the purpose of making arbitrary figures at which petroleum shall be sold to merchants—will meet success." Already there were signs that it might not. On December 17 a panic had seized the crude oil market and prices had fallen sharply. Even after the ratification of the agreement, the market remained weak. The two committees, acting under Section 9 of the contract, felt impelled to lower the base payment from the stipulated $4 to $3.25! The glut of oil increased, and well-owners began selling to speculators for $3, $2.50, and even $2 a barrel.

The complete collapse of the producers' organization was soon at hand. Independent producers at the beginning of 1873 were disposing of oil at $2.60 a barrel or less; treachery appeared in the ranks of the association, one member of the executive committee selling five thousand barrels at a cut rate the very first day of the agreement; and by January 15 it was clear that all efforts at control had broken down. That day, according to the Titusville *Herald* of January 16, C. V. Culver of the executive committee made a report to the Producers' Council in Titusville admitting failure. At the same time, he warmly praised the Refiners' Association for its loyal coöperation, terming them "the most honorable set of businessmen I ever met."

Culver spoke in special praise of Rockefeller, saying that when offered 5000 barrels at $2.25 a barrel, the Standard head had stoutly replied that he had agreed to take his quota at $3.25, and he would abide by his pledge. "We ourselves are at fault," said Culver sadly; and on his motion, the Council declared the contract with the Refiners' Association "inoperative and void."

Once more, disorganization and glut dominated the oil fields. The Butler and Clarion areas continued to pour out increasing floods of oil. In 1874 production reached a new record of

10,810,000 barrels, and the following year came the discovery of the great Bradford pool, which in 1880 alone produced about 22,000,000 barrels. The significance of the spectacle was not lost upon Regions refiners like Archbold and Vandergrift. They saw clearly that any further effort on their part to find stability would mean coöperation with fellow-refiners and not with producers.

The Association continued its effort to build an effective control of refining activity. But the lack of strong central authority began to be felt. The directors were continually passing resolutions which had to be ratified by the districts, dues were not paid promptly, and members frequently over-stepped the rules. The last minutes are for May 15, when the Association was clearly in a shaky condition. At a meeting in Saratoga on June 24, 1873, it was dissolved.

"It was apparent to me early after the organization of the Refiners' Association," said Rockefeller years later, "that among so many men untrained in business there were many who could not be relied upon to aid in solving a problem so difficult as the reformation which my associates and I sought to bring about in this industry." Probably the failure of the resolution permitting the formation of a company to buy or acquire by merger outside refineries was in his mind. He went on: "But it was deemed desirable to continue patiently the study of these same people . . . to confirm or disprove the impressions early formed of their unreliability. We proved that the producers' and refiners' associations were ropes of sand."

# CHAPTER IV

# LEVIATHAN

ALTHOUGH hurt by the glut of oil and the poor prices, refiners in general were in a happier situation than producers, and of all refiners the Standard was best off. It had reduced the total amount of refining in Cleveland, it had no important rivals for the Western trade, and it had placed its manufacturing operations on a foundation of unapproached efficiency.

While there is evidence that Cleveland was using somewhat less oil at this time than the many plants of the city had used in January, 1872, the Standard refined more than ever before— thirty-four per cent of the total industry! And the notable advance had been associated with earnings of 20 per cent upon capitalization, an additional fact which deepened the conviction of Rockefeller and Flagler as to the rightness of their policy.

The Standard had become national in scope. The acquisition of the Bostwick interests had laid a firm foundation for its Eastern activities. These had been further extended late in March, 1872, by the annexation of the Long Island Oil Company, one of the small but efficient refineries in the New York area. The works of this firm stood near the transfer facilities of the Standard itself at Hunter's Point, on the Brooklyn side of the East River roughly opposite Thirty-Fourth Street, Manhattan. The Long Island had been established in 1862, and at the time of purchase was capitalized at $200,000. Unfortunately, several months after the merger a disastrous fire swept Hunter's Point. Although the facilities were soon more than replaced, the disaster temporarily reduced the production of refined oil by the Standard in the New York area.

Its Eastern manufacturing capacity was again greatly increased, however, by a new acquisition early in 1873. On January 13 of that year a contract with Devoe Manufacturing Company made it a part of the Standard. This was a momentous step in expansion, for the Devoe works on Long Island, with a capitalization of $500,000, were extensive and efficient. They specialized in the export of "case oil," for which they made their own cans.

The vigorous New York properties were of the greatest value to the expanding Standard Oil. Although Cleveland was the ideal situation for supplying the Western markets, it operated at a disadvantage with respect to the East, and to the ever-richer export trade. Overseas sales rose in 1873 to almost 5,500,000 barrels, or more than a quarter of the entire output of refined oil. New York, Philadelphia, and Baltimore were the logical centers for Eastern and foreign marketing; the Standard would soon increase its New York facilities, and then move on the other two cities. William Rockefeller at once profited by the assistance of the experienced Devoe men in building up foreign sales. Meanwhile, relations with jobbers and middlemen had been strengthened and extended.

This marketing activity was a new departure of the greatest significance. Until 1873 the Standard Oil Company had remained almost wholly a manufacturing corporation. It had organized no retail selling agencies, shipping wholesale instead to a multitude of local jobbers, or to big regional distributors such as the Waters Pierce Oil Company in St. Louis and Chess, Carley & Company in Louisville. The Standard had been embarrassed by its complete lack of authority over this horde of middlemen. Some of them disturbed the market by speculation in oil, and threw quantities of cheap, dangerous kerosene into the market. They even adulterated the Standard's own products, thus endangering its reputation. The abuses and wastefulness of retail distribution had for some time irked the methodical Rockefeller.

In 1873 he suddenly invaded the field by acquiring half ownership of Chess, Carley & Co. This firm operated a Louisville refinery, which might become important if the wells of West Virginia and Kentucky increased their output; but its distributing business was more valuable. The combination opened up for Standard products a lucrative Southern territory, in which Chess, Carley rapidly increased their operations. As with the Devoe Manufacturing Company, the Standard continued this agency as an apparently independent organization.

Steps had meanwhile been taken to systematize the purchasing of crude oil. Bostwick, long a buyer, continued his activities nominally as an independent, but actually under the control of the Standard and with its funds; except that he was permitted to employ $250,000 of his own, on which he was guaranteed 7 per cent and commissions. His capable agents in the Regions, Joseph Seep and Daniel O'Day, were soon handling orders that ran into many millions monthly.

In the summer of 1873, newspapers announced the sale of the Union Pipe Line to the Empire Transportation Company, fast-freight subsidiary of the Pennsylvania, and already owner of the Mutual Line. Thus two of the longest pipe lines in the Regions were combined. Apparently startled by the transaction, Rockefeller forthwith undertook a new and highly strategic activity, which he had already been planning.

Up to this time the use of pipe lines for carrying oil had been chiefly local, although the threat of a conduit from the Regions to Cleveland had alarmed the Lake Shore and helped to give the Standard more favorable railroad rates. Pipe lines had been linked to little groups of wells and had run their oil to the nearest railroad. They had already driven most teamsters out of existence. Longer systems, like Abbott & Harley's Allegheny Transportation Company, had begun to indicate a greater scope.

In 1873 no pipe line company could command much capital. Their nominal charge was thirty cents a barrel, whether for half a mile or thirty; but competition often drove the rate down to five cents. Thirty or forty companies were operating, only six of which owned more than one hundred miles of line. Thus in the fifteen years following Drake's strike, the pipe lines and their facilities had not grown beyond the rudimentary stage. Yet they were explosive with potentialities, and for some time Rockefeller had been studying them with mixed feelings. Suppose the pipe line now fell into the hands of some determined opponent, who developed their immense possibilities? A pipe line monopoly might be far more dangerous than a producers' monopoly, for it would rest in fewer hands and be open to more unscrupulous manipulation. The obvious safeguard lay in Standard-controlled pipe lines, with accompanying storage tanks. That would help assure a steady supply of crude, and doubtless lower the cost of transporting it.

When the Empire purchased the Union Pipe Line, making it

clear that danger was at hand, Rockefeller leaped into action. Bostwick's genial but ruthless Daniel O'Day had a special knowledge
of transportation, along with the two-fisted fighting qualities that
a job of competitive pioneering required. Rockefeller turned to
him. Bostwick had strongly recommended O'Day to Rockefeller
as the best man to build a Standard pipe line system.

At Rockefeller's suggestion, Bostwick commissioned O'Day to
build a line from Emlenton to the new Clarion County oil fields.
By the fall of 1873 the energetic Irishman had put down about
80 miles. This property was soon consolidated with a short line
of the American Transfer Company, bought in 1874, and with
the holdings of Vandergrift & Forman, in which the Standard
purchased a one-third interest. In September, 1874, O'Day opened
a line from Turkey City in the Clarion field to Oil City, with only
one pumping station en route. In 1875 he ran a pipe line into the
new Bradford area to the northeast. From all these grew the great
gathering system soon known as the United Pipe Lines, which
were placed under the control of W. T. Scheide, an experienced
operator. The United Pipe Lines became one of the two cornerstones of the Standard's pipe line network. The other, the American Transfer Company, was soon completely owned by Rockefeller and his associates. On November 15, 1874, the Standard
paid $200,000 for it to Bostwick, Josiah Macy, Jr., A. J. Pouch,
and Rockefeller himself.

At the close of the year 1876 the two systems comprised 400 miles
of pipes, with a tankage capacity of nearly 1,400,000 barrels.
Rockefeller had thus blocked the formation of a monopoly by
the Empire or any other group. Indeed, he was already dreaming
of his own pipe line monopoly.

The panic of 1873, which was to usher in a national depression
of five years, broke like a thunderclap on September 18 with the
collapse of the powerful banking house of Jay Cooke & Company.
Banks closed their doors, stocks tumbled with a crash, unemployment became general, and breadlines formed in all the larger
cities.

Both branches of the oil industry felt the terrible blow. The
price of crude sagged late in 1873 to almost eighty cents a barrel,
and despite a partial recovery still averaged only $1.33 early in
1874. Refined, which brought 26 cents a gallon in 1872, sold just
after the crash for 13. In 1876, although the depression was at its

worst, the price of oil recovered. Production had fallen below world demand, and producers were prosperous once more.

For Rockefeller, even the wretched prices of 1873–74 had performed a useful service. They had helped him to promote the consolidation which he had long pictured as the one rock of hope for the industry. In difficult times his gospel had a stronger appeal. He renewed his former arguments. He pointed out that refining capacity was still absurdly excessive, that two efforts to reduce it and otherwise to control refining by a pool had failed, and that complete unification offered the one true road to prosperity. Even the doubters listened to him now.

Meanwhile the railroads, hard hit by the depression and their own rate wars, were struggling to keep their respective oil shipments high. The New York Central–Lake Shore system had entered into partnership with the Standard in acquiring the United Pipe Lines so that it could compete with the Pennsylvania and the Empire. The Erie was now to court the company in spectacular fashion.

During the year that followed the old rate agreement of March 25, 1872, even the pretence of renouncing rebates had been abandoned. Every oil shipper of any consequence now received one. Archbold and Vandergrift, so insistent during the South Improvement war that all such favors should be abandoned, had obtained concessions. Adnah Neyhart, an oil jobber who had taken as conspicuous a position, had collected $7000 in rebates from the Erie in the single month of September, 1872.

But even while making such payments, this road had not received the shipments of oil to which it felt entitled. An agreement with the Regions refiners in March, 1873, which it hoped would bring it nearly all their shipments from Titusville, Oil City, and other centers to New York, ended in relative failure; for the Empire promptly met all its cuts and was soon routing most of the coveted oil over the Pennsylvania's tracks. Since matters looked almost hopeless in the Regions, the Erie turned with something like desperation to Rockefeller and his associates.

The Standard's contract with the New York Central had expired on or about April 1, 1873, and apparently it had made another with that road of a more satisfactory character. But at some time during the summer of that year it was confronted by two emissaries from the Erie.

These were General James H. Devereux, formerly of the Lake Shore, who in June had assumed the presidency of the Erie's affiliate, the Atlantic & Great Western, and G. R. Blanchard. Devereux naturally knew the details of the Lake Shore–Standard agreement. The two made a vigorous protest. The New York Central and the Pennsylvania, they pointed out, were hogging the oil freights. The Erie was carrying only one-seventh of the output (final figures for 1873 showed that it received but 762,000 out of very nearly 5,000,000 barrels of oil). They asked for more.

"Give us a share equal to the Central's," they urged.

Rockefeller and Flagler were not unwilling to arrange for a more nearly equal division, but they raised an objection with respect to terminal facilities. They pointed out that ever since they had acquired the Long Island Oil Company, their main Eastern terminal had been at Hunter's Point on the East River. The New York Central delivered all shipments to Hunter's Point without additional charge. There the Standard could transfer crude oil to its refinery tanks, inspect barreled oil and make repairs when necessary, or draw refined oil from tank cars and barrel it for sale at home or abroad. The Erie had an oil terminal at Weehawken, N. J., where its own force inspected ready-barreled oil, drew off and barreled refined oil from tanks, and performed other operations. It charged shippers considerable fees for these services. Devereux and Blanchard had expected the Standard to pay such charges, but Rockefeller and Flagler declined to do so.

The Erie could not throw its expensive transfer plant into an already cluttered junkyard of bad investments. Blanchard and Devereux, however, quickly worked out a solution. They suggested that the Standard lease the Weehawken yard, and take over the entire business of cooperage, repairs, and transfer, both for itself and for other shippers. Paying so much a barrel for the use of the terminal, it could collect the usual fees from other refiners, and from jobbers and oil commission men. On this basis an agreement was worked out. The Erie guaranteed the Standard as low a rate on refined oil as the New York Central would make; the Standard promised that no other road or roads should receive more than half of its east-bound shipments.

The lease of the Weehawken yards by the Standard marked another step toward its control of the making and sale of refined oil. It soon enlarged the terminal facilities to provide for the routing of oil to New England or to the South. At the same time, it gained a full acquaintance with all competitive shipments over the Erie.

The important gains were the more convenient location and new facilities for shipping to certain Eastern points, the favorable freight rates and the check on the Central which they represented, and the advantage of a close alliance with the Erie. The agreement was dated April 20, 1874; Bostwick, familiar with the Weehawken yards, helped to knit the facilities quickly and firmly into the Standard's system. The new arrangement was scarcely pleasing to the Central. It lost a certain amount of valuable shipments, and was later to protest. But its quarrel was with the Erie rather than the Standard, and it could not offend its best customer. As a matter of fact, the agreement appears in perspective as the beginning of a loose but important triple alliance in which the Erie, the Central, and the Rockefeller interests became aligned against the Empire and the Pennsylvania.

Meanwhile, the Standard completed another significant stroke of expansion, when on January 22, 1874, it purchased the large Imperial Refining Company near Oil City, owned by Vandergrift, Forman, and other Regions men. It was the second largest plant in the area, Archbold's firm having somewhat greater capacity. Thus Rockefeller and his associates notably enlarged the foothold they already had in the Regions. But the winning of the burly, resourceful Vandergrift was more important than the acquisition of his company. He was not to end his days with the Standard Oil, for banking and the iron business in Pittsburgh later called him to other tasks. But for years he was a powerful ally, and the mere news that he had gone over to Rockefeller staggered the Standard's opponents in the Regions.

The Standard Oil Company had now become an imposing structure—a closely-controlled unit of widely varied and widely placed activities. It operated practically all the refineries in Cleveland except a few lubricating plants. It was well on the way toward building the strongest network of pipe lines and storage tanks in the Region. It had acquired large properties in New York: oil terminals at Hunter's Point and Weehawken; the refineries formerly owned by Bostwick, Devoe, and the Long Island Oil Company; and a great array of lighters, barges, and other properties. Under Bostwick it had begun to conduct the buying of oil with new efficiency. The purchase of control in Chess, Carley signalized the fact that it had started to organize its own retail marketing activity. It was developing an effective alliance with two of the great railroad systems. It had invaded the Regions as a refiner. It was improving its already superior manufacturing techniques; it operated the best barrel-making shops in the land under the incomparable McGregor; it was making its own acids and other by-products. Finally, under William Rockefeller it had built up a splendid export organization to compete for the European trade.

In its expansion it had acquired or developed not only immense material resources, but many talented executives. It had built for brains as well as plant. In this Rockefeller was always specially interested. He had his own way of studying men and ascertaining their talents. The Standard built carefully for defensive and offensive strategy; it was strong to attack or defend. Even in 1874 the Standard Oil Company was Leviathan.

As for John D. Rockefeller, each year had brought some new vindication of his business foresight. Not least among the evidences of his self-confidence and acumen was the assiduity with which he increased his Standard stockholdings. From the outset he had held by far the largest single block. In 1873 this amounted to between 3500 and 4500 shares; in 1875 it totalled 4549. Stephen V. Harkness with 2500, Payne with 2045, and Flagler and Andrews with 2042 each were then the next largest holders. From that year forward Rockefeller added rapidly to his holdings, until in 1882 he had 9500 shares. One of the large American fortunes was beginning to appear. Of course, it comprised other holdings besides Standard Oil stock.

During the later months of 1873 an event was impending which bore an important relationship to this growing fortune. The Euclid Avenue household was expecting an addition. On January 29, 1874, a fourth child joined the three daughters who already made a lively family. This time it was a son—the male heir for which both husband and wife had hoped. He was named John D. Rockefeller, Jr.

The father was inexpressibly happy. On the morning his son was born he burst into the office to tell his associates the news, and Flagler and Payne affectionately put their arms about him, while the room rang with their congratulations, and tears of joy stood in Rockefeller's eyes.

\*        \*        \*        \*        \*

At this time the refining industry remained badly overcrowded. Well-owners were even harder hit than refiners. The failure of the Producers' Association having destroyed all curbs on drilling and pumping, in 1873 the flow of crude oil reached almost ten million barrels. Prices went down and down. The outlook was grim. To be sure, the railroads were carrying increased quantities of oil. About three-quarters of all the refined oil of the country was going to the seaports for the European trade. But the carriers were fighting wastefully over the division of the traffic. General rail freight traffic had declined, and oil had become more important.

As a result of these conditions, refiners, producers, and railroad officials alike were feeling that more organization was needed.

The well-owners moved first. April, 1874, brought another definite drive to stop the drills and pumps. Hopeful producers argued that production was now in fewer hands and could be more easily controlled. With Butler County men taking the lead, a plan for a ninety-day stoppage was launched which appealed to the large owners and ignored the little fellows. A meeting at Petrolia on April 21 displayed marked enthusiasm. By the end of that month drilling had been stopped at 130 sites, owners of 27 drillrigs had promised to cease work for ninety days, and prices had risen sharply.

From the outset, however, the movement was opposed by many hard-headed oil men. They pointed out that it was fostered chiefly by large producers who had stocks of oil on hand and would realize handsome profits from an increase in prices. Was it fair to ask men who had no oil in storage to cease drilling in order that those with big reserves might coin money? By hundreds, such dissenters refused to sign. The result was that on May 15, at a new meeting of producers at Titusville, a resolution was unanimously passed releasing everybody from the ninety-day pledge.

It is evident that the ethics of a combination of oil producers to restrict output and raise prices does not differ from the ethics of a combination of refiners with the same objectives. At a later date Miss Ida Tarbell pictured the recurrent failure of the producers to organize as attributable to the machinations of the refining interest. Of course it was traceable primarily to the producers' numbers and to their rampant individualism.

It was now the turn of the railroads and the refiners to make an attempt at organization, and they succeeded a good deal better. The year 1874 found the Baltimore & Ohio and the Pennsylvania in a bitter war, the former cutting its through rates to the Mis-

sissippi by about one-third, and arranging for a fast-freight service
from Baltimore westward on this basis.

Moreover, the compact of April, 1874, between the Erie and
the Standard, had disturbed both the New York Central and the
Pennsylvania. The former had lost a considerable part of their
Cleveland oil shipments, and Scott had always feared the Erie.
The heads of both these roads complained that the new Erie rates
were too low to permit a profit, and therefore set a bad example.
Competition for oil traffic was again raging with implacable fury,
and the press agreed that it was likely to precipitate another general rate war.

And the roads agreed that freight and passenger rates were too
low and must be raised. They signed a number of rate agreements, of which that on oil alone concerns us. In enforcing this
agreement it was necessary to have the coöperation of the principal refiners, and the intermediary between the railroads and
oil men was Joseph D. Potts of the Empire. While his fast-freight
line was a subsidiary of the Pennsylvania, it also served other
roads, and held a nominally independent position. A member of
an old Pennsylvania family, he had acted as general manager of
the Philadelphia & Erie when it was leased to the Pennsylvania.
Then in 1865 he had been detached to organize and manage the
Empire, and he had done this with such brilliance that he had become an outstanding figure in the railroad world of the seventies.

Potts, equally fearful of a general rate-war and a continuance
of the attack on fast-freight lines, urged a compact among the
three great oil-carrying roads and the principal refiners. He was
extremely persuasive. A plan was soon hammered out to which
the trunk lines and a large body of refiners subscribed.

It had three main features. First it provided for an equitable
division of oil traffic among the Pennsylvania, Erie, and New York
Central, the first-named getting approximately one-half, the other
two a quarter each. The Standard and other leading refiners were
to act as "eveners." In the second place, it called for an advance
in freight rates. But it was the third feature of the plan that was
most startling; for this decreed that the entire Oil Regions should
be treated as a single station, and that a uniform rate should be
fixed from this station to the eastern ports *by way of all refining
points.* For example, the charge for transporting the crude to
make a barrel of refined oil from the pipe lines to a Cleveland,
Pittsburgh, or Titusville refinery, and then for taking the same

oil when refined from any of these places to New York, was made precisely the same as the charge for transporting the same amount of crude directly from the Oil Regions to a Philadelphia or New York refinery.

Under this arrangement, the Cleveland or Pittsburgh refiner could put a barrel of oil on the wharf in Philadelphia or New York for shipment to Europe just as cheaply, in terms of freight charges, as his rivals in the Regions or in the coastal ports themselves, although his crude-plus-refined haulage was much longer. This practice was already common among the railroads; it was applied in hauling coal from the anthracite regions to the seaboard, and in shipping fruit from southern areas to the North.

To "equalize" their freight charges, the Pittsburgh and Cleveland refiners were given a rebate. This completely wiped out the previous cost of bringing crude from the Regions to their doors; Cleveland, for example, had apparently paid 35 cents a barrel for this service—and now this charge was abolished. Rates on refined were similarly "equalized." They were made $1.85 a barrel from every inland refining point—Titusville, Erie, Pittsburgh, Cleveland, it was all one—to Philadelphia and Baltimore, and $2 to New York.

By these changes the railroad giants destroyed with one blow the advantage in short-haul transportation which the Regions refineries had enjoyed over Pittsburgh and Cleveland works. They destroyed the great advantage of the New York and Philadelphia plants in having no rail transportation to pay at all for export shipments—these being piped or carried direct from refinery to ship. These coastal refineries had only one haul for overseas trade —from the Regions east; Cleveland had two: first west, then east; yet the charge was the same! To the Regions the new schedule seemed utterly outrageous. For while losing their old advantage of position, they were still weighted down by the handicaps of poor labor supply, high fuel costs, higher charges for chemicals, and inadequate barrel works. They had poor terminal facilities in New York, while those of the Standard were superb. Under the name of "equality," they were receiving what might be their deathblow.

Who had devised this third feature of the compact? Very little doubt can exist. The Standard Oil and its allies were almost certainly responsible. By now the Standard was so powerful that when it called the tune, refiners and railroads both had to dance.

As for the railroads, the new plan suited them well. It raised rates on oil shipments and made them truly profitable. Moreover, the promise of the refiners to "even" the traffic, maintaining the division agreed upon, was invaluable. The pledges the roads made to each other never held for long; but those of the Standard were absolutely dependable.

The railroads having stablized their position, the principal pipe lines in the Regions soon united in making an agreement. Henry Harley, the eccentric pioneer builder of pipe lines, was apparently the moving spirit behind the compact. Probably four-fifths of the pipe line mileage of the Oil Regions entered this pooling agreement signed on September 4, 1874; only a few short lines were omitted. Each line was to charge 30 cents a barrel for piping. It was to keep 8 cents a barrel for itself, and hand the remaining 22 cents over to the pool. A central committee was to divide profits among the members at stated periods. The Standard controlled a little more than a third of the pipeage signed up, and its lines were to receive 36.5 per cent of the net revenue.

The plan brought in the railroads. All of them were to collect from oil shippers 22 cents a barrel, above other charges, upon all crude oil delivered to them. To the inside companies maintaining the 30 cent rate they refunded this 22 cents, but to the lines outside the pool they made no refund. Thus if an independent line tried to undercut the pool lines by charging a shipper 20 cents, or even 10 cents (for undercutting was often savage), it would be checkmated. Even if the shipper paid only 10 for piping, he would pay the 22 cent railroad charge, or a total of 32, and be the loser by 2 cents a barrel! He would do better to patronize the pool.

By the end of September, 1874, railroads, refiners, and pipe lines were ready to act together. If the new arrangements worked, they would mean the doom of both independent refiners and independent pipe lines in the Regions; they must either surrender or die.

That the arrangements were just or fair no one can argue. The strong were combining against the weak, and intended to trample them underfoot. But the men responsible for this situation did not believe in free competition, with a fair chance for all. They saw free competition as responsible for the heavy overproduction of crude oil, the excess refining capacity, the abysmal prices, the pipeline wars, the constant railroad dogfights. They wanted to replace its waste and lawlessness with order and assured profits.

John D. Rockefeller and his son in 1921.

Frederick T. Gates: Rockefeller's first great associate
in planning the benefactions.

If their new pools could be maintained, such would be the results. In fact, more would be accomplished than the South Improvement Company had attempted.

Rockefeller respected the necessity of both a fair division of traffic and higher rates. But these fitted into his own effort to control refining, in that he was able to suggest or dictate the "equalization" feature, so eminently favorable to Cleveland. While the railroad presidents were conferring in New York, Long Branch, and Saratoga, and the pipe line heads in the Regions, he was a dominant figure at a meeting of refiners in Saratoga. The two pools which resulted were quite to his liking. They favored Cleveland especially, and to a lesser extent the men in Pittsburgh, Philadelphia, and New York to whom he had already talked of consolidation. They did not favor the Regions refiners. Yet that fact might suggest to these very refiners the wisdom of uniting with the Standard.

Rockefeller at once renewed his suggestions for union with those competitors who seemed most favorably inclined to the idea. These were, in order, William G. Warden of Philadelphia; Charles Lockhart, R. J. Waring, and William Frew of Pittsburgh; and Charles Pratt and H. H. Rogers of New York. Rockefeller tells us that after the conference Warden, Lockhart, and Waring, who had been considering his suggestions about union for some time, came on to Cleveland to see the Standard's works and discuss the matter further. We can imagine Rockefeller and Flagler taking them carefully over every inch of Plants 1 and 2, and giving them a glimpse of the other four. Then in his offices in the new Standard Buildings Rockefeller would throw open the books of the company. The figures would have been the clinching argument. In 1874 the Standard was making extraordinary profits, while most of its competitors were wrestling with problems of the depression. In fact, on January 5, 1875, a dividend of no less than $115 a share was voted. Rockefeller later spoke of these Pittsburgh and Philadelphia men as "entirely neighborly and friendly." He impatiently denied that they had ever received an ultimatum from the Standard.

It was early in October, 1874, according to Rockefeller, that Warden, Lockhart, and Frew finally all decided to join the Standard. They were the first large group to come in at this time. However, Charles Pratt & Co. appear to have had the matter under consideration, too, and the Standard minutes give October 15 as the date for Warden, Frew & Co. (and apparently Lockhart, Frew, although it is not mentioned in that entry) and the Pratt organization.

These three groups owned refining facilities second only to the Standard's. Warden's chief plant, the Atlantic Refining Company, was a large property situated just below Philadelphia on the Delaware. The Pittsburgh works of Lockhart, Frew & Co. comprised seven separate units: the Nonpareil, the Brilliant, the National, the Lily, the Crystal, the Model, and the Standard. The works of Charles Pratt & Co., situated at Newtown, Long Island, had long held a position in the oil business out of proportion to their modest capital of $250,000.

Thus in what was a three-fold merger the Standard obtained the largest refinery in the Philadelphia area, more than half the refining capacity of Pittsburgh, and the most widely known of the New York independents.

Again its gains in personnel were as notable as those in property values. Warden, Lockhart, Waring, and Frew all entered the Standard's service, and helped notably with its continuing growth. So did Charles Pratt and the brilliant H. H. Rogers. The important roles of all six in the later history of the company fully support Rockefeller's assertion that they had not been threatened or constrained, but joined the organization freely and by deliberate choice.

The new transactions were kept secret. Within a single week the Standard had taken possession of the inner citadels of refining in Pittsburgh and Philadelphia, and had added a powerful strategic unit to its New York stronghold and nobody outside the group immediately concerned knew what had happened. This secrecy was later a ground of indignant and well-justified complaints by the Philadelphia and Pittsburgh independents. They declared that Warden, Lockhart, and Frew acted like free refiners, listened attentively to the talks of opponents of the Standard, picked up their confidential plans, and then hurried to the Standard Oil offices. Even if there were few secrets to learn, the duplicity was reprehensible.

In order to cover the mergers of October, 1874, Flagler, at a special meeting of the stockholders held in Cleveland on March 10, 1875, moved that the capital stock of the company be increased to $3,500,000, or by $1,000,000. The Executive Committee was authorized to receive subscriptions for the whole amount.

Some elements of the fabulous entered into this transaction. Walter F. Taylor of the Standard's legal staff states in his manuscript history of the corporation that Pratt & Co. paid $265 each for its 3125 shares of stock. Part of the payment was in cash—$250,000; while the remainder was presumably represented by the properties they put in. The cash being deducted from the total share value of $828,125, the properties might be assumed to be valued at $578,125, a fairly high figure. But apparently they were accorded a higher rating, and an ingenious device, very pleasant for Charles Pratt & Co., was employed to account for the balance of value. At a previous meeting of the directors of the company in New York on January 5, 1875, W. C. Andrews pointed out that by the contract of October 15, 1874, the $1,000,000 of new capitalization was to be "treated the same as present capital in respect to the past earnings of the company." But those earnings for 1874 had been voted a few minutes earlier into dividends of $115 a share! Therefore Pratt & Company received from this source $359,375, making their plant value $937,500. Or, if applied differently, this sum absorbed their $250,000 cash payment, and left them a profit of $109,375 in cash, in addition to the allowance of $578,125 for their properties.

Warden, Lockhart, and the others in their group fared similarly, except that as they took twice the number of shares, 6250, their plant value was set at $1,256,250, and after getting a dividend of $718,750, they were $318,750 richer in cash after having canceled their $400,000 payment. No wonder the new stockholders were willing to merge with the Standard!

Doubtless the advantages of participation were plainly seen by John D. Archbold when in 1875 he agreed, on behalf of Porter, Moreland & Company of Titusville, to merge with the Standard. The final date may be set as October 26, when the Acme Oil Company of New York was formed; this new establishment took in both Porter, Moreland and Bennett, Warner & Co., another Regions firm. They were the first and third companies in their area in refining capacity, and together had tankage facilities for more than 200,000 barrels of crude oil. Yet once more, perhaps more important than the properties were the high talents—associated, as we shall see, with faults—of Archbold. He was promptly made the head of the Acme Oil Co., formed to operate both of the former plants.

Impetuous, magnetic, brilliant, Archbold immediately became

one of the most active officers in the Standard; and the faith of many small refining firms in the Regions in his probity and talents helped bring them into the combination. In Titusville alone the Octave Oil Company, Pickering & Chambers, Teague Brothers, and Easterly & Davis all presently joined.

The crucial year 1874–1875 had built the Standard into something like the "one big company" of which Rockefeller and Flagler had dreamed. It was now dominant in every important refining area. Yet despite the power of the new Standard, it was a dominant force rather than a monopoly. Characteristically and patiently, Rockefeller set about the task of binding such remaining independents as he could—in New York, Pittsburgh, Erie, Baltimore, Parkersburg, the Regions—into a constructive alliance with his own great company. The Central Refiners' Association was born to revive in more effective form the lately deceased National Refiners' Association.

All refiners were asked to join. An Executive Committee, with one member from each of the five chief districts, was appointed. Twenty-five thousand shares of stock were to be issued at 25 cents a share (worth only $6250 in all), and divided among the five districts in accordance with their refining capacity: Cleveland, 7175; New York, 5375; Oil Creek, 4125; Pittsburgh, 5125; and Philadelphia, 3200. Owners of refineries took stock in the proportion which their refining capacity bore to that of their entire district, but not until they had signed such agreements and contracts as the Executive Committee might prescribe. Absolute control was to be assured by an ingenious system of leases.

The five directors were to apportion all refining among the various members, to control all purchases of crude and all sales of refined, to make all rate agreements with railroads and pipe lines, and to divide all profits. The president of the Association was John D. Rockefeller.

Altogether, the pool was remarkably well-planned, and promised to succeed. But its most remarkable feature was this: it was difficult to say precisely where the Standard Oil Company left off and the Central Refiners' Association began! Any member of the Association somehow soon found itself inextricably entangled with Rockefeller and his partners. Thus combination had dominated the year. Each step toward combination had contributed directly to the growth of the Standard Oil.

On March 10, 1875, the Standard stockholders enlarged their

Board of Directors to thirteen, electing, on Flagler's motion, J. J. Vandergrift, W. G. Warden, Charles Lockhart, and Charles Pratt to fill out the original nine. The stockholders at this time included the two Rockefellers, S. V. Harkness, Samuel Andrews, W. C. Andrews, O. H. Payne, John Pitcairn, H. B. Payne, John Huntington, Joseph Stanley, P. H. Watson, D. W. Harkness, S. G. Harkness, W. T. Wardwell, Benjamin Brewster, T. P. Handy, O. B. Jennings, A. M. McGregor, A. J. Pouch, F. A. Arter, J. A. Bostwick, Josiah Macy, Jr., D. P. Eells, S. F. Barger, and W. H. Vanderbilt.

The new refineries in the combination were thus well represented on the Executive Committee, although Archbold did not take a place there until October 1, 1878. The Standard's two railroad allies were represented by stockholders—Watson for the Erie, Vanderbilt for the New York Central. Cleveland banks were represented by Handy and Eells. The stockholders were a select group of successful, intelligent, and powerful men, many of them officials of the company, and the others it stanch friends.

In their drive to complete the unification of the refining industry, Rockefeller and Flagler had always contemplated the absorption by merger or purchase of practically all refiners. That they now had as partners the leading men of every refining area in the country was not enough. Nor did Warden, Pratt, Lockhart, Archbold, and Rogers disagree with them on this point. All these manufacturers had learned by personal experience that a few desperate rivals in any locality, cutting prices in their struggle to exist, could ruin the market for everybody. Consequently they were more than ready to join in a gigantic effort to coax in or buy out the remaining independents everywhere.

The first notable step taken by the Standard in its campaign for further expansion concerned the agencies for buying and shipping crude oil from the Regions, a vital element in the huge petroleum industry.

Under the alert Jabez A. Bostwick, the Company had developed an efficient force of its own for this work. Its largest rival was the firm of Neyhart & Grandin. Neyhart was now chief owner in the buying concern, which also held some pipe lines, but for some time he had been so ill that his assistant, W. T. Scheide, had carried on the business for him. When in February, 1875, Neyhart died, the Standard hoped for an opportunity to acquire his property. From Rockefeller's point of view, it had been uncomfortably useful to independent refineries. As early as 1874, the Standard had tried to induce the Erie Railroad to help it squeeze Neyhart & Grandin out of the oil-buying business. But the Erie, to its credit, refused the Standard's attractive proposal and went on carrying oil for other shippers.

However, Scheide by 1876 was having as much trouble with certain independents in New York as with the Standard Oil. In the months before and following Neyhart's death they were playing a double-dealing game. Some of them wished to sell out to the Rockefeller interests, but hoped for a high price. They would announce to the Standard that as Scheide would keep them supplied with oil, they had no wish to dispose of their property; and thus they would do their best to "bid up the price of their works on the Standard Oil Company." At the same time that they used Scheide's support, they shopped around among his rivals in procuring their crude. One refinery broke a contract with Scheide for $\frac{1}{128}$ of a cent a gallon! Much disgusted, the shrewd German resolved to abandon the field. In the spring of 1875 he sold out the shipping portion of Neyhart & Grandin to Charles Pratt & Co., blissfully ignorant of Pratt's recent sale to the Standard!

At the same time the pipeline holdings which the Neyhart organization controlled were incorporated in the Tidioute Pipe Company, part of the ownership being held by the Neyhart estate, part by the Grandin brothers, and part by the United Pipe Lines. Scheide did not work directly for the Standard until this jointly-owned pipe property was merged with the American Transfer Company early in 1880.

The Standard Oil thus absorbed its best-known competitor in the buying and selling of crude oil, and increase the pipeline mileage under its influence. Some of the refiners who had depended on Neyhart for raw materials now had to come to the Standard. The Standard was safe against an embargo, and was even in a position in which it could restrict or cut off the flow of vital supplies to some of its competitors.

As for pipe lines, the Standard was able to pick up several small independent units in this same period, 1875–76. The time was soon ripe for a consolidation of the entire network controlled by the Company. Early in 1877 a new corporation under an old name, the United Pipe Lines, was formed with a capital of $3,000,000. Some properties of the American Transfer Company, the old United, and various lesser lines were merged in it. The Standard acquired a heavy majority of the stock and exercised control, although Amasa Stone and W. H. Vanderbilt held nearly a thousand shares each. Only two pipe line systems of notable strength now shared the field with the new United—the Columbia Conduit Company and the Empire Transportation Company. The latter, backed by Pennsylvania Railroad money and influence, constituted the chief rival of the United.

Rockefeller soon took a notable step in enlarging the Standard's transportation contacts. It was nothing less than the invasion of an extensive producing and refining territory which had heretofore lain outside any direct contact with either the Pennsylvania Railroad or the Standard Oil. Southwest of Pittsburgh an oil-producing region had existed since the days following Drake's strike in 1859. It comprised a considerable district about the neighboring river towns of Marietta, Ohio, and Parkersburg, West Virginia—towns about halfway between Pittsburgh and Cincinnati. Activity in the field had grown in the early 1870's, and a number of small refineries had sprung up in and near the two towns. The amount of oil produced in this Ohio River district was very slight compared with the Pennsylvania yield. But it was oil; it might increase in volume; and what was more important to the Standard, it was in regions tapped by the Baltimore & Ohio Railroad, the one trunk line with which the Rockefeller group thus far had no dealings.

The situation had a broad strategic importance to the Standard Oil Company. Under the vigorous leadership of Robert Garrett, the B. & O. had pushed its rails to St. Louis and Chicago, and through the Connellsville branch had reached Pittsburgh. The road was thus flung across the entire Southern front of the Standard. Rockefeller perceived that the West Virginia and Baltimore areas were a potential threat to the Standard in the East, West, and South. Should the B. & O. develop both producing territories and refineries, the independents it served might even invade the Northern markets. In any event, here was an activity that might and should be consolidated with the Standard. Rockefeller and his associates decided upon action.

Their strategy was the same as that used in Cleveland, in New York, in Philadelphia, in the Regions: to ally themselves with the strongest leader among the refiners of an area, and with his aid to bring in the others.

The choice fell upon Johnson Newlon Camden of Parkersburg, part owner of the largest refinery in that town, and also a well-known lawyer and prominent Democratic politician. He was far-seeing and adroit in manipulating men, whether in business or politics. Despite his good humor he could be vigorously blunt, and in an emergency was a realistic and hard-hitting as Flagler. Colonel W. P. Thompson, one of Camden's partners, was a man of different but comparable abilities—a former Confederate officer who showed a fine courtesy and judgment, and marked executive ability.

The fact that when 1875 opened, Camden's refinery was not doing well, was not to his discredit. The mixing of Pennsylvania oil with the local crude had proved an expensive process. The new railroad rates had closed all the eastern markets except Baltimore to the company. Camden had been watching the situation in refining, knew of the Standard's moves to organize the industry, and admired the capacity of its leaders. One plausible story is that he himself made the first overture. However the agreement was reached, a contract was signed May 12, 1875, between Rockefeller and Flagler on the one side and Camden and his associates on the other. This resulted in the formation on May 29 of the Camden Consolidated Oil Company, successor to the former firm of J. N. Camden & Co. The new organization was actually a unit in the Standard system, but of this vital relationship the outside world as yet knew nothing. The company bore the Camden name; that gentleman and his former partners directed its activities; and complete secrecy shrouded the fact that the majority of the stock in the new company was held by the Standard Oil, while Camden and Thompson were paid in part for their property by shares of stock in the larger corporation.

A clear understanding hand been reached between Rockefeller and the Camden Consolidated as to the immediate function of the company. It was to unify the refining industry in all B. & O. territory east of Cincinnati and south of Pittsburgh. When the Camden unit had finished its work, the West Virginia-Ohio-Maryland area would be a Standard domain, a protection to the Company's existing activities in the North, and a convenient instrument for their expansion into the South. The Camden Consolidated had good working arrangements, a capitalization of $200,000, and a vision and energy which were not less valuable than its more tangible resources.

Camden proceeded vigorously with his work. As early as June 17 he acquired one refinery—sold in bankruptcy proceedings—and later added two more. Camden continued to absorb independent refiners in the Marietta and Parkersburg areas, and as the year 1875 advanced, cast an appraising eye on Baltimore. In February or early March, 1876, aided by the Standard's Executive Committee, he purchased 600 feet of waterfront at Locust Point, Baltimore, in order to build an oil wharf and a warehouse. Soon the Consolidated had its offices in Baltimore: the stationery read: "The Camden Consolidated Oil Company and Consolidated Oil Wharves." By December 21, 1876 a complete agreement had been worked out. And Camden did not hesitate to snap up another Baltimore refinery, the Merritt & Jones plant, for $40,389.95.

Meanwhile, representatives of the Standard in other areas had been equally busy. Archbold had been working in the Regions. During 1876 he had purchased five Titusville firms and leased another, the chief being the John Jackson Refinery, the Octave Oil Company, and Easterly & Davis. He had also purchased the Aurora oil works at Olean; Fairfield, McRae at Petroleum Center; and half a dozen other plants in Pennsylvania and New York. Lockhart in Pittsburgh had acquired some refineries in 1875 and 1876. One was the plant of Augustus H. Tack and his partners. Tack, like other Pittsburghers, had suffered from the discriminatory policy of the Pennsylvania against his city; his refinery sank into a desperate condition, and his partners bought it, representing a $300,000 investment, as a public sale; from them it came to Lockhart.

In Philadelphia, Warden began the year 1876 by absorbing Franklin Oil Works of Stewart, Matthews & Pennington, while such other refiners as W. L. Elkins, Waring, King & Company, Malcolm Lloyd, and the Harknesses made arrangements with him by early autumn. In New York the only acquisition was made by Pratt & Rogers, who bought a half interest in James Donald & Co. on June 15, 1876; within a few years this company was completely owned by the Standard.

During this period the Standard units had steadily profited by the arrangements Flagler had made with the railroads. In the spring of 1875 the Pennsylvania reduced rates on refined oil to Pittsburgh shippers to meet the menace of the Baltimore & Ohio. Scott in an angry letter to Garrett promised "to give to Baltimore a line in every respect equal both as to rates and facilities to any the Baltimore & Ohio may be able to offer."

Meanwhile, the Erie accused the Pennsylvania of granting secret rebates to the Empire Transportation Company, a charge undoubtedly true. Jewett's road turned to the Standard, giving it a favorable agreement. This could not be kept secret, the Pennsylvania and New York Central protested, and the four trunk lines finally met at Long Branch and again in New York, seeking a new general compact. The final arrangement gave the Pennsylvania about 51 per cent of the total traffic to the seaboard, the Erie and Central about 20 per cent each, and the B. & O. about 9 per cent. The Standard was to act as "evener," and was granted a small commission for its services, which really required considered trouble and expense. This was the first arrangement of the kind which Rockefeller and his associates had made with Scott's road.

The concession angered Joseph D. Potts of the Empire Line. He was not satisfied to nurse his bitterness in frustration. Within a few months, on November 4, 1875, he had signed an elaborate new contract with Pennsylvania, which granted him a special rebate in return for extending his pipe lines to Olean and giving all his through traffic to the road. Meanwhile the Columbia Conduit Company cemented its relationship to the Baltimore & Ohio, and the Standard's United made a counter-alliance with the Erie and the Central, delivering half its crude to each line. The United received in return a 10 per cent rebate! The recent railroad pool was thus actually although not nominally broken, and two hostile forces were mobilizing around the Pennsylvania and the Standard respectively.

The truth was that Scott and Potts were alarmed by the Standard's growing power. Most of its acquisitions of 1875–76 were known to them, for they had excellent sources of information. They pondered the Standard's amazing record. The consolidation of Cleveland plants in 1872, the expansion of the New York branch in 1872–73, the absorption of the strongest refiners in Philadelphia, Pittsburgh, New York, and the Regions in 1874–76—all this startled and aroused them. Now the earlier acquisitions had been topped by the capture of Parkersburg and the partial conquest of Baltimore. When, they asked themselves, would this process of consolidation come to a halt? And how would the revenues of the Empire and the Pennsylvania be affected? Was it safe to let nearly all oil be refined, and its transportation allotted, by a single company?

The two leaders felt compelled to answer these questions. And when they did, their reply took the form of boldly hostile action.

# CHAPTER V

# A NEW KIND OF MONOPOLY

A N AGREEMENT between the Pennsylvania Railroad, party of the first part, and the Empire Transportation Company, party of the second, was signed by Tom Scott and Joseph D. Potts in January, 1877. It began:

> The second party agrees to enlarge its control of petroleum refineries, partly by investing its own capital in constructing refineries at or near the Eastern termini of lines controlled by the first party in which it will have a majority and controlling interest (as it already has in one existing refinery) and partly by contracting with other domestic refineries on the Eastern Seaboard and with foreign refineries or their representatives to supply them with crude petroleum at the seaboard and by contracting with them to furnish transportation for the petroleum they require.

Scott knew that this was a drastic clause. A subsidiary of his railroad was undertaking, by compact with that railroad, *to enter the field of oil refining and expand its activities there.* It was as bold a step as if Warden, Frew had contracted with the Standard to build a railroad from the Regions to New York; and Scott could easily picture the indignant faces of Flagler and Rockefeller.

The contract included provisions as to rates—the Pennsylvania Railroad was to charge the Empire no more than similar shippers were charged, all concessions and rebates deducted. The Pennsylvania was not required to help finance the refineries, and could buy them when and if its management chose to exercise the option the railroad held on the other properties of Pott's fast-freight line. Finally, if the Pennsylvania reduced its petroleum rates to the Empire in any month, the latter would repay the railroad from its profits (if any) for the losses thus incurred. This clause looked toward a rate war. Both Potts and Scott anticipated an eventual struggle with the Standard, and that meant battling with its allies, the Erie and Central.

If either Potts or Scott had been asked why he had signed, doubtless he would have said that the step was forced upon him. Potts later described the feeling of alarm which he shared with his associates in the Empire as they watched the growth of the Standard in the middle 1870's. "We reached the conclusion," he testified before a Congressional Committee, "that there were three great divisions in the petroleum business—the production, the carriage of it, and the preparation of it for the market. If any one party controlled absolutely any one of these divisions, they practically would have a very fair show of controlling the others." That is, if the Standard controlled all the refining of oil, it could divert that oil where it pleased.

Potts was not inclined to trust to the Standard's sense of fairness. He felt that its all but complete monopoly was a threat not only to the Empire, but to his own personal career.

When the young Colonel, fresh from the Army, had organized the Empire in 1865, it was one of a number of similar fast-freight companies. But the company had quickly developed under Potts's astute management from a sub-subsidiary (attached to Philadelphia & Erie, leased by the Pennsylvania) into an important feeder for the entire system of the great trunk road. Other fast-freight lines were being absorbed by express companies or becoming parts of the railways they served. Under Potts, however, the Empire quietly but impressively rose to a position of semi-independence.

The resources and activities of the Empire by 1877 were varied and impressive. It controlled two lines of passenger and freight steamships on the Great Lakes, twenty vessels in all; they poured an important stream of traffic into the Pennsylvania's cars, including large shipments of grain. The fast-freight company owned nearly 5000 cars; its 1500 tank cars for oil, painted a bright verdant hue, were known as the "Green Line." Some 520 miles of pipe line helped to bring crude oil from the wells to the Empire's depots, where receiving tanks holding as much as 20,000 barrels per unit stood ready to store the product until time of shipment. Most of the oil sent to Philadelphia and much going to Baltimore and New York went by Empire cars. The Company's terminal at Communipaw on New York Bay occupied half a mile of water front and was equipped with modern tanks, warehouses, and pumping appliances. In fact, the Empire did everything for the oil sent by the Pennsylvania Railroad except haul the cars. Its oil traffic, on which it fixed the rates, was one of the chief elements which accounted for its $11,000,000 annual gross earnings, and its 10 per cent dividends on a capitalization of $4,000,000.

Yet the Empire was legally a creature of the Pennsylvania Railroad. Officials of that carrier owned most of its stock; the trunk line held an option which permitted it, on notice, to buy the fast-freight line, snuffing out its life like a candle's; the Pennsylvania heads not infrequently suggested policies for Potts to adopt.

However, so able and widely respected had the Colonel become that he exercised a remarkable independence, and he thought more of this than of the option Tom Scott held—an ax dangling over his head which he expected never to fall. Potts knew that as the president of the Empire he occupied a unique position in the transportation of oil. His cars went by a much shorter route than either the Central's or the Erie's—in fact only half the distance of the Central's. His terminal at New York was the most modern in that area. He had the best rolling stock for carrying oil on any of the trunk lines, and he had more of it. Indeed, Vanderbilt's road owned no tank cars. Finally, Potts had built up an organization notable for its compactness, efficiency, and high morale.

But he saw a future even brighter than the present. Why should the Empire not continue to grow in public esteem and independence, until eventually it could act as a kind of regulator of national railroad traffic?

Neither the Standard leaders nor those of the Central, Erie, or B. & O. accepted the Empire and its president as impartial. They knew that Potts eagerly took rebates and other concessions, and that he could drive a bargain that was sharp to the very verge of trickiness. Vanderbilt, Jewett, and Garrett would never tolerate Potts as an arbiter of railroad affairs.

Potts's feeling of hostility to the Standard was enhanced by the fact that for some time independent refiners who feared the combination had been coming to him. "Buy an interest in our plants and give us your protection," they begged. The Colonel realized that to answer these calls for help meant taking his company down a wholly strange road. "Our business was transportation and nothing else," he testified in telling his story later. Yet here were lambs at the mercy of a lion, and the idea of protecting them appealed to him. A strong company like the Empire must enter the field of refining and build up a bloc there which could resist the rising monopoly. With the independents forming a "nucleus," as Potts termed it, an alliance could be made with the remaining "free" refiners in New York, Pittsburgh, and the Regions. The Pennsylvania would protect this flourishing group, monopoly would be prevented, and adequate oil consignments would be guaranteed to the Empire and its mother road.

Scott, with less immediate cause for concern (for he must have felt fairly sure of getting oil consignments regardless of the Empire's fate), apparently hoped for a greater triumph. He occupied an almost fabulous position. The Pennsylvania was the largest freight carrier in the world; its shadow covered the state house at Harrisburg; it paid dividends of $25,000,000 a year. While no longer president of the Union Pacific, Scott still controlled the Texas & Pacific, and dreamed of making a vast continental railroad system. Since his salaries from various offices sometimes totaled $200,000 a year, he was rapidly piling up a great personal fortune. When he encouraged Potts to go into refining, a vision of leadership in the petroleum industry must have danced before his eyes.

It seems certain that Scott (and perhaps Potts as well) counted on two favorable factors. One was the ability of the Empire, by moving swiftly and quietly, to build up a considerable refining power before the Standard realized what was happening. The other was the tendency of Rockefeller to negotiate. He had always been patient, and better pleased with an agreement than with a battle. He should be the more hesitant now, when opposed by the most formidable array of power he had ever encountered. If such were Scott's calculations, he miscalculated twice.

In the first place, he underestimated the alertness of the Standard. In the second place, Scott's confidence in Rockefeller's hesitation proved to be utterly misplaced. It is evidence of the latter's business genius that instead of being slow in this emergency he was swift, bold, and uncompromising. Doubtless Flagler, too, favored quick, forceful action.

The two went directly to Scott and Vice-President A. J. Cassatt, probably not long after Scott and Potts had made their final agreement, telling the Pennsylvania officials that they knew all about the Empire's activities, and presenting an ultimatum. "The Pennsylvania and its subsidiary the Empire," they said in effect, "are carriers. The Empire has no business whatever in the field of refining. We ask for its immediate withdrawal." There was no need to remind Scott that about 65 per cent of all the oil carried by the Pennsylvania came from Standard refineries.

Some of Potts's defenders have remarked that Scott could have retorted: "The Standard has no business in the field of transportation, yet it owns pipe lines." But of course that was no answer, for the pipe lines were a special interest long controlled in part by refiners. Naturally, the Empire had a right to go into refining, or the Standard to build a railroad. Yet neither could expect to go outside its province without meeting instant opposition, and this was the Standard's real point.

Rockefeller and Flagler already knew that the New York Central and the Erie supported them to the extent that these roads also objected to the Empire's new activity. President Jewett of the Erie later testified that his road would have fought Potts's company alone if necessary. "Whether the Standard Oil Company was afraid of the Empire Line as a refiner I have no means of knowing," he told the Hepburn Committee in 1879. "I never propounded the question. We were opposed to permitting the Empire Line, a creature of the Pennsylvania Railroad, to be building refineries, to become the owners of pipe lines leading into the oil fields and leading to the coast, without a contest.

Jewett and Vanderbilt conferred, they too remonstrated with Scott and Cassatt, and when they did so, the Standard renewed its representations. For a time Cassatt wavered. He even talked with Potts about leasing the Empire refineries to the Standard, or selling them to third parties. But Potts indignantly refused. He exhorted both Cassatt and Scott to stand by him.

There is no evidence that Scott ever wavered. If he did, he was probably reassured not only by Potts, but also by his own appraisal of the power of the Pennsylvania and the Empire. The Standard, after all, was a loose, recently formed organization, with leaders from six different regions who had never fully merged their interests and abilities so far as Scott could see. The Company had never faced a big fight in its whole existence and had come up by absorbing weaker competitors. Could it stand against the Pennsylvania? And as for the Erie and the Central, had they not been at each others' throat not long ago? They were competitors by nature, not allies. Scott, believing that a stiff battle would see this fantastic alliance quickly shattered, stood firm. The Empire pushed on with its refining program.

But Scott's analysis of his opponents represented a third miscalculation. The Central and the Erie were absolutely at one in opposing him, and were never to falter; and they were the more resolute because in striking at the Standard Potts and Scott struck at their one real source of oil. At this particular time both roads happened to be financially well armed for a contest. So was the Standard, for although he had spent considerable sums for mergers, Rockefeller was prepared for this greater emergency.

The moment Scott made it clear that he would support Potts, in March, 1877, Rockefeller canceled the contract of 1875 with the Pennsylvania. Then he struck hard. He cut the price of kerosene in all markets reached by the Empire. He rushed the construction of 600 new tank cars for the "northern lines." Standard buyers bid actively for crude oil. The Erie and the New York Central cut their freight rates; the Pennsylvania retaliated; the others cut again. Rockefeller closed down his Pittsburgh plants and ran the Cleveland refineries to full capacity, so that he need not ship a drop of oil over the Pennsylvania. Then, when he had made a contract for shipping refined eastward over the Baltimore & Ohio, he opened the Pittsburgh units again. His sellers were active in every export market in trying to close the field to the Empire refineries, and Standard agents were equally active in all domestic markets.

Potts and Tom Scott, for their part, filled the Regions with buyers clamoring for crude. The prices paid for the oil were of small consequence; to get it was the important thing. At the same time, the Pennsylvania moved oil to New York for a song or even for nothing. Indeed, Cassatt later testified that Henry G. Ohlen had his oil transported under a contract made with the Empire on April 2, for eight cents less than the cost to the road.

At the same time Potts was industriously wooing all the independent refiners as well as all independent producers. The conflict automatically imposed one loss upon Potts and the Pennsylvania: they might buy crude, but for refined they must depend on friendly manufacturers of that product. There were few of these, for the simple reason that the Standard and its allies already refined the great bulk of oil produced. If Scott had gained time before Rockefeller struck, Potts might have built up a respectable group of plants; but the fight had been started abruptly, and the Empire lived chiefly on hopes, not performances. The Standard's output of refined was at least from three to five times Potts's. Thus the Pennsylvania was constantly deprived of one source of revenue which it had enjoyed while serving the Standard plants in the Regions, Pittsburgh, and Philadelphia. A state investigator later declared that the road had lost a million dollars in this fashion during the short span of three months.

While the Empire and the Pennsylvania were thus under a constant strain, the Standard scarcely felt any ill effects at all from the battle. Its position was made additionally strong because of its considerable cash reserves and complete freedom from debt. On the other hand, the Pennsylvania had no great reserves, nursed a considerable debt, and had paid out high dividends on outrageously watered stock. It was therefore in a vulnerable position if anything happened to shake the confidence of its financial backers. And during the year 1877 fate dealt it two heavy blows.

The first was not unexpected: a rate war between the Eastern trunk lines. Then with midsummer the great railroad strike of 1877 exploded and reached its climax on July 18 with rioting on the Baltimore & Ohio, which spread through western Pennsylvania and into New York. The strike was justified, for the men had been overworked and underpaid. When they finally acted, nowhere were they so fierce and implacable as along the Pennsylvania lines. In the following months governors were to call out militia, President Hayes to send federal troops for the restoration of order; dozens of men were to be killed and millions in property destroyed.

Tom Scott now reaped the destructive harvest of the hate provoked by his interference with the state government and his callous labor policy. Not only had he reduced wages 20 per cent since the depression began, but he had tried to double the freight cars per train, causing many discharges. Everyone in Pittsburgh knew that the Pennsylvania had discriminated against the industries of the city, increasing the unemployment and economic distress.

Here the disturbances became a flaming popular revolt. Other laborers and small shopkeepers joined the railroad employees in an attack on stations, shops, and rolling stock. The police, help-less before the fury of the crowd, were at length aided on the afternoon of July 21 by a force of state militia; but this body of troops was driven to shelter. They vainly fired on the resolute mob, killing twenty-five persons and wounding many more. By nightfall they were forced back into machine shops and a roundhouse.

Here they were besieged. To the east, the yards and sidings were crowded for several miles with freight cars full of merchan-dise, oil, coke, and coal. While part of the crowd grimly stalked the buildings in which the troops were massed, others set fire to the cars. As flames roared, the fire department rolled out with engines and hose and ladders; but the purposeful rioters warned the firemen back from all railroad property, which they swore to destroy. They promised to harm nothing that belonged to private citizens, and actually helped save a lumber pile belonging to such an owner. Meanwhile they pushed cars of blazing coke down the tracks against the roundhouse, and poured volley after volley in upon the militia, for they had armed themselves with guns taken from gun-shops. Finally the soldiers, worn-out and half-suffocated, retreated under a hail of bullets and missiles across the Allegheny River.

The loss of the railroad was catastrophic. When the uprising ended, more than a hundred locomotives and fifteen hundred passenger and freight cars had been destroyed. Innumerable buildings had been gutted. Eventually the Pennsylvania made claims upon Allegheny County for $4,100,000 of which it finally collected $2,765,891, by settlement. Meanwhile it had to ride the storm alone. It borrowed huge sums, passed its dividends in August and November, and saw its stock fall sharply.

By August, Scott and Cassatt were eager for peace. The latter came to Cleveland twice during that month to discuss a solution with Rockefeller and Flagler, who were there for the summer. The Standard leaders took a relatively mild position, although they were firm on one point. "They insisted," Cassatt testified later, "that the first condition of their coming back on our line . . . must be that the Empire Transportation Company . . . must cease the refining of oil in competition with them." Of course this had been the Standard's original demand, and the Pennsylvania was not in a position to oppose it further. With Pott's company gravely complicating the road's precarious position, its president would have had difficulty standing by it and continuing his battle with the Standard while angry voices were lifted within his own organization.

Rockefeller and Flagler encouraged Scott and Cassatt by promising to restore the Pennsylvania to its former position as a shipper of Standard products, crude and refined. But when Potts was told of the demand that he withdraw from refining, he protested. He declared that if the fight were maintained, he and the Pennsylvania could win it. Was not his refining capacity growing? Was he not showing a profit? He would never haul down the flag; the railroad would have to buy him out if it wanted to surrender. Apparently there was a stormy quarrel, for Scott was a realist, and must have thought that Potts talked like a fool. Potts on his side seems always to have felt that Scott betrayed him.

The Pennsylvania's president was pressed vigorously by the Standard officials. "Very well, if it is necessary to buy the Empire out," they declared, "then between us we shall buy it out." The Standard agreed to take refineries, pipe lines, oil terminals, most of the tank cars, harbor tugboats and barges, and let the railroad take rolling stock only. On September 17 the Pennsylvania directors formally approved the purchase.

Flagler and Rockefeller had gone to Philadelphia before the action of the Pennsylvania trustees, and were away from New York up to October 17, Flagler part of the time and Rockefeller all of the time. He was in Cleveland, where William asked him on October 15 to borrow money on short term. John said years later that all the money was raised in New York and Cleveland. None came from Lockhart, Pratt, Warden, or the other parties. He himself climbed into his old buggy, drove from bank to bank, asked at each for the president. "I must have all you've got!" he told each official. "I need it all! It's all right! Give me what you have! I must catch the noon train."

Rockefeller has piquantly described the scene at the St. George Hotel in Philadelphia where the negotiations were closed. A number of Standard and Pennsylvania officials had assembled, but Tom Scott was late. "I can see him now, with his big soft hat, marching into the room in that little hotel to meet us; not to sweep us away as he had always done, but coming in with a smile, walking right up to the cannon's mouth. 'Well, boys, what will we do?' Then he sat down and signed the papers."

The Standard paid $3,400,000 all told. Of this $1,094,805.56 was the cost of the Empire's pipe lines, $501,652.78 went for the Sone & Fleming Company, $900,000 for its share in the Oil Tank Car Trust, and $900,000 more for personal property and settlement with outside refiners, the chief of which was the Philadelphia Refining Company. Both Cassatt and Rockefeller later testified that the Standard took the pipe lines reluctantly, and only on the insistence of the Pennsylvania; but we need not accept this statement at face value. Contrary to news reports of the time, full payment in cash was made at once; moreover, the Standard loaned the Pennsylvania money with which to purchase the cars of the Empire. The properties in question were nominally transferred to various individuals, not to the Standard Oil Company of Ohio. The agreement was signed on October 17. At the same time, the Standard paid $1,050,000 for the Columbia Conduit properties owned by Dr. David Hostetter.

Few sales of such magnitude had hitherto occurred in American business. But Rockefeller seems not to have haggled over terms; such was never his practice when an acquisition opened up great earning power. This one did, for the Empire had offered the one great threat to the Standard's quasi-absolute control of refining; the Company would still face competitors, but none of such size and power. Moreover, the new properties could be made highly profitable.

The Standard won a victory that was literally epochal. It took over every asset of the once menacing Empire that had to do with the piping or refining of oil. It even took over most of the famous green tank cars. The acquisition of the Hostetter properties brought it additional pipe lines, storage tanks, and refineries.

The total number of the latter acquired from both the Empire and the Columbia Conduit was not large. The Columbia refineries numbered at least three, perhaps five. The real triumph of the Standard as to refineries lay in its having taken out of the oil business two big organizations which might have built up blocs of manufactories to threaten its control of the piping and refining of crude. Now there were *no* strong companies in the field to which the remaining independents could turn for aid. Strategically, this fact was of an importance difficult to magnify.

With the pipe lines, the victory was more complete and dramatically overwhelming. Only a few small units remained outside Standard control. For the moment, it dominated almost completely the means by which oil must go from the wells to the railroads.

To a great extent it now also controlled storage. Hostetter's many tanks, some of the Empire's facilities for receiving and holding oil—both were now Standard property.

Finally, the agreements signed with Hostetter and the Pennsylvania on October 17 were not the only ones executed on that date A new trunk line pact was concluded at the same time. It provided oil shipment quotas for the roads: 47 per cent of all shipments to the Pennsylvania, 21 per cent each to the Erie and New York Central, and 11 per cent to the Baltimore and Ohio. The Standard was specified as "evener."

In becoming a party to the arrangement, the Rockefeller group agreed not only to apportion the oil shipments among the roads, but also to guarantee certain quantities—for example, to the Pennsylvania not less than 2,000,000 barrels a year. For this service the Standard was to receive a commission of 10 per cent on all its own shipments *and also on whatever other freights it might control.* No such commission was to be paid to any other shipper unless he furnished oil which brought the same total amount of profit—a manifest impossibility. Later, in the Federal courts, the Standard's lawyers argued that ten per cent was not then regarded as an exorbitant charge for the work of "evening," that the obligations fully offset the advantages, and that it is doubtful whether the Standard reaped any real profit from the contract. Any impartial historian must reject these contentions and pronounce the arrangement iniquitous.

Quite as important as the pact itself was the corollary that the Pennsylvania again acknowledged the Standard as its most favored shipper. It was a new relationship which would strongly influence the history of oil production, refining and transportation.

The Standard leaders recognized that the strategic hour had struck for pressing their campaign to absorb the "outsiders" by lease, merger, or purchase. Accordingly in Baltimore, in the Regions, in New England, in Pittsburgh, in the New York City area, and in up-state New York the Rockefeller captains raised the tempo of their activities.

Numerous and far-flung acquisitions in 1877 and 1878 lifted the Rockefeller organization to a position close to monopoly. This was true of both pipe lines and refineries. On April 10 of the latter year, Flagler in a letter to P. H. Judd estimated the total refining interest in the United States to be worth $36,-000,000. If we include independents operating on lease or quota, the Standard probably controlled $33,000,000 of this great investment. A letter from Rockefeller to Warden on January 5, 1878, confirms this probability, for he speaks of a $200,000 valuation (for McKee's plant) as "a little less than $1/150$" of the total Standard holdings—not counting leased interests.

The realization of the great plan left "the one big company" in a confused, almost chaotic state. Yet such was Rockefeller's vision, and Flagler's, that the Standard never ceased during these distracting days to make plans for spectacular enlargement. These new calculations looked beyond refining. They carried the great organization into new fields.

Looking back over the record since 1870, any careful reader of Standard history must be impressed by the quiet, efficient channeling of domestic activities into three branches: refining, pipe lines, and terminal activities. True, a few steps had been taken in other fields. The Standard had turned out its own barrels, had manufactured lubricating oil, and a few other by-products, and had entered distributing in Louisville and St. Louis. But it had never sought a dominant control of such activities. Now, despite the problems of intra-organizational control, it took steps toward a vigorous expansion in all the fields mentioned and in others as well, such as gasoline and paraffin production, and expanded distribution.

How, from an ethical point of view, had the Standard conducted itself in these extensive and sometimes furious campaigns? Had it won unfair advantages through its pressure on the railroads? Had it employed deceit in a reprehensible fashion? Had it intimidated the men and women whose properties it purchased, and had it by underpaying them and shutting off their means of livelihood, brought many to ruin?

At the time and more emphatically afterwards it was accused of all these misdeeds. While the general question of its practices will be considered later in a broader framework, certain particulars deserve attention now.

Like Potts and the independents, the Standard took rebates and commissions from the railroads during the entire period we are discussing. Yet from 1875 to October, 1877, it cannot be said that the advantages it gained by doing so were always continuous or effective. The Pennsylvania for the greater part of these two years gave comparable or superior advantages to other shippers. So apparently did the Baltimore & Ohio. In the end, Flagler and Camden were glad to accept the peaceful routine of open rates.

Thus the Company was continuously fighting for its position of superiority, and not always with success. Until the purchase of the Empire it was never consistently successful with the Pennsylvania or the B. & O. After that event, for a few years, its position improved immensely. The contract of October 17, 1877, gave the Standard an overwhelming advantage. The commission was excessive for the services performed. It was ethically indefensible. In addition, as will be shown, the Standard exacted special rebates which gave it sharp advantages over its rivals. Again, early in 1878 Daniel O'Day demanded of Cassatt (and received) 20 cents a barrel on all oil piped to the Pennsylvania, pointing out that the Erie and the New York Central had been paying comparable commissions. Thus the Standard collected on both its own oil and that shipped by competitors.

To be sure, the Standard was ready with an excuse for this exaction. Flagler testified that the American Transfer Company Pipe Line had been built to serve the New York Central. That railroad had no tracks south of Titusville, and O'Day's organization collected and pumped the oil to the railhead. The Erie had used the line in a similar fashion. On November 30, 1877, the American Transfer Company had completed a thirty-mile line between the southern oil belt and Pittsburgh, and could feed oil to its refineries there. This made the Standard independent of the Alleghany Valley branch of the Pennsylvania. Nevertheless, as "evener," the Rockefeller organization protected this branch road, seeing that it got its full proportion of oil traffic; and it was for this service that O'Day demanded his 20 cents per barrel.

Although the argument was ingenious, it is clear that the charge was excessive, and the collection of money on the oil of rivals could never be justified. The fact was that the Standard had won its battle for supremacy, possessed the strength to collect, and used that strength ruthlessly. This was Rob Roy's code:

> The good old rule, the simple plan
> That they should take who have the power
> And they should keep who can.

Other corporations of the day, such as the meat-packers and the railroads, exerted power as and when they could. The Standard should have set a better example. Today we must condemn the misuse of power as not only a crushing blow to the Company's competitors but an indirect tax on the public.

In its employment of secrecy, the Standard again used the same weapon as others, but used it more extensively. We have seen examples of secrecy. The policy was maintained from 1872 on. Early in 1878 he complained bitterly to Lockhart about the indiscretion of an employee who revealed the real facts as to E. I. and R. G. Waring, just bought out by the Standard.

To present-day students this elaborate deception is reprehensible. Yet it was justified by the Standard officials as a practice used by others (they detected Potts, the Pennsylvania, the Baltimore & Ohio and many of the independents employing it) and as a practical necessity. These facts considered, the extent to which the Company used secrecy and subterfuge still leaves anyone who knows the full record with a sense of distaste.

The period of 1875–1878 is particularly interesting because of the many absorptions of independent refiners. What can be said, on the basis of the Company's letter-files and minute-book, of the Standard's attitude and approach to its rivals, of its fairness in making terms, and of the treatment of opponents once they had surrendered?

One fact can be accepted as certain: the approach to any independent with whom the Standard treated was courteous. This seems to have been true no matter who was the negotiator. Archbold may have been outspoken, but he seems also to have been friendly. Camden, Hutchins, and Rockefeller were uniformly pleasant, earnest, and reasonable. Even Payne and McGregor, both stiff-minded and somewhat cold, never seem to have shown the least threat or bluster. However, all tacitly used the advantages of their position.

What of the prices paid for the properties of "outsiders"? The point has already been made that there was often bound to be a gap between the total investment made in a plant and either replacement value or earning power value when bought. Occasionally the value, associated with good will, was greater than the full cost; in most instances it was less. The owner usually asked for as much as he had put into his works, and sometimes demanded a great deal more.

Although the Standard objected to paying such prices, it usually offered a generous use-value figure. Often it ended by paying much more than any impartial evaluator would have held to be fair. This was enlightened self-interest. Better to pay $1000, $5000, or even $25,000 too much than to prolong costly competition! The result was that many independents received a price that pleased them, plus stock in their reorganized company or in the Standard, plus jobs or "pensions." Few could have felt that they had not had full opportunity to plead their cases, and when it is remembered that thousands of men were affected, the subsequent protests appear relatively few.

Naturally, in closing out a competitor, the Standard was insistent on a guarantee that he would not take his money, build a new plant, reëstablish himself as a rival, and thus become eligible to sell again. Such guarantees sometimes occasioned trouble. A number of the former independents found it difficult to resist the attractions of refining. They saw the prosperity of the Standard, forgot their feelings when hard-pressed and willing to sell, and believed that they could try again and succeed. Somewhat naïvely, they did not recognize that Rockefeller and his associates were flourishing because of efficiency of operation as well as favorable railroad rates.

Accordingly, some broke their pledges and built refineries. Scofield, Shurmer & Teagle, bought out in 1872, launched themselves anew in 1875, erecting a $65,000 plant with a yearly capacity of 180,000 barrels of crude oil. In the first year they made $40,000. But they felt unjustly treated by the railroads, and in the spring of 1876 sued the Lake Shore, alleging that its "unlawful and unjust discrimination, partialities, and preferences" had enabled the Standard to obtain "to a great extent" the monopoly of the Cleveland oil trade. Rockefeller made no effort to "crush" these competitors, but quietly concluded a leasing arrangement, fixing a yearly quota for the rival firm of 85,000 barrels a year, and guaranteeing them $35,000 per annum.

Some recognition should be given here to the Standard's reputation as a business organization as reflected in the comments and actions of other companies which had relations with it. The railroads, for example, trusted Rockefeller and Flagler when they would not trust each other. The banks relied upon and trusted them. Many refiners, distributors, and manufacturers of by-products received overtures from the Rockefeller group with apparent cordiality. Many firms made overtures themselves, sometimes inviting Standard control. Even in the Oil Regions the Company drew to its support an increasing number of friends.

What is the final conclusion so far as these years are concerned? The story offers the picture of a vigorous, realistic, superbly-led organization, rising swiftly to a power greater than any other American corporation had won. This organization zealously pursued its interests in a new, ill-organized, chaotic field, sometimes allying itself with and sometimes combating the yet unregulated railroads, whose practises were unstandardized and frequently unscrupulous. The Standard Oil by 1879 held a position new in economic history. It had attained monopolistic power in a great industrial field by its own efforts, and not by state grant, patent rights, exclusive control of raw materials, or special geographical position. The means by which it had gained this power offered wide scope for criticism. It had been ruthless at times in exploiting its advantages in transportation rates; it had frequently been tyrannical in making competitors "sweat" or "feel sick"; it had employed deception in a reprehensible manner. Criticism was certain to find voice and grow in volume. As for the end-result, the monopoly itself, the healthy instinct of English-speaking peoples since Tudor days had been to detest monopoly, and the stronger the monopoly the greater was the detestation.

Saying all this, and he can say no less, the historian must add that two great considerations palliate the record. The first is that extreme disorganization of the oil industry in 1870 made heroic measures necessary to end its over-production, price-slashing, and competitive savagery, with their consequences of waste, bankruptcy, and suffering. Drastic remedies were demanded; the oil-producers and oil-carriers both tried monopoly by pooling; and if Rockefeller and his associates, so much abler and so much more successful, overshot the mark, their fierce impetus had some justification. The second consideration is equally basic: in sometimes employing ruthless methods, they to a great extent acted according to the economic ethics of the time; if they had not used these weapons, still more ruthless men would have used them against the Standard organizers. In this early stage of the American industrial revolution, the moral code of bankers, manufacturers, railroadmen, merchants, and entrepreneurs was in process of evolution and formulation. The Standard leaders had to act by the rules of the game as men generally played it, or be knocked out. This, of course, does not alter the fact that they accepted or even depressed the code when they might have raised it.

It was inevitable that the Standard should presently be judged not on the basis of the law and the business code of the 1870's, but by an improved sense of what was fair in business and industry—by a more enlightened economic conscience. By 1879 this conscience was already more sensitive on a number of points. It condemned discriminatory railroad rates; it objected to acts by which one firm deprived a competitor of materials or markets; it censured deception. Above all, as the industrial revolution developed, as business advanced, and as markets became national instead of local or regional, the fear and hatred of monopoly grew deeper.

Meanwhile, the conscience had not yet become law—had not even become fully accepted by opinion. While it was not law, Rockefeller and his associates did not bow to it. In the beginning it was impracticable that they should, and when they had won control they still tended to carry some of the unfortunate practices of a moderate-sized, struggling business forward into the activities of a great combination which had become affected, in all its relationships, with a public interest.

The sheer volume of labor in the gigantic and almost chaotic company cried out for a Hercules; its intricacy asked for an industrial surgeon with unique powers of observation and surpassing skill.

For never had any corporation faced a situation comparable in magnitude and confused variety with that of the Standard in the fall of 1877. Even before the purchase of the Empire its leaders had been struggling to develop coherence in their scattered organization. The Standard Oil Company of Ohio in 1872 had possessed full unity. Its plants in Cleveland and New York were completely controlled by the Cleveland office. But even in that year new plants had been brought in—not only the firms absorbed in the Cleveland drive, but many others. A small Regions concern, the Portage Oil Works, had been purchased, along with one in Toledo. Jabez A. Bostwick & Company, the Long Island Company, and S. Freeman & Co. of Jersey City, New Jersey, came in between March and September of 1872.

Altogether, thirty-one units had been absorbed before the end of December.

To these had been added in the ensuing three years the Devoe Manufacturing Company; Chess, Carley & Co.; the American Transfer Co.; the United; Waters Pierce of St. Louis; the Philadelphia plants grouped about the Atlantic Refining Co.; the Pittsburgh plants with the Standard of that city as a center; the Imperial Refining Co.; Porter, Moreland of Titusville; the Camden Consolidated in Parkersburg; the Eclipse in Franklin; the Economy in Oil City; the Philadelphia and Pittsburgh plants acquired in the first nine months of 1877, and the New England refineries and distributing companies. This list does not include dozens of small firms purchased throughout the country. In addition, the Standard had operating agreements with firms like Merriam's paraffin works, the Pioneer Oil Co. (Frank Rockefeller's firm), and Scofield, Shurmer & Teagle.

It is not clear just how many of these many organizations were still operating under separate names and officers in the fall of 1877. There were at least dozens. After the Empire sale the complex of lines, refineries, and terminals belonging to that organization and to the Columbia Conduit were added—eight or more separate organizations. Acquired or soon to be acquired were new Parkersburg plants, the eleven Baltimore plants, and new units in Pittsburgh, Philadelphia, the Regions, New York, and New England! Many of the Standard officials brought in since 1874 were still adjusting to their jobs in the monster corporation, and additional men were thronging in during the late months of 1877 and the new months of 1878. Knocking at the door were dozens more of plants and officials, some already marked for induction, others still unheard of or only vaguely considered.

As October passed into November of 1877, a score of urgent tasks needed to be performed. Most pressing of these was a merger of the pipe lines, for the three systems which the Standard now controlled could not continue to operate separately without the greatest annoyance and confusion. Meanwhile, plants must be scrapped or provided with new personnel acquainted with Standard policies and routines. Contracts also demanded attention. These were held by individuals; because of tax laws the Standard could not hold them, yet the existing arrangement was a makeshift. Some of the new companies in turn had their own contracts with pipe lines and railroads—a complication which Flagler found most vexatious. A whole new schedule of railroad rates had further to be adjusted to the new units.

Such questions in turn called for a new division of work among the Company leaders. Beyond the immediate matters demanding action loomed also what might be called the king question: could the scattered, many-headed organization be put through a miraculous series of operations from which it would emerge with a single head and body?

The Standard leaders were aware of the gravity of these problems. They bent with resolute energy to the task of finding solutions. Already the officials who had entered the Company in 1874, and 1875 were coming forward to shoulder some of the burdens. Warden, Lockhart, Pratt, Rogers, Vandergrift, Archbold, and Camden were the men most ready and able to do this. They worked, of course, with John D. Rockefeller, Flagler, Payne and William Rockefeller, who at this time were the four top-level men. Quite as important as any of the first group in function, however, was Ambrose McGregor, now acting informally as technical expert and trouble-shooter for the whole great complex of firms. Others who were taking an increasing amount of responsibility were Colonel Thompson, Camden's partner; Hutchins, the sales head in Cleveland and fieldman for the Western trade—Payne's left hand if McGregor was his right; Daniel O'Day, increasingly prominent in pipe line affairs; Vilas, an able negotiator and finance expert; and Chester, the Company's chief although not wholly adequate legal aide.

As yet these newer officials were only beginning to assume the important roles most of them would soon play in Standard affairs.

Vandergrift had by 1878 become the Company's chief pipe line man. He was to preside over the new United when it had digested the Empire and Columbia properties, and would discharge this and larger tasks efficiently until he left the Company early in 1889, after fifteen years of service.

As the organization's purchasing agent in the Regions, Bostwick was a sober but energetic representative. He brought shrewdness, expert knowledge, and unflagging diligence to his important task. His aide Joseph Seep, slow, genial, full of

Teutonic common sense, in whose name much of the oil was bought, had a capacity for mollifying complainants and bringing quarrelsome people together.

As for Archbold, his emerging prominence was the result of his natural ability and his increasing maturity. At twenty-nine he already had a long and rich experience, and he had just begun to acquire the greater dignity and deeper judgment which a young and brilliant man is likely to find at the threshold of early middle age. Aggressive and optimistic, he still swept a project to success partly by sheer energy and animation, but he was showing an unobtrusive sagacity which he had previously lacked. This and his unfailing good nature were soon to make him an admirable conciliator among divergent members of the Standard group.

Lockhart, a native Scot, was a rock of caution, hard sense, and resolution. Rockefeller later spoke of him as "one of the most experienced, self-contained, and self-controlled men in business." The refining companies he helped to establish in Pittsburgh prospered steadily. Rugged, hard-minded, alert, to John D. Rockefeller he was a symbol of security. He could be counted upon to sound a warning if the Company turned down a dangerous path.

In contrast, H. H. Rogers was a man who might lead the way down such a path. The considered judgment of some later Standard leaders was that the organization would have been better off had he never entered it. He was a man of electric personality and inexhaustible energy. Except for Rockefeller himself, no member of the group was to put a sharper impress on the public mind. For Rogers was adventurous and speculative by instinct, he threw himself into many enterprises, and in half a dozen fields he made a spectacular record. A year younger than Rockefeller, he had wandered, after an impoverished boyhood in Fairhaven, Massachusetts, into the Oil Regions. Here he had entered refining, eventually allying himself in New York with the quiet but dynamic Charles Pratt. Rogers was attractive, dashing, magnetic. His keen mind, quick wit, and alert physical presence were like Flagler's, but with even more sparkle. The moment he entered a roomful of men, they awoke to a richer sense of life—and some of them in the end were likely to be the poorer for it! He was a natural leader, particularly in aggressive enterprises. As yet relatively quiet in the Standard, he was soon to supervise its oil purchasing, then direct its pipe lines, and finally become chairman of its manufacturing committee.

Kaleidoscopic was an appropriate word for Rogers, as any one could agree who watched his handsome head for an hour in some conference or at an investigation. At one moment he was genial and talkative; the next frigid, sarcastic, or jeering. He passed in an instant from democratic cordiality to freezing hauteur, from beguiling kindness to cutting harshness or blazing anger; and each mood was natural. Wall Street called him "Hell Hound Rogers," yet Mark Twain could write that he was a saint on earth. He paid for Helen Keller's education, was a patron of the arts, and loved to be the brilliant center of an intellectual circle. But his competitors in business—and some associates—knew him as exacting, cold, relentless, and tyrannical.

In contrast, Charles Pratt seemed a colorless man, yet in fundamental strength he was perhaps a greater man than Rogers. A Massachusetts Yankee now in his late forties, he had pushed his way up in New York by industry, integrity, and an imaginative shrewdness. Establishing his own refining company in 1867, he had been a pioneer in the export trade. "Pratt's Astral" was long a familiar brand of kerosene in Europe, Asia, and Africa. His chief said of him later: "Mr. Pratt had shown ability as a merchandiser." He could meditate incisively on Standard policy, and he expressed with illuminating vigor what he felt, even if it led him into opposition to Rockefeller himself. Indeed, on occasion he swung the Executive Committee behind his proposals and against his chief. He demanded loyalty from his employees, and his friends and followers came to be known as the "Pratt clique."

William G. Warden presented a different type from Archbold, Pratt, Rogers, or Lockhart. He was a big, genial, but earnest man, and was popular in Philadelphia, whither he removed in 1870. As Rockefeller remarked: "He was effusive. He would sit up till two in the morning writing me a long letter." Yet he was so devoted to his work, that his sons testify that he never took any recreation. His active spirit led him into numerous enterprises, so that in Philadelphia he is even better remembered as the founder and head of the United Gas Improvement Company and as a reformer in city politics than as a partner in the Standard Oil Company.

In general, Warden took charge of any Standard enterprise in

Pennsylvania outside the Regions—political, legal, or industrial. His acquaintanceship, his skill in conference, his persistence and force of personality, always brought results that were acceptable and sometimes won notable success.

But in this distinguished group—perhaps the ablest in the history of American business—Rockefeller and Flagler were tacitly accepted as the supreme leaders. Flagler was the authority and master in the Company in any matter relating to the railroads. Sometimes John D. Rockefeller joined his chief associate at an important meeting with the trunk line heads, or consulted with him on a point of policy. But Flagler was the principal strategist who planned new steps in this field, and the bold tactician who won acceptance for them from the roads. He was also the director of the routines by which the Standard carried out its part of each new compact, and the watchful observer who saw that the carriers fulfilled their obligations. The master intellect directing Standard officials in all tasks affecting the obligations of the various companies in their relationship to the central organization was Flagler's. He was the supreme guide in dispelling chaos and establishing order during these crucial months of 1877–1878.

All through these troubled months Rockefeller was clearly the watchful over-all strategist, adviser, and director. Although he was still in his thirties, officials everywhere wrote to him outlining their problems, and their relationship to him is impressive. They wrote to Flagler also where railroad rates or matters of organization were concerned, but they wrote to Rockefeller about *everything*. They told him what they had done and asked his judgment about what had not been done. One feels that each said to himself: "He will straighten me out—give me the answer"; or, even more frequently, for the Standard lieutenants took a large initiative, "He will tell me if my idea about this business is the right one."

Rockefeller often sent approval for proposals made to him, with a few suggestions as to modifications of plan. Sometimes he carried complaints or disputes to his New York associates and had them satisfactorily settled. Sometimes he raised pertinent questions. Again, he counseled delay, to wait with time for more light. On occasion he told his troubled associates to make their own decisions without his aid. But his replies were always helpful. It is an indication of his remarkable justness and wisdom that dozens of talented and even brilliant men who served the Standard turned constantly to this young, vigorous, but sagacious leader as a trusted confessor and guide.

It was in relation to manufacturing that Rockefeller began about this time to ask questions or request information, both designed to put various officials on their mettle. Thus in February, 1878, he wrote Vilas, after studying reports on Cleveland production, that he found an increase in costs of 33 cents a barrel during the second six months of the year as opposed to the first, although production had been greater. "How is this difference accounted for?"

One earlier story of Rockefeller's attention to the details of manufacturing is at once simple and impressive. It indicates that his activities in 1877 and 1878 were merely a more highly organized continuation of previous ones. At Long Island City in the early 1870's he inspected a building in which refined oil was being packed for shipment abroad. One employee has told us what happened:

He watched a machine for filling the tin cans. One dozen cans stood on a wooden platform beneath a dozen pipes. A man pulled a lever, and each pipe discharged exactly five gallons of kerosene into a can. Still on a wooden carrier, the dozen cans were pushed along to another machine, wherein twelve tops were swiftly clamped fast on the cans. Thence they were pushed to the last machine, in which just enough solder to fasten and seal the lid was dropped on each can.

Mr. Rockefeller listened in silence while an expert told all about the various machines used to save labor and time and expense in the process. At last Mr. Rockefeller asked:

"How many drops of solder do you use on each can?"

"Forty."

"Have you ever tried thirty-eight? No? Would you mind having some sealed with thirty-eight and let me know?"

Six or seven per cent of these cans leaked. Then thirty-nine drops were used. None leaked. It was tried with one hundred, five hundred, a thousand cans. None leaked. Thereafter every can was sealed with thirty-nine drops.

Another story, perhaps authentic, tells how a memorandum was sent from Rockefeller's office to one refinery reading approximately as follows: "Your March inventory showed 10,750 bungs on hand. The report for April shows 20,000 bungs bought, 24,000 used, and 6000 bungs on hand. What became of the other

750 bungs?" As a matter of fact, a "daily stock report" was exacted of various units; we have such reports from the American Lubricating Oil Company, for example, showing daily the exact quantities on hand of more than fifty different kinds of oils and greases.

In addition to watching the dozens of Standard units, John D. Rockefeller supervised the campaigns for the absorption of rival manufacturers. Each move was reported to him, and the terms in all cases had his approval. Furthermore, it was he who seems to have led in developing the varied techniques of negotiation which his lieutenants employed. Flagler only occasionally entered this difficult area, and then as an agent and not as a commander-in-chief.

Rockefeller maintained the same supervision over sales. He discussed prices with men on half a dozen fronts—Payne, Camden, Warden, Lockhart, Archbold, and his own associates in New York. His was the most influential voice in determining if a drive should be made or no. He studied carefully the retail quotations in various cities in relation to such factors as manufacturing, shipping, and negotiations with rivals. The four were related, and except for shipping all were his special provinces.

Finally, he was the central figure in all matters affecting personnel. Payne, Camden, Archbold, Flagler, Warden, Hutchins, McGregor made their recommendations; then Rockefeller picked the men. He seems to have felt keenly that each choice affected the Standard for years to come; a new employee was a brick, a board, or a beam in the edifice that would be the Company of the future.

The Standard's president not only selected men, but kept the keenest interest in their work and advancement. He made suggestions for shifts, keeping the welfare of the individual in mind as firmly as the welfare of the Company (he would have said that the two went hand in hand). He was no less concerned on occasion about humble workers.

It is revealing of Rockefeller's character that not only did the scope of policy and the least detail of manufacturing simultaneously command his interest, but that even in these difficult days, his attention and sympathy were directed to his troubled associates, his former competitors, and individual workmen of his company. Of all the Standard officials, he undoubtedly carried the greatest and most varied load. His labors were not in vain.

By the summer of 1878, thanks to resolute efforts of the Standard leaders, a measure of order began to appear in the Company's affairs.

On November 20 or 21 of the preceding year Flagler had effected a merger of the pipe lines. According to what he wrote Payne on November 7, while arrangements were still in process, this action gave the Standard "with what we held before . . . substantially ⅚ (perhaps a little more) of the entire stock of the pipe lines." The plan was to issue both stocks and bonds. The latter would be taken by all parties to the merger in proportion, the United at the same time distributing some of their stock (16 per cent in all) to the newcomers. In addition, some $2,000,000 worth of stock seems to have been available for distribution, as the capitalization was raised from $3,000,000 to $5,000,000. The name "United" was retained, and along with the merger the management of the various lines was centralized.

This merger cleared up the pipe line tangle, and the situation was further improved early in 1878 by the creation of the Tidioute and Titusville Pipe Line with the Grandins and Scheide (for the Neyhart estate) and the United taking the $300,-000 worth of stock, as earlier described. The company was dominated by the Standard; Scheide acted as secretary.

Meanwhile the various new refineries that had been acquired were scrapped, or assigned trustworthy supervisors and officials. Warden continued to watch both the Philadelphia and Pittsburgh situations; Archbold presided over the Regions, Payne over Cleveland. In New York both John D. and William Rockefeller guided developments, with Rogers and Pratt as their frontline deputies. These steady advances toward order coincided with the recovery of the United States from the long depression of 1873–77, and the opening of a period of general industrial prosperity. The depression had extinguished a multitude of small businesses; and as the industrial revolution was completed, consolidation became an irresistible tendency in most American industries.

Already there was an overall coördination between the groups of companies, with McGregor watching the technical aspects of their work, and constantly reporting to John D. Rockefeller. Measures were taken for various units to help others, although some friction developed from overlapping activities. But the unity achieved by top-level coöperation was loose and fugitive, and the leaders increasingly felt its disadvantages. The seed of a device for a more effective control had actually been sown as early as January 25, 1873, when the directors of the Company appointed an Executive Committee of three—John D. Rockefeller, O. H. Payne, and Henry M. Flagler. An advisory committee of two, William Rockefeller and Jabez A. Bostwick, was established at the same meeting. These committees were continued from year to year. The former carried out a number of tasks assigned it by the directors, among them the establishing in Baltimore of facilities for storing and shipping. This was done in January, 1876. Two years later, on January 9, 1878, the Executive and Advisory committees were merged into a larger Executive Committee. At the same meeting Pratt, Jennings, and Bostwick were appointed "to examine and audit the stock certificates of other companies (which are owned by the Standard Oil Company) as also the securities, properties, and titles thereto, and finances of this company, and report at each quarterly meeting of the Board."

As will be seen later, each of these actions fitted into future plans for greater unity. Possibilities for achieving it were undoubtedly being discussed. An uneasy sense of the inadequacy of existing arrangements filled the minds of the higher executives; Flagler, exasperatedly collecting and filing dozens of contracts, must have been especially sensitive to the need for further centralization. In a relatively short time he and others were to devise a method of control which would satisfy them. Unfortunately, it would also alarm and anger the citizens of the United States.

# CHAPTER VI

# THE PIPE LINE REVOLUTION

ON NOVEMBER 13, 1877, D. Armstrong, Grand Organizer for the Petroleum Producers' Union, sent out a call to the lodges of that organization. They were to elect representatives for a Grand Council to be held in Titusville eight days later. Armstrong had no need to declare the purpose of the gathering, which related to the events of the preceding month. These had brought almost all the tanks that stored the producers' oil and almost all the pipes that carried it into the hands of one organization: Rockefeller's. About 175 delegates answered the call on November 21, representing, it was asserted, some 2000 well-owners and property worth hundreds of millions.

The dominant emotion of the producers on hearing of the Empire and Columbia Conduit sales had been anger; but the news had alarmed them, too. *Rockefeller now controlled all the pipe lines—all the outlets for oil from the producers' wells to the world market.*

The sessions of the November 21 gathering were secret, but soon everybody knew that they had been notable for two proposals. One was for a renewal of the union of producers and independent refiners—a somewhat forlorn undertaking, since the latter were small and few. The other was a plan for building a great pipe line which would break the monopoly the Standard had apparently just achieved.

This latter scheme was practicable. A seaboard pipe line would soon knock the monopoly element out of that alliance, giving the producers their own outlet. Once built, it would permit crude to be refined by existing independents or by new plants established by the pipe line itself.

The fertile-minded Lewis Emery, Jr., had already moved to construct such a line. In his Equitable Petroleum Company two hundred producers of the new Bradford field held stock. Emery proposed to gather oil from this flourishing northern area by branch pipes, which would feed into a trunk line leading to the Erie Canal at Buffalo. This would provide a cheap route to the seaboard. He was already charting his right of way.

Another group told the Council of a route from Brady's Bend on the Allegheny River southeast across the mountains to Baltimore. It covered a distance of 235 miles, and crossed high altitudes. No pipe line had ever pumped oil so far or so high, but the Seaboard Pipeline Company, with General Herman Haupt as their engineer, felt confident of success.

A second meeting of the producers on December 11 found them in a stern mood. They voted encouragement to both the proposed pipe lines and urged that the organizing of producers be pushed with all possible speed and energy. At the same time, the Council took steps to draft a free pipe line bill, which they hoped to have passed by the legislatures of New York, Pennsylvania, and Maryland. Finally, they arranged to prepare a bill for the federal regulation of interstate commerce, prohibiting all discriminatory rates by carriers.

Unfortunately, the angry producers did nothing meanwhile to check the avalanche of unwanted oil. From a record-breaking production in 1877 they moved recklessly toward another and far greater in 1878, and to a new record in 1879. Thirteen and a half million barrels, fifteen and a third million, almost twenty million —such was the American output for these three years. Consumption could not keep pace. Already in 1878 some ten thousand barrels of oil a day, more than three and a half million a year, were piling up in storage tanks.

The effect of this glut on transportation and tankage was appalling. In 1878 the pinch was severe, and it produced agony and conflict. On December 28, 1877, the Standard's pipe line officials warned their customers that daily production was exceeding shipments by 22,000 barrels, and that storage facilities were overtaxed. But the oil poured in upon them in increasing quantities, and most of it had to go to market as fast as the glutted railroads could provide cars. Meanwhile a number of producers were selling at a discount from market prices to get rid of their oil: that is, in return for immediate shipment they undercut the current price. Much of this cheap oil went to rivals of the Standard.

Within a month of its warning, the United acted to meet this situation. It announced that it would not run more than one-fourth of any man's production into tanks; the remainder would be taken only on an "immediate shipment" basis, and consequently at a lower price—from two to twenty-five cents a barrel less than the market quotation. Ample precedent existed for this order. Similar ones had been issued by the pipe lines during periods of excessive production in 1872 and 1874. They were intended to discourage production and encourage the building of tanks. But naturally they had a further result—they provided cheap oil to the buyers, who, in 1878, were primarily Standard agents.

As a result, the Regions boiled with indignation, and the meeting of the Council early in 1878 brought a torrent of denunciatory speeches against the Standard. Yet it is significant that even at this time there were oil men who turned to the Standard with a hope that a way out might be found through coöperation. One was H. L. Taylor of the firm of Satterfield & Taylor. He had some common interest with the Rockefeller group in certain producing properties, and while he had spoken harshly of the Standard during the crisis, on January 8 he had a long talk with Daniel O'Day.

Apparently O'Day and other Standard agents (Seep, Barstow, and William Brough, for example) were consulting with the moderates among the oil men. On January 19, writing from Oil City, O'Day told Rockefeller of a long conference he and Seep had held with no less a person than D. Armstrong, the Grand Organizer of the Council! They talked with him in Titusville, and found him ready to consider plans for coöperation.

Both at the time and later the Standard protested that it had sought to deal with an overwhelming situation in the best way it could. Rockefeller later declared that only the frantic exertions of the United Pipe Lines had saved the Regions from a worse calamity than that which they endured. "Had it not been for the interposition of the Standard Oil interests in building tankage, making pipe lines, and otherwise providing for this surplus of oil which came gushing from the earth these producers, many of whom had no working capital, would have seen their oil go into the ground." The logic of the extremists among the oil men, according to Rockefeller, ran as follows: "We have disregarded all advice, and produced oil in excess of the means of storing and shipping it. We have not built storage of our own. How dare you refuse to take all we produce? Why do you not pay us the high prices of 1876, without regard to the fact that the glut has depressed every market?" Rockefeller felt that if the Standard had obtained a profit from the discount on "immediate shipment" oil, it was only a just return upon its emergency construction of hundreds of miles of new pipes and millions of barrels of tankage in the Bradford district.

The first acts of the Grand Council were constructive. By its third meeting on January 9 the Regions extremists had perceived the value of seaboard pipe lines. Accordingly, the support of both Emery's Equitable line to Buffalo and the Brady's Bend-Baltimore route were publicly announced at the conclusion of that gathering. Indeed, subscriptions for the latter project were circulated among the delegates, and two members of the Council accepted posts on the board of directors.

Meanwhile the press announced that Herman Haupt had almost completed the purchase of a right of way from the oil fields to Curtis Creek, a few miles from Baltimore, where he had bought three hundred acres as a site for a great independent refinery and barrel plant. The pipe line was expected to bring down two million barrels of oil a year. If free pipe line bills could be carried through the New York and Pennsylvania legislatures, both companies seemed assured of early success.

Tremendous battles at once developed in Harrisburg and Albany. In Pennsylvania, monster petitions supported the bill, while the Regions interests lobbied aggressively. The Pennsylvania Railroad at once opposed the measure, and the Philadelphia Commercial Exchange, after two public hearings, joined it. After a stormy infancy, the bill received a setback when the Senate voted to postpone consideration indefinitely; and though it had better luck in the House, where it was passed on April 30, eight days later it was killed in the Senate. At Albany, the producers were more successful. Despite hard lobbying by the Standard and the Erie, with the New York Central apparently not exerting its full influence against the measure, a bill was finally passed by both houses. There was a question as to its constitutionality, and on April 30 Governor Lucius Robinson finally let it become a law, announcing that while he believed it unconstitutional, the courts ought to pass on it.

Three-fourths of the well-owners were convinced that the Standard had them by the throat, and was using its control of pipes, tanks, and rail transportation for the grossest extortion. They knew that the Standard had not only opposed the free pipe line bills, and thus blocked one avenue of relief, but had also put every impediment in the way of the Equitable's success, even bringing pressure on pipe manufacturers to withhold supplies. They had another genuine grievance in some of the details of the system by which the Standard used privately owned tanks as part of its general storage facilities. At any rate, they had been blocked and thwarted at every turn; and they refused to believe that the car shortage was real, or the immediate shipment order justified.

The main cause of friction lay in overproduction. A secondary cause was the arrogant insistence of the producers that the United bear the full burden of supplying storage facilities. The Standard had no responsibility for overproduction, and cannot be blamed for the shortage of storage tanks, which it strove heroically to remedy. However, some aspects of its management were open to question. It tacitly conceded the justness of one complaint when it modified its contracts for controlling privately owned tankage. Nor is it certain that its use of the immediate shipment device was always as necessary as it declared.

But the important aspect of the episode is the passionate hostility to the Standard which it bred among a large group of producers. These men believed that they struggled for their lives against a heartless tyranny. The Producers' Union went so far as to issue an address on July 14 proposing a great pool for oil. Numerous meetings discussed the project, but it came to nothing. Meanwhile other meetings bitterly denounced the railroad rebates that were being paid to the Standard through the American Transfer Company.

At the same time, the indignant Regions leaders resolved to turn to the State Government for redress. It had acted to destroy a threatened monopoly in 1872; why not again in 1878?

Few episodes in American business history are more dramatic than this appeal of the bitter men of the Regions to the executive and courts of the state of Pennsylvania.

It had three aspects. First, they requested that the Governor and Attorney-General bring *quo warranto* proceedings against the United Pipe Lines to compel that agency to perform its duties as a common carrier. Second, they demanded suits in the state supreme court to enjoin the Pennsylvania Railroad, the lines of the Erie and New York Central in Pennsylvania, and the Standard Oil against discriminating in favor of any shipper either in freight rates or car distribution. Finally, and later in time, they asked the indictment of the principal officers of the Standard Oil for criminal conspiracy.

In calling for *quo warranto* proceedings, the Producers' Union laid their grievances before Governor Hartranft, who was so much impressed by the description of the Standard's tremendous power that he demanded: "How has all this been produced?" At his suggestion, the Regions men drew up a memorial which reviewed the checkered history of the oil industry since 1872, while they also called for an extra session of the legislature—a mere gesture. The Attorney-General asked for a writ of *quo warranto* against the United, Judge Charles E. Taylor granted it, and hearings shortly began. In these the Regions men made no progress. They were answered by a demurrer and faced endless delays.

Prominent oil men therefore filed with the Secretary of Internal Affairs, William McCandless, formal charges that the railroads and the Standard had fixed discriminatory freight rates. A series of hearings ensued, which elicited much indignant testimony. But after studying it, the Secretary reported on October 14, 1878, that the allegations had "not been substantiated in any way that demanded action." This opinion threw the Regions into a new fury. In various towns McCandless was hanged in effigy.

The uproar in the Regions echoed across the country. Meanwhile, the Attorney-General had filed bills in equity against the Pennsylvania, the Atlantic & Great Western, the Lake Shore, and the United Pipe Lines, charging an unlawful combination to control the entire oil industry and a refusal to offer proper transportation facilities. He asked for injunctions.

Public hearings on these suits began early in 1879, under J. B. Sweitzer as master examiner, and from the producers' point of view proved extraordinarily successful. The whole story of the special rates established both before and just after the downfall of the Empire came out, and made a profound impression upon the public. The revelations of the size of the Standard combination, of the functions it had assumed as an "evener" of railroad traffic, and of the heavy drawbacks, rebates, and special concessions granted by the railroads, excited astonishment and indignation.

Danger signals were meanwhile raised in other states. A free pipe line bill found its way into the New Jersey legislature, but was postponed as probably unconstitutional. Much more seriously, West Virginia concluded its investigation of railroad rates, which had started with the appointment of a joint committee in 1877 to investigate travel and transportation.

By March, 1879, an investigation of railroad rates had begun in Ohio. Payne, who took charge of the Standard's interests, was alarmed to find that the matter had been transferred from the Committee on Railroads, where he had well-wishers, to that on Corporations—"a very unfriendly committee." As a result of his maneuvers, the inquiry was restored to the first agency. "This puts the investigation in the hands of *friends*—and will probably not hurt us much," he wrote Rockefeller on March 5. He was right. The affair came to little. The Standard succeeded in getting sympathetic independents, like James Corrigan, to evade the subpoena servers. Rockefeller pleaded business in New York, but submitted answers to questions sent him.

Flagler, however, went to Columbus early in May to testify. "Eight of the nine members of the committee were present upon my examination, and I think that every one of them was thoroughly satisfied that whatever the railroads may have done for others, our Co. has no contract providing for discriminations or rebates." This was an amazing statement. Doubtless it represented the theory Flagler had now developed that the favors which the Standard received were all in the nature of "commissions" for its services as "evener" or for maintaining oil traffic.

The most notable of early legislative inquiries, the great Hepburn Investigation, was already being organized when Flagler returned from Columbus. It grew out of a long agitation culminating in a memorial drawn up by New York business organizations and endorsed by Mayor Edward Cooper of New York City, asking the State Assembly to investigate railroad practices. The

committee of nine which that body appointed was headed by
Alonzo Barton Hepburn, a young lawmaker of energy and insight.

The first steps toward the Hepburn Investigation were taken
in February, 1879; the actual hearings began on July 12 in New
York City, with the general freight manager of the New York
Central as first witness. They produced an immense amount
of information, for a host of independent refiners and oil dealers
testified, and the Committee brought Jewett, Vanderbilt, Vilas
(of the Erie), Pratt, Archbold, Rogers, Bostwick, and Flagler
to the witness stand. For both the railroads and the Standard
they were devastating—at least so far as public opinion was concerned.

While the free pipe line bills were being considered in New
York and Pennsylvania, the Company maintained a paid lawyer,
A. N. Cole, at Albany. He was a wretchedly garrulous, boastful,
and ineffective creature, but diligent. Flagler paid money for
"expenses" in dealing with both the New York and the Pennsylvania free pipe line bills. In New York he sent $10,000 to
Blanchard of the Erie, and offered $5000 more. In the other state,
he made a loan to the Pennsylvania "to enable them to thistle
[pay] up matters at Harrisburg." A year and a half later Warden
wrote to Rockefeller in some perplexity about a Pennsylvania
politician who needed $15,000. Warden had "lent" the man a
third of the sum, and didn't know whether to do more or not.
"I feel that Mr. Quay might be of great use to us in the state,"
he sighed, "but he is fearfully expensive."

The Standard never took more than what might be called a
discreet rôle in political affairs, according to the practices of the
times. The railroads were far more active. But Rockefeller and
his associates were by no means disposed to play the rôle of timid
nonresistants while action was pushed against them.

The Pennsylvania and Hepburn investigations, following the
various attempts at free pipe line legislation and the sturdy
propaganda of Regions sympathizers, had a cumulative effect.
The general public was aroused. Thoughtful observers did not
miss the point that the Standard was exacting a drawback upon
other men's shipments of oil as well as on their own. Such observers noted grimly that in one case alone a toll had been taken
on 30,000 barrels in two months. These practices looked like a
revival of the hated South Improvement scheme. The demand

for effective railroad legislation was immensely strengthened.

Meanwhile the Regions men, although much heartened by the first results of their injunction suit, asked themselves what practical effect the startling testimony would have. The answer was that aside from arousing public opinion, it would merely bring the issuance of restraining orders. But the Producer's Council wanted more than that—they wanted punishment. Why not a charge of criminal conspiracy? On April 29, 1879, the grand jury of Clarion County indicted nine Standard Oil officials: John D. Rockefeller, William Rockefeller, Bostwick, O'Day, Warden, Lockhart, Flagler, Vandergrift, and the cashier of the American Transfer Company, George Girty.

The eight counts of the indictment included the following charges: (1) an attempt to achieve a monopoly in buying and refining petroleum, (2) an attempt to oppress and injure the producers, (3) a conspiracy to prevent others from refining, (4) a combination to prevent the Pennsylvania Railroad and its branches from obtaining their natural oil traffic, (5) a conspiracy to extort unreasonable commissions and rebates from various roads, and (6) an effort to control by fraudulent devices the market prices of crude and refined oil. The grand jury gave the defendants no preliminary hearing, nor were any of them present when the indictment was found.

Naturally these charges produced an enormous sensation. They also produced prompt action by both public officers and the officials of the Standard Oil Company, Warden, Lockhart, Vandergrift, and Girty, as Pennsylvanians, were arrested and gave bail. The others, not being residents of the state, did not answer the charges. When Governor Henry M. Hoyt was urged to request their extradition from Ohio and New York, the Standard officials and lawyers at once opposed this move, and began to work upon their own governors to deny any such request if made. John D. Rockefeller and Warden were particularly active. At the same time the Standard marshaled an array of lawyers drawn from Cleveland, Pittsburgh, New York and the Regions, to initiate plans for their defense.

Rockefeller in New York had taken steps to prevent extradition even before the indictment was returned, for the Standard received advance knowledge of the producers' intentions. On April 25, he had written to Chauncey M. Depew, who, while serving the New York Central, seems also to have acted for the

Standard upon request, mentioning the possibility of an attempt
at extradition. "The object of this letter is to ask, if you will
please call upon Governor Robinson, and inform him of this
possible action, and request . . . that no such requisition be
granted for any Director of our Company, without giving these
gentlemen ample time to answer." Depew acted promptly, and
wrote on the 29th: "I telegraphed you yesterday the Albany matter was all right. I write now to assure you by repeating that I
have a letter promising all needed protection."

These paragraphs show that by Standard's plan of action in
the civil suit Vandergrift, Warden, Archbold, and O'Day would
all profess to have no connection with the Standard. They would
be evasive about rates and rebates. Their records on the manipulation of prices were actually clean. How could conspiracy be
proved? Fortunately for these officials, they were not even called
upon to follow this shrewd but essentially misleading procedure.

In the meantime Warden sent a letter to Rockefeller outlining
a move suggested by Cassidy of the Pittsburgh counsel. "It is, to
get the Gov. to postpone any hearing in the civil cases, until after
the criminal conspiracy case has been tried. And Cassidy gave
legal opinions & cases that would sustain the Gov. in doing so."

The Standard attorneys saw Governor Hoyt, and the Attorney-
General, and while doubtful for a time of the outcome, eventually found it quite as happy for their clients as they had prophe-
sied. O'Day and Vandergrift were to testify in the civil proceedings on May 14. They had earlier refused to answer, but now
protested that any testimony they gave might be used against
them in the criminal action, and asked a postponement until
after the conspiracy trial had been held. The state had to grant
their request, and promptly moved for an indefinite adjournment
of the civil case. The producers had thus outsmarted themselves
and had to prove their criminal charges before the other action,
which had been so promising, could be resumed.

The Standard proceeded vigorously to seek to have the sus-
pended civil case removed from the Clarion County court to the
state supreme court. The plea for a change of venue caused a
series of delays. Finally, early in January, 1880, after a full
argument, it was ordered that the trial should take place in the
Supreme Court; but one of the seven judges was ill, and the case
was postponed.

Meanwhile, the Standard representatives had been working

for a peaceful adjustment. A number of producers favored it; the peace party quietly grew in strength. As over-production raged, oil fell to 70 cents a barrel in June, yet the well-men ignored all pleas to curtail the supply.

During this period the United was working desperately to increase tankage and ship oil. In replying on August 15, 1879, to a group of independent tankers, it asserted that 9,000,000 barrels of oil were in storage. This doubtless represented the total tankage capacity available at the time, for it was all in use. The greater part of it was in the Bradford area, so that the increase there from a little more than a million barrels' capacity in April, 1878, had been astounding. In October, O'Day reported to Rockefeller that 54,000 barrels of wooden tankage alone (iron tankage was also in process of construction) had been completed in the first twenty days of the month. But, he added, during that time the American Transfer Company had connected with 110 new wells.

On December 24 the United Pipe Line announced suspension of its "immediate shipment" order. As a result of the suspension, pressure for a settlement grew stronger on the producers. Rockefeller was pleased with the situation. "I know the producers will ascertain who their real friends are," he declared in a remarkable burst of optimism, "and that the time will come when they will carry us about upon their shoulders to express their gratitude."

That time was never to arrive. But the end of the immediate struggle came quickly. In mid-February, D. T. Watson of the Standard's legal staff reported to Rockefeller the termination of the conspiracy suit. Faced with further delays, the necessity to plead before an impartial court, and a weakening support even in the areas of their power, the Council leaders had at length made their peace with the "combination." In return for certain important agreements, the Council would withdraw both its civil and its conspiracy charges.

The producers had not come off empty-handed. The Standard agreed to make no opposition to the abolition of rebates, drawbacks, and secret rates; to accept no rates that the roads were not free to give to other shippers; to make no objection to full publicity for freight charges. It agreed further that the United should make no discrimination between shippers, should not fix different prices from one field to another, except as based on quality, and should give thirty days' notice of any rate increase. The United was to make every effort to store and transport all oil delivered so long as production did not exceed 65,000 barrels a day during fifteen consecutive days. Even if production exceeded that amount, the United agreed not to buy any so-called immediate shipment oil at a discount, provided it was not sold at discount rates to others.

Thus the Standard was pledged to reform the practices of its pipe lines, and conditionally to abolish "immediate shipment" purchases at less than market rates. Its commitments on railroad rates were less specific. For example, the railroads were "at liberty" to give favorable rates to others. But would they? The roads also agreed not to discriminate in the allocation of cars. But despite such concessions it was clear that rebate discrimination would still exist. This was the bitter fact that the Grand Council had to swallow.

Rate discrimination had come to be the symbol of everything the producers detested. That they had gained much was almost forgotten in their humiliating recognition of what they had failed to gain. Seven years later, in the Interstate Commerce Act, they were to see a first installment of their demands substantially met. Meanwhile, they were to suffer less than before from the old abuses. The American public had been deeply impressed by the testimony in the Pennsylvania injunction suits and the New York and Ohio investigations, and Rockefeller realized it. Officers and attorneys of the Standard later asserted that from this time forward it never took rebates. Some students of Standard Oil history have disagreed violently with them. In a sense, both are right.

The Standard officials are right to the extent that beginning in 1880 the Company received open rates, and no rebates. By 1882 there was no need to use the trunk lines for the greater part of crude oil shipments. If railways were still employed to a considerable extent, thereby the railroads and not the Standard were favored. On the other hand, the railroads were still highly useful for local shipments and the general situation was such that the interests of the Rockefeller group and of the roads were practically identical. Therefore the trunk lines at times took measures to discourage independent refiners. The Standard profited in such cases much as it had profited from the older type of discrimination; it received the equivalent of rebates.

As for the settlement of 1880, the important point is that thereafter the practice of discrimination in railroading stood condemned as never before. It was now threatened with legal extinction. As a result, both the trunk lines and the Standard Oil were wary of provoking public indignation further, and they abandoned or sharply curtailed the measures that had aroused nation-wide anger. This was a moral and to some extent a practical victory for the producers. Because the roads and the Standard still coöperated in many ways to help each other, the practical victory was limited. So far as crude oil shipments went, the building of pipe lines was soon to make it all but pointless anyway. But the moral victory helped to bring about federal legislation which forbade monopoly and banned many vicious trade practices; and to this extent it was real, momentous, and enduring.

At Coryville, Pennsylvania, on the afternoon of May 28, 1879, the Tidewater Pipe Line put into operation a 110-mile trunk line, three times the length of any previously built, connecting the tanks and pumping station at Coryville with Williamsport, across the Allegheny range. So began the pipe line revolution. The line made direct railroad connections with the seaboard. To the Regions it represented the blow of a giant chisel striking from the producers the shackles which they believed the Standard and the rail chiefs had fastened upon them. Actually, the event was far more momentous. It was the beginning of an industrial change which in a few years would turn three-quarters or more of all the crude oil produced away from the rail heads into silent channels underground.

The audacious pipe line enterprise owed much of its success to its chief engineer, Herman Haupt. A graduate of West Point in the same class as Meade of Gettysburg fame, later a professor of civil engineering, one of the architects of the Pennsylvania's main section and for five years in charge of the Hoosac Tunnel, he pushed the pipe line to completion despite the opposition of both man and nature. The Standard tried to thwart him by purchasing a right of way north and south across Pennsylvania. But Haupt outwitted them. Working secretly, with various ruses and the most careful legal procedure, he found a gap in the supposedly tight line, foiled the Pennsylvania Railroad with an injunction which protected him in laying pipes under one of their culverts, and brought his six-inch conduit to its terminal.

As to the technical problems represented by distance and terrain, Haupt had full confidence in his ability to solve them, and wholly confounded his critics. The great pipe line worked from the start. In a week the oil was pouring into immense new tanks at Williamsport, and the imagination of every man in the Regions was stirred. The days of the railroads as crude oil carriers were clearly numbered, and the grip of the Standard on the producers seemed to be broken. Everywhere men talked of the astounding feat: oil had been pumped 1900 feet above sea level, to drop 2100 feet by gravity to Williamsport. Two pumping stations did all the work. Soon the pipes were discharging much more than the 6000 barrels a day which had been their initial load. Williamsport tanks with ten times that capacity were receiving it, while the Reading was filling thirty-car trains in minutes instead of hours.

By mid-June more than 50,000 barrels had been pumped, and new tank cars, of which the Reading had 200, were carrying the oil southward into Chester on Delaware Bay, where stood an independent refinery. Meanwhile, construction was being pushed rapidly on the Solar Oil Works at Williamsport, which would soon aid in disposing of the green torrent that poured steadily from the pipes.

Neither the railroads nor the Standard Oil could afford to watch the brilliant beginning and rapid expansion of the Tidewater without a desperate effort to check or control its activities. What could Rockefeller do? The trunk lines still controlled the long-distance transportation of oil. They provided advantages greater than any pipe line could offer: if the Standard built one, it would exchange existing advantages for competition with an aggressive rival. Therefore until the pipes demonstrated their superiority over the rails, Rockefeller was naturally reluctant to risk offending the roads by embarking on an experiment which would challenge them as carriers.

But Rockefeller was never a man to fail to see the economic handwriting on the wall. As soon as the Tidewater was pouring crude into Williamsport and its ability to continue its deliveries was clear, he moved promptly to meet the emergency. The Standard met the threat in three ways: by securing cheaper rail transportation rates; by purchasing additional independent refineries in the East, thus shutting out some purchasers for the crude oil delivered by Tidewater pipes; and by launching a new and extensive pipe line construction program for connections to Cleve-

land and New York. Rockefeller was determined to control the
Tidewater, but was willing to make a place for it in the overall
pattern of transportation and refining. His opponents in turn
desired a compact with him. They wanted to pump a considerable quantity of crude, and to dispose of it. But there were sharp
points of difference on the amount of crude the Tidewater should
pump, and the proportion of this which it should sell to the
Standard.

The two chief units in the oil industry continued to face each
other as competitors, and the struggle for power continued. The
Tidewater sought to enlarge its activities; the Standard resolutely
bent itself to the task of forcing an arrangement which would
limit the scope and disruptive power of its smaller but vigorous
rival.

As the year 1880 came to a close, the Tidewater seemed to be
in a fairly promising condition for waging a defensive war, with
the hope of winning the arrangement with the Standard which
it desired. Its pipe line was an engineering success. Its arrangements with the Reading and the Jersey Central enabled it to
reach the chief eastern markets. A number of independent refineries continued ready to take its crude, and it could sell
abroad. It had strong support in the Regions and from independents elsewhere.

Unfortunately for its promoters, events now began to break
down this promising position. Internal dissension sapped the
company's vitality. Meanwhile, as the Tidewater was losing
strength, the Standard was gaining it.

As to pipe lines, it was not satisfied to rest upon its recent
notable advances. While the trunk lines were being pushed, it
went on acquiring various shorter ones. Some time in the sum-
mer or fall of 1880 it bought the Pennsylvania Transportation
Company, the former Abbott & Harley lines, which it had
operated on lease since 1876. On September 1, 1880, it leased the
Fox & Fink Pipe Line; after long delay it purchased the Karns
Pipe Line on November 12, while the Emlenton Producers' Pipe
Line was picked up the final day of the year. These were all
Regions lines of small length. In December, 1881, the Buffalo &
Rock City Pipe Line was also acquired, a $120,000 property in
Buffalo which had worried both Benson and O'Day.

Thus the Standard was leasing or buying all the pipe line
properties it could lay its hands on. And by January, 1881, a

much larger project was being contemplated which, it was hoped by Warden, Rockefeller, and Archbold (to name the leaders most closely concerned) would sweep all independent pipe line activity outside the Tidewater into one mighty company which would also include all Standard pipe line properties. The Rockefeller group would naturally hold control, but the new interests would have a voice and share in the company management.

In this vision of a pipe line colossus no less a person than Joseph D. Potts shared and worked for a fulfillment! H. L. Taylor, Houston, Roberts and Cassatt of the Pennsylvania, William Thaw, and others were figures in what became an exciting drama of negotiations.

Potts had lent counsel to Tidewater during the preliminary stages of their enterprise. But the Standard's former antagonist had interests of his own. When the Standard bought out the Empire, it did not buy all the properties that this company had controlled. One of those not acquired was the National Storage Company, to which Potts seems to have devoted his chief energies from 1877 to 1881. He was a large stockholder; so were Roberts of the Pennsylvania, and C. A. Griscom, also prominent in the International Navigation Company, a line owning ocean steamships for carrying of oil.

The National Storage Company in 1877 seems to have restricted its activities to the area its name suggests; it had tanks for storing oil and doubtless a few local pipe lines. But Potts had not collapsed with the sale of the Empire. He was the same shrewd, statesmanlike industrialist who had built up a great fast-freight company. He now proceeded to develop the property he had retained. He planned a refinery to use the crude oil the storage unit held. A pipe line then seemed logical. We know that this line was well out of the dream stage in January, 1881, for the hard-headed O'Day wrote Rockefeller on the 21st of that month, saying that the right of way was being purchased from Bradford to Driftwood "on the Grade Rail Road and Philda. & Eries RR." O'Day knew that both Potts, apparently in charge, and the Pennsylvania were interested. "I believe it will be constructed," he declared, "unless recent negotiations stop it."

These negotiations were even then under way in Philadelphia, where Archbold and Warden had been discussing with Potts the valuation to be put upon the National Storage Company, with its projected and perhaps partially constructed pipe lines and refineries. The negotiations went forward, the two sides drawing nearer to each other. The big "new company" finally came into being as the National Transit Company, a $30,000,000 corporation which included all the United Pipe Line system, the American Transfer System (five trunk lines and two small ones), one steamship, the *Vaterland,* for the European oil trade, and Potts' National Storage Company. Essential agreement was reached April 14, 1881, and the transfer of titles took place May 25.

Joseph D. Potts completely abandoned his hostility to the Standard, and apparently would have come into the organization as Warden, Lockhart, Archbold, and Rogers had previously done, but for limitations on his time and strength. The Standard leaders wished him to assume the presidency of the new organization, and although he refused, for the next few years he advised them on many questions, was a director of the National Transit Company, and undertook negotiations for this organization.

In the formation of the gigantic new unit, the National Storage Company was valued at $3,450,000, the *Vaterland* at $750,000, and pipe line properties of the Standard at $25,200,000— $600,000 being reserved for other pipe lines which it was hoped would be acquired. Eventually C. A. Griscom became the first president. A special franchise, that of the Southern Railway Security Company, had been bought on March 21, 1881, for the use of the new organization.

Thus the Standard had taken a stride in pipe line affairs which paralleled to a considerable extent its unification in refining. It had pooled all its own interests under a central authority, and had acquired the largest single competitive organization outside the Tidewater.

What exactly were the Standard holdings at this time? They comprised, of course, all the lines of the United (as distinguished from the American Transfer Company, technically a part of it). These covered the Regions to bring crude to the railheads, and altogether, with their multiple local connections, represented more than 12,000 miles of line. Their storage tanks, pumping stations, offices, and telegraph lines constituted an immensely valuable property. By early 1883 the Standard's pipe line empire had grown to new dimensions.

The day of the pipe line had fully dawned. It was no longer merely an ingenious substitute for the mule teams which in early

days had splashed through Regions mud, carrying oil from the
wells to the railheads; instead, the long-distance conduit would
inevitably supersede the tank car and the locomotive. It was the
custodian of millions of barrels of tankage into which oil was
poured, to be held until shipment—in which function it invaded
the financial aspect of the industry, helping to check ruinous
speculation. It was an iron artery which lowered the cost of
transportation to the consumer.

Everywhere oil men were talking of pipes. The producers saw
in them a weapon against monopoly—a means of transporting
oil to friendly independent refineries. The independent refineries
saw them as potential or actual sources of supply which would
permit continued competition. The Standard saw them as a new
device for serving its many units and maintaining its low transportation costs. Foundries were casting pipes; manufacturers were
building tanks and pumps for storing the oil and speeding it on
its way; engineers were plotting maps, and routes were being
charted by brisk surveyors. Rights of way were being discreetly
purchased by busy agents scouting and buying passage rights,
aided in their work by the advice of distant lawyers and executives.

After the scouts came the construction crews, who strung pipes
along the route, dug ditches, and erected pumping stations. The
impact of activity was often dramatic. The little town of Cameron on the New York line was to be the site of a station, but
the grasping officials tried to exact too high a price. Cameron
Mills, near by, offered land at a reasonable price and won the
station. The local paper published a jubilant description of
what was happening:

Eight acres of land have been purchased here, and is being prepared
for the tanks, two in number, each having a capacity of 25,000 barrels;
and the pumping house which is to be of brick; 600,000 being already
ordered. A contract for 300 perch of stones has been let; also for an
indefinite amount of lumber, estimated, however, at 150,000 feet. There
are now about 50 men in town. The carpenters are coming Monday,
and the masons and riveters soon after. The engines are to be 150 horse
power. This is a six-inch pipe, and will go on through here directly
east. Its destination, no one here knows. It has become a saying with
us, "Mum as a pipe line man."

Once the pipe lines were placed, they gave little evidence of
their existence: only the tanks and shacks, and engines at the

pumping stations, and the "walkers" patrolling the lines day and night. The pipes were underground. Few Americans realized that even by 1882 some 14,000 miles of iron webbing lay beneath their soil, silently carrying the heavy fluid that would light the homes of their land, lubricate their machinery, and provide them with dozens of products from paints and vaseline to candles and chewing gum! Here was a transportation unit the length of four transcontinental railways, yet for the most part hidden from men's sight. It had grown to maturity in fifteen years, had revolutionized the carrying of oil, and was already taken as much for granted as the humble kerosene can which had suddenly become a household article around the world.

Meanwhile the Tidewater had been resolutely pushing its line eastward toward the seaboard. It had worked under great annoyance and difficulty. Doubtless the Standard's tactics of purchasing refineries, contracting for all available tanks, using all available railroad cars, and possibly competing for crude had constricted its efforts.

From late 1881 forward, after the Standard made a loan to the Tidewater, Archbold and other Standard leaders seem to have been in fairly close touch with the Tidewater officials. The fall and winter of 1882–83 witnessed a complicated series of transactions, attended by not a little garish melodrama. Two New Yorkers, the banker George F. Baker and the speculator James R. Keene, helped market bonds and loan certificates for the Tidewater on terms of cruel harshness. They did more to weaken the company than the Standard could ever have done. But the Standard also played an unfriendly role; it induced a Regions man named E. G. Patterson, to whom Archbold paid $20,000, to try to throw the Tidewater into bankruptcy by asking the courts to appoint a receiver—a maneuver which was defeated when Judge Pierson Church in Meadville dismissed the petition with a scathing condemnation of Patterson.

Meanwhile, a minority under the leadership of H. L. Taylor tried hard to wrest control of the Tidewater from its founders; and an arbitrary coup at the annual meeting was defeated only by the hasty barricading of the company offices in Titusville, and by another clear-cut decision by Judge Church.

The result was a compromise. It was not easily effected, and for a time the Standard leaders seem to have believed that they would win complete control of their rival. Both had to give way.

Several events may have induced the Standard to make concessions. One was the establishment in December, 1882, of the National Petroleum Exchange at 57 Broadway, New York. Up to this time the Regions had held the chief trading points for oil—at Titusville, Oil City, and finally at Bradford. But the New York center, with its 500 members, introduced a new era. When President C. G. Wilson rapped with his gavel to open its first session, and a member shouted, "I'll give 94¾ for 5000 barrels," while another responded, "I'll sell 5000 for 94⅞," an exchange was inaugurated which promised to surpass any in Pennsylvannia. It marked the expansion of the petroleum industry and perhaps indicated that this complex activity would be more difficult to control in the future than it had been in the past.

The passage of a free pipe line bill by the Pennsylvania legislature may also have had an influence. It was a limited bill, in that it provided that all the lines it affected must have their terminals within the state. Still, it seemed likely to encourage more pipe line ventures. Would not an agreement between the Standard and the Tidewater be likely to discourage competition and protect both of the established interests? The Standard had often agreed with competitors on a quota basis.

It made such a compact now with the Tidewater. On October 8, 1883, it signed a contract by which its pipe lines would take 88.5 per cent of the business from the Pennsylvania fields eastward, and the Tidewater 11.5 per cent. Charges were to be kept uniform at 40 cents a barrel to Philadelphia and 45 cents to New York. Local lines in the Regions were to receive 20 cents a barrel for collecting from the wells. Both parties hailed the treaty as a victory. For the Tidewater it meant a final recognition of independence; for the Standard it represented a guarantee that the Tidewater would make no plans for marked expansion, and would not attempt to build up the refining interest which must form the basis of such projects.

Under this arrangement the Tidewater prospered. It continued its operations as before until its line reached Bayonne in 1887. Then the Chester refinery was consolidated with the Ocean refinery at Bayonne, and in 1888 the Tidewater Oil Company was formed, absorbing the Ocean Oil Company and Lombard, Ayres. Important Bradford wells owned by Satterfield and Taylor were bought by the new company when it went into oil production. As a combined producing, transporting, refining, and exporting corporation the Tidewater did about a tenth of the whole American business in petroleum. Its existence gave the Standard some ground for denying that it held an absolute monopoly.

But Rockefeller and his associates had prospered more than their rivals. To be sure, the competitors were established, but they were also established within prescribed limits. The building of the Tidewater had been a brilliant stroke opening possibilities for turning the flank of the Standard combination. Other pipe lines might have been laid by independents, refineries might have been built to take their oil, and the entire structure of Rockefeller plants might have been forced to contract its activities, its dominant position seriously impaired. But the Standard leaders had moved swiftly and masterfully to occupy the new field of trunk pipe lines. They had outbuilt the Tidewater, absorbed the Potts properties, and bought out Taylor's pipes and storage units. Finally, they had constricted the Tidewater's activities and forced it to become a partial ally. The result was less dramatic and crushing than the outcome of the battle with the Empire. Nonetheless it was notable, and from the Standard's point of view quite effective. That the Tidewater had been dealt with gently did not disturb Rockefeller. He was an apostle not of demolition but of stabilization, which he had achieved.

It was really an improved type of control. The pipe line revolution had pushed the railroads into a subordinate position. Transportation and refining were both dominated by the Standard. As the sources of oil moved westward, Rockefeller laid pipes from the new Ohio fields to Cleveland and Chicago. He doubled and in some cases tripled the pipes of his original trunk lines. Competition increased rather than diminished, but he was in a position to check and regulate it, and to maintain unfractured the massive structure which he had so carefully and boldly erected.

# CHAPTER VII

# THE FIRST GREAT TRUST

W HENEVER the heads of the Standard Oil combination
met after the middle seventies, whether in the crowded
Cleveland offices or the more specious Pearl Street quarters in
New York, they were troubled by the question of legal organization. They were building up a huge interstate combination of
many companies and properties, efficiently organized under one
direction; and though such far-spreading combinations were
soon to become numerous, state laws as yet impeded their growth.

The Standard Oil Company of Ohio, the nucleus of the group,
chartered to manufacture, ship, and sell petroleum products, was
confined by the terms of its incorporation to the single state in
which it had been established. It had no legal right to own plants
in other states, and no right to hold stocks in other companies. If
the Standard were to expand on a national scale, the officers
of the company would somehow have to be clothed with power to
participate in manufacturing and marketing enterprises in other
states. This power should if possible be given them in such a
fashion that each new acquisition or enterprise in other states
would not attract general publicity. How, under the restrictive
corporation laws of the time, could such interstate activity be accomplished?

In buying the New York properties of Bostwick & Company
in 1872, Rockefeller and Flagler had resorted to a simple expedient. Paying for the holdings with cash and Standard Oil
stock, they made an agreement by which Bostwick carried on
the business under his own firm name but for the account of the
Standard and under its direction. That is, although the Bostwick
profits went at the end of the year to the Standard, legally it re-

mained a separate unit. This loose arrangement would not prove a satisfactory model for extensive acquisitions, and would not serve at all for the purchase of properties to be amalgamated with each other. Accordingly, in the second New York purchase a significant new procedure was followed. The stockholders of the Long Island Oil Company received a certain sum in cash and Standard Oil stock. In return, all the securities of the Long Island were transferred to Flagler, secretary of the Standard, as *trustee*.

This was a radically different method from that followed in the Cleveland acquisitions, where the properties were intrastate and were easily welded together under the Standard's Ohio charter. But the Ohio company had no right to take physical possession of New York manufactories and operate them. Nor, as the law was generally interpreted in America and had until recently been interpreted in England, did the company have any right to hold stock in a concern incorporated elsewhere. Railroads had held and operated insterstate companies and lines, but in general only by special statute. It was not until 1889 that New Jersey began legalizing the practice of intercorporation stockholding, and so ushered in the day of great holding companies controlling businesses in several or many states. The Standard would be open to heavy attack if it asserted stock ownership in companies outside Ohio. The obvious recourse was to depute an officer to take personal possession of the stock, denominating him a trustee.

But a trustee for what? Up to 1879 the various trustees holding stocks did not execute any papers in the nature of declarations of trust. No statement was recorded on the stock-books or elsewhere to show who was the beneficiary of the trustee's property. The strongest hint on the subject, given for example in the arrangement made with Charles Pratt & Company, was that the stock was put in the name of "H. M. Flagler, Secretary, Trustee" —for Flagler was secretary of Standard Oil. Later this question was explored in the courts. Standard officials then declared that the stocks standing in the names of trustees had *not* been held for the Standard of Ohio, but for its stockholders just as though equitable interests in the various stocks had been distributed in dividends. Rockefeller himself was always emphatic on this point.

This device of placing new acquisitions outside Ohio in the

hands of a trustee was followed for some years. The device at first seemed effective. It partially protected the combination under state laws. It maintained a veil of secrecy over the Standard's expansion; even on the witness stand the officers, from Rockefeller down, could flatly deny that the Standard owned or controlled a given corporation. This was juggling the truth, but they could quiet their consciences by thinking that technically the trustee was owner. The device made possible the welding of many properties into an effective alliance.

Nevertheless, as the Standard absorbed one holding after another, it became clear that the system of individual trustees had grave defects. If one of the important partners—Rockefeller, Flagler, Pratt—died, difficult legal questions might arise. Moreover, the trustee system was too loose; it interfered with the proper unification of the management of the mighty congeries of plants, pipe lines, and marketing agencies. And what if a trustee some day wished to make trouble for his associates?

In the Standard's early years the able Myron Keith of Cleveland had been Rockefeller's principal legal adviser. "Rockefeller never made a decision without consulting that man," said a Standard official familiar with the Cleveland office in the seventies. "Mr. Rockefeller would write a letter or draft an agreement and hand it to Flagler. Henry would rewrite it, often interlining. He wrote a beautiful hand. Then, if important, it would go to Keith. When it was finished, it was a *document*." Judge Rufus P. Ranney of Cleveland, a shrewd, experienced, ingenious attorney, with considerable breadth of vision, also performed many legal services for the Standard.

Keith and Ranney had a lucid grasp of the problem, and also, like Rockefeller, a powerful instinct for simplification and coordination. These men and Flagler knew that the principal contrivance thus far employed for uniting corporations in different states, the pool, was highly defective. Under the common law, all pool agreements for dividing trade, traffic, or revenues were unenforceable; they were therefore constantly being broken. The four men also perceived that the expedient of transferring stock to a trustee, invented by Flagler, offered possibilities for elaboration. The word trust, as then used in law, referred almost exclusively to an instrument by which one person held property for the benefit of another or others. A court might assign the property of a minor in trust to a guardian, or several partners might assign some joint property to a bank as trustee. It was natural first to think of improving the original expedient.

With this end in view, someone, probably Flagler, prepared a trust agreement which Judge Ranney put in general form an April 8, 1879, and revised the following November. Instead of a single trustee for every company, a small body of trustees was named for all of them; instead of men scattered all over the map, the trustees were made a little group inside the head office. Three Cleveland officials, Myron P. Keith, George F. Chester, and George H. Vilas, were selected. The Standard Oil Company, its thirty-seven stockholders, and all the former individual trustees executed an agreement transferring to this trio all the stocks acquired in subsidiaries, and "all other interests of every kind and description held by the Standard Oil Company or in which it has an interest, which can or by right ought to be divided and distributed among the parties entitled thereto without affecting its proper, legitimate, and efficient operations as a corporation." They were to manage the stocks and other interests for the exclusive benefit of the Standard Oil stockholders. Of course they were merely dummies, behind whom stood the real managers.

The trust agreement shows that the Standard at this date held all the stock of nearly a score of corporations, and part of the stock of a baker's dozen or more.

"The effect of the Vilas, Keith, and Chester agreement," as Walter L. Taylor says, "was that the Standard Oil Company of Ohio ceased to be the owner of the stocks and interests transferred to Vilas, Keith, and Chester, if it had been the owner of them before." They were now held by the three Cleveland trustees for the benefit of the thirty-seven Standard Oil stockholders. The Standard Oil stock was not placed in the trustees' hands; there was no reason why it should be. Under the agreement the trustees were instructed to divide the shares of the Standard-controlled companies among the Standard stockholders, but this was difficult and was never seriously attempted. The main duty of the trustees was simply to divide profits annually in the proportion to the number of Standard Oil shares held by each of the thirty-seven, this bookkeeping task falling to Vilas.

At that time, Rockefeller was the principal holder of Standard oil stock, with 8984 of the 35,000 shares. Flagler stood next with 3000 shares; then S. V. Harkness with 2925, Charles Pratt with 2700, Oliver H. Payne with 2637, J. A. Bostwick with 1872, and

William Rockefeller with 1600. Vandergrift held 500 shares, Archbold 350, Camden and C. M. Pratt 200 each, and Ambrose McGregor 118. It will be seen that the Cleveland group held a majority interest, the two Rockefellers, Flagler, Harkness, and Payne alone owning 19,146 shares. Samuel Andrews, Amasa Stone, and Peter H. Watson had ceased to be stockholders. Inasmuch as the stockholders received dividends not merely from the Standard, but from all the subsidiary and allied corporations, every share was worth far more than its face value of $100. The actual worth of Rockefeller's shares, capitalized upon dividends from the controlled companies, was estimated by Standard men in 1879 at about $18,000,000, and by outsiders at much more. He was, therefore, among the richest men in the country, although few yet suspected the fact.

The veil of secrecy about the Standard's acquisitions was still impenetrable by any legal searchlight. Rockefeller, in a Cleveland suit in 1880, made solemn affidavit: "It is not true, as stated by Mr. Teagle in his affidavit, that the Standard Oil Company, directly or indirectly, through its officers and agents, owns or controls the works of Warden, Frew & Company, Lockhart, Frew & Company, J. A. Bostwick & Company, C. Pratt & Company, Acme Refining Company, Imperial Refining Company, Camden Consolidated Company. . . ." Legally, this statement might be defended. The three trustees held ownership and Rockefeller could say they acted not for the Standard but its stockholders. Actually, to call the statement disingenous would be putting the matter mildly; it was equivocation. Such evasive tarradiddles were then too common in American business.

But while the action just taken was a step in advance, it was only a short step. It did much to clarify the ownership of the Standard-controlled properties; it furnished a clearer legal status; it brought all the legal strings together in the Cleveland office; and it facilitated the distribution of profits. But it left many problems still unsolved, and as the combination increased in scope, wealth, and power they grew more acute. We find W. P. Thompson writing Payne on April 23, 1879, that better integration was a necessity. "In my judgment it is important that we endeavor to induce the parties holding interests of a private nature in the various companies now under our control to release them, and let the whole be put into some common interest . . . this condition of conflict will grow as the business grows—it will prevent harmonious pulling together until we do develop the business to its highest magnitude." By the time that Rockefeller, Flagler, and other officers decided to transfer the main headquarters from Cleveland to New York, some new action had become imperative. Fortunately for Rockefeller and Flagler, an attorney of remarkable ability, Samuel C. T. Dodd, had not long since been added to the Standard's staff. Here was the man who, becoming its leading counsel, was to brood over the gloomy abyss of American corporation law and to evolve from it an idea which not only gave unity and power to the Standard, but profoundly influenced an entire era of American business.

Even before he joined the Standard he seems to have been convinced that, as he later put it, "just in proportion as combination and concentration of capital have taken place, have prices decreased, wages increased, wealth been created, and the individual been benefited." By May, 1879, he was a member of the Standard's legal staff. Dodd soon took general direction of the Standard's legal affairs, and went to New York in 1881 as its general solicitor. First, however, he made his position clear on a vital point. "I am bitterly opposed to the whole system of railway rebates and discriminations," he told Rockefeller and Flagler. They assured him that they had long been willing to forego rebates if the railways would only discontinue them universally. "We ask only to be treated the same as our competitors," they said. From that date until his retirement in 1905 on a pension which he was asked to fix for himself, he remained in charge of the growing staff of Standard lawyers.

Immediately on coming to New York, Dodd was asked to report upon ways and means of reorganizing the Standard holdings under a single ownership and direction. In an undated letter of 1880 or 1881, he advised Rockefeller and Flagler that three possibilities existed. The first was the creation of a central corporation or holding company which should own the stocks of corporations in different states and make the business of these scattered corporations subsidiary to the business of the central unit. The second was the formation of a partnership by the stockholders of the various corporations. The third was a careful development of the plan of holding the stocks in trust, while the business was managed by elected representatives of the beneficiaries.

The main obstacle to the creation of a holding company, he

pointed out, was the difficulty of obtaining a charter which conferred the necessary powers. Plainly, the holding company device was not available. Indeed, it did not become available until New Jersey led forth the long procession of states legalizing it. But what of the other two expedients?

The legal objections to a copartnership of stockholders were many. Such a copartnership could not have a common seal, nor make a deed in its corporate name. Its internal arrangements were not binding upon outside parties. Each partner was the legal agent of all the others. A transfer of his interest by any partner, or his insolvency, or his death, operated as a virtual dissolution of the firm. Dodd noted that New York had a peculiar law which obviated most of these objections—the law governing unincorporated stock associations. While such associations were partnerships and had no franchises, they possessed nearly all the essential elements of corporations. They had corporate immortality; their capital could be divided into shares like those of a regular corporation; death, insolvency, and transfer of stock did not work a dissolution of the firm; they could sue and be sued; they could buy and hold real estate; they might devolve the sole management of the business upon three or more trustees. But—and here Dodd touched a vital point—they lost all the advantages of secrecy; for "such associations are required to make reports and are subject to taxation the same as corporations."

As for the third possibility, the trusteeship, Dodd felt that its advantages and disadvantages were too familiar to Standard men to need much comment. He merely noted that any device for holding the stocks in trust must necessarily be associated with either a corporation or a partnership. "If the beneficiaries of the trust carry on a joint business they are partners. It seems to me not so important, in case of a trust, to decide whether the trustees shall be a corporation or an individual as to decide in what manner the beneficiaries shall conduct their business." He added:

In regard to the question which plan renders the parties least liable to the charge of forming an illegal combination, I do not think it makes any difference unless the combination is specially legalized by a special charter in the mode above stated. It is not the mode of combination which makes it illegal, but the extent, purpose, and tendency of it.

For a time Rockefeller and Flagler seriously entertained the idea of creating a large central corporation or holding company.

But to do this it would be necessary to dissolve the Standard Oil
of Ohio, a step which Dodd told them would be more difficult
than they thought. Dodd did not like the proposed attempt to
establish a single great holding company. Dodd's plan was to
create a corporation in each state where the Standard had important properties or affiliates, to hold and manage most or all of
these assets. Then no danger of double, triple, or quadruple
taxation of the same property would arise. No corporation in one
state would be in any way subject to the legislature of another
state. With a Standard Oil Company of New York, a Standard of
New Jersey, a Standard of Pennsylvania, and so on, the intrastate
business could be well unified, while the trust device could weld
these corporations together in a great interstate combination.
Dodd explained the advantages of the scheme:

The objection to this plan is that with separate corporations there
must be separate stocks, separate boards of Directors, and separate
books. There is no way of avoiding this. There is no way to perfectly
consolidate the corporations of different States. It may be done by the
legislatures of the different States to the extent of creating a community
of stock and interest, but for the most purposes the law treats corporations thus consolidated as still separate and distinct. But you could have
a common name, a common office, and a common management by
means of a common executive committee. The stock can be made in
effect common by placing the corporation stock in the hands of Trustees
who shall issue certificates of interest in the Trust estate, which certificates will be entitled to their due proportion of the various stock
dividends, and may be made assignable freely or subject to such restrictions as may be agreed upon. If the Directors of one of the companies and their successors shall be made Trustees of all the stock, you
thus procure a practical unification of all the companies.

Here, in a nutshell, was stated the solution of the problem. In
the end, Dodd's plan for the unification of properties within
each state, under the aegis of trustees who would issue certificates
of interest in the trust holdings, was adopted.

The new trust agreement, signed January 2, 1882 (with a
supplementary agreement dated two days later), marked a new
departure in the history not only of the Standard, but of industrial organizations in the United States. The signers were
the stockholders of the Standard Oil of Ohio, now forty-two in
number, and Messrs. Keith, Chester, and Vilas. They agreed to

set up a board of nine trustees, and to place in their hands *all* the properties owned or controlled by the Standard. That is, the nine men were to take not only the stocks of the subsidiary and allied companies, but the 35,000 shares of the Standard Oil of Ohio itself. For each share of stock in the Standard of Ohio and the corresponding interest in the stocks and partnership equities held by Vilas, Keith, and Chester, twenty trust certificates of a par value of $100 each were issued. The profits of all the component companies were to be sent to the nine trustees, and the certificate-holders were to receive such dividends as the trustees might deem expedient.

The first trustees were designated by the trust agreement itself, three serving for one year, three for two, and three for a triennium. They were John D. Rockefeller, Oliver H. Payne, William Rockefeller, Jabez A. Bostwick, H. M. Flagler, William G. Warden, Charles Pratt, Benjamin Brewster, and John D. Archbold. It will be seen that whereas the three trustees of the 1879 agreement were men of minor executive standing, the nine trustees comprised the chief active managers of the combination. Power to elect successors was vested in the certificate-holders. The trustees were to have their principal office in New York. They were charged with the early formation of Standard Oil companies in New York and New Jersey. Additional companies with similar names might be organized in other states and territories whenever the trustees thought proper. Finally, a sweeping grant of authority was made to the nine leaders. They were to "exercise general supervision over the affairs of the several Standard Oil Companies," and were to elect the directors and officers of all the companies in which they held a complete or controlling ownership.

In effect, though not in law, one great company, the Standard Oil Trust, had been created; a company represented by the 700,-000 new hundred-dollar certificates, and managed by the nine trustees. While it is true that the trust agreement did not bring together separately-owned properties, for they had been under common ownership before, the birth of this unprecedented entity was an epochal event in business organization; for it showed how, at a time when interstate holding companies were outlawed, an interstate business involving numerous companies and properties could be efficiently welded together and managed.

Other combinations—first a few, then scores—were soon to follow the path thus blazed. In the end the states were to abandon their antiquated, unworkable prohibitions. Meanwhile, the public was quick to show its grasp of the momentous innovation by utterly changing the meaning attached to a venerable English word. A trust had hitherto meant a trusteeship, or something confided to another. But it now came to mean a great monopolistic or semi-monopolistic corporation, and this meaning it has retained. Even when holding companies were generally legalized, any of them which attained great size was certain—though it had no trustees of any type—to be termed a trust.

Thus what still had been in some ways a rather loose confederation was transformed into a tight unitary state, with the nine men at its head possessing full means for control. The trustees and the Executive Committee were substantially identical. They created the Standard Oil of New York on August 1, 1882, with William Rockefeller its president, J. A. Bostwick its vice-president, and Benjamin Brewster, O. B. Jennings, and Charles Pratt as the leading figures. Almost simultaneously (August 5, 1882), the Standard Oil of New Jersey was incorporated, with H. M. Flagler its president, Thomas C. Bushnell its vice-president, and Paul Babcock, Jr., and J. M. McGee (who soon took Flagler's office) prominent in its affairs. The trust agreement provided for the creation of a Standard Oil company in every state or national Territory; and although the plan was never fully executed, in due course Standard companies were established in Kentucky, Indiana, Nebraska, Kansas, and California.

As the last vestiges of the period of chaos disappeared, the dream of Rockefeller was converted into an empire grander than he had imagined, and more efficiently compact. The trust certificates made it possible to buy and sell shares in the trust, even though it had no legal existence; and they also made possible a regular machinery of elections. At last the necessities of the Standard Oil combination had been met. Unquestionably Rockefeller grasped the full significance and possibilities of the trust. We may doubt if Dodd, its chief creator, quite shared his comprehension or his approval. For Dodd, writing in later years his pamphlet on "Combinations: Their Use and Abuses," declared that his intention had been merely to set up an effective trusteeship in the old sense, and not to aid in creating a centralized monopoly.

As long as possible the nature of the trust was kept secret from the American public. As for the trust in the sense of a great interstate combination of monopolistic tendency, centrally directed, the officers simply denied its existence; and in fact, legally it had none.

They long maintained, with how much accuracy the reader can judge for himself, that the companies were still essentially separate and largely competitive. In 1888 Rockefeller told a committee of the Federal House that the trust kept no books—"We have no system of bookkeeping." It is true that the nine trustees kept no records. It was also true that the combination known as the trust had, both for its separate units and its general annual balance-sheet, one of the most elaborate and efficient bookkeeping systems in the world.

The years 1879–1882 inclusive had witnessed a steady continuance of the Standard's acquisitions. As a result, no fewer than fourteen organizations joined as complete units in executing the trust agreement, while twenty-six more became parties through a portion of the stockholders and members. Never before in history had such an imposing array of industrial units been banded together in a single organization. Never before had any really great industry come under so nearly complete a control, for in the early 1880's the trust comprised about eighty per cent of the refining capacity of the nation, and about 90 per cent of the pipe lines. The percentage of refining controlled was less than it had been in 1879, but the volume was much greater, and while the number and capacity of the independents were notable, the Standard dominated this branch of the industry.

The trust was nominally first capitalized at $70,000,000; that is, its certificates represented that amount. In 1874 the $3,500,000 capital stock of the Standard of Ohio was really valued, in exchanges of that year, at about $10,000,000. Since then highly valuable refineries in all the main centers had been added. The trust's great pipe line company alone, one of its most profitable divisions, was now capitalized at $30,000,000. Colonies of tanks, fleets of oil cars, elaborate export facilities, had steadily grown. Beginning in 1883 we have explicit statements of assets and earnings which show the conservative nature of the capitalization:

| | Net Assets | Total Net Earnings | Total Dividends |
|---|---|---|---|
| 1883 | $ 72,869,596 | $11,231,790 | $ 4,268,086 |
| 1884 | 75,858,960 | 7,778,205 | 4,288,842 |
| 1885 | 76,762,672 | 8,382,935 | 7,479,223 |
| 1886 | 87,012,107 | 15,350,787 | 7,226,452 |
| 1887 | 94,377,970 | 14,026,590 | 8,463,327 |
| 1888 | 97,005,621 | 16,226,955 | 13,705,505 |
| 1889 | 101,281,192 | 14,845,201 | 10,620,630 |
| 1890 | 115,810,074 | 19,131,470 | 11,200,089 |

Rockefeller and his associates, it will be seen, followed their tested rule of plowing a great part of net earnings into improvements and expansion: in 1883 nearly seven millions, and in 1890 nearly eight. It was also the policy of Rockefeller and his associates to keep indebtedness low and maintain complete independence of bankers. The trust became in fact a great reservoir of capital.

It is fair to say that the Standard in the eighties was the largest and richest of American manufacturing organizations—the largest and richest in the world. The fact that ownership lay mainly in the hands of the executives removed any temptation toward stock-watering or stock-manipulation; but in any event Rockefeller would have detested such practices. In the rigid honesty and economy of its financial structure the Standard contrasted sharply with many other American aggregations. Jay Gould and "Jim" Fisk watered and manipulated the stock of the Erie shamelessly. The builders of the Central Pacific capitalized that road at $139,000,000, although federal investigators reported that $58,000,000 would have been a generous valuation. William H. Vanderbilt's South Pennsylvania Railroad, actually worth six or seven millions, became the basis for $40,000,000 in bonds and shares. One trust modeled on the Standard, the American Tobacco Company, between 1890 and 1904 capitalized its good will alone in $110,000,000 of stock. But holders of Standard Oil Trust certificates—and Rockefeller at once took steps to distribute them widely among major employees—paid for no fictitious values.

The nine original trustees comprised the whole group, with one exception, who had done most to build up the Standard combination. Charles Lockhart alone was omitted, probably because his varied banking, mining, lumbering, iron, and glass interests made it impossible for him to leave Pittsburgh or give the Standard much time. Together, the nine men represented great material power. Of the 700,000 trust certificates, they held 466,280, or nearly two-thirds. Rockefeller since 1879 had been quietly adding to his holdings of Standard of Ohio stock. He had bought from Payne, Bostwick, and Flagler at $375 to $450 a share. As a result, when the new trust agreement was signed in 1882 he had 9585 shares, which were converted into 191,700 trust certificates. He alone had more than a third of the trustees' holdings, and almost two-sevenths of all the certificates; while he, William, Flagler, Payne, and Harkness—the Cleveland group— held very nearly four-sevenths.

The fact must be reëmphasized that the trust was not, as many later supposed, a great unitary organization with Rockefeller as its despotic head. It was an association of companies and executives in which Rockefeller, by virtue of his greater abilities, personal force, and holdings, was the chieftain. He was *primus inter pares.* Neither among the nine trustees nor in the Executive Committee did Flagler, Pratt, Warden, or Archbold, strong men all, have to obey his orders. Actually he did not work by orders, but by suggestions and by efforts to obtain an agreement, often after protracted argument. Sometimes his views were rejected. In short, the trust was an oligarchy rather than a dictatorship, and a hierarchy of committees rather than an oligarchy.

What the new giant would mean to the country was not even dimly comprehended in 1882, but in perspective we can define its primary significance. After the depression of 1873–79 the country was emerging again into the sunlight of prosperity. Old industries were soon flourishing, new industries like electricity were springing up, immigration was increasing, investments were expanding. The better times continued until 1893. Meanwhile, because of improved transportation, the development of power machinery, new inventions, technological improvements, the economies of mass production and marketing, and other factors, industry was tending strongly toward concentration.

Ever since the Civil War, industrialists had been searching for a mode of interstate combination at once legal and workable. Leaders in various businesses had seen as early as Rockefeller that the savage price-cutting and other practices often incident to unlimited competition must be abated. They also saw how valuable were the advantages of large-scale combination. Great manufactories could make larger use of cost-saving machinery;

could arrange for the subdivision and specialization of labor; could buy materials at wholesale prices; could set up branch plants at advantageous points for serving specialized markets; could utilize by-products; and could establish research departments quite beyond the reach of small companies. All this the Standard did. But how were units scattered through several states to be combined? In the railroad field the pool had achieved some success, but elsewhere it was usually a failure. Its status was illegal, and no matter how definite the pledges of its members, its compacts, being unenforceable by law, soon broke down.

In numerous industries the excesses of competition repeatedly brought prices to a ruinous level. Manufacturers everywhere were searching for an effective means of combination. This was not evidence of wicked greed, as some agitators held; it was evidence of an irresistible business law. In the "trust" Rockefeller, Flagler, and Dodd found the answer. To be sure, it was legally vulnerable, but years were required to prove that, and meanwhile imitators became numerous. The distillers, standing on the verge of bankruptcy, soon set up another trust. The sugar refiners and tobacco manufacturers followed suit. Then, as the eighties progressed, came a crowd of other businesses. The leaders of the Standard had fashioned the mould in which much of American industry was reshaped until New Jersey passed her holding company law.

The creation of the new instrumentality coincided with—indeed, it had an integral relation to—the removal of the headquarters of the organization from Cleveland to New York. This was effected by a series of steps in 1881–84. One after another, Rockefeller, Flagler, and most of the other important partners and executives became legal residents of the metropolis. The able Oliver H. Payne, the meticulous Ambrose McGregor, and their assistants stayed in Cleveland, which remained an important center, long dominating Western trade; Warden continued to live in Philadelphia, commuting to New York. But Archbold came east, and many more. Once, early in 1883, a special car transported about a score of subordinate Standard officers from Cleveland to New York. Rockefeller met them, took them to breakfast, and then turned them over to guides who were ready to show them available homes.

Although Rockefeller had been busy in New York since early November, 1877, and the offices there were rapidly becoming the center for Standard activity, Cleveland was the center of his personal world. There he had two spacious residences, there his friends and relatives lived, and there was his church (as yet he had made no selection among those in Manhattan). Naturally he felt that the Company works and offices in Cleveland were still particularly his. At Forest Hill, his new estate by Lake Erie, he was also building stables which would be the permanent home for his horses, and the roads near Cleveland were better than Manhattan's for driving.

Rockefeller's stature as a business leader was already impressive. He was undoubtedly the richest man in Ohio and one of the richest in New York, though this fact was not yet widely known. Actually, his fortune may already have rivaled Vanderbilt's or William B. Astor's. When the Trust was formed in 1882 the total of the certificates he received had a value of $19,170,000. His other securities—railroad and industrial stocks—his real estate, government bonds, and so on, may have approached his Standard interest in value. All told, his possessions made one of the first five or six American fortunes of the day.

The John D. Rockefeller who celebrated his fortieth birthday in 1878 was a man of sturdy physique, almost six feet in height, with a full head of light brown hair and a thick reddish mustache. His blue eyes were keen. He carried himself with an air of authority, yet his manner was quiet and friendly and only at moments would an observer be aware of a penetrating glance that surprised and disturbed him.

To a number of unfriendly observers he was merely a big figure in the hated "combination." In Cleveland and in the Oil Regions many competitors knew or suspected that he spoke the final word in Standard councils, and they detested him because of its acts and his power to shape them. In later years some pictured him as cold, hard, humorless, and grasping. But many men opposed to the Standard or critical of it turned to the Company's president in moments of desperation with an apparent faith in his justness and essential kindness. While these men wished to reach the final source of power, they probably also hoped for both justice and generosity. It is further worth observing that outside of the relatively few independents who had direct contact with Rockefeller in these years, he was long a rather vague figure even to men in his own field.

Doubtless Rockefeller himself was partly responsible for the confusion and vagueness which surrounded him. He was still relatively unknown because he was quiet and reserved in his manner, leaving scant basis for evaluation; he was self-contained and enigmatic to a disconcerting degree. He had matured early. Since his teens he had been laden with business burdens and family responsibilities. He championed an idea of industrial concentration which was repugnant to nine Americans in ten. The result was that he drew in to himself, cultivating reticence and making it his rule to "expose as little surface as possible." While his subtle, ruminative, daring mind solved large problems by an acid process of thought, he presented to the world a front of silence which was like smooth steel. But behind this armor plate his associates and friends saw a person very different from the baffling figure known to strangers or opponents.

The Rockefeller whom his friends and associates knew at forty had grown into a man of broad outlook, less concerned than formerly with detail, and more interested in the major problems of his company. Of course, his eye remained lightning sharp, for to note significant facts was a part of his nature. But as he grew he made a different selection of details: those he noticed after 1878 always affected the larger aspects of Standard activity.

Even so, the burden he carried was almost crushing. His was always the planning brain and the central responsibility in the ceaseless advance of the Standard. Business crises in manufacture, in competition, in administration, in litigation or governmental investigation would force him to labor almost with frenzy for weeks at a time. Yet he bore his pyramiding burdens with patience; no associate has recorded one instance of petulance or anger. On the contrary, many have testified to his serenity. His associates were not afraid of Rockefeller. They brought complaints to him, they suggested better methods, and they did not hesitate to challenge his accuracy or judgment.

Just as he welcomed suggestions and criticisms and was quick to acknowledge his mistakes, so he was greatly concerned when his associates showed the penalty of overwork. To Bushnell, to Warden, to Barstow, to Archbold, to Thompson, to Benjamin Brewster he wrote urging vacations. "Your health is more important to you and to us than the business," he wrote Bushnell, and exhorted a weary Camden to "break away three, six, nine, twelve, fifteen months. . . . Your salary will not cease, however long you decide to remain away from business."

One group in particular had come to know Rockefeller as an understanding and helpful friend: the large body of ministers and reformers whom he had begun to count as fellow-workers. Some were men of high standing, like Dr. Augustus H. Strong, head of the Rochester Theological Seminary; Dr. T. W. Goodspeed of the Baptist Union Theological Seminary of Morgan Park, Chicago; Dr. S. W. Duncan, the former pastor of Rockefeller's Cleveland church; Dr. John E. Clough; and the Rev. George Thomas Dowling, the Cleveland minister of this particular period. Others, like D. C. Potter and H. L. Morehouse, were hard-working missionaries or humble ministers and social workers.

But Rockefeller's true personality remained almost unknown to the world, for his secrecy encouraged misapprehension. Early in 1880 Payne was considering the prospects of a measure he wished to see enacted by the Ohio legislature. "There is such a prejudice against our company," he wrote Rockefeller on February 27, "that should we attempt to get such a bill through I am satisfied it won't do to have it known we desire it."

This was no exaggeration of popular feeling in a number of states. Rockefeller had been under pressure from his associates to promote a better understanding of the company's attitudes and acts. But Rockefeller had established a policy. It was better to "keep sawing wood," as he later put it. "A man cannot concentrate his faculties at the same time on two opposite things; and I was concentrated upon extending and developing and perfecting our business, rather than on stopping by the wayside to squabble with slanderers." Other Standard men winced under attacks or even the prospect of attacks. "John, you must have a hide like a rhinoceros!" Flagler exclaimed on one occasion. But Rockefeller was imperturbable. "No, I will not engage in controversy," he would reply, although in old age he confessed how much the attacks had sometimes hurt him. "I can wait; the truth will justify me."

For a man under the strain of an enormous and exacting business, the estate at Forest Hill offered both release and a healthful activity. Rockefeller had bought part of this large tract lying just east of Cleveland as early as 1873. At the time he had no intention of building a country home. The plain but roomy house on Euclid Avenue seemed to be adequate for the family's full needs. But after 1878 it was pushed into the background and used little except for Sunday dinners or on short spring or autumn visits to Cleveland.

Forest Hill began to play a part in Rockefeller's life in the spring of 1875, when he and three others incorporated the Euclid Avenue-Forest Hill Association. They intended to establish a hydropathic sanitarium. Capitalized at $250,000, the corporation bought the land from Rockefeller and began erecting a large building. But times continued so hard that the three associates lost heart and Rockefeller had to repurchase the land with the white-elephant structure of an almost-finished building on the crest of the hill.

In the summer of 1877, he and Mrs. Rockefeller tried to run it as a club hotel. But, as Rockefeller subsequently told his son, "I found that the guests expected Mother to entertain them and act as hostess. Therefore, we discontinued the club at the end of the first year.

The next step was to create a summer home. The busy executive had fallen in love with the wooded hillsides and rolling patches of open, which reminded him of the western New York of his childhood. If the passionate delight he later felt in planning roads and paths, in planting and moving trees, had not stirred him when he bought the tract, it now came quickly to life. In 1877–79 the building was remodeled, an ice house was built, and quarters were provided for the horses, grounds-machinery and vehicles which from this time forward furnished a large part of his recreation.

His growing family invested the life at Forest Hill with a bubbling energy and gaiety. The four children in 1880 ranged from six to fourteen, with John the youngest. They flung themselves into the activities of the estate with happy abandon. Rockefeller's parents spent much time there. The old "doctor" was now away for long periods in the West, nobody knows where, apparently peddling medicines and giving treatments. Indeed, he was so little in Cleveland that not many years after the marriage of their daughter Mary Ann in October, 1872, Eliza Rockefeller began to spend most of the summers with John and most of the winters with Frank or William.

Horses, always a favorite recreation with Rockefeller, became almost a passion as he developed Forest Hill. On summer mornings, sometimes taking Sambrook along, he would drive from

Forest Hill to the Standard block, covering the six miles at a fast trot. There he would hand the team over to the young man to be brought back later at an appointed time. He had stables in New York and at Forest Hill, both heated in winter. He recalled later that whenever he was worn out, an hour's fast driving—"trot, pace, gallop, everything"—with a rest and dinner, would rejuvenate him. "I was able to take up the evening's mail and get the letters off."

The Rockefellers never went to the theatre; good stock companies and famous stars played in Cleveland, but the Rockefellers were not in the audience. They seldom listened to lectures except at church. Of first-rate music performed by distinguished artists they heard little or none before they removed to New York, where they regularly purchased season tickets for orchestral concerts.

While Mrs. Rockefeller and her sister bought and read a good many books, her husband cared little for any literature outside the Bible. He sometimes listened in the evening while others read aloud novelists like Scott, Dickens, or Harriet Beecher Stowe, new books like Helen Hunt Jackson's *Ramona,* and some biography and history. Later his son recalled that he read with avidity Lew Wallace's *Ben Hur.* He took it with him on his first trip abroad and devoured it even when walking on the streets of Paris.

However, it should be remembered that Rockefeller, like an early Puritan, used his church intensively. To a large extent, it was a substitute for the theatre and lecture hall. He listened to many eloquent speakers, saw lantern slides, discussed the problems of missionaries, and met many distinguished and highly-educated ministers, both at church conferences and as guests in his house. If his religion had its narrow aspects, it was educative also. And the Standard's president was broadened still more by his business and industrial contacts. These gave him a first-hand knowledge of the many activities of his fellow Americans and of his own industry and the railroads. His business brought western Europe, Russia, Mexico, and the Far East to him.

Despite his complex business responsibilities and his personal burdens, Rockefeller remained a devoted religious worker. He was still the principal trustee of the Euclid Avenue Baptist Church, and this was *his* church; for at the end of the year 1884, although attending the Fifth Avenue Baptist Church in New York, he had not joined it. When in Cleveland, Rockefeller never missed a service. He was always prominent at church suppers and picnics, and still felt a close fellowship with many other members of the congregation.

Rockefeller, as we have seen, had begun giving to worthy objects as soon as he earned a salary. He had continued to give, increasing his donations as his income increased, until in 1869 he had donated $5489.62. In 1870, probably because his capital was needed to help launch the Standard Oil, he gave only $2695.79. But the next year the total climbed again to $6860.86, and in 1872 to $6930.68. In 1873 came the panic and depression, and for 1873 and 1874 Rockefeller made recorded gifts of $4770.58 and $4841.06 respectively. Then comes a period during which he apparently did not keep full records. After 1877, we have full data on his gifts:

| | | |
|---|---|---:|
| In 1878 | ........................... | $ 23,485.65 |
| In 1879 | ........................... | 29,280.16 |
| In 1880 | ........................... | 32,865.64 |
| In 1881 | ........................... | 61,070.96 |
| In 1882 | ........................... | 61,261.75 |
| In 1883 | ........................... | 66,722.97 |
| In 1884 | ........................... | 119,109.48 |

It is thus clear that as Rockefeller's wealth increased, his giving kept pace with it. As he once said, many men in becoming rich fail to develop any sense of trusteeship for their money, and think of it as entirely their own; he, on the contrary, always regarded giving as a plain duty. His benefactions in the early eighties were becoming highly varied. He gave to "colored students for the ministry"; to various colleges; to the Charity Organization Society, newsboys' homes, old ladies' homes, hospitals, the Y. M. C. A.; to missions, to fresh air farms, and day nurseries; to the W. C. T. U., to a school in Italy, and repeatedly and generously to a theological seminary in Hamburg, Germany; to immigrant societies and Indians. He supported several "home" missionaries, and of course contributed to churches and to annual religious conferences. The items for 1884 varied from $31,800 for the Baptist Union Theological Seminary to $10 "for poor family" and $5 for a poor man's medicine.

He insisted also that any cause or institution to which he gave should have a "stickative quality" that would lend it permanence. Too often he was left with a haunting sense of uncertainty about his benevolences. Characteristically, he was seeking guides and principles for action. By 1886, when he had become a resident of New York, we find him insisting that all doubt about a project must be dispelled in advance. "I haven't a farthing to give to this or any other interest," he wrote bluntly in answer to a request made at that time, "unless I am perfectly satisfied it is the *very best* I can do with the money."

It is important to remember the variety, persistence, and number of the demands made upon him in the early eighties, for they stimulated him to study philanthropy, just as he had studied the chaos of the oil industry, and with results as striking. In sending $3500 to Dr. George Goodspeed of the Baptist Union Theological Seminary in 1881, he wrote: "I must shut down brakes for a time, having made so many other promises of like character." "I have numerous calls from all over the country," he declared in another letter. In dispatching $1000 to Doctor Duncan, doubtless for the Ohio organization of his church, he remarked: "I am prepared to do as I stated in respect to the Chicago Seminary, providing they raise One Hundred Thousand Dollars there." This sentence is an indication that even in 1882 the germ of the future University of Chicago existed. Later that year we find Rockefeller paying the last part of a $20,000 pledge to Denison University. The extent of his growing donations is suggested by a letter in 1884 in which he mentions exceeding his gift budget by "some thirty or $40,000.

However, even as he moved toward systematizing his benefactions he did not cease making many highly personal contributions. These gifts to persons and organizations which he knew at first hand gave him particular pleasure. By 1881 he was apparently paying almost half the expenses of the large Euclid Avenue Church. A letter of 1883 to a collector for some minor fund related to that institution shows with what care he approached even small matters. He enclosed pledge cards "signed as follows":

| | |
|---|---|
| Mrs. Rockefeller ............... | $10.00 each week |
| Self ........................... | 30.00 each week |
| Each of our four children ........ | 00.20 each week |

"My family are much interested in the work," he declared, "and the 20¢ from each child will be earned by the sweat of their brows, pulling weeds, etc."

To the world at large in the 1880's Rockefeller did not appear as a brilliant or attractive figure. Most business leaders regarded him as the politicians regarded the glacial Benjamin Harrison or the austere John Sherman. We can understand this appraisal of Rockefeller, for both his background and his personality were of a type to leave all observers save those who knew him intimately with a sense of limitation and aridity.

The Rockefeller household made such an impression. It was an admirable household, dominated by two earnest, moral, and religious persons. There was no arrogance about it; the Rockefellers respected the least of their fellow Americans. But his home reflected a certain intellectual and aesthetic sterility: it was not a household of ideas, of artistic impulses, of spontaneous enthusiasms, and it lacked the graces of living. Forest Hill, while comfortable and cheerful, impressed most visitors as a rather ugly house. The big rooms had a gaunt look. Rockefeller, who liked sunshine, kept many of the windows without curtains or hangings. The furniture was not beautiful nor harmonious. He and Mrs. Rockefeller, caring much for utility and less for attractiveness, lacked a gift for combining the two, and neither showed any marked taste for collecting artistic objects. In its strength and stiffness, its earnestness and angularity, their home was Puritanical; not Puritanical in the harsher New England sense, but rather in the friendlier yet bleak tradition of the Baptist West.

Rockefeller's personality was finer and more complicated than his home. His humor, his patience, his breadth of vision and originality of outlook gave it a greater pleasantness, force, and dignity. Yet it possessed essential limitations which, quite as much as his deliberate reticence, explain his failure to kindle the imagination of his contemporaries. He had genius, yet despite its force it possessed little fire or gusto. He had abundant good will toward his fellow men, as his many gifts testify, yet he could not express it freely. He was democratic, but without affability. All his fine qualities were grayed and cooled by a nature fundamentally patient, meditative, and detached. About great men like Whitman and Lincoln there was an aura of radiance which shone from an inner core of love and warmth. Rockefeller could project nothing comparable to this, for the inner man was reserved and ascetic.

This want of warmth and likability was to cost Rockefeller dear. It made the public of his day unwilling to recognize fully his original outlook and high talents. It has remained for later generations, with a fuller knowledge, to do him greater justice.

# CHAPTER VIII

# THE GIANT MACHINE

ROCKEFELLER himself never felt any doubt that the creation of the Trust was a contribution to the good of the whole industry. He had been passionately convinced of the necessity for a general combination to help save the oil business from competitive chaos. During the hard struggle for unification he had never wavered in his faith. And in later life he believed that the accomplishment loomed ever larger in the perspective of time. "The movement was the origin of the whole system of modern economic administration," he declared with a touch of pride. "It has revolutionized the way of doing business all over the world. The time was ripe for it. It had to come, though all we saw at the moment was the need to save ourselves from wasteful conditions. . . . The day of combination is here to stay. Individualism has gone, never to return."

The trust was an efficient instrument for governing the complicated and far-scattered parts of a fast-growing industry of nationwide proportions. But precisely what was the machine to which it was geared? We have seen how the immense combination was created; just how did it work?

A crude right-angled triangle drawn upon the map of the northeastern United States would as late as 1885 have circumscribed the territory intensively concerned with the production, refining, and transport of oil. This triangle would have covered the area bounded by Boston, New York, and Philadelphia on one side, Baltimore, Pittsburgh, and Wheeling on another, and Cleveland, Erie, and Buffalo on the third. From this territory about 21,500,000 barrels of crude oil flowed yearly into the markets of the world.

By 1889 the Standard had acquired a number of wells and an impressive amount of potential oil-producing territory. This was a defensive and not an aggressive move. Distant expansion was avoided. In 1878 C. D. Angell, a producer of Regions experience, had investigated what he called the belt line of Southern California, and had urged Rockefeller and Archbold to send an agent to gain control of the field. But he made no headway with the Standard; such far-off commitments still seemed undesirable. However, eastern oil lands were bought or leased by the Trust, partly to insure a future supply, partly to limit the number of active wells and reduce the overproduction of crude oil. Having once begun to acquire oil-producing properties, the Standard was bound to press rapidly forward.

While its original holdings of wells were in Pennsylvania and West Virginia, during the middle eighties it began to buy largely in the new Lima field of Ohio, where the first discoveries were made in 1885. Had it not been for the purchase of this supply of Lima crude, which bridged the long period between the heavy decline of Pennsylvania oil and the development of the mid-continent field, the Standard would have been badly pinched for raw materials. Nobody then foresaw the great new fields across the Mississippi, and few dreamed of the automobile.

The leaders of the Standard had set up a manufacturing empire; but it might fall with the slickening flow of crude, or Europe might discover rich new fields, or the electric lights twinkling ever more numerously on city streets and village roads might be improved until they drove kerosene lamps to remote hamlets and farms. Rockefeller showed courage and vision when he acted to guarantee the Standard a great supply of crude oil.

From the wells ran the local network of pipe lines, emptying into the great trunk systems. For although the sources of oil were shrinking, the supply still outran the demand, and the demand was increasing. Already the Lima field was piped locally, and oil from this region would soon be pumped into the Buckeye Pipe Lines, organized March 31, 1886, with its Macksburg gathering division for southeastern Ohio, the Cygnet division, and its connections at the Ohio boundary with the Indiana Pipe Line Company and to the east with the Northern Pipe Line. In 1888–89 a trunk line would reach Chicago, and the World's Fair in 1893 would burn Lima oil for its buildings. Earlier in 1890–91, the

Eureka Pipe Line would be laid from the Kentucky border through West Virginia to Pennsylvania, and the Southern Pipe Line from West Virginia to the Coast. In 1893 the Standard purchased the Crescent Pipe Line from Pittsburgh to New York Bay. These various units, with their tanks, pumping stations, supply yards, and offices dominated the transportation of crude. In 1885 the National Transit Company represented a capitalization of $31,495,000, or nearly one-third of the Trust's total holdings.

Once crude oil entered the pipe lines it was part of a great common pool; no possibility of separating the product of different wells or localities existed. The management guaranteed merely that all oil pumped was of good refinable quality.

So steadily did the manufacturing facilities of the Standard grow, and so numerous were the changes and consolidations of units, that it is difficult to enumerate the refineries existing at any given date. As of March 30, 1883, the Standard Oil Trust embraced, along with many other elements, more than thirty refining companies. The largest were then nationally known— the Standards of Ohio, New York, Pittsburgh, New Jersey, the Atlantic Refining Company, the Acme of New York, and so forth. Despite mergers, the Trust in 1885 still embraced more than twenty component companies.

These companies operated in 1885 fully forty refineries. The largest single group were the twenty-three or twenty-four in and about New York and Brooklyn. Pittsburgh had fifteen or sixteen works, while Cleveland and Philadelphia each had five or six. The greatest single refineries included the parent plant in Cleveland (No. 1), which had been steadily enlarged; the Charles Pratt works, the Kings County refinery, and the Long Island works in the Brooklyn area; the great Bayonne plant of the Standard of New Jersey; the Standard Oil of Pittsburgh; and the Atlantic Refining works below Philadelphia.

Like the pipe lines, the refineries made a highly complicated mechanism, with scores of able executives, a growing corps of chemists, engineers, and other technicians, and a small army of office workers and laborers. The task of coördinating the work of the various plants was one of intricate difficulty. Just how should crude oil be apportioned? Which units should produce for certain markets? What mixture of various types of crude should take place? How could one refinery be stimulated to fuller operation when another reduced its flow? What special by-products should be assigned to a given refinery?

Control over such matters was exercised by the Manufacturing Committee in New York, which relied considerably upon the judgment of Ambrose McGregor, its most experienced member, as a general coördinator. In addition to the refineries, the trust owned or controlled a great variety of allied manufacturing properties. They included the Elizabeth Acid Works, constructed at the instance of the Standard in 1879, and the Bergenport Chemical Works, built a year earlier by Charles Pratt & Company and Osgood & Company. They included the American Wick Manufacturing Company, organized in November, 1883, by the trustees to make wicks; and barrel works. They also comprised the case and can works and the export oil yards of the Devoe Manufacturing Company in New York harbor; the Communipaw oil yards of the National Storage Company, once a unit of the Empire Transportation system. Indeed, they included almost everything that appertained even distinctly to the refining, packaging, transporting, and marketing of oil. Just as in Cleveland a score of small refineries had been concentrated into several large units, so at other points various plants were consolidated. The plants around New York city far outstripped those in any other district.

Inevitably, the manufactures based on oil marched westward. Production in the Lima-Ohio field no sooner became important than a refinery was needed there; and in 1885 the Solar Refining Company was organized to erect a plant at Lima. Four years later (June 11, 1889), the Standard Oil of Indiana was formed to build a refinery at Whiting, Indiana—for a long time one of the greatest in the world.

Inevitably, too, refining tended to decay on the northeastern periphery of the domain of oil. First it disappeared in New England, then in the Regions. A few refineries were kept there, but by 1890 the area counted for little as compared with Cleveland and the seaboard. Pittsburgh also continued its comparative decline.

Whenever one element in the great Standard machine moved inefficiently or laboriously, Rockefeller and his associates promptly sought the cause of the difficulty. In the years 1883–85 the Cleveland plants made a poor showing as to costs and quality. To bring Cleveland up to the mark, two of her technicians were sent east in 1883 to examine the facilities for making high-test oil. Much pressure was brought to bear upon Payne and his aides to keep stricter accounts, improve their car-ordering system, avoid the leakage of oil into the Cuyahoga, and in general improve their efficiency.

A system of auditing for the Trust was built up by George H. Vilas, and vigilantly applied to every part of the machine. Detailed periodical statements of costs, profits, and stock were required of all works. Sometimes the emphasis on auditing and inspection seemed overdone. Vilas, who had general charge, Joseph Bushnell, who supervised audits in the New York area, Dan Leslie, who came to do the same in Cleveland, and others were ceaselessly busy. Now and then an harassed executive protested. Instructions were issued in 1879 that all the different units should take inventory each quarter, drawing up balance-sheets. Many offices disregarded these orders, and Ambrose McGregor finally wrote Rockefeller that as the preparation of quarterly statements was burdensome, the requirement should be changed to one of semi-annual statements. Yet Rockefeller's instinct was to insist upon unsleeping watchfulness.

The Standard plants manufactured a steadily widening variety of products. Although illuminants were the staple, naphtha and gasoline grew increasingly important, the best-known brand of the latter being "Pratt's Spirit." Cleveland developed a particularly successful gasoline trade, and therefore protested against letting other Standard units in on the secret of its success! However, the Executive Committee insisted on its doing so.

The combination early began the large-scale manufacture of lubricants. The lubricating plant in Cleveland, with Silas H. Paine long in charge of sales, became an important source of revenue. In Parkersburg, where Camden had constructed some facilities, the Standard was soon making the best lubricants in America. It developed a dozen chief types—engine oil, valve oil, cylinder oil, spindle oil, motor oil, and so on—with no fewer than a hundred and fifty subordinate varieties.

A wide array of by-products was brought forward by the Standard. From the oil works came an increasing variety of greases: axle-grease, gear-grease, cup-grease, graphite, and others. Vaseline was one of the finer products made from the residuum. The Chesebrough Manufacturing Company, which was organized in 1880 to take over a vaseline business already established, with the Standard holding a majority of the shares, specialized in this article. Soon few American households were without it. Nor were many homes without paraffin, though for years the Standard found it difficult to sell its huge stocks. Much of it, mixed with stearic acid for firmness, was made into candles; we find the *Oil, Paint and Drug Reporters* of August 3, 1881, stating that Standard paraffin and wax were so good that British candle-makers already largely depended upon them. A Cleveland manufacturer named White bought large quantities to make chewing gum. Some went into matches and some into candles. The Standard soon learned to produce anthracine, component of beautiful aniline dyes, and rhigolene, used in ice manufacture. It made a variety of paints, varnishes, and wood-fillers. It turned out paint-remover and polishes. Before many years passed it was selling about three hundred by-products, many of which no smaller organization could have made, and it distributed them through much the same channels used to market illuminants and fuel-oil.

Rockefeller, enumerating the most important of these products years later, remarked: "Every one of the articles I have named to you represents a separate industry founded on crude petroleum. And we made a good profit from each industry."

By and large, the Standard as the years passed turned out better kerosene than its competitors. It had more efficient plants, better experts, and improved methods. In the lubricating field in particular it boasted that it had improved the quality of the oils and drastically cut the costs of greasing the nation's fast-expanding machine industries. Here the trust was the inheritor of methods first devised by the American Lubricating Oil Company. Under the primitive system, the residual fluids left after the lighter oils had been distilled away could not be raised to high temperatures (as they had been to get the maximum yield of kerosene) without impairing the viscosity essential to good lubrication. But heating in stills under powerful steam pressure avoided the dissociation of the oil; and the Standard greatly improved this method. In taking over the American the Standard gained the valuable services of P. S. Jennings, one of the best lubricant experts in the land.

The trust had vigorous competitors in the lubricant field, like the Valvoline Company, which deserve much credit for improving the product. Rockefeller, however, always asserted that the Standard had played the principal role from 1875 to 1900 in evolving better products and in lowering prices. Making the most of new technological processes, operating on an unprecedented scale, and using to a great extent the same marketing machinery employed in selling illuminants, it could sell improved oils on narrower margins. "And when customers found," said Rockefeller, "that they could buy for twenty or thirty or thirty-five cents a gallon products that they had been made to believe were difficult to produce at seventy or eighty, they were not slow to avail themselves of the advantages offered by the Standard Oil Company."

Careful cost sheets were kept for each of the many petroleum products. Only by degrees, and by the bold use of such innovations as vacuum refining and the cracking process, was the yield of high-quality products enlarged. Whenever a new device or method was tried in one plant, reports were sent to the others. Sometimes, too, the Manufacturing Committee asked a plant to make a special experiment. All major experiments had of course to be approved by the Executive Committee under Rockefeller. And experiments were continuous; the Standard, for example, was the first company to build tanks for refined oil (1881).

Meanwhile, it was the ambition of Rockefeller and his associates to make the great combination as nearly self-contained as possible. From an early date it manufactured its own sulphuric acid in Cleveland. The establishment of the Elizabeth and Bergenport acid factories was a response to the pressing eastern demand for chemicals. By 1885 the Standard made its own pumps in Oil City and its own tank cars in Buffalo. J. N. Camden & Company (before its merger with the Standard) had a large cooperage establishment at Parkersburg—a good point, for West Virginia could supply much of the lumber required. We find Camden writing Payne on June 11, 1875, that he had 2,800,000 staves coming in, and six days later that he had contracted for three million staves annually for three years. He was then able to manufacture 1200 barrels daily. The chief buyer of empty barrels for the Standard was Gust Heye, who would sometimes purchase 300,000 in a single month.

For a number of years George H. Hopper supplied a large quantity of barrels on contract. It presently struck the head of the Standard that the combination might save money by doing

the work itself. McGregor had made the contracts, but Rockefeller interfered, as Orville T. Waring tells us:

On a high hill some miles outside Cleveland stood a large and handsome house, dark green with white trimmings, which could be seen for
miles. It was built by George Hopper, who furnished barrels for the
Company. Passing in the train, I pointed it out to Mr. Rockefeller.

"You wish to know who owns that house?" he asked. "It's our Mr.
Hopper, who makes barrels for us. Whew! That's an expensive house,
isn't it? I wonder if Hopper isn't making altogether *too much* money?
Let's look into it. When we get back we'll go over the contracts."

It was found that the profits were out of proportion. Mr. Hopper accepted a proposition made to him, his business was appraised, and he
received full value in stock of the Standard Oil Company.

The Standard always prided itself upon its economies, precision, and foresight. "We had vision," Rockefeller said later.
"We saw the vast possibilities of the oil industry, stood at the
center of it, and brought our knowledge and business experience
to bear in a dozen, in twenty, in thirty directions." Quantity purchasing became of ever-growing importance, and wood, iron,
coal, and machinery could all be had at quantity discounts. A
great economy was effected in the wood used for the cases holding two five-gallon cans each. The original practice had been to
buy perfect lumber. But Paul Babcock questioned the employment of these flawless planks. "What's the matter with wood
having a few knots?" he asked. "If a can leaks, the case won't
hold the oil. And the wood holds and protects the can just as
well whether it is perfect or not." Rockefeller accepted the suggestion. "We saved many thousands of dollars a year," he recalled later; and since the boxes ran into tens of millions annually, this may well be believed. Indeed, in the five years 1894–98
inclusive the Standard manufactured 223,166,660 tin cans, which
required well over a hundred million wooden cases in addition
to almost five million metal cases.

Everyone in the organization became imbued with Rockefeller's own zeal for economy and efficiency. The total effect of
the constant drive for savings, applied by the best technologists
and managers procurable, can readily be imagined. Even by
1879 it had done much to place the Standard in advance of all
competitors.

The committee system which managed the far-branching Standard interests was a natural development. As the aggregation of companies and plants grew, the only way in which the leaders of the various regional units could effectively unite their talents was by frequent informal meetings. Out of these meetings the Executive Committee was born. Though it is impossible to fix an exact date for its inception, it was certainly in full if somewhat informal operation by the time in 1877 that the Empire Transportation Company was forced to surrender. The eastern executives, with Camden from Baltimore, would come by overnight train to the Cleveland offices and there decide upon general policies; or they would all meet in Warden's Philadelphia office; or Rockefeller, Payne, Flagler, and others would join the eastern heads in New York. After 1877, the business of the combination came to be transacted more and more in the cramped headquarters in Pearl Street.

In the late seventies Rockefeller and his family began spending a varying period in New York during the colder months, and beginning with the fall of 1882, he took up legal residence there. From then on, the Executive Committee was a metropolitan institution. Its composition was roughly identical with the group of Standard trustees designated in 1882: John and William Rockefeller, Payne, Bostwick, Flagler, Warden, Pratt, Brewster, and Archbold. Sometimes a trustee was not a member; sometimes a valued executive not a trustee *was*—but in general the two bodies were substantially the same.

This powerful body drafted general policies, directing the management of wells, pipe lines, refineries, by-product factories, marketing units, and export organizations. Every non-routine expenditure of $5000 or more had to have its approval. Among other affairs, it dealt with the buying of crude, the purchase of chemicals, piping, and lumber, the relations with railroads, the provision of shipping, and all financial problems. It fixed the quotas for different refineries, and different types of oil. It was the last authority on price-quotations. Usually it met five days a week, and prized the secrecy of its proceedings—for it wished to be protected from pressure or criticism within the huge organization.

Obviously the Executive Committee could not carry on detailed administrative work for the scores of refineries, the forests of producing wells, the tens of thousands of miles of pipes, the vast marketing system, and the other enterprises. A single subsidiary like the Consolidated Tank Line Company was a little world in itself. This marketing agency sold its lubricants to hardware and grocery stores scattered among the Dakota wheatfields; it supplied light to bustling towns from the Wabash to the Kaw; it sent wagons rumbling through the streets of Paducah and Little Rock. Sometimes its annual account with the Standard of Ohio ran to $5,000,000, and Jim and Alex McDonald, who had founded the company out of which it was formed, were millionaires.

Yet the Consolidated was merely one of a hundred Standard units, some far more powerful. Their direction had to be delegated to special committees, each made up of one or several trustees and some additional experts, and each entrusted with an important branch of the Standard's work. Usually eight or nine of these bodies were busy in the New York offices. They received a steady flow of reports from refineries, jobbing companies, buying agencies, and other concerns; they had thousands of messages every month from the petroleum fields, the manufacturing centers, and the steadily-expanding markets. They assembled the data in proper categories and used it to fix sagacious lines of policy.

However, while the special committees were indispensable and authoritative, all their work was reviewed by the Executive Committee. They reported to it constantly and received authorizations, admonitions, or (on certain matters) downright orders. And in the case of important intra-company disputes, the Executive Committee spoke the final word. It did so after the fullest and most impartial examination. It is clear that the entire committee system brought East and West together in the organization, and made for unity.

The various committees did their utmost to see that information and skills were pooled. Statements upon all plants and companies were regularly made available to Standard managers wherever situated, so that each might see how his accomplishments compared with those of others. But the names of the various establishments were seldom given; the cost and profit sheets were presented simply by number. Nothing was done to humiliate or penalize any group of men in the sight of others (though Rockefeller sometimes reprimanded people in private). The great object was to foster a healthy spirit of emulation, loyalty, and zeal—the "Standard spirit"—by personal attention, praise where deserved, and tangible rewards.

Rockefeller was much concerned with recruiting able new men for the organization, with keeping them there, and with developing their capacities. Confidential reports on personnel flowed constantly to his desk. Young officers were given opportunities commensurate with their talents. In general the Standard paid moderately high salaries, to which it added bonuses for specially efficient officers. Rockefeller's own original salary (1873) as president was only $12,000; he, however, fell in a special category, for he was compensated as stockholder. George B. Burton, who was borrowed from the Standard of Ohio in 1878 to reorganize New England marketing, and whose work was much prized, received $3000 a year in 1879–82 inclusive (equivalent to at least $12,000 today), to which were added bonuses rising from $500 the first year to $1000 the fourth. This was low pay for the Standard, and Burton asked for, and was granted, $5000. Occasionally one of the higher executives asked for an increase. O'Day did so on March 2, 1880, and Rockefeller graciously met his request.

The Trust made a point of looking after the physical and moral welfare of its principal employees. Rockefeller would see that an executive transferred to a new city was given aid in finding a house; he took pains to provide adequate office facilities; he wanted everyone in the force happy. Officers were encouraged to hire assistants to look after details, so that they could themselves attend to large policies. Employees were rigidly forbidden to speculate in oil. Now and then an officer who thought he could make some money in the crude-oil market applied for permission to do business on the exchanges; it was always curtly refused. Irregularities of any kind were discouraged. Archbold had one weakness—intemperance; and in 1881 Rockefeller required him to take the pledge. For some time thereafter he sent Rockefeller every Sunday a brief certification that during the previous week he had touched no intoxicants—completing the thirty-second week in May, 1882.

It need not be said that the trustees and their aides had to stick to the job day in and day out, with no truancies and no relaxation. An executive who found other cares soon withdrew, as Camden did not long after his election to the Senate in 1881.

The labor was intense and sustained. But at one hour of the day the leaders met in more relaxed mood—at noon.

The luncheon table for officers had its beginnings in 1876. At that time the Standard's quarters were at 140 Pearl Street, but lunch was served above the offices of Charles Pratt & Company at 128 Pearl. The Standard removed its New York offices in 1882 to 44 Broadway, and in 1884, after buying for $450,000 the properties at Nos. 24–28 Broadway, erected there a massive building of which the trust became the best-known tenant. Although its existence was little known publicly, in 1885 the name appeared in the New York Directory: "Standard Oil Trust, 26 Broadway." This building was the brain from which peremptory orders were flashed to every department of the intricate organization. Here the luncheon table became an important agency for centralizing the activities of the company. The various subordinate committees, which met daily or almost daily, could exchange views; officers from outside, brought in as guests, could furnish news; letters of interest could be handed around.

Rockefeller had a way of anticipating and averting potential clashes between members of the Board. Whenever differences of opinion appeared, he insisted on having all the facts and all the tenable views lucidly presented. He was always careful to procure the opinion of every important executive on any issue of magnitude, and, if uncertainty remained, was likely to urge a delay for more study. His deference to others had a happy effect. As we have said, the committee system was essentially a system of management by discussion.

Yet in crucial matters Rockefeller's leadership was not questioned. Everyone who has occasion to sit in conferences of a dozen able men, where the discussion grows warm and arguments are exchanged with unflinching directness, knows that they offer the best possible test of intellectual superiority. If, in the conferences of the Standard executives, dealing with highly intricate problems, Archbold or Warden or Pratt had possessed a keener mind and riper sagacity than Rockefeller, he would soon have established his primacy. But the testimony is unanimous that Rockefeller, by virtue of his intellectual force, prevision, and patience, was always the head. He ruled by agreement, and his view was sometimes rejected, but he was captain of the ship.

It was an admirably officered ship. Abraham Flexner once asked him the secret of the Standard's uninterrupted march to power. "We had a group of strong men from the outset," replied Rockefeller. "There were Flagler, Harkness, Colonel Payne, Andrews, my brother—later others. Our general rule was to take no important action till all of us were convinced of its wisdom. We made sure that we were right and had planned for every contingency before we went ahead." Yet Rockefeller's personal qualities, ideas and aims permeated every corner of the organization. His spirit became the Standard's spirit. The machine grew greater, and always operated smoothly. By 1885 the Standard Oil Trust was one of the most powerful, complex, and efficient business organizations ever created by man.

Its success was built in the main upon superior efficiency. To be sure, its record had dark pages; the rebate contracts of 1877 and the relentless extinction of some refineries—these were not to be condoned. But so severe a critic of the Trust as Charles J. Woodbury pointed out that the Standard employed only the same weapons used by its rivals; methods which "men of business at large have not disapproved . . . because they are American." To have been ultra-moral would have invited ruin. The companies with which the Standard competed, writes Woodbury, large and small, "kept down production, sought partial and discriminating rates and rebates, appropriated processes of manufacture, exercised an elastic scale of prices, gave commissions to purchasers, were down to all the tricks of the trade. The number of those who would not have done much of what the Standard has been arraigned for is minute." In internal administration the Standard was almost faultless. Its management was as safe and steady as the government itself, it met every business obligation, it benefited every investor, and it treated its labor with generosity. "Chicane," concluded Woodbury, "still taints the ways of the Standard, but its main foundation and business structure are of better material. Tricks may build a small business—never a large one."

The time was to come when the Standard would be praised for its pioneering qualities and for its demonstration of the useful possibilities of efficient large-scale organization. When Nathaniel S. Shaler published his three-volume work, *The United States of America* in 1894, Charles Francis Adams, Jr., contributed a chapter on the rôle of corporate organizations; and he paid tribute to the Standard Oil as a magnificent achievement in the large-scale integration of industry for efficiency and expansion. Later Miss Tarbell included in her history a long chapter on the Standard's "legitimate greatness," ungrudging in praise of its feats. Walter Hines Page wrote early in the new century that "one of the best pieces of constructive practical work ever done to accomplish its purposes" was that done by Rockefeller in building the Standard. And in 1915 Charles W. Eliot, publishing an essay on national efficiency, selected as his industrial illustration the Standard Oil. "The organization of the great business of taking petroleum out of the earth, piping the oil over great distances, distilling and refining it, and distributing it in tank steamers, tank wagons, and cans all over the earth, was an American invention."

The marketing organization of the Standard grew fitfully and unevenly, but rapidly. It was of course dependent upon the formation of the big combination itself, which had been practically achieved early in 1878. However, long before this date marked progress had been made in marketing activities. All the major Standard units had from the beginning been distributors in that they sold much of their oil direct to local or small regional dealers. They also sold in larger lots to independent houses, particularly those more remote from the refining centers. Between 1873 and 1884, the marketing structure had been undergoing a tightening process as it expanded. The Standard companies in Cleveland, Pittsburgh, Baltimore, Philadelphia, and New York had been putting their dealers under contract and regularizing all their practices that involved the handling and pricing of oil. The absorption of independents or the organization of new companies also meant the extension of such policies as the Standard found to be efficient and profitable.

But the various distributors who operated for the Trust, even after they were absorbed and were supposedly obedient agents of the Standard, evinced a degree of independence and occasionally of irresponsibility which is startling. Chess, Carley and Waters Pierce, for example, both committed acts which at times shocked the Standard officials. The two companies had been built up by strong, ruthless men who wished to continue their old policies, resisted dictation, and sometimes yielded only a partial, grudging compliance with the suggestions or directives of the Trust. Pierce and Carley, in short, were feudal barons who had gained their domains by the mailed fist and who liked to give orders much better than to take them. They made independent decisions and carried them out. The Standard put representatives of good salary and high ability in both offices and doubtless through them kept informed of the distributors' activities, but the Trust could not properly control these dynamic and unscrupulous men. The saving fact, from the Standard's point of view, was that they made large profits.

With other marketing agencies such as Alexander McDonald & Company and the Consolidated Tank Line Company, difficulties arose on various matters of policy. In 1883 Rockefeller wrote to Payne to find out if the McDonalds were actually selling oil at the prices decided upon by the central offices. The Standard was never sure of the loyalty of the Consolidated until it bought out the minority interests in 1890. The Standard had particular difficulty in getting these quasi-independent agencies to work as team-mates. They invaded each other's territories; they quarreled about quotas and prices; they showed constant jealousy.

Step by step, the Standard made its organization more systematic. Rockefeller's policy was to buy out allied and satellite marketing companies, dispense with such pioneer merchants as the refractory Carley and ageing Hanford, reorganize the selling in large territorial units controlled entirely from Cleveland and New York, and give marketing ever more system and efficiency. By 1890, and still more by 1895, the goal had been largely achieved. Of the major associated companies, only Waters Pierce remained. The Domestic Trade Committee at 26 Broadway and in the Standard Building overlooking Lake Erie after 1895 issued orders which except in rare instances were never questioned.

By 1882 the Standard had 130 bulk stations, each with its special marketing machinery; by 1886 the number had risen to 313; and steadily it went above 1000, then 2000, then 3000—reaching 3573 in 1906.

The tank stations in the period 1880–1900 sold in general to jobbers—that is, dealers who took carload lots for sale to retail distributors—on thirty days' credit. A firm like Hanford's sold direct to merchants in the cities of Chicago and Milwaukee, and to jobbers in the smaller cities and towns of Illinois and Wisconsin. Large mercantile houses were not infrequently supplied straight from the refineries; thus the Standard in Cleveland for years shipped oil and by-products to McCulloch, McCord & Com-

pany in La Crosse. Traveling men who were employed to take
orders for lubricants sometimes also booked orders for small lots
of kerosene or gasoline.

Nothing like the Standard's elaborate machinery for the nationwide wholesaling and jobbing of an industrial product had
previously been known in America. Gustavus F. Swift had shown
the meat-packers how to establish a similar organization, but it
did not compare in scope or efficiency with that of the Trust.

The field in which the Standard had perhaps the least difficulty
in holding and enlarging its markets was that of lubricating oils.
It swiftly established an unassailable position in supplying railroads and steamships. In 1899 it advertised in the *Official Railroad Guide* of the United States that its Galena oils were being
used on ninety-five per cent of the railroad mileage of the United
States, Canada and Mexico. It boasted that its headlight oil was
the best in the world. According to its detractors, railroads paid
high prices for the lubricants because if they took competing oils,
the Standard would deny them freight. But according to the
Standard, the railroads purchased Galena oils because they de-
monstrably did more work for less money. These lubricants were
usually sold on a three or five year guarantee that the costs per
train-mile would not exceed, or would fall below, those of oils
previously used. That is, the Standard found from the railroads'
books how much the cost of lubricating freight cars, passenger
cars, locomotives, and other equipment was, and usually guaranteed a reduction—at any rate, it guaranteed better service at
equal costs. No other company offered this train-mile guarantee
on a long-term basis.

We may here note that about 1887 two large internal combustion engines made by the Otto works in Germany were brought
to America, one for the Cramp shipbuilding yards in Philadelphia and one for the Detroit Shipbuilding Company. They attracted Rockefeller's attention not only because they used gasoline but because they presented novel lubricating problems. The
Otto works had recommended castor oil, but this clogged the
engines. A Standard expert on lubrication, George A. Burke, the
first highly trained mechanical engineer employed by the trust,
was sent to Detroit. He took out the pistons, washed them with
kerosene, and prescribed No. 2 Red Oil, five gallons of which
he had brought from Cleveland. The Standard was proud of
this oil, a lubricant having a gravity of 23, a viscosity of more

than 200, and a flashpoint of about 410 degrees. Pressed out of paraffin, its qualities specially adapted it to engines of great dry inner heat, and its application ended all trouble with the Otto motor.

During the next ten years numerous large internal combustion engines were installed in American plants, proving especially popular in the electric light stations rapidly being built. The Standard supplied them with gasoline, or a distallate between kerosene and gasoline, while it also found in them a widening market for lubricants; and this lubricating market was systematically developed.

Burke, going on to one large plant after another, whether of steam or gasoline power, made surveys of the machinery, drew up charts, and offered recommendations of the proper oils. Early in the nineties he established a school for salesmen, giving them a drill of three to six months in the correct use of oils and then sending them out to study plants, make charts, and recommend oil-types. The result was soon evident in increased orders and in warm expressions of satisfaction with the Standard's service. As time passed the Trust encountered sharp competition from other makers of oil—notably Valvoline, Pure Oil, and Kellogg's—who paid their expert salesmen (really lubrication engineers) as much as $15,000 a year. But until after 1900 these firms were interested mainly in heavy oils for machinery, leaving the Standard foremost in distributing lighter lubricants for internal combustion engines. When Henry Ford began operating his first car, a Standard salesman named Charles Ross sold him a can of Atlantic Red Oil which he found excellent. The development of lubricants kept pace with that of internal combustion engines, for Rockefeller and his associates saw that it did so.

Oil and oil-vapor stoves came to have a great vogue in the two last decades of the century, and the business of supplying them with fuel grew to be an important branch of Standard activity. Rockefeller gave it much thought and effort, for it offered perplexities. Crude types of oil stoves were sold as early as 1870, though a year later Professor Charles F. Chandler in his famous *Report on Petroleum* condemned them all as criminally dangerous. Most were so constructed that the naphtha flowed from a small tank into a very hot chamber or tube, where it was vaporized—the vapor then passing by suitable orifices into burners. Explosions were frequent. "A keg of gunpowder in a building is not as dangerous as one of these stoves," was Chandler's wrathful comment as he described how New Yorkers had been mangled or roasted alive. Yet the devices were so cheap and convenient that the demand increased, and beginning about 1880 the gasoline stove had a rapid rise.

Naturally, all refiners were interested in encouraging this demand. During the seventies and eighties there was little market for naphtha or gasoline as distinguished from kerosene; though some was used in gas-making and some burned under refinery stills, much was left; and oil companies looked anxiously for outlets. Late in the seventies Rockefeller suggested that the Standard negotiate with a Cleveland manufacturer of vapor stoves, M. L. Hull, and learn if by united effort they could not design an apparatus that would be safe and that could be sold in quantity throughout the vast plains region, from Iowa and Kansas north to the Dakotas, where wood was scarce. C. M. Higgins was sent to the Middle West to survey the potential market and talk with Hull. He found local dealers enthusiastic over the idea, and Hull willing to coöperate. A better stove was soon being manufactured. Then, since Hull's work did not prove wholly satisfactory, other manufacturers were approached, and still better designs were put on the market. After the early eighties the Standard had a large business in the Middle West and on the Great Plains selling stoves and fuel.

By 1885 both oil-vapor stoves and kerosene or gasoline stoves were widely distributed. Since the former required the vaporization of a light oil and were dangerous in careless hands, New York and many other cities prohibited their sale. Yet a competent authority declared: "For those able and willing to exercise a reasonable degree of care, the oil-vapor stove is by far the most agreeable and economical means for light cookery as yet available." With naphtha at only three dollars a barrel or six cents a gallon, the cost of using a vapor stove was small. Kerosene and gasoline stoves were more popular, and many good designs were soon on the market. As most of them burned heavier oils than the vapor stoves, they were relatively safe, and it was generally agreed that a few simple precautions would have prevented ninety-nine in a hundred of the occasional accidents. The worst fault of the oil stove in the eighties was that after perhaps months of efficient service, it would fall into a mysterious fit of sullenness and sootiness. But as steady improvements were made, it was soon found in most farm and village homes, for it was convenient, kept kitchen temperatures down in summer, and was cheap—the cost of running most models being only about a cent an hour.

In 1891 Rockefeller brought C. M. Higgins to New York to develop a New England market. Within two years Higgins had attained a marked success. But just as he was rubbing his hands over the volume of orders, Rockefeller and his associates perceived that the demand for gasoline to feed the new internal combustion engines was growing at a rate which would not permit the Standard to increase its stove-oil sales. There would not be enough gasoline or naphtha to go around! The campaign in New England was temporarily discontinued—so abruptly that Higgins had to persuade the Chicago stove-manufacturers to take back a large consignment they had shipped him. Later, of course, the Standard resumed its efforts to sell gasoline stoves, placing T. J. Williams in charge of a gasoline stove department in New York in 1897. The noted manufacturer and reformer Edward Atkinson boasted that in his "Aladdin Oven" a little more than a quart of kerosene, burned with an ordinary lamp wick, did as much roasting or boiling as 120 pounds of coal in an ordinary kitchen range.

Meanwhile, since the middle seventies there had been a steady increase in the demand for oil as an ingredient of carburated water-gas, which might better have been called petroleum gas. This new industry grew out of experiments performed by a number of Europeans and Americans, chief among them T. S. C. Lowe, who had won fame during the Civil War as chief of the aeronautic section of the army and who later went into the manufacture of artificial ice. Obtaining a series of patents, he developed the industry courageously. In Lowe's process hydrogen was mingled with carbon oxides, the mixture then being combined with richly carbureted gases, taken usually from petroleum. The first plants to use it, opened at Phoenixville and Conshohocken, Pennsylvania, in 1873–75, proved so successful that others sprang up in the East. For several years makers of coal-gas vigorously opposed the new process, but in time many of them adopted it. Not only did water-gas cost less, but it gave greater illumination. By 1900 more than three-fourths of all the gas consumed in America was carbureted water-gas, requiring nearly two hundred million gallons of oil or oil distillate; and much was manufactured abroad. Rockefeller and his partners always evinced a keen interest in this particular market. It explains why William G. Warden (whose United Gas Improvement Company bought Lowe's patents) became one of the principal figures in Philadelphia utilities, and why William Rockefeller and H. H. Rogers went into gas manufacture in Boston and New York.

Indeed, no outlet for oil was missed by Rockefeller. One market alone he disliked—it was his policy to sell as little crude oil as possible. "He thought it much too valuable," a subordinate has said. After the Frasch process was perfected the Standard sent no more Lima crude to Chicago mills, and Rockefeller was not pleased by the fact that the Chicago World's Fair burned crude. Great efforts were made by the Standard, however to sell fuel oil to factories, ships, and railroads.

The Standard had developed a marketing organization covering the whole United States. But the system was neither so tight nor so personal as some have assumed. Over a long period many units in the complicated organization were refractory or difficult to manage. Again, decisions on policy were not the personal decisions of Rockefeller; he took counsel with many associates, while committees of the Trust usually made the final decisions.

Finally, the Standard as a marketing force was no irresistible giant striking down at a blow the puny weaklings in its path. The Standard's opponents dealt it many a shrewd stroke; and if it often struck below the belt, so did its enemies. Rockefeller and his associates at 26 Broadway must sometimes have seen a vision out of *Gulliver's Travels:* the visions of a giant pinned to earth by a swarm of pygmy antagonists, bound fast with packthread, and facing death from poisoned darts. Its struggles with competitors cast new light on the question of how effectively the Standard could use its enormous strength.

For two main reasons Rockefeller and his associates always regarded competitors with a jaundiced eye. They had replaced a savage competition which meant ruin for the weak and losses for the strong by a unified control which lifted the oil business to a highly profitable level, attractive to outsiders. If the independents were permitted to spring up on every side they would soon disorganize the markets again, and the Trust with its heavy fixed investment would suffer calamitously. The Standard, of course, never possessed a complete monopoly. Its spokesmen declared in 1879 that it did about 90 per cent of the refining business of the country, in 1888 about 80 per cent, and in 1893–99, just 82.3 per cent—figures subject, as we shall see, to some modifi- cation. To maintain "order" in the industry, the Standard leaders felt that they must prevent outsiders from doing more than one- fifth of the business.

Then, too, Rockefeller regarded many would-be competitors as essentially blackmailers, who erected plants merely to sell out at high prices. The Standard in purchasing refineries always made careful inventories, but it often paid generous extra allow- ances for good will, potential earning power, and the services of executives. Many oil men knew that in buying out Clark, Payne & Co., it had given almost $150,000 in stock for "volume of busi- ness" and for Payne's services; they knew of some similar arrange- ments. That a number of designing men set up refineries, pressed their competition in the markets, and appealed to public opinion for support, hoping to compel the Standard to buy them out at high prices, is incontestable.

A number of independent-spirited refiners were especially per- sistent in maintaining competition with the Standard. All over the map, in fact, these threats kept cropping up. Sometimes a rapid settlement was made. In other instances an unimportant invader was ignored. But little independent plants did arise everywhere: in Cleveland, in the Regions, in eastern Ohio, in West Virginia, in New York.

In the repression of competitors, the Standard relied upon two main weapons over and beyond its superior efficiency: its transpor- tation advantages and its ability to make local or regional price- cuts. Most independent refineries had to depend upon railroad shipments of crude, while the Standard had its trunk pipe lines from the wells to Cleveland, to New York, to Pittsburgh, to Philadelphia, and later to Baltimore. The maintenance of stiff rail rates for crude oil was, therefore, always important to the Trust.

This fact emerges clearly from a letter which Warden sent Charles Lockhart in Pittsburgh on March 1, 1880. The Standard had learned that some Cleveland refiners were getting crude by way of Pittsburgh in cars of the Allegheny Valley branch. "It might be very proper for you to see Mr. John Scott and tell him we shall expect him to keep his proportion of the rate from the oil regions to Pittsburgh at 35¢." Warden's letter revealed the spirit of the relationship between the Standard and the Pennsylvania. "We do not ask him not to haul the oil," he continued, "but of course we prefer he should not. It is a great injury to us to have him do it and we feel that we have been working to build up his interest, and in all justice to us he should see that this is done" (i.e. that the rate was maintained). Warden added: "The parties getting the oil are a new competitor, very bitter against our people and making a desperate effort for a large blackmail." This sentence may have referred to Heisel, to Scofield, Shurmur & Teagle, or to Clark, Childs. The point is, the Standard wanted to be sure that the railroad rate was severely maintained.

However, the railroads also gave concessions to the Standard's competitors, or let their subsidiaries do so. The Allegheny Valley was permitted by the Pennsylvania to make the independents low charges. And Henry Lewis, head of the crude oil purchasing department of the Standard of Ohio, after a trip to Cleveland, reported to Rockefeller on January 15, 1881, that favorable terms were being offered to the "outsiders" there. Joseph Stanley told him that these refiners got a 20¢ rate on crude from the Regions, and that "the Railroad had offered to make them an open rate to New York of 50¢ per bbl. on Refined Oil." The Buffalo, Pittsburgh & Western made a special rate for independents early in 1882. And of course, the Tidewater had a favorable alliance with the Reading and the Central of New Jersey. Yet year in and out, the Standard in general apparently had marked advantages in the shipping of both crude and refined.

Many examples of favoritism, both to the Standard and to its competitors, could be cited. As the Standard had the greater bargaining power, it was more generally the beneficiary. After the Hepburn investigation, however, the railroads pursued a much more careful course, and following the Interstate Commerce Act of 1887, the Standard, as careful observers generally agree, came close to a general obedience of the new law, and asked no outright rebates.

The other principal weapon in the elimination of independents, the use of price-cutting, was attended by certain limitations of an interesting character. It is an error to suppose that by drastic price-slashing the Standard could drive any rival out of a given market for kerosene, lubricants, paraffin, or other products. To be sure, price-slashes frequently were effective: doubtless they were the chief cause for the collapse of such rival firms as the

Solar, Denslow & Bush, and the Brooklyn refineries which Arch-bold and Pratt bought up on Newtown Creek. Price cutting also held the Tidewater and the Cleveland independents within strict bounds.

But the independents were not and could not be finally and completely routed by price-cuts or allied measures. The reasons for the continued ability of the independents to compete are complex, for a number of factors permitted them to operate.

One was the growing size of the Standard organization, and the expanding nature of the oil business in the United States. This business now covered the entire country from the Atlantic to the Pacific, from the Lakes to the Gulf. Aside from the East and part of the Middle West, the Standard in the early and even the middle eighteen-eighties did not have direct control of the territories it served. The distributors who dealt with the market-ing of oil products usually did not want independents in their territories, but they were not so keenly concerned as Payne, Warden, and Rockefeller about the total control of the oil busi-ness. They were reluctant to cut their prices. Quite early in the development of the Standard as a nationwide colossus, Rockefeller became aware of this natural but in his opinion dangerous atti-tude.

It is true that Rockefeller and his chief associates seem to have supposed for a time that by cutting costs and lowering prices they could force a collapse of their opponents everywhere. But the situation had another and less cheerful aspect, sharply in contrast with these exuberant hopes of complete victory: *price-cutting meant profit-cutting.* Rockefeller was willing to accept this fact and cut if he could see even the ultimate results of such a sacrifice. But were the results certain? Could competitors be priced out of the refining business?

At moments, Rockefeller felt that perhaps they could be. On one occasion he suggested to Payne that the latter "see how much we could afford to decline the market if we could get the entire business in refining, taking into account the profit and the extra crude we would thereby pump." This was written on April 21, 1883. Payne, although he, too, had seen the vision, feared that even if the Standard cut to cost, the independents would con-tinue to make oil, holding it until prices were raised.

Rockefeller seems to have accepted this judgment. All along, he had recognized the importance of even the fraction of a cent per gallon in the piling up of profits. And as Payne had pointed out with respect to the Consolidated and its competitors, the Standard gained or lost on a titan's scale while its opponents did so on a pygmy's. It was clear enough that if prices were slashed to the bone, the independents might simply suspend operations for a period, while the Standard through the cuts lost revenues amounting to a fortune. Then when the titan tired of this expensive experiment, the pygmies would start up again and take what profit they could.

The prospect was not inviting. In the end the Standard chose to compete in a much more complex manner. When "outside" oil appeared, its agents cut enough to hold their own trade; and occasionally, when they wished to give some audacious rival a lesson, or protect a territory never previously invaded, they made greater reductions. The Standard chiefs watched carefully the stocks held by the independents, and took sharp note of their transportation difficulties; whenever they felt that only a small amount of oil could be shipped into a given market, or that their competitors were selling near cost, they boldly maintained their prices and profits.

The execution of this policy was a delicate and often harassing activity, demanding the fullest possible information on many points and the promptest action. Rockefeller watched prices with infinite care and patience. He was completely realistic. On one occasion he felt that "the prices will afford encouragement to our competitors sufficient to cause them to increase their works, and we can afford to do the business considerably closer." However, even in this situation he was willing to "delay along from day to day in making further concessions [to the retail dealers]; but on the other hand if they rush in to do business, would not delay to reduce."

The Standard had a system of private concessions. It seldom gave its distributors or dealers *carte blanche* to meet "outside" prices, but studied their reports and acted as it felt was judicious. Sometimes it dropped the open price; sometimes it maintained it, but gave important discounts. This policy was designed to confuse the independents, who never could tell what the Company was charging its distributors, or what the distributors were charging the dealers. Occasionally the Standard let "outside" oil come into a market and made no reductions at all.

Always, regardless of the price policy of the moment, Rockefeller preached the gospel of low costs and moderate prices. These, he felt, should be the Standard's norm of practice, so as not foolishly to invite competition, as he felt Waters Pierce and the Consolidated sometimes had done. "Let us do the large volume at the smaller profit"—this counsel to Payne in the spring of 1883 on benzene manufacture was characteristic.

A mammoth organization following such a policy naturally left some room for competitors. The shrewd independent could slip into a territory, make a considerable number of sales, and take a neat profit before his big opponent began to slash prices. At times, if he did not offer too much oil for sale, he could keep on doing business over an extended period, for the Standard agents preferred to let him carry on his relatively slight activity rather than to take the large losses on their own sales which price-cutting would have involved. So the independents persisted and even prospered.

Their number and strength grew. The Standard, too, was growing. However, with the Tidewater representing a respectable island of independence, and dozens of smaller competitors putting their oil into many localities, Rockefeller was concerned about his rivals. The size of the Standard, its extensive marketing area, and the number of its distributors made for a certain looseness of organization and action which, with the reluctance to make cuts, permitted many small operators to survive.

Late in 1882 Colonel W. P. Thompson began sending Rockefeller bulletins from the Cleveland office on the total shipments of the independents. He reported that in October they had shipped 18½ per cent of all the crude produced. In January, 1883, they shipped 20.72 per cent, and in February 24.90. This seems to have been the top figure, as the percentage diminished slightly in succeeding months. But the outsiders had a pretty firm control of between one-fifth and one-fourth of all available oil. It was a startling change since midsummer of 1878, when they had handled not more than ten per cent of the total.

Several episodes in the history of the Standard's dealings with competitors have received an emphasis somewhat out of proportion to their real importance. George Rice of Marietta in the spring of 1881 sent a Louisville merchant seventy barrels of kerosene from his independent refinery. At once F. D. Carley of

Chess, Carley tartly rebuked the general freight agent of the Louisville & Nashville, of which he was a director, writing: "We suspect [the car] slipped through at the usual fifth-class rate—in fact we might say we know it did—paying only $41.50 freight from here. Charges $57.40. Please turn another screw." This turn-another-screw letter was destined to echo down through Standard history. Nearly four years later a worse incident occurred. Daniel O'Day had a long-standing feud with Rice. Acting as manager of the National Transit Company, O'Day forced the receiver of the bankrupt Cincinnati & Marietta, a small railroad serving the Macksburg, Ohio, oil field, to haul the Standard's crude for ten cents a barrel, to charge all independents thirty-five, and to turn the extra twenty-five cents over to the National Transit Company. This outrageous arrangement went into force in March, 1885, and was stopped later that year only by threat of court action. Thereupon the National Transit Company immediately refunded $340, the amount collected on Rice's oil.

In each instance Rockefeller and his associates, condemning the action taken, placed the blame upon irresponsible subordinates. Carley was always a law unto himself, and had sent his arrogant message without consulting anybody. O'Day was reckless and unscrupulous, and had similarly acted on his own initiative. Rockefeller, commenting on O'Day's drawback scheme, told the New York *World* on March 29, 1890: "We repudiated the contract before it was passed upon by the courts, and made full recompense. In a business so large as ours, conducted by so many agents, some things are likely to be done which we cannot approve." S. C. T. Dodd made a corroborative statement: "It was the fault of an over-zealous agent in Ohio." Accepting these statements, history must censure the Standard for inexcusable negligence. But the main point is that the Carley and O'Day episodes were unique and untypical; nobody ever seriously asserted after 1881 that the Standard made a *practice* of demanding drawbacks upon competitive shipments.

The same point applies to the much-discussed charge by Charles B. Matthews of Buffalo that in 1881 Hiram B. Everest and his son Charles, operating the Vacuum Oil Company in Rochester, had committed various criminal acts, including attempted sabotage, against Matthews' struggling refinery. The Everests had sold a three-quarters interest to the Standard, but kept a free hand in the day-to-day operation of the Vacuum Company. They may or may not have committed harmful acts against their competitors; the evidence is murky and conflicting. Matthews himself came into court with unclean hands—he and his partners had acted to take the Vacuum process, copy the Vacuum machinery, and use the Vacuum's list of customers. The judge let the Everests off with a fine of $250 apiece. It is quite certain that the high executives of the Standard had nothing whatever to do with the acts for which the Everests were arraigned; the indictments of Archbold, Rogers, and McGregor were without a shred of justification, and the judge promptly ordered them dropped. As for Rockefeller—who was called as a witness for the *prosecution!*—he knew nothing whatever of the affair. But here again the main point is that the episode was unique and untypical. Nobody ever seriously asserted that the Standard made a *practice* of sabotaging rivals; such acts were common enough among Regions producers, but the idea would have been abhorrent to the Standard leaders.

A very different character attaches to the complaints against the Standard's usages in marketing oil. These outcries came in the 1880's and 1890's from all parts of the country, they were incessant and long-continued, and they build up the picture of a policy involving frequent price-cutting, espionage, dictation to dealers, and other rough tactics. To be sure, the Standard's competitors, when able, did the same. Again, just what *was* unfair was by no means so clear in 1885 or 1895 as it became a generation later. Throughout this period the use of underselling to drive out competitors presented a thorny legal and ethical problem. Many states placed no restraint upon it; others found their laws and court decisions against local and temporary price-slashing hard to enforce. Nevertheless, public sentiment in most communities emphatically condemned the Standard's marketing department for occasionally reducing local prices until an independent was eliminated, and then restoring them. It condemned the recurrent use of spying, intimidation, and detraction.

The fact was, however, that by the mid-eighties the Standard had reconciled itself to the continued existence of independent refiners who did from a fourth to a fifth of the whole domestic business. The Trust to that extent was content to fall short of being a complete monopoly. "Probably you are aware," runs a letter of F. Q. Barstow (vice-president of the Acme) to Rocke-feller March 20, 1886 (a letter typical of many), "that the Oil Regions refineries are shipping quite largely to Philadelphia at present. These refineries, including Pittsburgh, have shipped to Phila. some 11,000 barrels in the past 10 days."

# CHAPTER IX

# THE RISING STORM

"IT WAS not the Romans that spread upon the world," wrote Lord Bacon, "but the world that spread upon the Romans; and that was the sure way of greatness." It was the world that spread upon petroleum. For twenty years after Drake's discovery man saw little in oil but the means of banishing night. Then invention began to make it an instrument of power and speed; the gas engine, the automobile, the Diesel motor, and the airplane rendered it the principal propulsive force of civilization. The search for it spread over all the continents, until new fields had been opened in every clime. Great Powers came to depend upon it, guarding their pipes and tankers as fiercely as their food supply. As it thus rose to world-wide puissance, the Standard Oil Company rose with it to a strength and wealth of which its heads had never dreamed, and Rockefeller's fortune became perhaps the greatest the world had yet seen. The powerful and efficient organization Rockefeller and his partners had created was by 1883 one of the most dynamic oganizations in the world and its expansion in the next decade was continuous.

The first great oil discoveries beyond the Regions, we have noted, were made in the Lima field in northwestern Ohio. The area was eagerly developed. In 1886 more than a million barrels of oil were obtained; in 1890 more than fifteen million; and in 1896 more than twenty million. As this flood of sulphur-tainted or "sour" oil poured into the market, prices dropped to the lowest levels since 1861, even touching ten cents a barrel. Yet profits were frequently high, for some gushers yielded from 7000 to 10,000 barrels a day. With the same feverish haste, the Lima-Indiana field just across the Indiana state line was opened;

during the panic year 1893 about five hundred wells were drilled and some 2,300,000 barrels of crude were produced.

These new resources became available at the very time that the flow of Pennsylvania oil began to decline; at the very time, moreover, that invention demanded great supplies of gasoline and lubricants, and that the United States needed cheap oil to meet Russian competition. Sunset was descending upon the Regions, so long a fountain of gold. Although West Virginia produced vigorously in the eighteen nineties, had the United States depended solely on the Appalachian pools the price of crude would have shot upward, new industries built on the gasoline engine would have been retarded, and Russia and the Dutch East Indies would have captured the world market.

While still vaster oil pools lay in the West, it would have required years to discover them and provide transportation. Most oil men as late as 1885 were incredulous of any large deposits beyond the Mississippi. The output of Kansas until 1904 never exceeded a hundred thousand barrels, and that of the Gulf Coast field was equally negligible before 1901, when Spindletop, brought in near Beaumont, Texas, marked the beginning of a big "salt dome" production. In Kentucky the flow did not touch ten thousand barrels a year until 1899; and though California produced half a million barrels in 1892, most of this was used for fuel.

During the early years of Standard Oil, Rockefeller had taken no particular interest in the ownership of oil wells. Crude oil production, speculative and uncontrolled, was chronically in excess of demand. It was unnecessary for refining interests to own oil lands in order to get needed supplies. With the discovery of the Lima field, however, Rockefeller's views sharply changed. He knew that Pennsylvania would not furnish oil forever. Above all, the sulphur-tainted crude offered a technological challenge. Here was an opportunity to buy or lease large tracts at low prices, tank huge quantities of cheap "sour" oil, and by finding new methods of refining it, make it as valuable as the paraffin-base oils to the eastward. From this time forward the business was to be integrated vertically downward into oil production. The shift, which reflected a change in basic conditions, not a reversal of Rockefeller's judgment, was at first on a moderate scale; well-ownership remained a minor part of the whole Standard oil business. Nevertheless, it was an important change.

The story of the utilization of the sulphur-laden Lima oil by Herman Frasch is one of the romances in the Standard annals. At first it was necessary to sell much of it for fuel oil. But Rockefeller ordered tankage built to hold the fast-accumulating stocks, until by the end of 1888 the Standard possessed about ten million barrels of it. Frasch, an erratic, explosive little man, full of energy, determination, and hot temper, was "a most uncomfortable critter to work with," but he was a genius. A native of Württemberg, he had come to the United States soon after the Civil War, specialized in the then new field of industrial chemistry, and in 1876 had patented an improved process for refining paraffin wax. The Standard purchased it, and Rockefeller induced Frasch to remove to Cleveland in 1877 to experiment in petroleum and its by-products. After a time the chemist went to Canada to found an oil company; and though the Ontario oils were also "sour," he soon devised a process for eliminating the sulphur. Then the Standard purchased his plant, his patents, and his services, and Rockefeller brought him to No. 5 Plant, where in the early summer of 1886 his labors were crowned with partial success. Within three years the process was perfected; meanwhile, he received help from several hardworking Standard men, notably John W. Van Dyke. Later William M. Burton, a brilliant young Clevelander who held a doctorate in science gained at Johns Hopkins, came in as the techniques and mechanisms were being perfected.

It has been said that when Frasch and his aides began their work the Lima field was yielding thirty thousand barrels a day at fourteen cents a barrel, and when they ended it produced ninety thousand barrels a day at a dollar a barrel. This exaggeration has an essence of truth. For seventeen years the Standard had the exclusive use, thanks to its patents, of the Frasch process, based on the use of copper oxides to precipitate the sulphur. Its competitors in the Lima field had to employ the costlier and less efficient lead oxide process.

Rockefeller and his associates confided the development of the Lima-Ohio lands to the Ohio Oil Company, organized September 2, 1887, with a capital of half a million, of which the versatile W. T. Scheide was an early president. They had a great refinery built in Lima 1886–87 by the Solar Refining Company, whose total investment grew within five years to about two millions. John W. Van Dyke, who had been manager of the old Sone & Fleming plant, took charge of the new works. In the spring of 1888 the Trust began laying an eight-inch pipe from the Lima field along the right of way of the Chicago & Atlantic Railroad into Chicago, the railroad making a free grant of the ground in return for the profit from the carriage of pipes and other materials. The National Transit Company had charge of the enterprise. Though the pipe was 225 miles in length, costs of pumping oil from the Lima district to the lake front terminal in South Chicago proved only about five cents a barrel.

Before long work began, through the Standard Oil of Indiana, on the new oil refinery at Whiting, Indiana, a situation advantageous for western markets. The pipe line to South Chicago had at first supplied fuel oil to steel mills and other industries. When the mephitic smell of early shipments aroused Chicagoans to hold mass meetings of protest, the Standard heads realized they must build their refinery in a less populous area. Chicago taxes were high, and available land was limited. They found a site just across the Indiana line, in a flat district of sand, wilderness, and small glacial lakes, better known to hunters and fishermen than farmers. Three trunk railroads and one belt-line crossed the island-like strip, about three miles long and one wide, which Standard agents selected. Early in May, 1889, laborers commenced clearing away trees and brush. By the fall of 1890 a mighty plant had been built, with eighty crude-oil stills, a paraffin works, and a large force of executives, technicians, and workmen. Its daily capacity was then 24,000 barrels of crude.

Shiny perfection of machinery, the most up-to-date methods, marked the Whiting establishment. Frasch's assistant, Dr. W. M. Burton, was placed in charge of a laboratory to experiment with better refining methods; in time he rose to be assistant superintendent of the refinery, and later president of the Standard of Indiana. At Whiting Dr. Burton later introduced the process of "cracking" petroleum which so heavily increased the yield of gasoline. Indeed, the inspection or testing laboratories which Rockefeller had had placed in all the refineries (and on the top floor of 26 Broadway) were encouraged by Frasch's work to undertake more and more experimentation.

As the Lima production increased, the Whiting refinery became one of the largest in the world. Another six-inch pipe line was laid in 1890 from the Ohio fields to the works. For a time the Whiting men concentrated upon kerosene, gasoline, and naphtha, but their list of products steadily grew. Quantity manufacture of paraffin and candles began in 1893. Grease works commenced operations three years later, an elaborate lubricating establishment was opened about 1900, and other by-products followed. Shipments of light oils were made chiefly in tank cars, and in lake tankers that ran up to Duluth and there unloaded for the Minnesota-Dakota-Manitoba country. And cooperage shops were built to furnish barrels for lubricants, and a can factory to provide oil containers for the Rocky Mountain country, while the Grasselli Chemical Company hastened to throw a factory into East Chicago to provide sulphuric acid. Until 1906 the refinery used Lima oil almost exclusively, and found it quite satisfactory, but it of course turned later to Illinois and mid-continent crudes. Nearly the whole Midwest, Northwest, and Far West came to depend on the Whiting works, which also sent its waxes and other products into the markets of the Orient.

The profits of the western business, while not colossal, remained satisfactory, and came in at a time when general business conditions made profits desirable. From 1890 onward the oil trade, like other commercial lines, was in a nervous state, and in 1892–93 was hard hit by various adverse factors pointing to the great depression of 1893–97.

The Standard Oil of 1895, after this vertical integration downward, had a pattern of functions and earnings very different from that of a decade earlier. A new source of income had been added; the interrelationship of other sources had been changed. It is difficult to obtain precise figures for the earning-power of the various divisions of the business, year by year. We can say, however, that in the early history of the Standard the refining of oil furnished its largest single source of income; that after the acquisition of the huge pipe line and tankage system, transportation and storage furnished the greatest income—this being in proper proportion to the net value of the investment in the system; and that after the middle eighties the receipts from wells and from marketing rose very decidedly.

One reason why new seas of petroleum were indispensable lay in the constant discovery of new uses, a process which by 1895 had opened dazzling new vistas to the industry.

In the Paris Exposition of 1867 much attention was attracted by a little engine using an explosive mixture of illuminating gas and air, ignited by an electric spark—perhaps the world's first successful internal-combustion engine. The Lenoir gas engine had in fact been patented in France in 1860 and in America in 1863. Already an American had suggested that the vapor of light hydrocarbons might propel machinery. After 1870 many experiments were made with petroleum as an engine fuel. It was easily burned under steam boilers, while oil residuum was often utilized in refinery furnaces, and a little later crude oil or fuel oil in steel mills and other plants. In 1875 a steam automobile employing kerosene for fuel was running about the streets of Paris, and three years later was driven to Vienna. For oil refineries, however, the significant experiments were with internal combustion engines.

The practical history of these motors begins with Dr. N. A. Otto of Cologne, who in 1876 invented an engine in which gas (either illuminating gas or gasoline vapor) was first compressed and then exploded with a spark; an engine embodying the main four-cycle principle of all gasoline engines of today. From gas he turned to a distillate of oil. But the heavy motors manufactured by the Otto Engine Works and soon sold all over Europe were used exclusively for stationary power. It was left for another Württemberger, Gottlieb Daimler, to take an epochal step. An expert engineer, he left the Otto Works in 1882 to establish a shop of his own at Cannstadt, where he built light gasoline engines and soon began attaching them to bicycles, tricycles, and other vehicles. On March 4, 1887, he ran a motor car propelled by gasoline. Already, in 1885, Karl Benz of Mannheim had put an effective single-cylinder engine into a three-wheeled automobile. These were inventors' experiments, hardly more than playthings to the rest of the world. Who could read their implications?

The stationary internal combustion engine had definitely affected the oil market by 1900. The Otto Works sold about fifteen thousand engines in their first decade, 1876–86, nearly all of them using some form of petroleum distillate. After 1886 production increased, while the Otto factory had numerous competitors in various lands. Among gas motors in America, Dugald Clark's two-cycle engine (patented in Britain in 1877 and soon made in both Glasgow and Philadelphia), the Continental engine (1884), and the Parker engine of the Yonkers Manufacturing Company became noted. Among gasoline motors successful models were in no long time put on the market by Westinghouse, Olds, Fair-banks-Morse, and Allis-Chalmers. R. E. Olds, indeed, used his successful manufacture of such engines, begun in 1890, to support his work on the automobile.

Soon every progressive farm, shop, and feed-mill had its one-cylinder engine chugging away, pumping water, sawing wood, grinding meal, and doing other small jobs. The "naphtha launch," a small craft equipped with an engine of two or more horsepower, can be traced back to 1884 in the United States. By 1890 such launches were familiar on all waters, their pop-pop identifying them even in a fog. The motorcycle came in rapidly on the heels of the bicycle craze of the 1890's.

Even in 1895, however, it was clear that the two great uses of the future were to be the internal combustion engine and the burners of ships, locomotives, and power plants. Although the Standard resolutely pushed the sale of fuel oil, its use made no such spectacular advances in the United States as in Great Britain and Russia; British naval experiments with oil began in 1864, and the Russian navy and merchant marine were partly converted to oil in 1875–85. With gas and gasoline engines, the story was more creditable to America. The census of 1900 showed that more than 18,500 internal combustion engines were manufactured in the United States, with a total value exceeding five and a half millions. Factories were widely scattered over the country, and the size of the motors was increasing. Whereas the largest such engine at the Chicago World's Fair in 1893 developed 35 horsepower, the largest at the Paris Exposition of 1900 boasted 1000 horsepower. These motors rapidly grew familiar to Americans. They drove boats, they whirled dynamos, they sputtered away in barns and shops, their staccato in motorcycles and "horseless carriages" was soon to rise above the other traffic noises of cities.

In the first five years of the twentieth century the automobile manufacturing industry grew from origins so unimportant that it was not separately reported by the United States Bureau of the Census in 1900 to a business with products valued at $26,645,064 in 1905. The 57 establishments manufacturing automobiles in 1900 had risen to 121 in 1905; the capital invested from $5,768,-857 in 1900 to $20,555,247; the wage-earners from 2241 to 10,239. Detroit had become the automobile capital of the country, with 12 establishments and an investment of $2,982,949. Chicago and Cleveland came next, with seven establishments in each city, though Cleveland's factories had capital of $2,653,837 compared with Chicago's $376,886. Already the demand for gasoline was delighting refiners. By 1905, even ordinary men could see that the Age of Coal was ending, the Age of Oil was opening.

Since until the rise of the automobile the export market was much more important to the Standard than the home consumption, Rockefeller and his associates paid assiduous attention to its development and defense. In the seventies the United States stood almost alone as a producer of oil for Western Europe and Asia, its exports of kerosene rising in that decade from 97,900,000 to 367,325,000 gallons. The early eighties witnessed the sudden and powerful entrance of Russia into the world market, while the nineties saw the oil fields of Burma and the Dutch East Indies becoming formidable competitors in certain areas. Nevertheless, American kerosene exports rose to 551,000,000 gallons in 1890, and to 740,000,000 in 1900. Rockefeller for some years stood alone, the one giant in the world's refining industry. Then lesser but important figures rose beside him—Alfred Nobel, Henri Deterding, Marcus Samuels. Only by keeping prices low and quality high did American manufacturers maintain their unquestioned supremacy. In doing this the Standard played the leading role, and to its enterprise, system, and shrewdness must be given credit for the maintenance of American primacy.

Since in the export trade the Standard had to meet a double competition, that of American independents and that of foreign refiners, margins were nearly always narrow. The independents were handicapped by the smallness of their operations. They could not make up full ship-cargoes with assured delivery dates, as the Standard could. They had to export in comparatively small lots, and to deliver abroad at uncertain intervals. Nevertheless, as much the greatest part of American oil *had* to go overseas, they made frantic efforts to find profitable foreign outlets. When Russian and Galician kerosene came into the market, the Standard found itself competing against heavily-capitalized refineries using very cheap crude. In 1881 Rockefeller's combination was selling kerosene to Europeans at levels which allowed it a profit of only one-eighth to one-fourth cent a gallon, which meant a margin of one to two per cent on the price. The margin continued so slender that it was only the great volume of the Standard trade which made it lucrative. Benjamin Brewster in 1885 laid before Rockefeller figures which showed that the Standard was maintaining its high percentage of the American exports, the independents have gained only .61 per cent in the previous nine months.

Step by step, the Standard, impatient of dependence on foreign oil-buyers stationed in New York and the Regions, and on the long-distance efforts of William Rockefeller, Pratt, and the Devoe Company, established well-organized selling agencies abroad. In 1882 it created the West India Oil Refining Company, which both refined and marketed oil in the Antilles. About 1885 it launched Bushnell & Company as a Canadian marketing branch of the Standard Oil of New York, and a little later created the Eastern Oil Company to cover marketing in part of the Maritime Provinces. The highly important Anglo-American Oil Company, Ltd., was organized April 27, 1888, to carry on marketing in Great Britain. Though wholly owned by the Standard, its extremely capable officers were partly British, partly American. Before long it acquired a number of shipping companies, liquidated them, and took over the vessels.

A Danish marketing company (Det Danske Petroleum-Aktieskab), which was organized in 1888 by Scandinavian merchants, soon admitted the Standard as a shareholder; it had many Scandinavian subsidiaries. Another very important corporation, the Deutsch-Amerikanische Petroleum Gesellschaft, was set up on February 25, 1890, with headquarters in Bremen, to carry on the North German business; here the Riedemann firm, which evinced great ability and energy, were partners of the Standard. Next year (March 11, 1891), the American Petroleum Company was brought into being with Dutch and Belgian shareholders and managers, their offices in Rotterdam, to deal with Netherlands trade. The Società Italo-Americana del Petrolio, which represented a union with the powerful oil-distributing firms of B. Walter Company and the Wedekind family, was organized under Italian law in 1891, the Standard holding three-fifths of the stock.

This enumeration of foreign corporations owned or controlled by the Standard might be greatly lengthened. Their relations with the New York offices were kept fairly simple. Of course general marketing policies were established by the two Rockefellers and the Executive Committee, and carried out by the Export Committee; but within their own areas the foreign companies enjoyed a large degree of autonomy. By 1895 they formed an enterprising phalanx which steadily pushed Standard products all over the globe.

The foreign trade of the Standard had many romantic aspects. Sampans poled by coolies carried "case-oil" far up the streams of China; oxcarts laden with it lumbered along the great North Road that Kim traveled in India; it lighted the compounds and palaces of the barbaric chieftains whom Sir Hugh Clifford has described in his books on Malaya. Joseph Conrad in his days under the red ensign doubtless watched many a boatful of Standard products unloading in the ports of Oceania. Our consul in Singapore in 1887 stated that the Standard, as yet unworried by foreign competition, transshipped oil for all the wide regions roundabout. It was sent to the east coast of Sumatra, to the Isthmus of Malacca, to British Burma, to Siam, to French Cochin-China, and to the greater part of Borneo. The consul described its distribution to numerous harbors and islands of the Dutch and British possessions by small steamers, Chinese junks, and Malay prahees. Tens of millions of gallons of kerosene were sent by 1890 to all parts of Latin America, being distributed from coastal cities to river towns, plantations, ranches, and mines.

But in many areas the romantic phases of the business were quickly eclipsed by a savage struggle for survival. After 1880 Rockefeller and his associates felt a mounting concern over the threat of Baku oil. Up to that time the field, hampered by poor transportation, had fallen short of meeting even the Russian demand. As the flow of oil increased so did Muscovite competition, yet much American oil was steadily shipped into the Czar's domain from the Baltic. But Russia's importations dropped from 2,700,000 poods (a pood is thirty-six pounds avoirdupois) in 1873 to 1,700,000 in 1877, and to 1,445,000 in 1880. Evidently the vanishing point lay just ahead. Evidently also Russia was fast gaining a position which would enable her to throw a large surplus upon foreign markets.

This point was attained in the middle eighties; and although few histories mention the great Russo-American war of 1885–1914 in oil, that conflict raged relentlessly. The battle was of necessity long and hard fought. The grand strategy that kept the Standard largely successful throughout years of struggle against Russian competition had four main elements. First was the formation of the great marketing companies in foreign countries, a process at its height in the years 1887–92. The extension of the Lima business as a source of cheap exports after 1895 was another. The creation of great fleets of tankers was a third.

A fourth element in maintaining the Standard's position abroad was the development of a distributing system as highly finished as that in America. In Great Britain, for example, central depots were set up at various points: at Purfleet on the Thames, Birkenhead opposite Liverpool, Avonmouth, Plymouth, Hull, Newcastle, Belfast, and Dublin. Each usually held a three or four months' supply, keeping the oil in bulk as long as possible, lest the barrels affect its quality. By the end of the century the company had about three hundred small storage depots in the British Isles, and was making deliveries by some six hundred tank-wagons.

The efficiency and success of the Standard's marketing system naturally aroused jealously and enmity both in America and in foreign lands; an enmity increased by its price-cutting, its use of espionage, and some other practices which its opponents attacked, and which sometimes were highly censurable. Most great corporate aggregations in the United States did not compete with jobbers and retailers, and did not directly touch the consumer; the Standard did, and it paid the penalty in widespread popular dislike and fear. The bad name it had acquired at home by 1885 was so quickly carried abroad that when it established its network of European marketing companies, the foreign press and representatives of certain sections of foreign business expressed great uneasiness.

The treasurer of the Standard defended its steady expansion abroad. "We are pursuing a legitimate business and furnishing oil to Europe and Asia cheaper than any other producer," he said. "The only parties who appear to be dissatisfied are the Russian agents. The consumers have not objected. They want to get oil as cheaply as they can, and we can furnish it to them at lower rates than the Russian houses do." But great numbers of Continental and especially German jobbers, brokers, and retailers were much alarmed by the formation of the large European marketing agencies, wielding enormous power. They feared, as *Bradstreet's* remarked, "that their trade and occupation may become completely swallowed up by the gigantic maw of the Standard Oil Company." Meanwhile, in America the hard struggle of independent refiners and of countless retailers who used their kerosene attracted constant attention from the press, and inspired growing demands for governmental investigation and action.

Rockefeller was keenly aware of the rising public antagonism to the Standard Oil. Scarcely a week went by without some thrust by an editor or politician at the "anaconda" or "octopus." As hostility to the Standard spread, expressions of distrust or condemnation came in an intermittent stream from the New York *World,* Springfield *Republic,* Philadelphia *Press,* Chicago *Tribune,* and other liberal sheets.

The Standard by no means stood alone; it shared its position as target with the major railroads, with banking interests (notably Morgan and the Rothschilds), with Carnegie's steel company, and with other aggregations of wealth. At one point it was exempt from attack: managing an export industry, it could not be accused, like most manufacturers, of grabbing extortionate tariff favors. But as the first trust, as a mighty aggregation bestriding a dozen cities, as the object of the clamorous wrath of oil producers, and as a source of rich profits to a restricted body of men, it held a special prominence. We may distinguish between the general and the specific roots of this massive hostility, which was destined to grow until the dissolution of 1911.

Fundamental in the situation were certain large social factors. This was a decade of ferment, revolt, and germination. The Western agrarians, caught under the harrow of world gluts of meat and grain, price deflation, high freights, and heavy mortgage charges; labor groping blindly for an effective organization; idealistic intellectuals and reformers—all found their spokesmen. It was the decade of Edward Bellamy's persuasive exposition of utopian socialism in *Looking Backward,* which sold a million copies in a few years; of Henry Adams's *Democracy,* so caustic an etching of politics and society in Washington; of E. W. Howe's *The Story of a Country Town* and Joseph Kirkland's *Zury,* grim, hard depictions of the frustrations, crimes, and discontent of rural communities. The 1880's gave the country James F. Hudson's *The Railways and the Republic,* a passionate indictment of transportation abuses by a Pittsburgh attorney; D. C. Cloud's *Monopolies and the People,* an equally passionate agrarian indictment of combinations; and Richard T. Ely's *The Labor Problem.* The later eighties witnessed the rise of one Farmers' Alliance in the South under C. W. Macune, and another in the Northwest under Milton George, both dedicated to a long list of radical reforms. As the decade ended Mary Ellen Lease, the voice of the embattled Populists of Kansas, was proclaiming that the people were at bay: "Wall Street owns the country."

In this period of ferment and revolt, one central element was a fervent revival of the age-old hostility of the common people for monopoly; a hostility which embraced many railroads because of the obvious fact that transportation abuses did much to create and bulwark monopoly. By 1885 the rapid growth of strong industrial combinations had struck millions with alarm. Arthur T. Hadley that year pointed out that dozens of monopolies or quasi-monopolies were arising; in anthracite, in iron, in machinery, in hardware, in tobacco, in whiskey, in many other fields. "For lumber and for paper, for cattle and for milk, for cartridges and for matches," he wrote, "in each business there is an organized combination, fixing rates and often limiting production."

Alongside the monopolies stood the railroad corporations, arraigned for discriminating in favor of large shippers and picked cities, for levying excessive rates on farmers and small business men, for corrupting legislatures, and for enriching inside "rings." The Standard was the earliest, the greatest, and the most successful of the industrial combinations; its railroad bargains were the most notorious; its chieftains were the most mysteriously puissant. As the movement which produced those twin efforts at governmental control, the Interstate Commerce Act of 1887 and the Anti-Trust Act of 1890, gained force, so did denunciation of Standard Oil.

"It's many a day since I have troubled you with a letter," wrote Warden to John D. Rockefeller on May 24, 1887, "and I would not do so now could I justify myself in being silent. It is very much impressed upon me, that we have as a company approached one of those times . . . when we are being placed in balances to be weighed. . . . We have met with a success unparalleled in commercial history, our name is known all over the world, and our public character is not one to be envied. We are quoted as the representative of all that is evil, hard hearted, oppressive, cruel (we think unjustly), but men look askance at us, we are pointed at with contempt, and while some good men flatter us, it's only for our money and we scorn them for it and it leads to a further hardness of heart. This is not pleasant to write, for

I had longed for an honored position in commercial life. None of us would choose such a reputation; we all desire a place in the good will, honor & affection of honorable men."

The letter remains as a striking testimonial to the effect of public opinion on one Standard leader. Others—Rogers, Flagler, Archbold, to name a few—to some extent shared Warden's sense of hurt. In doing so, they responded to the most sweeping and savage attack which had ever been made upon an American corporation.

We have noted various aspects of the onslaught, which really had its roots in the South Improvement episode of 1872. However, its acute phase began in 1879.

The first of these stronger onslaughts was the Hepburn Committee's inquiry. It had been stimulated by the demand for a study "of unjust discriminations and other defects existing in the management of railroads chartered by the state." Although nominally the work of the Committee covered such practices alone, actually it took in much more.

It did not explore a number of notorious evils charged to railroad management, such as stock-watering, speculation in securities, and political activities. Rather it concentrated on the abuses that grew out of the relationships between railroads and huge corporations—flour-millers, meat-packers, salt-makers, and oil-refiners. Many observers were becoming convinced that such industrialists found the railroads only too willing to waltz them down to a rose-leaf path to monopoly.

The Hepburn investigation showed that the special rate contracts made on the New York Central alone between January and August, 1879, were estimated by its officers at six thousand in number. Indeed, for local freight in bulk a uniform tariff did not really exist; every rate was a special rate. Between the same points these rates varied widely from day to day, from shipper to shipper. Rebates flourished. Favored shippers often got discounts ranging from 50 to 80 per cent.

Such disclosures, proving once more the universality of rebating, are of incidental interest to us, but our chief concern is with the role of the Standard. In one sense the sessions of the committee were disappointing, for the inner secrets of railway offices and of the Standard (and of other big shippers) were fairly well preserved. Men like Vanderbilt and Archbold skirted the edges of perjury. Jewett's pretended lapses of memory were simply not credible. When Archbold said of the Standard: "Their interests are principally at Cleveland and New York; I know of none outside of those two points in connection with the Standard Oil Company," he was flouting the truth. He knew that the Acme was a Standard "interest." Rogers' denial of any connection between the Standard and Charles Pratt & Company was equally close to perjury. Nevertheless, the committee brought forth a mass of important information about the practices of the railroads, and pried some new facts even from the close-lipped Standard men. To an increased extent the general public realize how universally rebates and other discriminations had been granted by the railroads.

Although special rates had gone to literally thousands, the Standard emerged as the chief symbol of monopolistic tendencies fostered by rate-discrimination. Its huge size was more fully revealed than ever before. H. H. Rogers had admitted that nine-tenths of the refiners of the country were "in harmony" with it (a statement which new refineries about New York, in Cleveland, and in the Regions would soon make untrue). E. G. Patterson, still an enemy of the combination, furnished the committee with a fairly accurate list of Standard-controlled companies, including the Acme and Charles Pratt & Company. The fact that the Standard controlled the oil terminals of all four trunk-line railroads was established. New light was thrown upon its former services and rewards as an "evener," and the joint role of the combination and the railroads in working together to eliminate almost all the New York independents was made clear.

In its final report, submitted to the Legislature on January 22, 1880, the committee bluntly declared that the relations of the Standard with the carriers stood in violation of railroad economy and social justice. Calling the Standard "a unique illustration of the possible outgrowth" of railroad discrimination, it also termed the combination an object-lesson in "the colossal proportions to which monopoly can grow under the laws of this country." It declared that since the Standard had gained control of the refining industry, the railroads had obtained much less revenue from oil shipments than they deserved, with the result that they had to increase their rates upon other products to meet this loss. It estimated that of the 12,900,400 barrels shipped from the Regions in the first nine months of 1879, that part which was sent to the seaboard could, and should, have borne a dollar a barrel more in freight charges. In other words, both the railroads, and indirectly investors and other shippers, were being deprived of millions of dollars annually for the enrichment of the combination.

This part of the report was quickly rendered academic by the completion of the trunk pipe lines. Along with other passages, it was regarded by the Standard men as *ex parte* and unfair. But the testimony before the Hepburn Committee and the committee's report impressed New Yorkers even more than the injunction-suit testimony had impressed Pennsylvanians, and in addition powerfully influenced public opinion throughout the country. The New York *Shipping and Commercial List,* the chief business organ of the city, on October 18, 1879, pronounced rate discriminations "illegal, unjust, arbitrary, and tyrranical."

Hard on the heels of the Hepburn investigation came the Scofield, Shurmer & Teagle lawsuits. In spite of the fact that they broke an agreement with Standard, the Cleveland independents won public sympathy by defying the combination, and, of course, gained legal confirmation of their right to do so. In their later suit against the Lake Shore to compel it to give them the same rates as the Standard, they were also applauded by the public and sustained by the courts. It was small comfort to the Standard officials that two years later, in October, 1886, the Illinois Supreme Court ruled differently in a comparable case.

Scofield, Shurmer and Teagle prospered, acquiring in addition to their original plant two refineries in Cleveland and producing property, a pipe line, storage tanks, 63 tank cars, and loading racks at Lima, Ohio. They seem to have procured railroad rates as good as the Standard's to and from many points. In February, 1891, the Scofields and Teagle dickered with Frank Rockefeller (Mark Hanna acting as their representative), and estimated their properties as worth $439,799.11—a third refinery not chiefly theirs raising the total for a proposed "package" of the main Cleveland independents to $583,899.75. Frank did not think the estimate much in excess of actual value, but regarded some $185,000 of refinery construction as of little use to the Standard.

In any event, the Scofields and Teagle combined seem to have been worth about $400,000 at this time; they had prospered as independents. During a part of this period they leased two of their plants to the Standard on an allotment basis, thus return-

ing to the relationship against which they had so bitterly protested in 1881!

However, to all haters of monopoly, Scofield, Shurmer &
Teagle were seen through lenses which magnified their virtues
and ignored their faults. They loomed up as little less than
heroes, and the publicity which they brought to the Standard's
affairs gravely injured the reputation of that firm. It was particularly damaged by several witnesses who seized the opportunity
provided by litigation to offer testimony or submit sworn affi-
davits.

One witness in particular, Mrs. Fred M. Backus, told a malig-
nant story which reverberated for years to the injury of Rockefeller's reputation. She was the widow of a Cleveland manufacturer of lubricants. Fred Backus had developed a special
market for his products, was never in competition with the
Standard, and remained unaffected by its Cleveland acquisitions
in 1872 and 1873. He died the following year, and Mrs. Backus
carried on the business, supporting three children. However,
after a time the Standard itself turned to making lubricants, for
which it controlled nearly all the raw materials, and in 1878 it
bought the Backus plant. Mrs. Backus's story was that Rockefeller's competition, together with the general business depression, convinced her that she could not continue. She declared
that she had asked for $200,000, "much below what the stock
was worth," but in the end was offered only $79,000, and in
sheer desperation accepted this figure. When she begged permission to retain $15,000 in stock, it was abruptly refused. Accord-
ing to her tale, Rockefeller had ruthlessly taken advantage of a
defenseless widow, and appropriated her business for little more
than a third of its value!

But Mrs. Backus misrepresented the entire transaction. This
was indicated at the time by evidence which Rockefeller presented in court. Later it was completely established by the testimony of Mrs. Backus's attorney, her works superintendent, her
husband's brother, H. M. Backus, who was an employee and
stockholder in the refinery, and Charles J. Woodbury, another
responsible employee.

This evidence shows that Mrs. Backus's own valuation of her
works was $150,000 not $200,000. Two years earlier, when the
business was fairly prosperous, she had been ready to sell for

less, but could obtain no assurance of the would-be purchaser's financial status. The $150,000 she asked contained as its principal item $71,000 for "works, good will, and successorship." There were additional items for oil on hand, cash, bills receivable, and accrued dividends. The Standard paid $60,000 for works and good will, and $19,000 for the oil on hand, leaving the other items, valued by her at $60,000, to Mrs. Backus. Her brother-in-law wrote: "She got as much more out of these accounts as the Standard Oil Company had given her for the business." She thus received or retained $139,000 for assets which she asserted to be worth $150,000—a difference of only $11,000. Rockefeller's appraisers declared that this was a generous payment. "She had a business dwindling; we bought it from her on liberal terms," said Rockefeller later. And again: "In this case particularly I was moved by kindly consideration of an old employee, Fred Backus, who had been a bookkeeper in my office, who had been for years a consumptive, and who had been a mission Sunday School teacher with me in our boyhood days." For good measure he had added $10,000 to the appraisers' figure.

Woodbury, who had been trained by Backus, asserts that the payment for the plant "far exceeded its value." Mrs. Backus, according to her attorney, was well pleased at the time. She had not been denied permission to retain stock in her company; on the contrary, Rockefeller suggested that she keep part ownership, but she replied that she wished to get out of the business entirely. This "poor widow" conserved her money shrewdly, and according to Clevelanders died worth about $300,000.

Equally baseless was the story of a Baltimore widow, Mrs. Sylvia C. Hunt, who in 1877 leased her refinery to the Camden Consolidated Oil Company. The lease provided that for a generous rental, and the assumption of all risks and taxes, this Standard subsidiary should control the refinery for a number of years. Here again the known facts wholly refute the accusation. Mrs. Hunt was anything but crushed. While drawing handsome payments from the Standard, she joined a former agent of hers, John W. S. Brady, in developing the Monumental Paraffine, Machinery Oil and Wax Works. In the spring of 1881 she and Brady enticed a Baltimore United employee, Neilson, to join them, and with his aid built a naphtha plant. Eventually she and Brady tried on several occasions to sell both establishments to the Standard, but by 1884, when these efforts were made, the combination, guided by Archbold, was wary. Apparently no sale was made. However, Mrs. Hunt seems to have been as prosperous and active, or more so, after her arrangement with the Standard as she had been before. Nor did she scruple to compete with them, although this involved a questionable moral point, if not a technical infringement of her agreement with the Rockefeller group.

Then, as time passed, the inevitable happened: a hostile publicist seized upon the facts and suspicions which had darkened the Standard's name, and wove them into a coherent indictment.

About 1880 a Chicago journalist and lawyer, Henry Demarest Lloyd, then only thirty-three, began to display a critical interest in the larger American corporations. The son of a New York minister, a graduate of Columbia, he had won admittance to the bar eleven years earlier, had lectured on political economy, and finally had gone west in the early eighteen seventies to join the staff of the Chicago *Tribune*. He had been fired by various reform movements of the time—the anti-Tammany revolt, the Liberal Republican onset, the free-trade uprising, the demand for remonetizing silver. In the *Tribune* office he was inspired by the paper's liberal editor, Horace White, and its part-owner, William Bross, whose interest in the commercial growth of Chicago led him to hate railroad greed. Lloyd married wealth in the person of Bross's daughter, but this did not lessen his reformist fervor. Possessing a highly emotional temperament and a rhetorical pen, he found ample material for invective in the iniquities of business. His editorials for the *Tribune* vehemently assailed the anthracite monopoly, the railroad scandals, the stockyards combine, and other evils. In 1880 he read to the Chicago Literary Club a plea for railway regulation called "A Cure for Vanderbiltism." Studying the railroad strike in 1877 and the Hepburn Investigation, he fixed his attention on the Standard Oil. As yet his acquaintance with finance was elementary; he knew nothing of economics; he was credulous and cocksure. But when he sent the *Atlantic Monthly* his article called "The Story of a Great Monopoly," which he wrote with passionate haste from the evidence he accumulated on the Standard group, William Dean Howells gave it the leading place in the magazine for March, 1881.

Until this time criticism of the Standard, though frequent and sometimes bitter, had been sporadic and generally local. The Oil Regions had produced passionate denunciations, the *Oil, Paint, and Drug Reporter* had assailed the combination, George Rice and others had promoted state and national investigations, and miscellaneous comments and editorials had slashed at the rising colossus. Lloyd's article now drew national attention to the subject. He furnished, moreover, the first brief, comprehensive, and readable statement of the main allegations against the Standard. Whereas few readers had explored the five thick volumes of the Hepburn Committee hearings, the *Atlantic* article reached a thoughful and potentially influential audience from Maine to Oregon. That issue went through seven printings. The London *Railway News* reprinted it and distributed thousands of free copies to English investors. It was read in lands as remote as Australia. Even Herbert Spencer, speaking in New York in 1882, referred to it: "I hear that a great trader among you deliberately endeavored to crush out every one whose business competed with his own."

Seldom has an article been better timed than Lloyd's. The years of depression had destroyed a multitude of weak businesses. The larger corporations were emerging with renewed strength and pushing on toward near-monopoly or monopoly. Meanwhile the position of the farmer, unprotected from Canadian, Argentine, and Russian competition, and as a debtor badly hurt by poor credit facilities and gold-appreciation, was one of grim hardship. That of the workingman, without adequate unions or strong leadership, was equally desperate. While the lords of industry amassed enormous wealth, took control of legislatures, and by the time of McKinley and Hanna became intolerably arrogant, the social strains and stresses within the nation became ever more acute. One of the few weapons of the discontented was the printing press. Lloyd's article was the first loud stroke in what soon became a mighty tocsin of protest—not the first, for *Chapters of Erie* deserves that title, but the first heard throughout the land.

"That article," wrote Charles Edward Russell, "was a turning point in our social history; with it dawned upon Americans the first conviction . . . that the republic could no more endure an oligarchy of capitalists than an oligarchy of slave-holders." It would be more accurate to say that Lloyd resumed the protests of the Jacksonian era, of William Leggett and Peter Cooper, against the injustices of large-scale capitalism. Already, in 1879, Henry George had published in *Progress and Poverty* a stirring indictment of the inequitable distribution of wealth; already Simon Sterne had written effective articles on railway abuses; already Abram S. Hewitt had called upon his fellow capitalists to promote labor organization and profit sharing. The demand for railroad regulation had been voiced both by Eastern commercial groups and Western agrarian interests, and was caught up by a thousand pens. In 1890 the Populist movement was laying the foundation for Theodore Roosevelt's progressivism and Woodrow Wilson's new freedom. Lloyd could claim a place among the numerous vanguard of an irresistible uprising.

Yet his attack had glaring errors and falsehoods. Indicting the Standard's monopolistic practices, the writer charged that an evil combination between the Standard and the Pennsylvania had been largely responsible for the fierce Pittsburgh riots of 1877—although the Pennsylvania had been generally anti-Standard, and that was the very year in which Tom Scott and Rockefeller were locked in battle! Throughout the article *ex parte* statements were accepted without scrutiny.

Gross carelessness as to fact was equally prominent. "Of the fifty-eight refineries in Pittsburgh in 1867 twenty-eight have been crushed out and dismantled, and of the remaining thirty twenty-nine have been bought up or leased by the great monopoly." When the Standard began its absorptions in Pittsburgh during 1874 that city had between twenty-two and thirty refineries only (the computation varies), and it of course had nothing whatever to do with "crushing out" weak plants between 1867 and 1874. They died of bad management and over-competition. Lloyd blamed the Standard for the low prices of crude oil caused by the great Bradford field glut. "In 1878," he wrote, "oil went down to 78.75 cents a barrel at the very time the shipments from the wells were 56,000 barrels a day, the largest ever made till that time." Evidently he thought the price of oil should have gone *up* at the very time that production broke all records! He also calmly twisted statistics to suit his purposes:

The average cost, last December, of the one and one-third barrels of petroleum needed to make a barrel of kerosene was $2.05 at Cleveland. The cost of refining, barrelling, and all expenses, including a refiners' profit of half a dollar a barrel, is, according to the testimony of experts, $2.75 a barrel. To bring it by rail to Chicago cost 70 cents, making the total cost $5.50 for a barrel of fifty gallons, or eleven cents a gallon. The price the Standard charges in Chicago is nineteen and three-fourths cents a gallon, in which . . . there is a tax on the public of eight and three-fourths cents. . . . A family that uses a gallon of kerosene a day pays a yearly tribute to the Standard of $32, the income from $800 in the four per cents.

Now the Standard's profit was high, but it did not remotely approach this exorbitant figure. Lloyd includes nothing for the heavy cost of distribution and marketing, for capital investment, for plant-depreciation, for cost of barrels, or for risks and incidentals. And his figures differ amazingly from those of better authorities. The New York Chamber of Commerce states that in 1878 the average market-price of crude in that city was 6.38 cents a gallon, and of refined, 10.78 cents a gallon. The margin between the two was thus but 4.40 cents per gallon, instead of Lloyd's alleged 8.75, and this did not allow for refining costs, waste, transport, and marketing! Actually the profit per gallon, when such items were figured, was often not half a cent. Colonel W. P. Thompson in a letter to John D. Rockefeller on August 15, 1883, estimated the profit per gallon to be but .413 a cent!

But inaccurate and biased as it was, the article in one respect hit the mark squarely. It reëmphasized the now well-known fact that great railroads had granted secret rates to industrial allies, and that those special privileges had enabled some corporations to strike down competitors and erect gigantic near-monopolies or monopolies. It showed further that the monopolies sometimes used the money they took from the public to influence newspapers, legislators, and even courts. It argued and this was widely accepted although a highly debatable point that the growth of great combinations shut out competition and increased prices to the consumer. What could be done? Lloyd concluded that it was hopeless to push reformative measures in the state legislatures, for these were controlled by the corporations; the tiger must be caged by the federal government.

Lloyd's attack helped create the legend of a ruthless and extortionate Standard Oil, pausing at nothing to destroy competition and mulct consumers—a legend that was to grow steadily during the next thirty years. The picture had just sufficient truth to be effective. Some acts of the Standard were indefensible. But Lloyd, paying no attention to the creative aspects of the Standard's work, projected on his screen the image of a frightful monster,

all horns, hoofs, and scales, ramping in crime; an image whose
exaggerations made all the more vivid a stereotype upon the
national mind. It was a picture which demagogues, sensational
journalists, cartoonists, and muckrakers were to keep constantly
before the public eye.

The volume of attack now rolled up like a gigantic snowball,
gathering size as it moved along. The attempt of the state of
Pennsylvania to collect taxes from the Standard on the basis of
its capital stock and dividends from the time it first engaged in
business in Pennsylvania to the autumn of 1880 had got well
under way before the *Atlantic* article appeared. Failing to receive
information from the Company, the Auditor-General had made
a rough estimate and sent a bill of about $3,200,000 for taxes
and penalties.

To this the Standard filed a list of twenty-five objections. It
had a strong case. "If this principle were adopted by all states,"
declared William Rockefeller, amplifying Flagler's original objection, "it would put a stop to all interstate commerce."
Actually the claim that the entire capital of an Ohio corporation
was taxable by Pennsylvania was a piece of political vaudeville.
Of course, the physical properties of the Standard in that commonwealth, all plainly visible, were taxed by both state and local
authorities. So were the the capital and profits of those units, like
the Standard Oil of Pittsburgh, the Acme of Titusville, and
Warden, Frew, which were the holders of Pennsylvania charters.

"In our tax fight," wrote S. C. T. Dodd to Flagler on July 23,
1881, "we do not deny the *power* of the state to tax except in a
single instance. We say that the Pennsylvania Act *does* not tax
the entire capital, and that when the business is in the nature of
inter-state commerce the state cannot tax such business."

But the Auditor-General was seeking, on the basis of a statute
of 1868 to which he gave a novel construction, to levy on the
whole combination because it bought its oil in the state. Ohio
could as justly have tried to tax the Pennsylvania units because
the original Standard began its operations in Cleveland!

Early in 1882 the case was argued before the Court of Common
Pleas in Harrisburg. The Standard presented evidence that no
"foreign" corporation had ever before been so taxed. Its attorney
pointed out that if mulcted in this fashion it might be driven
from the state. "That may be little, but it may not be all. The
decision that drives this company from the State will drive

hundreds more that hitherto have contributed to our prosperity and have also borne their full share of the burdens of taxation. It will not stop there. Our own corporations are in every State. Retaliation will ensue. New York with an untried statute on her books is standing waiting this decision."

On April 4 Judge Simonton filed his decision—a complete victory for the Standard. Instead of $3,200,000, he ordered it to pay only $33,277.57 as taxes and penalties for the whole period of 1873–78. And, he declared, when a "foreign" corporation "comes into this state, and engages in business here, and brings just so much of its capital stock as represents the tangible property and assets invested or used here, this proportion and no more is subject to the taxing power of the state." An elementary principle of interstate comity had been upheld and clarified. Both the state and the company appealed the decision of the Dauphin County Court; and finally the Pennsylvania Supreme Court ruled in favor of the Standard, though three justices dissented. The amount which the Standard was required to pay was reduced by this decision to some $21,000. No penalties or interest were allowed by the Supreme Court, which declared that the state had never wished to "erect a judicial Chinese wall" around its resources.

At the same time, the suit had once more called attention to the Standard's size, and fixed in the public mind the range of its activities and its immense profits.

By prompt action the Standard might have done much to shatter in the making the horned-devil portrait of its enemies. It could have established the wastes and cruelties of the old cutthroat competition. It could have attacked its assailants as either ignorant or untruthful, and might thus have altered the ugly picture before it was accepted by the American public as a stereotype.

But the Trust could not have corrected errors, exaggerations, and lies without admitting to some abusive policies and indefensible acts; and this Rockefeller hesitated to do. The *Nation* stated (February 24, 1881) that Lloyd's article was sensational but apparently factual. The Standard could have exposed much of the sensationalism but would have had to admit damaging facts. It remained silent, with the immediate result that more assaults were made as the months and years went by. Thus the public belief in the Standard as a monster was fostered until with many it became a deep-rooted conviction. More than a decade later Lloyd boasted to a friend that his article of 1881 "remains unanswered to this day" and because it had gone unchallenged, he and others thought it unchallengeable.

The silence of the Standard was the more suspected because the company's well-known secrecy was believed to conceal malpractices. J. C. Welch wrote in 1883: "If there was ever anything in this country that was bolted and barred, hedged round, covered over, shielded before and behind, in itself and all its approaches, with secrecy, that thing is the Standard Oil Company." The statement, which was true, was accepted as a reproach and an accusation.

The only defense which the Standard explicitly sanctioned in the 1880's was a paper which the loyal hand of J. N. Camden contributed (1883) to the *North American Review*. The refusal to reply was a mistake, and primarily Rockefeller's mistake. Many Standard men felt the attacks on their organization keenly. Yet at this very time some railroads were responding effectively to their critics, and Godkin in the *Nation* was disproving the exaggerated charges of the Anti-Monopoly League.

The general silence of the Standard under attack doubtless requires a complex explanation. Some of the charges against it were so ridiculous that to well-informed men any reply seemed unnecessary. Again, both Rockefeller and his colleagues had long pursued a policy of being close-lipped about Standard affairs; the policy was now habit, and hard to break. In the past their silence had served the Standard well. As another consideration, to permit even friendly writers to champion their cause might have seemed dangerous. Such men or women wanted to ask questions, and where would their questions lead? There were various phases of its activities which the Standard did not wish to have explored. Its feeling on that point was not necessarily one of guilt. The Trust, the relationships among its various units, the rate and price policies—these to the Standard were justified by existing economic and political conditions. None the less, it knew that they would be subject to protest and attack. Similarly, for Standard officials to enter directly upon a public debate had perhaps even greater possibilities for harm. The temper of Americans generally was unfriendly to large corporations. To make answers to accusations might merely stir up more accusations, and the "howlers," as Archbold called them, would outshout the Standard. If it endured in silence, would not the furor die down?

This reasoning was essentially that of other industrial leaders of the day. Many were inarticulate; those who were not, like Carnegie, John Wanamaker, and Abram S. Hewitt, stood out as exceptions. So Morgan, Hill, Frick, Harriman, and Huntington, like Rockefeller, tended to shrug criticism aside. It was not until the attacks began to act like a great fulcrum upon the state and federal governments that they awoke to self-defense.

Rockefeller's own belief in silence was doubtless shared at first by men like Bostwick, Archbold, Flagler, and Warden. As the storm of protest and accusation rose, they seem to have been more doubtful than he of the wisdom of reticence. But Rockefeller was the rock of faith that held them all to the gospel of silence.

What neither he nor his associates perceived clearly was the depth of the public's feelings against monopoly. They knew that monopoly was unpopular. They hoped that this unpopularity would fade as the efficiency and positive virtues of consolidation became evident. This was, of course, a profound error. The more powerful and effective the Standard became, the greater was the public's willingness to believe the charges constantly repeated against it, and the stronger became the clamor for federal and state action. The time was approaching when the higher units of American government must grapple in deadly earnest with such powerful organizations as that which Rockefeller and his associates had built.

# CHAPTER X

# THE FOUNDING OF
# A UNIVERSITY

WHEN in the late seventies the Rockefeller family began spending the after-Christmas months in New York, their first residence was the quiet Windsor Hotel at Fifth Avenue and Forty-sixth Street, the home also for a time of Andrew Carnegie and Edwin Booth. But beginning about 1880 the family arrived soon after Thanksgiving to stay the entire winter, and made their abode the Buckingham, a residential hotel on the Avenue at Fiftieth. At first they used the hotel dining-room, but soon had meals served in their own quarters. Returning in early spring to Cleveland, they found two houses in readiness. The old Euclid Avenue house was used every Sunday, and for perhaps a fortnight each spring and fall, but Forest Hill was the principal residence.

During the early eighties the greater part of New York above Forty-second Street was still a brownstone-and-brick residential area. Fifth and Madison Avenues were lined with substantial and handsome houses, above which peered the spires of St. Patrick's Cathedral and the Reformed Church. An atmosphere of quiet pervaded the district. The reaches above Bryant Park remained well outside the commercial maelstrom.

In 1884 Rockefeller, who had become a legal resident of New York, looked about for a permanent home; and that fall he and his wife determined upon the four-story-and-basement house at 4 West Fifty-fourth Street, paying a reputed price of $600,000. Solidly built of brownstone, it was sufficiently imposing to be called a mansion, though too tall, narrow, and gaunt to be handsome. It already had some yard space, and Rockefeller bought an adjoining lot to give it more. The house, about twenty years old, had recently been occupied by Mrs. Arabella Worsham, who that summer married the railroad magnate Collis P. Huntington, and the Rockefellers took her furniture, rugs, and hangings.

For the side yards Rockefeller found a unique use. He was so fond of skating that in Cleveland he once got up a few minutes after midnight on a bitter Monday morning (he would let no work be done on Sunday) to direct employees in flooding a pond. In New York he had the space beside and behind the house cemented over and surrounded by a curved coping. In freezing weather the horseshoe-shaped space made an excellent skating rink. His children and friends delighted in it. The basement hallway was fitted up with boxes where sometimes a hundred guests kept their skates. At night, under gleaming electric lights, the yard offered a gay scene, while early in the morning passersby often saw Rockefeller, in overcoat and silk hat, taking some sedate turns on the ice before he went down to work.

From the beginning No. 4 West 54th Street was a center of hospitality for church people, charitable and temperance workers, and groups of Standard Oil executives. Dinners, teas, and musicales for these friends were frequent, but the house was never used for "society" affairs. Some of Rockefeller's associates have recalled the animated meetings and the gaiety with which he unbent at gatherings of his friends. He particularly liked breakfast conferences for Standard men. William Rockefeller, Henry M. Flagler, and Benjamin Brewster all lived for a time literally within a stone's throw on Fifth Avenue, and Rockefeller could see them by taking a two-minute walk. Other Standard associates and many church friends were near.

Home, church, and office—these were the three poles about which Rockefeller's life in the eighties revolved. He had three homes, the two in Cleveland and one in New York; two churches, the Fifth Avenue and Euclid Avenue Baptist; and two offices, the Standard Block in Cleveland and 26 Broadway. While burdened with labor and responsibility, he tried to keep his routine simple. He cared nothing for receptions and public dinners, seldom went to the theatre, and heard most of his music at home. Outdoor pastimes furnished his principal recreation; to driving, skating, and swimming he added horseback riding before 1890 and bicycling soon afterward.

All home activities were carried on with an eye to character-building. The parents set an example of courtesy and patience. "I cannot remember to have heard the voices of either Father or Mother raised in anger or complaint in speaking to any of us children," says the son. No coddling was permitted. The son, to improve his health, spent part of two winters in his teens at Forest Hill. He rose early and labored as hard as the men on the estate chopping wood, burning brush, and doing odd jobs.

Rockefeller's personal tastes remained for the most part extremely simple. He took no interest in clothes, and though he dressed neatly, his family found difficulty in getting him to renew his suits betimes. At table he always ate sparingly; he disliked hot dishes, and would usually wait for the food to cool, telling his family and guests to go right along while he talked. A favorite dish was bread and milk, which inspired stories about dyspepsia, though except for a few years in the early nineties his digestion was excellent. He was fond of eating an apple just before he went to bed, and for years kept a paper sack of them on the sill outside his bedroom window. The cuisine of the household was always plain, and they had no French chef.

The Rockefellers inculcated in each child the duty of giving to church and charities, these gifts being made from earnings. In time the children observed that many of their youthful friends did less work and had more money. This was true, for example, of William Rockefeller's children. "We felt we were in a terrible plight compared with them!" later recalled John D. Rockefeller, Jr. But their upbringing gave them a wholesome attitude toward life and a clear idea of the value of money.

When John D. Rockefeller, Jr., grew up and had children of his own he instituted the same discipline. One of his sons, becoming well grown, once admired a boat that a young friend of wealthy family had bought. He was frankly envious. "Get one for yourself," suggested the friend. "Why don't you have your father buy it?" The son rebuked the proposed extravagance with asperity. "Who do you think we are?" he demanded. "Vanderbilts?"

The three daughters were given their early education at home. Bessie then went to the Rye Female Seminary, founded at Rye, New York, by Mrs. Life, the former Susan La Monte, and later took some courses at Vassar. Alta and Edith also attended the Rye Seminary. At week-ends the three girls often made the West

Fifty-fourth Street house lively by parties of schoolmates. Edith's tastes were linguistic, artistic, and musical; Alta, who despite defective hearing sang and played the piano well, was interested in charities. In Cleveland she founded a settlement—Alta House —in the Italian quarter, which her hard work helped make a success. In New York she was active at St. Luke's Hospital, and managed a sewing-school for girls, while in both cities she was indefatigable in church work.

Bessie was the first to marry. An old friendship between the Rockefeller family and that of Dr. Augustus H. Strong, head of the Rochester Theological Seminary, repeatedly brought young Charles A. Strong to Forest Hill. John D. Rockefeller, Jr., recalls him sitting in a beech tree reading Gilbert's *Bab Ballads* to the Rockefeller children beneath. He took degrees and began teaching philosophy at Bryn Mawr; an attachment grew up between him and Bessie, and early in 1889 they were married at her home. Next day the couple sailed for Europe, where Strong wished to complete his studies—the bride, wrote Lucy Spelman, carrying "a face as bright as the sun above her." When they returned from Germany, Strong taught at Clark University and the University of Chicago, then briefly joining the staff at Columbia. He was a man of intellectual vigor, who wrote one notable book, *Why the Mind Has a Body,* and who, despite his retired, studious ways added a good deal to family life. Unhappily, Bessie Strong later fell into a prolonged illness.

Rockefeller decided that his son should be taught in schools where he would rub shoulders with boys of his own age, and the lad attended four of them, the most notable being the Browning School, founded by John D. and William Rockefeller. "Junior" found his school work hard, but was conscientious and industrious. "Father never expected more than that," he writes, "but he did expect *that*." As no study was allowed on Sundays he sometimes rose long before dawn on Mondays to finish his lessons. At nineteen, he finished his preparatory work and entered Brown University.

It would be different to overstate the affection, hope, and confidence that Rockefeller centered in his growing son. Never a demonstrative man, he now and then let his feeling creep into a letter. "Be assured," he wrote the youth on February 17, 1892, "the appreciation you show is ample payment for all we have ever tried to do for you, and I have not words to express our gratitude for what you show us in your daily life, and for the hope you give us for the future time when our turn comes to lean more on you." And on April 13, 1896, urging the young man to take care of his health, the magnate added: "I am looking to you and relying upon you to share my responsibilities with me on behalf of the family, as soon as you are ready."

Outside his home Rockefeller continued to find in church and office his principal sources of intellectual stimulus and spiritual refreshment. He belonged to two clubs, the Union League and the Driving Club; but it was in the Fifth Avenue Baptist congregation, where he immediately became a leading figure, that he found true comradeship. Indeed, he was now one of the most prominent Baptists of the country, acquainted with all the principal educators and ministers of a denomination rich in talent. His house was seldom without some clerical guest.

More and more time had to be devoted to his philanthropies, which were becoming extensive. In 1887 he gave away more than a quarter of a million dollars, in 1891 more than half a million, and in 1892 more than $1,350,000. The range covered by his gifts was large, with education receiving increased emphasis. Hardly a Baptist college in the land failed to get assistance, while he was giving to numerous other higher institutions. In making grants to Barnard, to Vassar, to Brown, to Oberlin, to Rochester Theological Seminary, and to Adelbert College in Cleveland he tried to interest other possible donors—the Harkness family, for example.

Gradually he hammered out a set of principles by which he tried to lend plan and system to his giving. (1) In assisting colleges, he would not contribute to buildings or current expenses, and would not pay debts; he gave to endowments. Of course, occasional exceptions were made (Vassar soon had a building which the authorities, much against his wishes, named Rockefeller Hall), but in general he stuck to this rule. (2) He refused to let himself be put in positions where he could be dragooned into giving; in 1892, for example, he resigned his trusteeship in Denison University and various colleges, and that same year he declined Seth Low's invitation to serve on Columbia's committee on site. He also resigned in 1892 the presidency of the New York Baptist Union for Ministerial Education. (3) Finding individual gifts to churches, hospitals, and other institutions often badly used, he tried more and more to work only through organized societies. Most of his college gifts, for example, were made through the Baptist Education Society. (4) He insisted that in general he would not give alone, but would expect others to do something toward matching his gifts. (5) And he also insisted that he would never give until he had been convinced that the money would be used economically and efficiently. That is, his money should stimulate philanthropy in others, not repress it, and should go to assist organizations that had vitality, not to bolster dying causes.

So far as possible his giving was done without publicity, and he frequently stipulated that his donation to an institution be anonymous. He had a strong conviction of the *duty* of giving. "I would," he wrote Andrew Carnegie on the occasion of the dedication of the Carnegie Library in Pittsburgh, "that more men of wealth were doing as you are doing with your money; but, be assured, your example will bear fruits, and the time will come when men of wealth will more generally be willing to use it for the good of others." He wrote T. P. Handy that his wealth was a burden mitigated by the pleasure of giving. "I realize that I am a trustee only and cannot shake off the weighty responsibility resting upon me; nor would I if I could." At a time when he had already spent nearly $300,000 in acquiring land for the park he gave Cleveland, the *Plain Dealer* published an attack upon him; but to L. E. Holden, who wrote him about the article, he replied patiently:

There is a great responsibility resting upon the possessors of wealth, and I believe there is on the part of many a growing appreciation of that responsibility. We must be very patient, and persevere in the endeavor to discharge our obligations, regardless of what may be said at the moment. I am willing to wait for a just record of History, and keep trying to do the best I can, with all the light I have. We must expect more or less of adverse criticism, however good our intentions, or correct our actions.

When he made this statement Rockefeller had founded one of the greatest American universities, and his general gifts ran into millions each year. At the end of the eighties he had still been open to some criticism for not realizing that, to keep pace with the growth of his fortune, he must greatly expand the scale of his philanthropies. In 1888 the dividends of the Standard Oil combination were exceptionally high, leaping to $13,705,505.50,

while Rockefeller's gifts were exceptionally low, only about $170,-
000. In 1890, when the Standard dividends came to roughly
$11,200,000, his philanthropies totalled just over $300,000. This
was not enough. He was slow in bringing his benefactions abreast
of the bounties bestowed on him; he was hesitant in recognizing
he must be a trustee on a grand scale. But there was perhaps
reason in his slowness; he knew that to give unwisely might be
worse than not to give at all. Large-scale giving had to be organized as carefully as large-scale business; in dealing with oil he
had worked by a grand vision, a set of practical plans, and a
group of able associates, and in dealing with his fortune he was
ready to wait for something like the same combination. He was
waiting, moreover, for his son to emerge from college and assist
with the burden.

Money is liberty, says Dean Swift, but great wealth is a jailer;
and long before 1890 Rockefeller could realize the truth of the
aphorism. By that year he found the task of dealing with the
applications for gifts exhausting. Every mail brought its crowding
appeals, every day its pertinacious callers. As a friend put it, he
was "constantly hunted, stalked, and hounded almost like a wild
animal."

As his wealth grew Rockefeller attempted constantly to obey
the principle which he repeatedly enunciated: "A man should
make all he can and give all he can." For evident reasons, the
organization best able to help him was the Baptist Church. He
had become its most powerful layman. It contained a number of
highly cultivated, disinterested, and sagacious men who were well
acquainted with social and economic issues; men like President
James M. Taylor of Vassar, Jacob Gould Schurman of Cornell,
W. H. P. Faunce, soon to be president of Brown, Augustus H.
Strong of the Rochester Theological Seminary, Thomas W.
Goodspeed and William Rainey Harper of the Morgan Park
Theological Seminary near Chicago. Already Rockefeller was
giving generously to Baptist missions and schools, and it was
inevitable that under church guidance his benefactions should
extend more and more heavily into the college field.

Between the Civil War and 1900 our colleges and universities
felt two great impulses toward renovation and expansion. Under
the leadership of such men as Charles W. Eliot, Andrew D.
White, and Daniel Coit Gilman, and with the aid lent `by the
Morrill Act, by the revolution in scientific thought, and by

technological advances, higher education was virtually remade. The second impulse appeared as the century entered its last decade. In 1890 the United States could still boast of but two really distinguished faculties, those of Harvard and Johns Hopkins. But by 1905 the scene had changed with startling rapidity. Leland Stanford opened its doors in 1891, the University of Chicago in 1892, and Clark University in 1894. David Starr Jordan, G. Stanley Hall, and William Rainey Harper appeared, and with them such other new statesmen of education as Nicholas Murray Butler at Columbia, Edmund J. James at Illinois, and Simon Patten at Princeton. The universities had shot up suddenly to maturity. Such swift and far-reaching innovations as distinguished new universities like Chicago and Leland Stanford, and old universities like Columbia and Harvard, were made possible by munificent gifts.

It was certain that Rockefeller would take a prominent place in that endowment of higher education which enlisted Carnegie, Armour, Stanford, Jonas Clark, Pulitzer, Duke, and many other men of wealth. He was one of the older figures in the group of business leaders which had arisen since the Civil War; by 1890 he was far on the road to the greatest fortune of them all; and he possessed an ingrained habit of giving in sums large compared with his resources. He was still in the thick of complicated affairs, but he was more and more aware of the duties imposed by the unexpected weight of his fortune. It presented two responsibilities to which he was keenly alive—the lesser of investment, the greater of philanthropy. For many years he had insisted that a large part of the Standard Oil profits be put back into equipment and expansion, while he had reinvested heavily in Standard stock. As late as the middle nineties he purchased large blocks from Flagler, then immersed in his Florida ventures. When the Trust was formed in 1882, Rockefeller had more than one-fourth of its shares, while fifteen years later he owned approximately three-tenths.

This Trust gushed forth such a stream of wealth as no other closely held corporation in the world's history had ever paid, and its annual dividends indicate accurately the rate at which income was flowing into Rockefeller's coffers. In 1887 they reached almost eight and one-half millions, and in 1888 they amounted to $13,705,000. Dropping back in 1889 to $10,620,000, they moved forward again in 1890 to more than eleven millions. For the six years 1885–90 inclusive, the total dividends paid by the Standard Oil Trust fell very little short of sixty millions, of which Rockefeller's share was between fifteen and twenty millions. In the next half-dozen years they totaled more than eighty millions, of which he received a similar proportion.

To invest this money he still possessed no proper mechanism. He depended on the advice of partners, bankers, and friends, with results that were often unfortunate. The lack of efficient system in his benefactions was equally distressing. He had progressed to giving hundreds of thousands annually in helping a wide variety of causes and institutions. With characteristic method, he had adopted careful rules for his philanthropies. But he needed an investigative and administrative office for the work.

It was inevitable that Rockefeller should give to education. But it was not at all inevitable that his first great gift should go to found a university; and for a time it seemed most unlikely that this institution would be established in the West. The steps by which he was led to create the University of Chicago constitute a story of absorbing interest, for it involves a clash of powerful wills and of determined sectional interests, and a division affecting Rockefeller's own family.

East against West; a specialized as against a comprehensive ideal of higher education; a sectarian as against a quasi-secular view—these were the lines along which the conflict between Rockefeller's advisers developed. The leaders of the church wished him to give to higher education. But one set of opinions found a champion in the vigorous mind and imperious will of Augustus H. Strong; an opposite set in the equally powerful minds and tenacious wills of William Rainey Harper, Thomas W. Goodspeed, and Frederick T. Gates. While Strong and his eastern supporters urged Rockefeller to create a great Baptist university in New York, Harper, Goodspeed, and Gates pressed him to establish it in Chicago. A third group spoke for Washington, but it hardly counted.

*A priori,* all the advantages of position lay with Dr. Strong. The friendship between Rockefeller and Strong dated back to just after the Civil War, when Strong, a vigorous young graduate of Yale, was pastor of the First Baptist Church of Cleveland. He was three years Rockefeller's senior. In 1872 he went east to become president of the Rochester Theological Seminary, then and during the forty years of his administration the principal citadel of Baptist orthodoxy. But the friendship remained close. Rockefeller could not but be impressed by the force and positiveness of Strong's stalwart though narrow personality. As we have noted, in 1888 young Strong married Rockefeller's daughter. Dr. Strong enjoyed opportunities of access to Rockefeller that were denied to most men.

Moreover, Strong's plan for a great super-university in New York had a nobility that appealed to any imagination. By 1880 he realized as clearly as Rockefeller himself that the latter was destined to amass one of the greatest of American fortunes. What was the principal need of the Baptist denomination?—indeed, of the United States? An institution of learning, church-controlled, possessing the richest endowment in the world; employing the most distinguished faculty in America; devoting itself entirely to post-graduate work upon a grand scale; drawing the most brilliant young men to its doors by hundreds of fellowships and scholarships, and turning out a constant stream of teachers, writers, ministers, and other professional men to lift American civilization to a higher level. This was Dr. Strong's vision. Before 1885 Strong had unfolded his plan, with eloquence and enthusiasm, to his friend. Rockefeller, he proposed, should give $20,000,000 to set up this great post-graduate university, rising full-panoplied on Morningside Heights in New York.

However, Rockefeller came to regard Dr. Strong, for all his learning, intellectual power, and fervor, as impractical, and to distrust Strong's vision precisely because too much grandiosity entered into it. It is true that Strong finally worked out his plan in some detail, laying down specifications for the highly paid faculty and the hundreds of graduate fellowships; but he did not correlate his super-university with the actual demands of the country and the church. He left that essential link unforged.

Meanwhile, by 1886 the first educational demands had reached Rockefeller from the West. They made little impression upon him at the outset for reasons connected with the minds and personalities of the petitioners. These first petitioners were the president and secretary of the Morgan Park Theological Seminary, G. W. Northrup and Thomas W. Goodspeed; men of ability, energy, and learning, but in Rockefeller's opinion, impractical.

As early as 1880 Rockefeller's pastor in Cleveland had called his attention to the needs of the Morgan Park school established thirteen years earlier. As a result, Rockefeller in 1882 became vice-president of the Theological Union of Chicago, a body which supported the Seminary, holding this post until early in the nineties. He gave generously to the Seminary—$40,000 the first year, and contributions of varying size thereafter. He maintained a large correspondence with President Northrup and Secretary Goodspeed. From them he heard much about the teachers at Morgan Park, including the young professor of Hebrew, William Rainey Harper, with whom he began exchanging letters in 1885. He heard much also of the old University of Chicago, founded by Stephen A. Douglas and others in 1856, with which Morgan Park Seminary was connected, and which was gradually collapsing under a mountain of debt. But his interest was in the Seminary, not in this so-called university— really a very weak fresh-water college.

Rockefeller was therefore a highly sympathetic spectator as in 1886 a double calamity fell upon the Morgan Park Seminary. The struggling little University of Chicago received its death-blow when an insurance company foreclosed a debt of $100,000 upon its site and buildings. Rockefeller had several times helped pay the current expenses of the University. At the same time Harper, the most precociously brilliant figure that western education had yet known, was invited to become Woolsey Professor of Biblical Literature at Yale. The Seminary, bulwarked by its endowment of a quarter of a million dollars, was in no immediate danger. But with its supply of students reduced, for the old University had been invaluable as a feeder, and with its most powerful teacher gone, it would face a troubled future. No one realized this better than Rockefeller. When he first heard, by way of New Haven, that Harper might be called to Yale, he had hastened to write a warning letter to Goodspeed.

Within the next few weeks Harper accepted the Yale offer. In June the first University of Chicago closed its doors. At this moment Rockefeller's fortune was steadily increasing; yet he did not feel justified in giving until a clearly practical plan, fixed in a clearly practical situation, and to be controlled by highly practical men, was offered. As late as February 4, 1888, Dr. George C. Lorimer wrote Rockefeller that, after patient effort, he had not been able to find a western Baptist willing to give even $25,000 to revive the old University of Chicago. "The difficulty," he wrote, "is to make a start in such a way as to inspire confidence and hope all along the line." It was plain that new elements must be introduced into the situation.

Fortunately, between May, 1888, and May, 1889, those elements appeared. In this year nothing less than a decisive revolution in the situation made possible the University of Chicago.

This revolution was initiated by the establishment in May, 1888, of the American Baptist Education Society. Many groups had become concerned over the feeble, chaotic condition of the Baptist colleges and seminaries, especially west of the Alleghenies. A convention was therefore called to meet in Washington to found a special society for raising funds and making plans to better the situation. The convention brought together 427 delegates from 36 states and territories. Its deliberations showed that while the Eastern churches controlled the more wealth, the Western churches had the more members and votes; and the Society was forthwith organized on a broadly representative basis.

The establishment of this society, important in itself, was still more important in bringing into the situation an entirely new figure, destined to exert a profound influence over Rockefeller's whole later career; a man whose importance in various spheres of American effort is yet to be properly recognized—Frederick T. Gates of Minneapolis. To Goodspeed and Strong, Gates was at first simply another Baptist minister with a strong interest in education. When he was appointed executive secretary of the new society it seemed to these men that nothing had occurred save the addition of another energetic cleric to the group studying educational problems. But from Rockefeller's point of view, it soon became clear that the addition of Gates had radically changed the whole equation. Rockefeller had probably never before heard of him. But the two men had not long corresponded, and had held only one or two conferences before Rockefeller realized that he could at last begin to discuss a great educational gift upon a practical, dependable basis; that in Gates he had found a man who, when assisted by Goodspeed and Harper, could build a firm bridge between visions and realities.

When this highly realistic man took hold of the situation, he was certain to bring some new result out of it. Gates steered the shrewdest possible course. As soon as elected, he informed Strong and others that he intended to do what they had previously advocated—make a survey of the Baptist educational field; and they promised him their support. He at once circulated an elaborate questionnaire on educational needs throughout the denomination. Then, taking the results and all the other matter on education he could find, he settled down at Racine to digest his data. He quickly became confirmed in the view that the primary need was the establishment of "a powerful college to become later a University, on the ruins of the old University of Chicago." He then wrote out an eloquent report which he laid before a Baptist Conference in Chicago on October 15, 1888: "The Need for a Baptist University in Chicago, as Illustrated by a Study of Baptist Collegiate Education in the West." Gates showed that the Middle Western and Plains states contained almost one-half the Baptists of the nation, but that the educational facilities of the church in this area were wretched beyond belief.

It is not too much to say that this report, with the instant approval which it evoked, made Rockefeller's choice of the West for his first gift inescapable. There his money *must* go if it went to higher education at all. On December 3, 1888, the executive board of the Education Society met in Washington, and unanimously approved Gates's proposals. Every one present understood that this action would have a powerful effect upon Rockefeller, who, as Gates put it, had been "waiting to hear the voice of the denomination."

Another factor of unquestionable importance in Rockefeller's changing views was the position taken by William Rainey Harper, whose genius, learning, and energy he fully appreciated. While Harper had told both Rockefeller and Strong that he would be ready to devote his life to a university in New York, his heart really lay with the Western enterprise—and Rockefeller saw it. With Harper, any university would soon become great; without him, its future might be dubious.

Meanwhile, the executive board of the Education Society had met in Washington in the last days of 1888, and Gates had submitted a report urging united support for the founding of a new university in Chicago. The board unanimously approved the Chicago plan. Then Gates sent Rockefeller a letter intended to resolve some of the last difficulties lying before the great project.

Rockefeller, as Gates learned, still felt two grounds for perplexity. Harper and others were urging him to give a large sum of money to erect a university of great immediate strength.

Others were advising him that only a college was needed. He inclined to some compromise action, partly because he did not have three or four millions immediately available, and partly because he believed in letting institutions grow from modest beginnings. He was also troubled whether Harper would take charge of the institution. Of course the Yale professor would gladly accept the presidency of a great university; but if Rockefeller established merely a college, would he consent to be its head? Gates suggested a way past these perplexities. In a long letter, he proposed that Rockefeller at once set up a college, but with plans for its early expansion into a university; and that Harper remain at Yale, giving his advice while the institution was in its formative stage, and then become head as it grew larger. Characteristically, Rockefeller gave no indication of his feeling about Gates's ideas. But he did write Harper that he had come to feel that it might be wisest to give Chicago a college, and leave the university to a later date.

A little later he had Gates and Morehouse lunch with him. After they had risen, Rockefeller suggested that since he was about to leave for Cleveland, and Gates was going back to Chicago, they take the same train. They did so.

"Of course I was on the crest of anticipation," the secretary wrote later, "expecting a long, interesting, and possibly decisive conversation." He thought it best to let the head of the Standard Oil open the Chicago subject. While waiting for him to do so, he studied his companion. "I observed the neatness of Mr. Rockefeller's clothing," Gates writes. "It was spotless but very quiet and inconspicuous, though of the costliest materials and workmanship. There was a conspicuous absence of jewelry and ornament. No watch guard or chain was visible, no rings, and not even a pin in his necktie." He was struck by Rockefeller's solution of the problem of tipping; he held out a handful of change and let waiters and porters take what they thought their due. All evening he waited vainly for his companion to open up the great subject. When they retired, Gates felt a miserable, disappointed man. But Rockefeller appreciated the educator's forbearance. Next morning he began to question Gates closely about the Education Society. After talking freely of its personnel and of Gates's part in the work, he remarked that the Society might "become a relief to him"; he thought of making important gifts through it. In parting he requested that the interview be held confidential. Gates was encouraged.

He had good reason, for the situation was now approaching its climax. On this trip Rockefeller was really appraising Gates, and assuring himself of the secretary's capacity and dependability. He was more than satisfied, and from that date the dynamic secretary began to take the leading part in the negotiations. Once Rockefeller was certain that Gates could be trusted as he already trusted Goodspeed, and once he felt a fair assurance that Harper's incomparable services would be at his disposal, he would be ready to move decisively. When Gates suggested that the executive committee of the Society should appoint a group to go to Chicago, talk with churchmen, inspect available sites, and discuss details, Rockefeller warmly approved the step. He wished this body to prepare a *definite* plan, including proposals for raising funds from other sources, and an outline of the departments of the university. He himself suggested several members of the committee, which, minutely advised by Gates began its work in March. Its nine members included Harper, E. Benjamin Andrews, President James M. Taylor of Vassar College, Dr. Henry Morehouse, head of the Home Missionary Society, and Charles L. Colby.

All the factors essential to a final decision by Rockefeller had now been, or were rapidly being, supplied. First, the existence of a genuine need and of a real popular demand had been established by Gates's telling report. Second, the denomination had been fairly united behind a course of action; Morehouse, Gates, and others had done that. Third, the scheme for a Western university was now being placed on that foundation of coöperative giving upon which Rockefeller based all his philanthropies. He would give but moderate sums until it had taken root, and others would be asked to give with him. Gates and Goodspeed would help find the funds. Finally, the personal elements that were all-important to action by Rockefeller had now been supplied. Three men stood ready to offer the new Western university precisely the leadership it would require. With Gates as principal money-raiser and guardian of funds, with Goodspeed to furnish his wide influence in the West, his learning, and his business capacity, and with Harper to supply his genius for creative planning, the university was assured of success. These three men, different yet complementary, were figures whom any institution might be proud to have in the forefront of its history; and their united enthusiasm for the project made Rockefeller feel that it was at last safe to act.

The final scene has been memorably described by Gates. In May, 1889, Rockefeller called him to New York just before the annual Baptist gathering, which was to be held in Boston. The report of the committee which had visited Chicago was now ready, and contemplated an expenditure of not less than $1,400,000 within four years. Rockefeller and Gates spent the evening together, and next morning Gates came back to breakfast. After the meal they stepped out upon the street and paced to and fro in front of the house. They agreed that at least $1,000,000 would be required to found the institution—that no smaller fund would command confidence. Rockefeller spoke of giving $400,000; but Gates told him that nothing less than $600,000 from him as against $400,000 from the denomination would furnish a real promise of success. They must go before the people of Chicago and the West with the task more than half done.

"At last," writes Gates, "at a certain point near Fifth Avenue, Mr. Rockefeller stopped, faced me, and yielded the point. Never shall I forget the thrill of that moment. I have since been intimately associated with him. I have seen him give $10,000,000, $30,000,000, $100,000,000, but no gift of his has ever thrilled me as did the first great gift of $600,000, on that May morning after those months of anxious suspense."

The date set for the meeting of the Baptist Education Society in Boston that year was May 18, and the place was Tremont Temple. Gates, journeying northward with an elated heart, found several hundred delegates present. The executive board had reported in favor of the establishment of a well-equipped college, later to become a university, in Chicago, and a motion was immediately made that this action be endorsed. Several speakers were heard. Among them was Dr. Strong, who declared that although he still believed that it would have been wisest to found a university first, he would give his cordial blessing to the college. The way was thus opened for unanimous approval of the report. Then Gates, as secretary, stepped forward.

"I hold in my hand," he said, "a letter from our great patron of education, Mr. John D. Rockefeller—" Here he was halted by wild applause.

"A letter," he went on, "in which, on the basis of the resolutions adopted by our board, he promises that he will give six hundred thousand dollars—"

Again he was interrupted by tremendous cheering. When order was restored, the assemblage rose and united in singing, "Praise God from Whom All Blessings Flow." Thereupon it sent Rockefeller a telegram announcing that the denomination had received "with unparalleled enthusiasm and gratitude" the announcement of his "princely gift."

Rockefeller had exacted from Gates a promise that the pledge of $600,000 should be kept entirely secret until the Education Society had committed itself to the establishment of the college in Chicago. If the Society had failed to do this, then the pledge was to be returned to him undelivered. He wished the denomination to make up its mind upon the new institution in perfect independence.

The two tasks of primary importance which now had to be faced were the raising of $400,000 to meet the stipulations of Rockefeller's gift, and the selection of a president. Within two months, the fund amounted to $200,000, given chiefly by Baptists. Then came the rub, and every new cent was won by hard effort and argument. But the victory was won at last. The Baptists of the city and its vicinity gave $233,000; businessmen of Chicago $70,000; and people outside the city area $116,000—making a total of about $419,000. Prominent among the donors were the alumni of the old University and a Jewish group. Finally, the merchant Marshall Field offered as a site a ten-acre tract valued at $125,000. Rockefeller's principle of conditional giving had after all been vindicated.

With an endowment assured, it remained to plan the institution's work and assemble its staff. This offered problems of a crucial character. Marshall Field's gift had determined the site of the school. The land fronted on the Midway Plaisance, between Jackson and Washington Parks, an ideal site; and an additional area of a block and a half was shortly purchased from Field. When the May meetings of the Baptist denomination were held in Chicago in 1890, Gates told the story of a year's progress with an eloquence which aroused the strongest enthusiasm. The

Education Society immediately appointed the Board of Trustees, two-thirds of whom were to be Baptists. Then important events followed in rapid succession. On July 9, the Trustees held their first meeting; on September 10, the University of Chicago was incorporated; and finally, the most momentous step of all was taken when on September 18 William Rainey Harper was unanimously elected to the presidency.

When Harper hesitated to accept the presidency, Rockefeller was seriously disturbed. Yale naturally made great efforts to keep the brilliant young professor, still only thirty-four. One reason why he hesitated was that, although a born executive, his heart was really in Biblical scholarship—or so he thought. Believing that he could not conduct a university and continue research and writing, he doubted whether he should give up his life's work.

But a larger reason lay in the fact that he did not believe a true university could be founded by a million dollars and ten acres of land. As soon as it was evident that he would be the unanimous choice of the Trustees, and that Rockefeller earnestly wished him to take the place, he made this fact perfectly clear. "There must in some way be an assurance of an additional million," Harper wrote Gates on July 31. "How this is to be obtained, or where, is the question. If Mr. R. is in dead earnest, possibly the case will not be so difficult as we may think." He discussed the situation with Rockefeller in Cleveland. Then, on August 17, he held a conference with Gates, and the two agreed upon an eight-point arrangement under which all of Dr. Harper's principal requests were to be met. The first part of it embodied a plan whereby he could become president of the University, and at the same time maintain his Old Testament research, criticism, and instruction. The most significant article of the agreement went tersely to the heart of the financial problem. "Mr. Rockefeller," it ran, "to give one million dollars as a new unconditional gift, a part of which would go for aid to the Seminary in carrying out the plan." The eighth article stipulated that Dr. Harper was to visit Rockefeller, and accept the presidency on the basis of this program.

Seldom, if ever, has a wealthy man been held up in this fashion! Rockefeller had committed himself to the establishment of a great university. He wished one particular man for president, and knew that the University could not attain its highest success without him. Now this man was coolly informing him that he would not come unless another million dollars was paid into the endowment.

But Rockefeller was quite willing to be held up! Gates laid the eight-point agreement before him at once, and found it acceptable. Harper spent September 4 and 5 in Cleveland, where he and Rockefeller devoted nearly the entire day to the discussion of details. The industrialist then wrote a letter promising an additional million and gave it to Harper for delivery to the Trustees, while Harper began to act upon the theory that he was committed to the presidency. The very day after the interview he wrote Goodspeed that he wished half a dozen acts performed. On the basis of this indicated willingness, the Trustees elected him president; and though he was given six months in which to make his final decision, everybody understood that his acceptance was certain. Indeed, he at once took in hand the plan of organization for the University. Always a terrific worker, he began to concentrate upon the institution the tremendous energy and zeal which, with his powerful brain, enthusiasm for scholarship, and wide knowledge of the teaching world, made him such an admirable choice for the presidency.

The founder had realized when he made his original gift of $600,000 that the sum would be only a small beginning. This fact accounted for the readiness with which he had added a million more as soon as Harper asked for it—a million which rendered possible the immediate expansion of the college into a university. His letter to the Trustees, dated September 16, 1890, declared that of the new fund, $800,000 was to be used as endowment for non-professional graduate instruction and fellowships, while the remaining $200,000 was to go to the Divinity School. In 1891 he gave another million, deliverable March 1, 1892, specifying that the "principal of the fund is to remain forever a further endowment for the University, the income to be used only for the current expenses and not for lands, buildings, or repairs."

He watched with equal interest the work now being done in Chicago to match his own donations. On April 7, 1892, Marshall Field offered to give $100,000 upon condition that a total of $1,000,000 were raised within sixty days; a period shortly extended to ninety days. At the end of the second month only a little over half of the amount had been subscribed. But within a few days a gift of $150,000 from Silas B. Cobb, an early settler of Chicago, lent a strong impulse to the campaign, and before the allotted time was up, $1,000,000 had been subscribed. Sidney A. Kent gave $235,000. The million-dollar fund assured the erection of eight buildings in addition to those already under way. With total resources of more than four million dollars, the institution now seemed certain of a place in the very front rank of American universities.

Thus the heads of the University with rising confidence, approached October 1, 1892, the great day on which it was to throw open its doors. Harry Pratt Judson writes that he spent the previous night working with Harper on details of the opening. They labored until nearly midnight. When they had finished, Harper threw himself back on the sofa and exclaimed: "I wonder if there will be a single student there tomorrow!" The next morning the bells sounded, the 120 members of the faculty waited in their classrooms, and nearly six hundred students began the work of the year. The University of Chicago had commenced its great career.

Before the University had completed its first year the panic of 1893 had descended upon the United States. The University of Chicago had undertaken a gigantic work, which would have taxed its resources to the utmost even in ordinary times. It could not have met the heavy strain so suddenly thrown upon it but for the generosity of Rockefeller and others.

Fortunately for the University, Rockefeller had made it a Christmas gift in 1892 of another million dollars. This new gift was not immediately deliverable, and no income from the bonds would be available until 1894. To meet the immediate financial exigencies, therefore, Rockefeller gave $150,000 outright, making it applicable to any University need; while Martin Ryerson, head of the Board of Trustees, advanced $100,000. Then in the fall of 1893, when the panic seemed at its height, Rockefeller unexpectedly made another large gift. The officers of the University had just launched a campaign to raise $350,000 more, and thus obtain a conditional gift of $100,000 from Martin Ryerson. Rockefeller wrote the Trustees on October 31, 1893, that he would contribute $500,000 with the proviso that the terms of the Ryerson grant should be fulfilled. Despite the terrible economic storm, the stipulations attached to this gift were met.

Even in these years of depression, the activities, the student-body, and the expenditures of the University all increased. The annual expenses went above $500,000, above $600,000, then in 1896–97 to nearly $700,000. The deficits went up, too; all efforts to hold them somewhere near the $50,000-a-year mark collapsed in 1896–97, when they amounted to nearly double that sum. Rockefeller was troubled by this inability of the University to make two ends meet.

The result was his $3,000,000 subscription of October 30, 1895. It gave one million outright, and two millions in amounts equal to the contributions of others, if paid in before January 1, 1900. Under the terms of this new gift, the University confronted the task of raising $2,000,000 from other persons within a little more than four years. It seemed a formidable undertaking. In fact, it remained an extremely difficult task even after Helen Culver, in 1895, turned over to the University properties which she valued at $1,000,000. Month by month, year by year, the fund grew—but not fast enough. Rockefeller extended the period until April 1, 1900. The last day but one arrived, with the Trustees and officers of the University in a state of intense anxiety. Then came a telegram from Gates which banished every apprehension:

"I have secured valid pledges from friends of University sufficient to cover whatever may be found on examination to be the actual shortage . . . and you can therefore announce the success of the movement."

The University never made any inquiry as to the identity of the "friends" thus mentioned. Its heads suspected that they were found in Rockefeller's own family. Thus as a result of his pledge of October 30, 1895, more than $5,000,000 was added to the resources of the University; an amount which, coming at a critical period in its adolescent growth, was simply invaluable.

Great as this accretion was, more gifts were to come. In December, 1900, as a new Christmas gift, Rockefeller gave $1,500,000 more, of which two-thirds was for endowment and one-third for general purposes. The following year came another Christmas gift of $1,000,000, and in December, 1902, $1,000,000 more; making in all, by that date, a total of almost $10,000,000 furnished to the University. And even this proved but a beginning.

Twice during the first ten years of the University, and only twice, Rockefeller visited the campus. He came first for the quinquennial celebration of July, 1896. It was a gala occasion for the University and the city. He watched the laying of several cornerstones, sat under two sermons, and heard the students sing:

> John D. Rockefeller, wonderful man is he
> Gives all his spare change to the U. of C.

Rockefeller was present again at the decennial celebration in June, 1901; a still more imposing occasion, for the University had grown steadily, and the cornerstones of three new buildings were laid. Once more he was the central figure at a convocation held on June 18 in a great tent set up in the central quadrangle. Once more he praised the work done by the University officers and its friends in the city.

His gifts continued. We may here note that by 1910, when he gave ten millions, they aggregated approximately $35,000,000, as against $7,000,000 given by others; while his son and the directors of his benevolent boards made additional grants from his fortune, until by 1941 the total well exceeded eighty millions.

As remarkable as the size of the gifts was the spirit in which they were made. Rockefeller asked and expected less from the University of Chicago than any other great benefactor of a similar institution had ever asked. He refused to let it take his name. He refused to assume the slightest voice in its management. He declined to visit it except on two great occasions when a refusal would have seemed ungracious; and then his visits were brief and his role was as inconspicuous as he could make it. Not until after his death was a building on the campus named for him—the chapel then becoming Rockefeller Memorial Chapel. He asked, in fact, for nothing, though he was deeply appreciative of what gratitude was shown him. He was one of the best friends of academic freedom in the country, for by giving the institution tens of millions without the slightest interjection of his own personality, he set a valuable example to all other wealthy men. When Edwin E. Slosson published his *Twelve Great American Universities* in 1912, he categorically declared that—as the whole intellectual world knew—the university which Rockefeller founded was one of the freest centers of research, publishing, and teaching on the globe.

# CHAPTER XI

# NEW AIDES:
# GATES AND THE SON

IN TWO respects, by the early 1890's, Rockefeller was need-
lessly overburdened. While bearing the still inescapable responsibilities of the Standard Oil, he had failed to find deputies
to help him with his ever more heterogeneous list of investments,
or expert guides in the field of philanthropy. His secretary
George D. Rogers in the summer of 1893 made up a rather appalling list of his principal holdings apart from the Standard,
natural gas, and his houses; they were no fewer than sixty-seven
in number, aggregating $23,375,000. Of this amount $13,750,000
was invested in sixteen railroads; $2,800,000 in nine mining
companies; $2,100,000 in various industries—paper, nails, soda,
timber, and so on; and $1,180,000 in nine banks and investment
companies. He had an interest in nine real estate companies,
six steamship lines, and two orange groves! Rogers quite properly
urged that Rockefeller stop putting large funds into enterprises
which others ran, either losing his money or using it to make
fortunes for themselves; he should control the principal businesses
he was financing through an able deputy or deputies.

If his investments were carrying him into one bog of detail and
confusion, the ever-mounting demands on his purse were leading
him into another. By 1890 he was constantly harried by requests
from men and institutions too important to be thrust rudely
aside. And, significantly, he first attempted a proper organization
for his gifts. One March day in 1891, conferring with Frederick
T. Gates at 26 Broadway upon University affairs, he stopped the

younger man as he rose to leave. "Sit down, Mr. Gates," he re-marked, "I wish to talk with you on another matter."

Rockefeller went on: "I am in trouble, Mr. Gates. The pressure of these appeals for gifts has become too great for endurance. I haven't the time or strength, with all my heavy business respon-sibilities, to deal with these demands properly. I am so consti-tuted as to be unable to give away money with any satisfaction until I have made the most careful inquiry as to the worthiness of the cause. These investigations are now taking more of my time and energy than the Standard Oil itself. Either I must shift part of the burden or stop giving entirely. And I cannot do the latter."

Gates agreed with strong conviction that he could not.

"I think you are the man," said Rockefeller. "I want you to come to New York and open an office here. You can aid me in my benefactions by taking interviews and inquiries and reporting the results for action. What do you say?"

Though Gates by no means realized the full extent of the responsibilities implied, he accepted without hesitation. In September, 1891, he took up his duties in an office on Nassau Street. He was soon appalled by the volume of the demands. The newspapers had now widely publicized Rockefeller's position as one of the world's richest men; an article on great American for-tunes in the New York *Herald* in 1892, for example, estimated the Rockefeller holdings at about $125,000,000. His employer had been driven almost desperate. Gates tells us:

Neither in the privacy of his home, nor at table, nor in the aisles in his church, nor on his trips to and from his office, nor during his busi-ness hours, nor anywhere else, was Mr. Rockefeller secure from insistent appeals. Nor, if asked to write, were solicitors willing to do so. If in New York, they demanded personal interviews. Mr. Rockefeller was . . . hounded almost like a wild animal. . . . But he had determined to escape. He meant what he said. And so, nearly all comers, near or remote, friend or guest, high or low, were blandly sent to my office at Temple Court. I did my best to soothe ruffled feelings, to listen fully to every plea, and to weigh fairly the merits of every cause. I found not a few of Mr. Rockefeller's habitual charities to be worthless and practi-cally fraudulent. But on the other hand I gradually developed and in-troduced into all his charities the principle of scientific giving, and he found himself in no long time laying aside retail giving almost wholly, and entering safely and pleasurably into the field of wholesale philan-thropy.

Rockefeller of course retained a very extensive private list of charities, but even in this the secretary weeded out numerous items. Of the huge stream of current appeals, Gates found that the great majority were personal, selfish, and unreasonable. They came from all parts of America and the world, and from all types of humanity. A large proportion were illiterate. Year by year they increased. Once, just after Rockefeller announced a large gift, Gates found that they totaled more than 15,000 the first week, and more than 50,000 the first month! A single steamer on one occasion brought some 5000 begging letters from Europe. No wonder Rockefeller had approached nervous prostration!

The man whom Rockefeller thus selected as his principal aide in philanthropy was as remarkable as any of his partners in business. In sheer ability he matched Flagler, Rogers, and perhaps even Archbold. Despite certain shortcomings, he possessed an unusual combination of gifts: insight, genuine imagination, analytical power, and vision, backed by unquenchable energy, courage, and an evangelistic fervor. At bottom, he was a businessman rather than a minister or social worker, and he soon gained a reputation for cautious, adroit, and hard-headed conduct in business affairs.

Gates possessed a varied experience. He had been student, teacher, farmer, bank clerk, salesman, minister, and money-raiser; he had become a leader in the Baptist denomination, and was one of the best-trusted advisers of the heads of the University of Chicago. Despite his enthusiasm, he was tough-minded, and never let personal considerations interfere with his business judgment. He combined strong altruism in some directions with strong self-interest in others. When he began advising Rockefeller in business as well as philanthropy his dualism of character increased, for he could be as cold, hard, skeptical, and adroit in managing investments as he could be warm, responsive, and enthusiastic in helping pour funds into some educational or social enterprise to which he had been converted. Altogether, he was a versatile, impressive, and electrifying man; and even while his associates saw his inconsistencies and foibles, they admired his dynamic energy and weight of character.

Inevitably, Gates was soon looking after Rockefeller's investments as well as his philanthropies. Shortly after he came to New York, Rockefeller suggested that whenever he happened on his frequent educational trips to be near one of Rockefeller's properties, he take a day off, visit it, learn all he could, and report. Gates was less reluctant than he seemed. In his *Random Reminiscences* Rockefeller explains that it was for strong common sense or sagacity that he chose Gates. Actually, however, the man knew more about finance and had a shrewder insight into business values than either he or Rockefeller at first realized.

It is not strange that Rockefeller quickly came to trust Gates implicitly. As he writes in his *Reminiscences,* he found in his new assistant "rare business ability, very highly developed and very honorably exercised, overshadowed by a passion to accomplish some great and far-reaching benefits to mankind." Gates was wont to lay his plans, always carefully thought out, in lucid written form before his employer. Once they were accepted, Rockefeller financed them without another word, and to whatever extent Gates asked. He provided Gates with every facility for conducting his work—with confidence, credit, information, and the best of office assistance. In this he simply followed a lifelong rule: to provide conveniences for any energetic, sagacious, and conscientious assistant, whatever his rank or place, which would make his work as easy, and his success as nearly certain, as possible. "I had every needed tool," asserts Gates, "and the machinery was well oiled and without the least friction. No man of serious business responsibilities ever had a happier business life than I. No man was ever furnished with more of the external elements of success, or given better opportunities."

For his part, Gates soon became convinced that Rockefeller was not only a business genius, but one of the most honest and public-spirited industrialists that America had produced. If he had ever questioned Rockefeller's probity or given any credence to the attacks upon him, his doubts completely disappeared.

"In all my acquaintance with him," wrote Gates at the end of his career, "acquaintance covering periods of trial and temptation, never have I ever known him to depart one hair's breadth from the best standards of business rectitude. Every newspaper story I ever have seen, of his supposed complicity in shady transactions, in doubtful mining promotions, in artificial booms, in conspiracies to create panic, in operations of the so-called 'Standard Oil crowd,' in the formation of monopolies, or in the manipulation of freeze-outs, have been falsehoods one and all without even a shred of semblance of basic truth. He has of necessity been annually a large investor. He has bought and he has sold stocks and bonds. It has been necessary for him to keep in touch with the market, to know its feel, and to interpret it as best he could. He has never been a 'bull' or a 'bear.' He has always followed the market, never sought to direct it. In every one of our great panics he did everything possible to sustain prices, and has always been a heavy loser. And when the panic was on and the credit of banks and individuals exhausted he has placed his securities at the . . . call of . . . distressed debtors." Of course Gates knew nothing of the early history of the Standard Oil.

In 1897 a new and still more important lieutenant took his stand at Rockefeller's side—his twenty-three-year-old son. John D. Rockefeller, Jr., was graduated from Brown that year. The young man was well trained. But what particularly distinguished the son was his remarkable earnestness and conscientiousness, and his sense of devotion to great objects. He had no thought of making a career for himself; he was anxious above all to be of service to his father—and to the public.

Early in October he reported at 26 Broadway. His father did nothing either to push or to guide the novice. By this time Rockefeller was withdrawing from the direction of the Standard, and seldom came downtown. The son had no difficulty in deciding that his career was to lie in dealing with the now colossal and constantly growing fortune—that is, in the work of investment and giving. He did represent his father's interests in the Standard's affairs, when necessary, as in other corporations, and for a year or two was vice-president and director of the Standard of New Jersey. But he took no active part in its control. Instead of going into Archbold's office, he entered that of Gates.

The younger Rockefeller gained experience in various ways, and went through much the same course of sprouts that most beginners have to hoe. He had his ups and downs, and one mishap was a bruising affair. It seemed important that he should obtain some acquaintance with security values by buying and selling; and his sister Alta and he became partners in stock investments, dividing their profits and losses. Somehow David Lamar, later termed the Wolf of Wall Street, became acquainted with several of young Rockefeller's associates and told them of certain attractive deals in leather stocks in which he said the very astute James R. Keene was interested. Little by little John D. Rockefeller, Jr., was drawn into a speculation in which he believed that he was acting with Keene. His commitments became greater and greater. Actually Keene had nothing to do with the matter; and when Lamar was supposed to be buying in Keene's name for the joint enterprise, he was really selling for his own account. At last, when called upon to produce certain amounts of stock, he was unable to do so. Young Mr. Rockefeller peremptorily asked him to call at his office. He appeared very tardily, and one look at his flushed face convinced the young man that he was a swindler. The total loss approached a million; but as the son writes, the elder Rockefeller showed an astonishing comprehension, generosity, and patience:

Never shall I forget my shame and humiliation as I went up to report the affair to Father. I had not the money to meet the loss; there was nothing else to do.

Father listened to the story. He did not utter one word of complaint or rebuke. He asked a good many questions—you know how hard he can bear down in asking questions—and probed into every detail of the transaction. It was hard to answer: "Why did you do so-and-so?" "Did you think to ask so-and-so?"

When he had heard the whole story, Father simply said: "All right. I'll take care of it, John." That was all. There was no reproach, not even a warning as to the future. But could any man have given his son a greater incentive to do right and try his hardest to learn the right than Father gave by what he did not say? He wanted me to learn in the hard school of experience how to protect myself, and he was so generous and big that he uttered no word of reproof for my costly mistake.

It happened that "Junior," as most people called him, appeared on the scene just when his services were most needed. The fortune had begun to grow with a tremendous new rush. By 1897 petroleum had become a spectacular source of power as well as light. Gasoline took its place beside kerosene as an indispensable commodity all over the world. The growth of the business was phenomenal. In 1900 and again in 1901 the net earnings of the Standard exceeded fifty millions. In 1902 they were almost sixty-five millions, and in 1903 more than eighty millions. Rockefeller, less and less interested in business, more and more interested in giving, was indeed in danger of being crushed by his accumulations. And he found in Gates and his son just the combination of qualities he needed: Gates endowed primarily with imagination, fire and vision, the son endowed primarily with hard sense, caution, public spirit, and conscientiousness.

Meanwhile, the flow of gifts was also being systematized and accelerated. Besides the grants to the University of Chicago, Rockefeller was making a steady succession of lesser donations. They included gifts to a long array of colleges and universities— Barnard, Wellesley, Vassar, Cornell, Brown, Denison, Lincoln Memorial, Nebraska, Syracuse; gifts to Newton Seminary, Rochester Seminary, and other divinity schools; gifts to the Y. M. C. A., to missions and settlement houses, and to other social agencies; gifts to churches, hospitals, and asylums. No grant was made without careful inquiry, or without guarantees of continuing usefulness.

In making these gifts, Rockefeller, his son, and Gates all acted on the same principle and were animated by the same spirit. It is now clear that in one sense the colossal fortune was largely an accident. Economic conditions would not have permitted such an accumulation before the Civil War, while our economic and social legislation would not have permitted it after the World War; it was a phenomenon possible only in a limited period of our history. Moreover, its ultimate magnitude far surpassed anything of which Rockefeller had initially dreamed. It constituted a tremendous responsibility, a vast opportunity for doing good; and he felt himself not so much its owner as its trustee or manager. He soon learned that the American public (perhaps because they felt that the fortune was largely an historical accident) did not express any special gratitude for the mere fact of its distribution. But discerning people did feel grateful for the care which Rockefeller put into his trusteeship. He, his son, and Gates were determined to employ it as scientifically and thoughtfully as possible. For the devoted labor, forethought, and imagination which they gave to this task, they deserved very warm thanks indeed.

We may add that there grew up in Rockefeller's mind, as the years passed, a semi-mystic conviction that God had lent him the money to be used for the welfare of mankind. He reflected that he had always been a giver, and had always given by the light of fixed rules, conscientiously and wisely; and it seemed to him that Providence had perhaps rewarded him by making him one of the largest distributors of its bounty in all history.

*CHAPTER XII*

# ROCKEFELLER, MORGAN, AND THE STEEL TRUST

AS THE panic of 1893 struck the United States, Rockefeller became involved with the Merritt brothers—"the seven iron men"—and others in the development of the rich new Mesabi iron range in Minnesota; and with this investment one of the most dramatic chapters in his career began to unfold. Chance rather than design led him into this new undertaking. For nearly ten years he had made minor ventures in iron properties. Under the guidance of Messrs. Colby and Hoyt, he had invested in an iron-ore holding near Santiago, Cuba; in several mines on the Gogebic range in northern Wisconsin, including two of the richest; and in Michigan and Minnesota properties. The iron and steel industry of the nation had rapidly expanded during the seventies and the eighties. One new ore field after another around the Great Lakes—the Marquette, the Menominee, the Gogebic, and the Vermilion—had been eagerly exploited. They remade the iron industry of the United States; and yet they represented but a beginning, for other rich fields were to be found. Of these the Mesabi was one of the greatest known to history.

In the spring of 1893 Gates visited Duluth, and went to the Mesabi range in a private car fitted up by Leonidas and Alfred Merritt, where he learned all about their history and their holdings. The Merritts—originally five brothers and three nephews —were a strikingly picturesque group. Interested in lumbering and in seafaring on the lakes, they had become lean, hard-bitten, indefatigable explorers for pine timber. Some of them were convinced that the Mesabi hills, full of iron-veined rocks, where the compass needle spun about like a whirligig, held richer ore deposits than any bed yet known. At various spots they came upon ochre-tinged dirt and felt certain that excavations would show iron. For years they had failed of any real proof, for explorers then believed that the ore would show itself in outcropping mineral veins, whereas actually it lay in loose flat beds beneath the surface dirt. But the Merritts never gave up. They went into the woods looking for pine and iron, and came out thirty days later "skin poor." Derision was hurled at them, but they kept on.

By methods too common in that day, but not fit to bear close scrutiny, the Merritts obtained control at preposterously low rates—less than a dollar an acre—to a great part of the Mesabi lands. They first tried to induce one of the northwestern roads to build into the ore field. Failing in this, they organized their own company, and by 1893 held part-ownership of a 66-mile line, poorly built and unballasted, connecting the Mesabi with the lakes at Superior. To achieve this railway, to lease land, and to acquire large equities in six separate mining companies along the range, the Merritts had run deep in debt. At the end of 1892 they owed fully $2,000,000 and probably much more; yet they planned to lay more track to Duluth, to buy hundreds of ore-cars, and to build costly ore-docks at the new Duluth terminal.

Obviously, the Merritts were headed for trouble, particularly as every omen early in 1893 pointed to the imminence of hard times. Yet nothing could restrain them, for Alfred and Leonidas had an indomitable faith in the mines and railroad which they partly owned. Their partners in the road, chiefly Minnesota contractors and bankers, sternly opposed the Duluth extension and the ore-docks. But the Merritts, with what their biographer calls "maniacal eagerness," broke with these partners and went ahead. By operations of a decidedly sharp character, which aroused lasting resentment in Duluth, they bought enough stock (paying in time notes) to gain complete control of the railroad.

In the very midst of the panic of 1893 when the Merritts were on the verge of catastrophe, Rockefeller came to their rescue. On Gates's recommendation, he had bought $400,000 of the first mortgage gold bonds of the railroad from the Mesabi field to Superior; apparently a sound investment, for in 1892 Henry Oliver of Pittsburgh had agreed to take out at least 400,000 tons of iron ore a year. Having invested so much, he and Gates reluctantly concluded that he might well go further in trying to save the line. Leonidas Merritt and his ally Charles H. Wetmore came to Gates with a series of proposals which meant the transfer to Rockefeller's broad shoulders of the load now crushing them. Their ideas were discussed, amended, and put into a set of agreements which were shortly bound together in one contract. The arrangement resulted in the formation of the Lake Superior Consolidated Iron Mines Company, a holding company chartered under New Jersey laws. To this company the Merritts turned over their equity in the six Mesabi mining companies and the railroad and ore-docks, while Rockefeller transferred to it his iron holdings in the Mesabi and Gogebic ranges and in Cuba, and in the West Superior Iron & Steel Company. He further advanced $500,000 to meet the immediate needs of the railroad, later adding $1,500,000 more, while he lent Merritt and Wetmore as partners considerable sums in cash, and advanced the Merritts personally $150,000 to enable them to hold their collateral. He was bailing them out.

The Merritts took stock in this Lake Superior Consolidated, thus controlling its operations to suit themselves; Rockefeller took first-mortgage six per cent bonds. Being ill-advised and greedy, the Merritts at once watered the stock heavily, issuing a total (at $10 par) of $26,050,000, of which they received about $10,000,000. That is, they had exchanged about $2,000,000 of mining and railroad stock, bought largely with other people's money, for five times as much in the stock of the new company. Watered though the issue was in values of 1893–94, eventually its par proved small in comparison with the actual worth of the Mesabi mines. The jubilance of the Merritts when they made this agreement with Rockefeller was unbounded. "The days are past when we rate ourselves as paupers," they declared. "Perfect confidence is restored." On July 12, when the vital contract was signed, Lon begged permission to visit Rockefeller's office and shake his hand.

The railroad was at once pushed to completion. Unhappily, Lon and Alfred Merritt, as managers of the Consolidated, at once fell into fresh difficulties. The iron-mining industry fell into a period, to use the words of one of its historians, of "ruin-

ous prices, contracted credit, limited consumption, sharp competition, ineffectual attempts at combination to hold up prices,
failure of the weak companies, and growth of the strong ones."
The Merritts failed to sell any large quantity of Mesabi ores.
Not only were most blast-furnaces cold, but even had demand
been high the Mesabi ores would have come into use but slowly.
When the loose powdery ore was charged in furnaces designed
for the old rocklike mixture, the results were unfortunate; sometimes it suddenly exploded, wrecking the furnaces, and sometimes
it blew out of the top in a fine hot dust, settling on neighboring
buildings and provoking lawsuits. A new type of furnace had to
be designed. Gates declares that "speaking with substantial accuracy," no mining company made a dollar out of mining Mesabi
ores in the first decade after their discovery.

Caught in these new pressures, Alf and Lon Merritt besought
Rockefeller for fresh help. This he felt unable to give; by the
autumn of 1893, with the panic at its worst, he had advanced
almost $6,000,000 to fifty-eight different men and companies, all
desperate and all unable to obtain money at the banks; and to
do this he had himself borrowed between three and four millions.
Thereupon the Merritts offered to sell him $900,000 worth of
Consolidated stock at par; and although this was fully $2 a
share above market value, and the stock was paying no dividends,
he took the block. In paying for it, he gave the Merritts an option to repurchase $550,000 worth within a year at the same
price, at six per cent interest; in other words, he gave them a
year—and would have given them more had they asked it—
to work their way to solid ground. Indeed, Rockefeller actually
carried two of the Merritts, Lewis and Hulett, for more than
seven years, until they sold their stock to the United States
Steel. Had Lon and Alf pursued the same course, they could
have delivered their 55,000 shares to the United States Steel
in 1901 for $9,190,000 in cash.

Instead, in 1894 they fell under the influence of a Duluth
attorney Anak A. Harris, who persuaded them to levy open war
upon Rockefeller. They still needed money; very well, Harris
would show them a cheap way out. Like all other mining properties, some of those which Rockefeller had put into the Consolidated had become embarrassed. Moreover, they had been
put in at inflated valuations; not such inflations as those attached to the Merritt's properties, but nevertheless substantial.

It is unnecessary to go into the litigation which Harris thus provoked. The upshot was that the suit was compromised out of court. The Merritts signed a complete retraction of the charges against Rockefeller; and Rockefeller—not because he felt he owed them anything, but because he wished to cut the litigation short, because he was anxious to help the innocent creditors to whom the Merritts owed money, because he needed the good will of Minnesota for his iron business, and because he wanted the brains and energy of some of the Merritts themselves—paid $525,000 in satisfaction of all claims. Subsequently a suit between Alf Merritt and the precious Anak Harris exposed some of the facts respecting what Gates calls their attempted frame-up.

Rockefeller's huge new iron-ore holdings furnished him one of the most interesting problems of his career—and also one of his most remarkable business opportunities. His wealth gave him great advantages in dealing with these ore fields. A process of business consolidation took place in this area with a rapidity which one historian calls "as inevitable as unexampled." At the outset, in 1891–93, the ore fields—rapidly being enlarged by new discoveries—were held by numerous individuals and companies. While for a short time the Merritts had exuberantly believed that they could control all the really valuable mines, they soon found that many other owners had obtained important sites. But the grim depression of 1893–97 worked a rapid transformation. When the economic storm ended, the ore fields were dominated by three great corporations: the Oliver Iron-Mining Company, the Minnesota Iron Company, and Rockefeller's Consolidated Iron Mines. A fourth large-scale producer, James J. Hill of the Great Northern, was just entering the field.

Rockefeller and Gates held long discussions upon the Mesabi deposits, which Gates had carefully inspected. Rockefeller also read reports from experts and debated the matter with various business advisers. His natural instinct was to increase his holdings in the field. He had followed the process of acquisition in the oil industry; now, having been led by accident into the iron-ore business, he found himself holding some of the finest ore beds. The railroad to Lake Superior was under his control. Should he back out or go boldly forward? His answer was never in doubt. He wished to find diversified investments for his enormous income, already perhaps above $10,000,000 a year and irresistibly expanding. He had acquired an important share in the cheapest sources of petroleum; why should he not turn to iron ore for a similar triumph?

"When the fright of the panic period subsided," he writes, "and matters became a little more settled, we began to realize our situation. We had invested many millions, and no one seemed to want to go in with us to buy stock. On the contrary, everybody seemed to want to sell. The stock was offered to us in alarming quantities—substantially all of the capital stock of the companies came without any solicitation on our part— quite the contrary—and we paid for it in cash." By these stock purchases he rapidly added to his holdings in the Consolidated, making his control absolute. Under Gates's astute management, the Consolidated increased its ore holdings by both purchase and lease. At the time this was done, the market for ore was wretched, and the future of the new range seemed to many experienced men a gamble.

The rise of Rockefeller as one of the potential chieftains of the steel industry was a spectacle which seized powerfully upon the imagination of most Americans. He and Carnegie seemed to confront each other like two armed barons of feudal days, meeting on the tented field with a crowd of retainers at their backs. Sensational newspaper writers attributed a grim personal rivalry to them. The ruler of oil against the ruler of steel, the two richest men in the world, the two strongest industrial organizations ever built, locked in implacable combat—this was a vision which excited a host of Americans.

As a matter of fact, Rockefeller and Carnegie were personally always on the best of terms, and equally averse to any "battle." Both always read with amusement the press comments on their supposed rivalry in benefactions. Charles M. Schwab later recalled their exchange of Christmas gifts one year—Rockefeller sending Carnegie a paper vest that had cost a few cents, and Carnegie favoring the abstemious Rockefeller with a bottle of his best whisky! Nevertheless, Rockefeller was not averse to making the most of his position.

"I was astonished," he later stated, "that the steelmakers had not seen the necessity of controlling their ore supply." Carnegie's biographer confesses this hiatus gave Rockefeller the opportunity of inserting an effective entering-wedge. "To slip between the steelmakers and their raw materials—here was another opening for the talent that had constructed the greatest trust in the world." Some of Carnegie's associates began to feel a decided nervousness lest the cool-headed oil magnate should decide to enter upon iron manufacture in rivalry with the Scot.

Rumors began to circulate to the effect that Rockefeller's agents were looking for the best sites on the Great Lakes— at Duluth, Chicago, Cleveland, and other cities—for new steel mills. Indeed, the circulation of these rumors by no means injured Rockefeller's position. The fields from which iron deposits could be shoveled out for a few cents a ton gave him a valuable asset; the brains of the "Rockefeller crowd" were hardly to be matched elsewhere; and Carnegie himself had publicly admitted that the Pittsburgh area was now less suited to steel manufacture than certain Northwestern districts. Adding to these advantages the ten to fifteen millions a year that Rockefeller had to invest, the powerful grip that he was fastening upon Great Lakes shipping, and his genius for organization, he held assets that gave the Carnegie group genuine reason for worry.

But Rockefeller, however carefully he masked his intentions, never for a moment thought of going into the manufacture of iron and steel. His desire was always to consolidate one domain before moving on to the conquest of another, and he perceived that to make sure of supremacy in ore and ore-transportation would require all his energies. He comprehended the bargaining advantage he gained from the reports which ran through the American press in 1895. "Within six months," declared a Pittsburgh dispatch, "it is quite probable that plans looking forward to the construction of a gigantic steel plant on the banks of Lake Erie, at a point near Cleveland, will be well under way."

Actually, however, he was anxious to decrease his business cares, and he knew that so strange, difficult, and speculative a business as iron and steel would be risky in the extreme. He would face the competition not only of Carnegie and Frick, so strongly entrenched, but of the fast-rising Illinois Steel Company under Elbert H. Gary, and other strong corporations. The result would be just such a mutually destructive warfare as he had abhorred in the early years of the oil-refining industry. He perceived that wisdom dictated an agreement with the Carnegie-Oliver interests by which, in return for his promise to abstain from competition in iron and steel manufacture, they should promise to refrain from unrestricted competition in ore production.

In December, 1896, an epochal bargain was therefore struck— and not so much a bargain as an alliance. The plan had been born in the fertile brain of Oliver. It was agreed that the Carnegie-Oliver group should lease the principal mines of the Rockefeller organization for fifty years at the low figure of 25 cents a ton. They were to take a minimum of 600,000 tons a year from these mines, and an equal amount from their own shafts, and to ship the total of 1,200,000 tons over Rockefeller's railroad and the great line of ore-carrying vessels that Gates had been building up. Thus, the Carnegie-Oliver interests attained a preeminent position in the control of cheap iron ores.

Under the new arrangement, while the Carnegie Steel Company gained an assured supply of inexpensive ore of high quality, Rockefeller gained an assured supply of freight for his railroad and steamship line. For the time being Carnegie kept out of transportation, and Rockefeller out of steel manufacture. It might seem that Rockefeller assumed the greater risk. The Carnegie group invested no capital beyond the mining machinery and similar outlays, and if any of the ore-beds became prematurely exhausted, Rockefeller would shoulder the loss. But the Carnegie Steel Company promised in writing that it would keep off the Mesabi range, would buy from Rockefeller alone so long as he could furnish the grade of ore required, and would purchase or lease no iron-bearing lands there. These pledges Gates, who conducted the negotiations for Rockefeller, regarded as "fundamental."

A situation thus existed which pointed to certain obvious conclusions. Further consolidation might be undertaken by Rockefeller, who owned the richest iron mines and the greatest fleet of ore-carriers, or by Carnegie, who controlled the strongest mills; but both were really too old, and too much interested in philanthropy. Others must do it. Meanwhile, the two aging leaders, credited by a great part of the public with ambitions which neither entertained, were maneuvering for position, each resisting encroachments, each anxious to exact a fair price for his holdings, but both ready to sell. For three years, 1898–1900, talk of buying and selling filled Wall Street offices, uptown clubrooms, and the financial columns of newspapers.

Only students of industrial and financial strategy would find a detailed rehearsal of the forays and hesitancies of these three years profitable. Nor is our information, despite the reams of gossip printed weekly, at all precise. It appears that in 1899 Rockefeller offered to sell all his mines, ore-field railroads, and steamships to the Carnegie Company for fifty millions, a bargain price which Carnegie should have snapped at had he been really interested in expansion. But he declined. According to Schwab, two factors besides his general reluctance to accept new burdens entered into this decision. One was Carnegie's innate caution, on which we need not dilate. The other involved the character of the Rockefeller lands. We have already quoted the opinion of the Carnegie experts, as reported by Schwab, that the ore was too powdery and the deposits were too meagre in Rockefeller's holdings.

It is also evident that the compact made in 1896 between the Carnegie-Oliver group and the Rockefeller organization by no means operated perfectly. Harry Oliver soon broke the agreement; he began buying Mesabi ores and shipping them east on independent vessels. This flat violation of the compact resulted for a time in an approach to open warfare. The Rockefeller organization intimated that it might set up its own steel mills in the Chicago area, to which it could bring ore cheaply, while it maintained a virtual monopoly of the ore-carriers.

Meanwhile, Carnegie, who from his thirty-third year had talked about an early retirement, had indicated quite clearly his desire to sell out. And in January, 1901, he did sell to J. P. Morgan and his associates, making possible the formation of United States Steel. The Morgan interests bought the Carnegie Company and all its properties for a colossal consideration—$303,450,000 in bonds, with stock worth about $144,000,000 in the market and nearly $200,000,000 in face value. Never before had the world witnessed a sale of such magnitude. Would it assure the country of industrial peace, and would the future justify so high a capitalization?

The pressure of circumstances now rapidly forced Morgan to attempt a union of nearly all the great iron-ore and steel manufacturing interests of the country. Above all, it seemed important for the Morgan group to obtain Rockefeller's Mesabi ore fields and his powerful Bessemer Steamship Company. The holdings built up by Rockefeller and his astute lieutenants constituted the greatest single potential menace to the new steel combination. They comprised the richest iron mines on the face of the planet, and the most efficient carrying fleet the Greak Lakes had yet seen; the Rockefeller organization had only to erect new mills at South Chicago or Cleveland to undersell any competitor. If Rockefeller sold to some third person the threat might become still more alarming. Morgan, prodded by Gary, made up his mind that it was all or nothing; every company of strong financial resources or connections must be included, and Rockefeller's holdings must be among them.

Morgan never like any rival, or any man who had acquired a degree of financial or industrial power which made him a great independent potentate. By nature he was arrogant and imperious, anxious always to play a dominating rôle, and unwilling to admit the equality of any contemporary figure. He had watched the rise of the Standard Oil with a dislike into which entered an element, probably unconscious but real, of jealousy. For his part Rockefeller had always of late years distrusted finance capitalism. The oil magnate, austere, self-contained, and coldly averse to the public gaze, also disliked Morgan's ways: his regal pose, his huge expenditures on his yacht, art treasures, and private library, his versatile interests, his lordly glittering magnificence. It was the Puritan against the Medicean prince, each incapable of understanding the other. In all the more desirable syndicates and promotions which he backed, Morgan never once admitted Rockefeller to the long list of initial participants—and Gates and the younger Rockefeller noted this fact in their tablets.

Apparently the two leaders had thus far met but once. William Rockefeller knew Morgan well, and since William was ready to show a proper deference, Morgan took an attitude of condescending friendliness toward him. Once at William's home on the Hudson, John D. Rockefeller and Morgan were introduced. "We had a few pleasant words," said Rockefeller later. "But I could see that Mr. Morgan was very much—well, like Mr. Morgan; very haughty, very much inclined to look down on other men. I looked at him. For my part, I have never been able to see why any man should have such a high and mighty feeling about himself." There is a world of meaning in those four words: "I looked at him."

The story of what now happened has some comic-opera touches.

Morgan swallowed enough of his pride to make an approach to Rockefeller, asking for an interview at 26 Broadway. To this Rockefeller replied that he had retired from business and never went down to his office, but that he would be glad to see Morgan at 4 West 54th Street, at the latter's convenience, for a purely personal talk. Morgan, taking the stipulation in a Pickwickian sense, went uptown and laid his business before the unresponsive Rockefeller. Gary's biographer tells us how the financier reported this interview the next day. He came in excitedly, throwing his arms up in exultation, and shouting to Gary, "I have done it." The latter naturally replied, "Done what?"

"I have seen Rockefeller."

"How did he treat you?"

"All right."

"Did you get the ore lands?"

"No. I just told him that we ought to have them, and asked him if he would not make a proposition. How much do you think we ought to pay?"

What Rockefeller had apparently done, when Morgan—for once masking his imperious manner behind a show of gracious courtesy—had asked for a "proposition," was to tell him that John D. Rockefeller, Jr., and Frederick T. Gates were in immediate charge of his investments, and that he must see them. Some incorrect accounts of the sequel have found their way into print. The true story of what happened is simple if in its way dramatic.

For some days the Rockefellers did nothing, but marked time. Morgan grew impatient. Finally, H. H. Rogers came to John D. Rockefeller, Jr., at 26 Broadway on the morning of February 25, 1901. He was closely in touch with Morgan, for as soon as plans for the great steel consolidation began to develop, the financier had called in important industrialists to advise him. "Would you like to go with me to meet Mr. Morgan?" asked Rogers, and young Rockefeller said he would. A discussion, since Morgan had asked for a "proposition," seemed much needed. The dapper Rogers, with the young man of twenty-seven, thereupon met by arrangement at 3:30 that afternoon in Morgan's office.

As they were ushered in they found Morgan talking with his partner, Charles Steele, about some legal papers. He took no special notice of their entry. Indeed, young Rockefeller wrote his father next day: "Mr. Morgan was exceedingly rushed with affairs and tired and nervous. He was just a little annoyed that you had not taken the matter up before, having desired to consummate the deal at once." Years later the recollection of John D. Rockefeller, Jr., was that Morgan had raised his head, and with a bull-like glare, had fiercely ejaculated "Well" (and his "Well" could be terrifying): "Well, what's your price?" No mention of this occurs in the letter to the father. Instead, the young man states that when Morgan showed his annoyance over the delay, he explained that an appraisal of the properties took time. Morgan rejoined that a decision must be made within twenty-four hours if Rockefeller was to come in under the existing plan for a merger, but that he might enter with others later. Then he asked for the price.

"He simply desired to have us make an estimate of the value of our properties and state to him on what basis we would exchange our stock for the stock of the consolidation. I replied that my understanding of the negotiations was that Mr. Morgan had come to you desiring to make a trade rather than the reverse; that while, if our minds could meet, we would prefer to be associated with these gentlemen in the consolidation, that we were nevertheless not seeking the trade and quite willing to have things go on as at present; furthermore, that I felt quite confident that you would not in any event wish to put a price upon your own properties; that Mr. Morgan could make whatever offer he thought fair after having become familiar with our properties and that you would either accept or decline."

At this point Morgan was called out. H. H. Rogers, present throughout, advised young Rockefeller not to take that tack; whereupon the young man declared that he had meant every word of it—that "we were absolutely indifferent about coming into the consolidation." It appears from Judge Gary's papers that Morgan had already requested Gary to compute a fair price, and that the judge had furnished him an "outside figure" of $75,000,000 for the Mesabi fields. Rogers now suggested that Frick might act as an impartial valuer. Young Rockefeller agreed that this seemed fair, and Morgan on his return to the office took the same view. His manner was still hurried and haughty. "The whole thing," wrote the young man to his father, "suggested the final sweep-up of the room and we seemed to be the crumbs around the edge which of course must be swept up and expect to be swept up and which it was most annoying to find at this late date still on the floor."

Then ensued some lengthy negotiations. According to George Harvey's life of Frick, that ironmaster went out to Pocantico Hills to talk with Rockefeller. Leaving his carriage at the gate he walked inside the grounds, and found the magnate strolling about. They talked for some time, Frick urging an agreement. "As my son told Mr. Morgan," Rockefeller said, "I am not anxious to sell my own properties. But as you surmise, I never wish to stand in the way of a worthy enterprise. I do frankly object, however, to a prospective purchaser arbitrarily fixing an 'outside figure,' and I cannot deal on such a basis. That seems too much like an ultimatum. . . . Do you or do you not agree that the price these gentlemen propose to pay is less by some millions than their fair value?"

But the Rockefeller papers show that this is a simplified version of what actually happened. Frick did talk with Rockefeller at Pocantico. The main negotiations, however, were with Gates and Junior at their New York office. At first the discussion revolved about various cash sums. Finally, on the morning of March 15, 1901, Gates and young Rockefeller agreed to ask $8,500,000 in cash for the Great Lakes fleet, and for one and four-tenths shares of preferred and one and four-tenths common stock in United States Steel for each share of Consolidated stock held by Rockefeller, amounting roughly to about twenty-five millions. This would mean approximately $41,200,000 par value in United States Steel preferred, $41,200,000 in common, and $8,500,000 cash, or $90,900,000 in all.

That afternoon at 1:30 Frick came in, heard the proposal, pronounced it fair, and posted off to consult Morgan. At three o'clock he returned bearing a counter-offer. Morgan was willing to give one and a quarter shares of both the preferred and common stock; one and four-tenths was too much. Finally, young Rockefeller and Gates told Frick that if he would close the deal that day, they would accept 1.35 shares for each share of Consolidated, and Frick returned to see Morgan. Late in the afternoon he telephoned that Morgan had agreed. "Mr. Gates and I feel well satisfied with the trade," Junior wrote his father. "While we might have gotten 1.40, we have shown a willingness to adapt ourselves and be yielding, which ought to leave a favorable and friendly impression on Mr. Morgan, and things are in such shape that neither he nor his people can ever suggest that you attempted to drive a hard bargain."

On April 2, 1901, the United States Steel Corporation sent out a circular to its stockholders announcing that the Rockefeller properties had been included in the amalgamation. Frick often expressed pride in having helped effect the arrangement. The price of roughly $80,000,000 (face value) in stocks for the Mesabi properties and $8,500,000 for the ore-carrying fleet was actually moderate. Naturally, many observers at the time thought it colossal. These Mesabi mines had never paid a dividend, and a few years earlier experts had talked of them as Rockefeller's folly. The total was approximately one-fifth of what Morgan had paid for all the far-flung properties of the Carnegie Steel Company, representing a lifetime of effort on the part of Carnegie and his partners; while Rockefeller's properties had been acquired within the last ten years, and represented an accidental and to him very subordinate line of endeavor. But as young Rockefeller told Frick, the office already had contracts for the coming year that promised to net $3,000,000 on the properties; and the ores and vessels proved worth far more than was paid.

It is clear from a review of the formation of the Steel Corporation that both Carnegie and Rockefeller were anxious to withdraw from the field. Carnegie later declared that he knew well that he could have exacted a far larger price for his holdings had he retained them some time longer. "I could as well have had $500,000,000 in a few years," he wrote John Morley while the sale was pending. Rockefeller similarly knew that he could have realized a larger sum than $88,500,000 for his ore fields and ore-carriers had he kept them some years longer. But both men were too old to care for the glory of conquering new industrial worlds. Both had large philanthropies in view, and valued the opportunity to obtain capital in forms givable to others. Both believed in industrial concentration, and had a strong faith in the economic and social utility of the work that Morgan was doing in integrating so much of the steel business.

One last incident—and not the least dramatic—remains to be recorded. The man who had done more than anyone else to seize the rich opportunities presented by the Mesabi field was Frederick T. Gates. It was Gates who was responsible above all others for the efficient construction and management of the fleet of ore-carriers. He had spent millions, and tens of millions had flowed into Rockefeller's coffers in return. In the negotiations with Morgan, as carried on through Frick, he had constantly been one of Rockefeller's chief representatives. Doubtless it was he, thoroughly conversant with the wealth of the ore field, who had insisted on the additional tenth of a share. When the deal was completed, and the final papers drawn for signing, he appeared before Rockefeller, and made a complete report. The president of the Standard heard him attentively, and as he paused showed genuine gratitude.

"Thank you, Mr. Gates—thank you!" he exclaimed, with cordial emphasis.

But Gates knew that his services had been worth a material return over and above his modest salary. He stood facing Rockefeller with a strange glint in his eyes.

" 'Thank you' is not enough, Mr. Rockefeller," he replied.

And Rockefeller saw to it that he received a reward commensurate with his sagacity and enterprise.

\*      \*      \*      \*

Early in the new century the simplicity which had characterized Rockefeller's life was decidedly modified by his creation of his wide Pocantico estate.

This new estate began modestly. He needed a place near New York for short summer sojourns and winter week-ends. In 1893 he therefore bought a little group of properties at North Tarrytown, New York, comprising part of the ridge which separates the Sawmill River from the Hudson. Seventeen or eighteen parcels in all, they cost a total of $168,705. On the slope of the principal eminence, Kijkuit Hill, was a comfortable wooden house of homely architecture, but with the broad piazzas that he liked. While it had few charms besides spaciousness and coolness, the views it commanded were magnificent, for anyone standing on the western veranda looked out over the Hudson just where it widens into the Tappan Zee. The main structure of the house was two stories high, with an attic. Simply furnished, the place gave Rockefeller a pleasant place of retirement.

It also gave him a new employment. Piece by piece, he rapidly increased the property, until before the end of the century it consisted of more than 1600 acres. Meanwhile, he was busy transforming its aspect. As plots were purchased he demolished buildings, whisked away fences, and removed unsightly boulders. Ragged clumps of woodland were sheared down, bushes uprooted, and lawns planted. At intervals he broke the open, gently rolling slopes with patches of native forest, or by trees and shrubs which he himself set in. He built many miles of winding drives and bridle-paths, making the most of the points overlooking the Hudson and opening wide vistas wherever needed. In his *Reminiscences* he wrote later that he had always delighted in this "old house where the fine views invite the soul and we can live simply and quietly."

Unfortunately, the house burned down in the summer of 1902. John D. Rockefeller, Jr., at once bought the furniture for another cottage on the estate, somewhat nearer to Tarrytown, and the family occupied this place for the next seven years. Meanwhile, the elder Rockefeller frequently spoke of placing a new house on the top of the Kijkuit Hill, but did nothing about it. He never liked to burden himself with the detail of building operations. His son finally suggested architects to draw plans, and Rockefeller and his wife determined the general arrangement. But when the plans were completed, he did nothing to utilize them. "After a while," writes the son, "I became convinced that the reason he did nothing was because he hesitated to build so large a house, with the additional care which its operation would involve, but on the other hand was too generous to suggest a smaller house, which would not adequately accommodate children and grandchildren. I therefore suggested that the plans be redrawn to provide a house that would fully meet his needs and Mother's, and provide for such guests as they might want to have but go no further in size. This met with Father's immediate approval and seemed to be a great relief to him."

The house, Georgian in style, was immediately erected. Its guest rooms were in the third story, with dormer windows. John D. Rockefeller, Jr., and his wife supervised the construction, and also bought all the furniture, china, silver, glass, and works of art, employing the best advisers. The younger Rockefeller frequently told the architects and decorator that his ideal was a residence so simple that friends coming from no matter how humble an environment, would be impressed by the homelikeness of the house; while those who appreciated fine design and beautiful furnishing would say, "How exquisite!" This combination of simplicity and beauty was attained; Rockefeller and his wife were delighted with it. But it is evident that Rockefeller derived his chief satisfaction at Pocantico not from the house, but from the grounds, which by 1908 approached 3000 acres in extent. To set out clumps of trees, to level hills, to build roads, to open wide views, delighted him more than anything else.

Here he could execute on sweeping lines what he had done at Forest Hill on a small scale. He grew young trees by thousands, especially evergreens, to be used in his planting schemes. When he bought a golf clubhouse at Lakewood, New Jersey, and converted it into another residence, he made a small fortune out of himself by selling it $1.50 or $2 trees which had cost but five or ten cents at Pocantico. He confessed his pride in moving large trees, ten to twenty inches in diameter. "We build our movers ourselves, and work with our own men, and it is truly surprising what liberties you can take with trees, if you once learn how to handle these monsters. We have moved trees ninety feet high, and many seventy or eighty feet. . . . Perhaps the most daring experiments were with horse-chestnuts. We took up large trees, transported them considerable distances, some of them after they were actually in flower, all at a cost of twenty dollars per tree, and lost very few." Careful records showed that the tree-moving campaign of a whole season was sometimes accomplished with a loss of only 3 per cent.

This passion for recontouring land and making fine vistas was one of the oldest and most constant of his life. Like Cyrus the Great, he always pointed with special pride to the trees planted by his own hand. His associates testify that he became expert in all the craft of the landscape architect. "I am thinking of moving that hillock," he would remark, and gaze at it appraisingly. "Offhand, I would say there are just about 650,000 cubic feet of dirt there." He laid out a drive through a deep rock cut; he built a stone wall to hide a railroad. In these years he often kept at his planting, tree-moving, and road building until he was exhausted. He would run the lines for new paths until darkness made it impossible to see the stakes and flags, and then tramp wearily home.

Rockefeller's other recreations had changed. Even when past sixty he continued his bicycle riding and skating. But after retirement he ceased to drive fast trotters in Central Park or on the speed-ways. The stables at Pocantico contained good riding horses for the children, while he and his wife liked to drive a steady pair on sunny afternoons around the estate. Racing, however, was out of the question.

He still went occasionally to concerts, Mrs. Rockefeller and he subscribing to the Philharmonic. He may have attended the opera, for William had a box. But he almost never went to the theatre. His son recalls that when in 1901 Weber and Fields were convulsing audiences with "Hoity-Toity," Rockefeller was prevailed upon to go to the Music Hall to see them. While spectators held their sides, he sat grimly impassive. But when De Wolf Hopper came on with Lillian Russell in a more dignified bit of comedy, he was amused beyond words. Some years later when Rockefeller was in Santa Barbara, his son took him to see William Gillette in "Sherlock Holmes," and that consummate bit of acting he greatly enjoyed. A taste for the theatre, however, was as little in his make-up as a taste for books. He still listened in the evening while Mrs. Rockefeller or Lucy Spelman read aloud, and the family recall his appreciation of Ian MacLaren's *Beside the Bonny Brier Bush.* Like Grover Cleveland, he was delighted by *David Harum.* He read the Bible, devotional or inspirational books, newspapers, and sometimes the principal Baptist journals. But his best books were people.

His principal new recreation was golf, a game now rapidly coming into vogue. The first golf club in America had been the St. Andrews of Yonkers, which built a six-hole course in 1888. A Chicago club completed an eighteen-hole course in 1893, and by the end of 1895 the country had more than a hundred links. By 1900 millions were taking a keen interest in the exploits of the Australian-born Walter J. Travis, who that year won the American amateur championship. The previous February, Rockefeller and his wife were staying at a hotel in Lakewood, New Jersey, with their friends the Johnsons of Spuyten Duyvil. Mr. E. M. Johnson, an enthusiastic golfer, often joined Rockefeller in playing quoits, and at last persuaded him to submit to some golf instruction on a grassy field remote from public view. They took a caddy and a bag of clubs, and Johnson explained the principles of the game. For some days the two men practised in the lonely field, until on April 2, 1899, Rockefeller played his first game on the nine-hole course of the Ocean Country Club. He showed no embarrassment before the curious spectators, and covered the nine holes, some 2800 yards, in 64 strokes; next day he did the course in 61 strokes. As his form improved he became enthusiastic.

He immediately put in four golf holes at Pocantico Hills, and in 1901 engaged one of the early golf architects, Willie Dunn, to lay out a course of twelve holes. A professional from Ardsley, Willie Tucker, came up regularly to give him lessons. At Forest Hill, meanwhile, he had a nine-hole course built, and was tutored by another professional, Joe Mitchell. Here the ground was much more level than at Pocantico. As it was the strokes, not the walking, in which Rockefeller was interested, he provided bicycles for all the players. "I like to play golf as much as possible," he explained, "so I save up energy." This practice he kept up at Forest Hill until the house burned down in 1918, and he forsook the place. In his last years there he even had men on the estate push his bicycle to save him exertion. His favorite companions at Forest Hill included Doctor H. P. Biggar, and the Euclid Avenue ministers.

Like Frederick W. Taylor, the father of scientific management, who braved a good deal of criticism by taking up golf in 1895, Rockefeller employed unusual methods to improve his game. At the suggestion of a friend, he had a photographer come out from Cleveland and make a series of snapshots of his stroke. Studying these, he learned how to get rid of a slice. For a time he hired a colored boy to ejaculate, as he teed off: "Hold your head down! Hold your head down!" To improve his long shots, he had a caddy place a stone slab on his toes to hold them straight as he teed off. When this did not work, he took a wire croquet wicket and fastened his foot firmly before driving. By 1904 golf was his principal amusement, and only very bad weather or an unusual pressure of business kept him off the course for at least an hour daily. E. M. Johnson writes:

Four inches of snow stopped us at Ardsley on December 4, 1904; so I was surprised three days later when Mr. Rockefeller telephoned me to join him at Pocantico Hills for a foursome with Mr. Rudd and Mr. McCormick. When I objected that we could not play in the snow Mr. Rockefeller said, "Just come up and see." I went up and found that on the day before he had sent out men with horses and snowplows and cleared the snow off five fairways, and that the five putting greens had been swept clean. We never had a finer game.

Henry Clay Folger became a frequent partner of Rockefeller's at Pocantico and Lakewood; he never talked about Shakespeare, but he played golf with enthusiasm. So did Father Patrick Lennon of Tarrytown, a young Irish priest. But Rockefeller had to choose his companions cannily. Once Gates, commenting on his apparent loneliness at a Southern hotel, remarked that many men of cultivation in the vicinity would make agreeable associates. "You should not keep to yourself so much, Mr. Rockefeller," he expostulated. "You should call upon some of these man, who naturally wait for you to make the first gesture."

"Well, Mr. Gates," said Rockefeller, emphatically, "if you suppose I have not thought about the matter you are mistaken. I have made some experiments. And nearly always the result is the same—along about the ninth hole out comes some proposition, charitable or financial!"

Landscape architecture, golf, and driving restored Rockefeller's health, which had never been as bad as newspaper articles asserted. In 1909, a writer for *Harper's Weekly* described him, then seventy, as "a hale and hearty athlete, bronzed by daily play in the sun, ruddy-cheeked and clear-eyed, as brisk and powerful and enduring as most men of fifty years." His muscular vigor sufficed for repeated drives of two hundred yards and more. Doctor Biggar liked to give the press brief statements upon Rockefeller's physical well-being. "He will live to be a hundred," he predicted. "He follows three simple rules. First, he avoids all worry. Second, he takes plenty of exercise in the open air. Third, he always gets up from the table a little hungry." Rockefeller sometimes spoke of golf as a touchstone for calmness and honesty. "One of the best places to test a minister is on the golf links," he told his Cleveland Sunday school after announcing that he and the pastor were playing next day. "Even the best of them often lose their tempers." And again he remarked sadly: "I am sorry to say that I have met ministers who did not hesitate to cheat a little on the links!"

Rockefeller still belonged to two congregations. In summer he faithfully attended the Euclid Avenue Church, but since he spent most of his time in the East, the Fifth Avenue Church received most of his attention. The Cleveland church went through serious financial vicissitudes. Under the Reverend L. A. Crandall, who served 1889–92, its building was reconstructed, while other expenses overtaxed its resources. When the Reverend Henry A. Applegarth took charge in 1893, the church, as its historian writes, was "at its lowest ebb." Applegarth, an able preacher who placed it on a solid financial foundation, became a favorite visitor at Forest Hill. But he was never so intimate with Rockefeller as his successor, the Reverend Charles A. Eaton, a gifted Nova Scotian who was pastor of the Euclid Avenue Church 1900–09 and later of the Madison Avenue Church in New York. Entering politics, Eaton finally became one of the leading internationalists in Congress.

At the Fifth Avenue Church Rockefeller always held a position more formal and aloof than that which he occupied in the Cleveland congregation; but the church nevertheless played an important part in his life. He, William Rockefeller, and Bostwick were all trustees. Mrs. Rockefeller took a class of boys and kept it for many years; she remained with a group until they became old enough to go to college, and then begin with a new one. Many of her pupils, looking upon her almost as a foster mother, spent much time at the Rockefeller house. Each spring her class went for an outing on the Palisades, crossing at the Fort Lee Ferry in a noisy body, while she followed in a landau, and a caterer brought a wagon of comestibles. Alta also remained active in the church. Besides managing her sewing school for girls, she taught a Sunday school class for boys which included Charles E. Hughes, Jr., and Albert Spalding.

The West Fifty-fourth Street house became a busy center for all kinds of Baptist work. It was used for missionary meetings, charitable meetings, temperance meetings, and prayer meetings. Young people's organizations met there, as did the board of trustees. Ministers of the Fifth Avenue Church almost became members of the family circle. The pastor when Rockefeller settled in New York was Thomas Armitage, another Englishman, who served more than forty years, and became a great favorite of the Rockefeller children. Visiting ministers were often invited to the Rockefeller house for Sunday dinner. Rockefeller would remark after the sermon: "You have fed us; now let us feed you!" Prominent Baptists from all over the land—Jacob Gould Schurman, President Taylor of Vassar, Doctor Harper of Chicago, and others—were often entertained. Missionaries came and went, some of them becoming familiar figures: Edward Judson, for example, son of the great Adoniram Judson, and John E. Clough, a noted missionary to India. Mrs. Rockefeller's zeal for temperance made Frances E. Willard and Frances E. Barnes frequent guests. The atmosphere of the house was full of religion and good works!

When Armitage retired from the pastorate, Rockefeller and

his brother William served on the committee to choose a successor. Hearing of a brilliant young minister in Springfield, Mass., William Herbert Perry Faunce, they and their wives went up one Sunday to listen to him. They were anxious to arrive and depart unrecognized. At the church door the usher demanded: "You are strangers, are you not? Will you please give me your names?" As the service was just beginning, Mrs. Rockefeller, hastily leaning forward, put her finger on her lips and said: "Sh-h-h! You will interrupt the minister!" A little later Rockefeller almost betrayed their identity. When the collection plate was passed he drew a ten-dollar bill from his pocket. Just as he deposited it he realized that the amount might attract attention, and hesitated. The result was that after the service an officer approached him, inquiring:

"Do you want change from that ten-dollar bill you put in the collection, sir?"

Dr. Faunce was called to New York, where he gave the Fifth Avenue Church fresh life. He was active in the world peace movement, and in various plans for social reform; he was fearless in assailing shams and corruption in the established order. But his administrative energies soon found a larger sphere. In 1899 the trustees of Brown University made him president, and there he remained for thirty years, completing the development of Brown to a true university. He also was often at 4 West Fifty-fourth Street. In view of Rockefeller's friendship with Harper, Schurman, Taylor, and Faunce, four leading educators of the day, the magnate could not be said to lack intellectual contacts. After Everett Colby and Charles E. Hughes became trustees of Brown, a liberal group under Colby's leadership undertook to eliminate the charter provision excluding Catholics and Jews from the board of fellows and board of trustees; and Rockefeller, his son, and Gates gave this successful movement earnest support.

Faunce's most notable early successor was Charles F. Aked, a man of remarkable eloquence, who was called in 1907 from Pembroke Chapel in Liverpool. For some years New York had no preacher of greater declamatory power. He was outspoken on all social questions, denouncing selfish plutocracy, and proclaiming his belief in Socialism "as the expression of human hope and zeal for human brotherhood, of the new spiritual life of the world." He was very different from the gifted man who succeeded him in 1911, Cornelius Woelfkin, a quieter clergyman who possessed rare cultivation and intellectual depth. To him Rockefeller always felt a special devotion.

No matter who was the pastor, the church always played a powerful part in Rockefeller's life. He found refreshment and sustenance in his simple elemental piety. "I can never be grateful enough for all that our church has meant to me," he told a friend in 1917. "Years ago in New York an associate of mine who was a member of a big and fashionable church was eager to have me go in with him. He said to me, 'John, you are too big for the Baptist Church.' I put my hands on his shoulders and replied: 'Henry, I *hope* I'm big enough for the Baptist Church.'"

As the children grew up the Rockefeller circle was expanded by marriage. Late in 1895 Edith, the most individual, artistic, and unconventional of the family, married Harold Fowler McCormick (younger son of the inventor of the reaper), who had graduated from Princeton. They had been brought together in musical and educational activities. Since the bridegroom was ill with a cold, the ceremony was performed at the Buckingham Hotel instead of the church, with a breakfast later at the West Fifty-fourth Street house. McCormick was soon occupied with his older brother in carrying on the harvester works. After the formation of the International Harvester Company he became vice-president, treasurer, and ultimately president of that corporation. Edith went to live in Chicago, where five children were born to them before the marriage ended in divorce in 1921. The union brought the Rockefellers some interesting connections, including the James G. Blaine family—one of McCormick's sisters having married Emmons Blaine. "Madame" McCormick, widow of the inventor, a supporter of numerous philanthropies and a witty, strong-willed person, often visited Pocantico or 4 West Fifty-fourth Street, bringing the breeziness of her vigorous personality.

Then in 1901 the two remaining children married. Alta had become engaged to E. Parmalee Prentice, an Iowan by birth, and a graduate of Amherst and the Harvard Law School. He was an attorney who had practised for a dozen years in Chicago, where he was general counsel for the Illinois Steel Company. He came to New York in 1901, soon joining the firm of Howland, Murray & Prentice, later Murray, Prentice & Aldrich. He became interested in questions of constitutional law, argued cases before the Supreme Court, and wrote two legal books, one on the commerce clause and one on federal power over carriers and corporations. Retiring in 1924 from the bar, he turned to scientific agriculture, making the Mt. Hope Farm near Williamstown, Mass., famous for his experiments, and writing some remarkable volumes on cattle-breeding and the conquest of hunger.

The marriage of John D. Rockefeller, Jr., to Abby Green Aldrich, daughter of Senator Nelson W. Aldrich, whose abilities were rapidly making him the undisputed leader of the Senate, was of course a notable occasion. A talented, attractive young woman, she had become a social favorite in Providence, New York, and Washington. It would have been difficult for many years to say which was the more unpopular with the American masses, the father of the bride or that of the groom; and the press naturally published reams of matter on the union. The Senator was not inclined to let the wedding be a quiet affair. A huge gray awning-pavilion was built at the summer home of the Aldriches at Warwick on Narragansett Bay. Here, in a chamber sixty feet wide and a hundred long, a thousand guests gathered. The same minister who precisely thirty-five years earlier had united Senator and Mrs. Aldrich, Doctor James G. Vose, performed the ceremony. Wine was served, and Doctor Faunce, a total abstainer, innocently remarked over a glass of champagne, "This is the most delicious ginger-ale I ever drank!" Thereafter, John D. Rockefeller, Jr., saw a good deal of the elder statesmen close to Aldrich, notably Senators Platt of Connecticut, Spooner of Wisconsin, and Allison of Iowa; and Rockefeller, who met Aldrich a number of times, heard more about governmental affairs.

The Rockefellers kept two of their children near them. John and his wife settled down at 10 West Fifty-fourth Street, next door, while the Prentices took a house just at the rear, No. 5 West Fifty-third. "Whatever are you going to do with this big echoing mansion?" a Brown classmate of John D. Rockefeller, Jr., asked his wife, soon after they moved in. "Why, fill it up with children!" she replied. Indeed, there were soon grandchildren in both domiciles. All of them thrived and grew except Edith's older son, John Rockefeller McCormick, who succumbed at Pocantico Hills to scarlet fever early in 1901, when not yet four. But the family circle steadily expanded. As child after child arrived in John's household—Abby in 1903, John D. Rockefeller III in 1906, Nelson Aldrich in 1908, and later still Laurance,

Winthrop, and David—the grandfather showed manifest pleasure in his patriarchal position.

To Rockefeller these were in many respects years of fruition and happiness. His health had returned, bringing an elastic vigor. His family grew more varied and interesting as the years passed. He had thrown off his heaviest burdens, and though still a very busy man, he was no longer driven by urgent tasks. He had found fascinating new recreations in his landscape work and golf. Only one dark cloud marred his contentment. Public antagonism toward the Standard Oil monopoly was mounting higher and higher. With Theodore Roosevelt in the White House, huge corporate aggregations were the target of increasingly heavy drives. The attack on Rockefeller personally, far from showing any abatement, was often clamorous in intensity.

But he did not take this popular hostility with tragic seriousness. Mrs. Rockefeller kept a scrapbook in which she pasted newspaper clippings that particularly interested her. Some abusive attacks upon her husband found a place there. Among the cutting was a cartoon which John T. McCutcheon had drawn for the Chicago *Tribune* in 1905. The American Press Humorists' Association had just met in Cleveland. Rockefeller had thrown the Forest Hill grounds open, and when they brought him a badge as honorary member, he conducted them, with a genial smile, to look at what he described as "a chestnut three, four hundred years old." McCutcheon depicted Rockefeller as saying: "Well, now that I have been elected a humorist, I suppose I must make a joke." He doffs wig and coat, and squares to his desk. In a moment he electrifies the group by holding up the joke he has composed: "Mr. John D. Rockefeller entertained a large company at a champagne supper last night. The guests of honor were the Reverend Washington Gladden, Miss Ida Tarbell, and Thomas W. Lawson." Evidently the Rockefeller family had enjoyed this good-natured fling.

# CHAPTER XIII

# ADVENTURES IN SPENDING

WHEN the twentieth century opened amid radiant national prosperity, Rockefeller's fortune was more than ever threatening (as Gates constantly warned) to overwhelm him and his children. At an early date in 1913, it totaled about nine hundred millions—the highest figure it was ever to reach.

This was much the largest fortune accumulated in America up to that time; and the man who held it lived in a way that Morgan or even Carnegie would have considered frugal. Always a giver, he now had both to expand the scale of his benefactions and to change their nature by endowing them with a more scientific quality. He had established the University of Chicago, but that was the merest beginning of his task. To spend hundreds of millions for philanthropic or pseudo-philanthropic objects representing personal whims and casual impulses would have been easy for some men, but intolerable to the systematic and conscientious Rockefeller. Fortunate it was that as he made philanthropy his main pursuit, he found two such aides as his son and Frederick T. Gates.

These two men shared Rockefeller's faith in the four fundamental principles of giving which he had developed during the preceding decades. First, his money should be given, whenever possible, to a work already sufficiently well organized to be of proved efficiency and usefulness. Second, it should, if feasible, be given on conditional terms, so as to stimulate gifts from others. In the third place, it should be used to foster in the beneficiary a spirit of self-help, not of dependence. Finally, the activity aided should in general be of a continuing character, promising to remain vigorous after the aid had been discontinued. Rockefeller had sharp limitations of education and outlook; he was not well read, not much interested in literature, science, or art, not expertly equipped to work with leaders in education and social welfare. But Gates and John D. Rockefeller, Jr., were able to help him plan his benefactions with sweep and imagination, to open epochal new undertakings, and to use his wealth in broad national and international channels. Like Rockefeller, they were able to create bold new designs. Like him, they were ready to put an unresting energy into making an unconventional and creative activity a success. Like him, they delighted in pioneering ventures; and they encouraged him to invest large sums in supporting new ideas, fresh patterns of action, and courageous leaders.

The collaboration of three such men in the work of planning was something new in the annals of philanthropy. Andrew Carnegie ventured into large-scale giving as early as Rockefeller, but his gifts either reflected his personal predilections—and in some degree, as in his building of Carnegie libraries, his quick vanity—or also took conventional lines. Rich men established colleges and universities, libraries and schools, museums and art-galleries. Probably the most original benefaction in America was the Union which Peter Cooper and Abram S. Hewitt had erected for adult education in New York. But the great benefactions planned by Gates and the two Rockefellers cast aside old conceptions and broke intrepidly into novel fields. The trio pooled complementary talents. Gates, with his enthusiasm, vivid speech, bursts of passionate feeling, and roving studies, was a discoverer; the younger Rockefeller had a cultural breadth denied his elders; and the multi-millionaire united precision in studying any plan with zest in bold new undertakings.

Of the three, Gates had the most ideas, and the most dynamic energy, coupled with rare skill in finding talented and influential men to translate plans into realities. He therefore played an outstanding part in organizing the philanthropies. Each of the others, however, played his part well. The young man just out of Brown gave faithful study to every proposal, and developed a keenness of judgment that was invaluable; while the elder Rockefeller brought his shrewd, critical, deliberate mind to bear on every proposal before he said the final word. As he had led in organizing the oil industry with consummate skill, so now he led in organizing the most effective use of private funds for broad human betterment that the world had yet known.

In fairly rapid succession, four great philanthropic institutions were established by Rockefeller and his two aides. The first was the Rockefeller Institute for Medical Research, founded in 1901; the second was the General Education Board, launched in 1903; the third was the Rockefeller Foundation, incorporated in 1913; and the fourth was the Laura Spelman Rockefeller Memorial, which began its ten-year career in 1918. The total of the funds given to these four agencies, estimated at their market value on the various dates of gifts, came to $446,719,371.22. The expenditures of the four, down to the summer of 1951, aggregated about $822,000,000.

Each of the four had its eventful history—a history in which many pages read like a sparkling romance. Each of them brought into fruitful activity a group of devoted and able men, whose gifts sometimes approached genius. It will be long before the world can forget what was accomplished in the Institute for Medical Research by Simon Flexner, William H. Welch, Hermann M. Biggs, and the scientists they recruited—Hideyo Noguchi, Alexis Carrel, Jacques Loeb, and others. The nation ought never to forget the accomplishments of Dr. Wallace Buttrick, Dr. Seaman A. Knapp, and Dr. Abraham Flexner, among others, in fructifying the resources of the General Education Board. The Rockefeller Foundation found brilliantly able heads in Gates, Dr. George E. Vincent (who became president in 1917), and Raymond B. Fosdick. Some men served on two or more of the agencies. For example, Dr. Wickliffe Rose as head of the Rockefeller Sanitary Commission, which later became the International Health Division of the Foundation, did a monumental work in ridding the South (and other lands) of the hookworm plague, and then served for six years as president of the General Education Board. In recent decades foundations of various types have multiplied. It has been generally conceded, however, that the early personnel of the various Rockefeller boards met a standard which has not been equaled by any other body of the kind.

"The most exciting thing in the world," said Charles W. Eliot of the Institute for Medical Research—and to many men it had become by 1910 precisely that. It had its origin in the conclusion of Gates, after a course of rapid reading, that medical science in the United States needed energetic stimulation and development.

In July, 1897, while Rockefeller was spending the summer at Forest Hill, Gates left New York to join his family in the Catskills for a vacation. Several conversations with a young medical student whom he often entertained at Montclair had led him to plan some reading in medical textbooks to ascertain what was the existing state of knowledge among physicians. William Osler's masterly *Principles and Practise of Medicine,* then six years old, was being used in the College of Physicians and Surgeons in New York, and he took a copy of the thousand-page volume with him. To his astonishment, he found it so delightful that he read every one of the close-printed chapters.

Osler's pages indicated that of hundreds of diseases then recognized, the best medical practice did not know any certain cure for more than a handful. For one reason, few disease germs had thus far been identified and isolated. Usually it was nature, and nature alone, that wrought a cure. Gates found a deep skepticism haunting Osler's pages. His chapter on any particular malady usually began with a definition, some account of its incidence throughout the world, and the history of discovery regarding it; he would then proceed to causes, symptoms, and probable course, using the results of innumerable post-mortems; "but when he came to the vital point, namely, the *treatment* of the aforesaid disease," wrote Gates, "our author . . . would almost invariably lapse into a feeble attitude of doubt, skepticism, and hesitation. He would suggest that such and such celebrated physicians at home or abroad had found this or that treatment to be helpful; such had not been his own experience, but perhaps this or that might be found to be useful in some cases." We need not accept Gates's summary of Osler or his gloomy view of the state of medical knowledge in 1897; both exaggerated. But his conclusion that medical science needed the help of advanced research was valid, and it was an important conclusion.

Most American medical schools at this time, even those nominally affiliated with universities, were proprietary money-making institutions, without real endowments or proper experimental facilities; their faculties were composed chiefly of prominent practitioners who taught but did not investigate. Few schools offered any laboratory instruction, and few individuals were engaged in the scientific study of medicine. Those who wished to do more than meet the low requirements for medical practice had to go abroad for their opportunities.

Gates became convinced that the advancement of medicine depended upon provision for advanced experimentation, permanently established, and carried on by groups of expert men with ample salaries and resources for uninterrupted investigation. The founding of an institute for medical research in the United States therefore seemed to present Rockefeller with an opportunity to do the nation, and perhaps the world, an immense service. Fortunately, Gates's overmastering enthusiasm was not dampened by knowledge of the difficulties to be encountered— the problem of finding experts, the great cost of research, and the opposition of doctors and laymen.

Returning from his vacation, Gates prepared for Rockefeller a memorandum setting forth the need for scientific research in medicine, expatiating upon the usefulness of the Koch Institute in Berlin and the Pasteur Institute in Paris, and explaining the inestimable benefits that might be accomplished by a similar agency in America, where progress in this field lagged so woefully behind that made in Europe. Both Rockefeller and his son were impressed, though for some time the pressure of other matters prevented action. Realizing that the project required the full time of an able man, Gates introduced to the Rockefellers a Montclair attorney, Starr J. Murphy—an able, agreeable, painstaking man, who always understood just what Gates wanted—whom they engaged to survey the leading medical schools of the country, to consult prominent medical men, and to study the foreign institutes. Most of the persons with whom Murphy talked gave only a chilly response to the idea, advocating instead the support of promising experimenters already at work in various institutions.

While Murphy continued his talks and studies with little progress, John D. Rockefeller, Jr., broached the subject to his family pediatrician, Dr. L. Emmett Holt—and matters took an entirely new turn. The famous authority on child care, the father of modern pediatrics, a man of dynamic personality and progressive outlook, saw at once the great opportunity presented. He brought three of his friends into the discussions: Dr. Christian A. Herter, Dr. T. Mitchell Prudden, and Dr. Hermann M. Biggs. Herter, who possessed inherited wealth, had a laboratory on the upper floor of his Madison Avenue house, where he devoted much time to scientific research; he was unfortunately destined to die young. Prudden, professor of pathology and bacteriology at the College of Physicians and Surgeons, had studied under some of Germany's leading investigators. Biggs, general medical officer of the New York City Department of Health, had been trained in Germany at the time when bacteriological research was making its most spectacular advances; he developed for the city the first scientific public health laboratory in the country, and became almost as stimulating a leader of medical education as Dr. Welch. All of them had a passionate faith in medical research.

Early in 1901, the four men met at the home of John D. Rockefeller, Jr., who asked them to consider what could be done to promote medical research if his father were to give $20,000 a year for ten years for the work. To answer this question the group felt the need to consult other medical leaders. They instinctively turned to Dr. William H. Welch of Johns Hopkins, then probably the foremost figure in American medicine. After a period as teacher of pathology in the Bellevue Hospital Medical College, where he had opened the first laboratory for instruction in that subject in the United States, Welch had gone to Baltimore in 1885 as the first professor in the germinating medical school of Johns Hopkins, and had become dean upon its opening in 1893. He had met Prudden when both were students in Germany; he had taught Biggs at Bellevue, and knew the other two men from his New York period. Herbert Hoover later called him "our greatest statesman in public health"; and he was truly great as teacher, leader, and inspirer of others, if not for original ideas or discovery. Dr. Theobald Smith, of the Harvard Medical School, was next brought into the group. Years before, while investigating the epidemic of Texas cattle fever for the United States Bureau of Animal Husbandry, Smith had demonstrated the principle of insect transmission of disease, opening an entirely new area of bacteriological research. He was considered by fellow scientists to be America's leading investigator. Finally, on May 25, 1901, Dr. Simon Flexner of the University of Pennsylvania was brought into the group.

Of all the men named, Flexner was destined to do the most important work for Gates's fundamental idea and for medical research. Born in Louisville in the midst of the Civil War, he had taken his medical degree in the University of Louisville and done post graduate work at Johns Hopkins under Welch, whom he all but worshipped. He had studied at Strasbourg, Berlin, and Prague, and had labored in the Pasteur Institute. Then, after teaching for a time at Johns Hopkins, he had joined the faculty at Pennsylvania, where he also directed the Ayer Clinical Laboratory of the Pennsylvania Hospital. Keen-witted, industrious, passionately interested in science to the exclusion of almost everything else, he was a born research worker.

Thus within a few months seven leading figures in American medical science had been drawn together as a group interested in using Rockefeller's proposed gift to the best purpose in research. Most of them were young—in their thirties or forties—and all were energetic. To Gates, who apparently believed that something like the institutes of Paris and Berlin could be created overnight, they at first seemed excessively timid. He had little patience with the general idea that it would be best, at least for a time, to employ the workers and laboratories already available; but this idea was accepted. During May the conferees agreed that Welch, who as editor of the *Journal of Experimental Medicine* had contact with the research in progress in the leading medical institutions of the country, should find out what problems were being investigated and ascertain the needs of the investigators.

By the end of 1901, incorporation papers had been received from the State of New York, naming the seven advisers as the board of directors, with Welch as president, Prudden vice-president, Holt secretary, and Herter treasurer. The elder Rockefeller executed a pledge of $200,000 upon which the directors might draw at any time during the next ten years. Although he offered no intimation that another copper would be forthcoming, everyone concerned knew that if the undertaking proved its worth, his purse strings would be loosed. It was in the Rockefeller pattern that the venture should start modestly and tentatively, letting experience show the way. It was characteristic, too, that Rockefeller was reluctant to let the board attach his name to the new Institute for Medical Research. The directors worked in entire harmony, all insisting on the severest standards of work. "It is not too much to say," states Dr. Abraham Flexner, Simon Flexner's brother, "that the moment these men were brought together for the purpose of governing the Institute, they were the group who determined the course of action which in a relatively few years resulted in the modernization of American medicine."

As a result of inquiries which Welch sent to directors of laboratories in the leading medical schools, the institute made grants-in-aid, ranging from $300 to $1200 each, in amounts totaling approximately $12,000 in 1901 and $14,450 in 1902. More than a score of research workers who received these grants eventually reported on their studies. One man was sent to the Koch Institute in Berlin and two went to the Ehrlich Institute in Frankfort. Of course, all discoveries were to be public property.

The directors met frequently with Gates, the younger Rockefeller, and Murphy to scrutinize the work and review financial arrangements. Gates alone felt discontent with the cautious exploratory program being pursued. The new institute was without a model. Whereas its European predecessors—the Pasteur, Koch, and Lister institutes—had clung to pathology and bacteriology, the American organizers wished freedom to investigate any problem whatever in biological science which might bear upon medicine. Inevitably, many doubts attended the early work, and observers continued to express uncertainty whether an able research group could be assembled in an American center.

The phase of cautious exploration, however, soon ended. The directors quickly found that scattering small subventions among research workers was not enough. They determined to build up a staff under an expert head, and, making certain of Rockefeller's willingness to support a research center, they formulated a proposal for him. In June, 1902, Rockefeller promised a million dollars to build, equip, and operate temporarily a research laboratory in New York. Again he offered no guarantee of further aid, but everyone knew that when needed it would be forthcoming. The directors, after careful thought, chose Simon Flexner as head of the laboratories. No other single step did so much to assure the success of the Institute. He was reluctant to accept, for he was devoted to his work at the University of Pennsylvania, while he doubted whether American science had really gained sufficient strength and elevation to support an ambitious institution for medical research. But the board, with Welch's enthusiasm as the strongest factor, finally won him over.

In a rented and modestly equipped building on East 50th Street, a small staff quietly began work on October 15, 1904. The members of the group, besides Flexner, were Drs. Hideyo Noguchi, Eugene L. Opie, and J. E. Sweet, pathologist; Dr. S. J. Meltzer, physiologist and pharmacologist; and Dr. P. A. Levene, biological chemist. Although care was taken to avoid overlapping or duplication of work, no preconceived plan of investigation had dictated the choice of these men. They had been selected with confidence that their initiative and talents would lead them into profitable activities. Each member was to have complete freedom, under Flexner's general guidance, to pursue a problem within his special field.

Early in 1903, Rockefeller had purchased a site for a laboratory building on the brow of the rocky plateau overlooking the East River at Sixty-sixth Street. Here a carefully-planned four-story brick and stone building was opened on May 11, 1906. It furnished excellent facilities for the work already undertaken in pathology, physiology, pharmacology, and biological chemistry, to which experimental surgery and experimental biology were added later. As the laboratories expanded and the staff grew in numbers, more money was needed, and Rockefeller always anticipated the need. "We never asked Mr. Rockefeller's representatives for anything," Flexner recalled. "They always came to us and asked, "Suppose you had more money, what could you do with it?' "

Assured that the Institute was a success, Rockefeller in 1907 gave it more than two and a half million dollars as permanent endowment. Growing rapidly, the organization now needed a more complex administrative arrangement. By amendment of the charter in 1908, the original directors were named "scientific directors," and confined themselves to scientific duties, while the business and general policies were transferred to a board of trustees composed of Gates, John D. Rockefeller, Jr., and Starr J. Murphy, representing the Institute's fiscal interests, and Welch and Flexner, representing its scientific work. With the completion of this reorganization in 1910, another body was formed, called "the corporation," which consisted of the board of trustees and the scientific directors. Through the ensuing years these two groups, scientific and financial, worked together in remarkable harmony. The research staff, with absolute control of their own expenditures, managed to keep within their budget. Rockefeller always scrupulously followed his hands-off policy. In fact, he was so anxious to respect the freedom of the scientists that he visited the Institute only once, when he and his son happened to be in the neighborhood. Dr. Flexner wrote:

The Institute . . . has been expected to explore, to dream. Our founder and his advisers have said to us again and again, in effect: "Don't be in a hurry to produce anything. Don't worry about making good. We have faith that you will make good, and if you don't, the next fellow will. . . . This thing may go on for generations; then suddenly somebody will give us a practical result."

Beginning in 1908, a series of gifts by Rockefeller provided for a sixty-bed hospital and a nine-bed isolation pavilion, which were opened in 1910 under the direction of Dr. Rufus Cole. The hospital, with ample laboratory facilities, was staffed exactly as were the laboratories—by salaried physicians who gave their full time to their work, engaging in no outside practice and accepting no fees. Only patients whose diseases were being studied by members of the Institute staff were admitted, and they were treated entirely without charge.

As the Institute grew, more buildings were constructed. In 1914, Dr. Theobald Smith accepted the directorship of a department of animal pathology which, in 1917, began its work on a 780-acre farm near Princeton, New Jersey. With the appointment of Dr. Louis O. Kunkel as its head, a department of plant pathology was established on the farm in 1931. These two departments were later moved to New York, the transfer of the plant pathology laboratory being completed by January, 1949, while by September 30, 1950, the animal pathology laboratory had been installed. New greenhouses were built to house the plant pathology department, and a new wing to the hospital was opened in February, 1951. By 1952, eleven buildings, not including the greenhouses and auxiliary facilities, stood on the Institute grounds bounded by York Avenue, the Franklin Delano Roosevelt Drive, and Sixty-third and Sixty-eighth Streets.

The first great discovery at the Institute was Flexner's serum for the successful treatment of epidemic meningitis, a deadly malady that raged in New York in 1905 and spread throughout the country. Flexner found that the disease could be transmitted to monkeys, and that the serum he produced in horses would cure the infected monkeys. The serum was then applied to the treatment of children, the commonest victims, and of the first 400 cases treated, nearly four-fifths recovered. With all possible speed, the Institute sent the serum throughout the country and to every foreign land where the disease cropped up.

Other discoveries of great value followed, while fresh techniques of research, developed by imaginative investigators who worked with passionate zeal but without any pressure for quick results, opened promising paths that were followed by other workers the world over. A list of the Institute's achievements and those who made them would be impressive but tiresomely long.

Any historian of the Institute would have to deal at length with the achievements of Hideyo Noguchi of the original staff, one of the most gifted research pathologists of his time, who lost his life in the investigation of yellow fever; of Alexis Carrel, from the University of Lyon, whose contributions to arterial surgery opened new fields of operational and experimental surgery and won for him the Nobel prize; of Jacques Loeb, the brilliant experimental physiologist; of Karl Landsteiner, whose work on infantile paralysis in Vienna was basic to the later important work done by Flexner and others at the Institute and who also won the Nobel prize; of Peyton Rous, discoverer of the fact that certain cancerous tumors in fowls and small mammals are caused by viruses; of Rufus Cole and his associates in the hospital, who found that the germ (pneumococcus) causing pneumonia could be divided into many immunological types, and who developed sera for the highly fatal type No. 1 and others.

The historian would have to deal, too, with a number of men of hardly lesser luster, for the list could be continued to great length. A comparative glance at the bibliography of Flexner's scientific writings and the literature of pathological and bacteriological investigation during the years of his productive work shows how many problems he explored and inspired others to pursue, with results of inestimable value to the world.

One of the greatest contributions which Flexner made as director sprang from his understanding of the essential unity of all branches of science. From the first, he recognized the importance of breaking down the barriers between even the few special fields represented by the small original staff. As he drew more and more highly-trained specialists to the laboratories, and as with the expansion of scientific knowledge, departmentalization became more difficult to avoid, he paid ever greater attention to the need for integration. He saw to it that informal contacts, discussions, and pooling of results were brought about at the daily lunch table and at staff meetings. A list of important discoveries that have come from the joint work of, say, a chemist and a bacteriologist, or others of equally unlike training, would make a fascinating record. After the opening of the Institute's hospital, the union of pure and applied science became fruitful. New knowledge acquired in the laboratory could be applied to the prevention and alleviation of disease by a hospital staff which had worked in close harmony with the laboratory specialists through all the steps of their research.

The Institute, like the University of Chicago, gave Rockefeller a use for tens of millions of dollars. Yet he and his two aides sought still larger avenues of expenditure. Soon after the beginning of the century he began the work of creating the General Education Board, which at the outset operated largely for the benefit of the long-handicapped South.

For some time, just before the beginning of the century, Rockefeller had talked with his son and Gates about establishing a generous trust fund to stimulate Negro education. He knew of the work of the Alabamian J. L. M. Curry. He knew also of the aid given to Negro education, and the other work to benefit the South, by Robert C. Ogden, long a business associate of John Wanamaker and a director (later chairman of the board) of the Union Theological Seminary in New York. In the summers of 1898 and 1899, these two men brought together at Capon Springs, Virginia, a number of persons interested in southern education, organizing a body of which Curry was president and Ogden vice-president. In the spring of 1901, the younger Rockefeller joined a group of influential men invited at great expense—and with a fanfare of publicity—by Ogden and Curry to travel by special train through the South, visiting Hampton and Tuskegee Institutes and other schools. Among the guests were Walter Hines Page, George Foster Peabody, Albert Shaw, John Graham Brooks, Bishop Doane, and William H. Baldwin, president of the Long Island Railroad. Rockefeller talked at great length with Curry, Page, and Baldwin, and brought his father a glowing account of the trip.

In the ensuing months of 1901 John D. Rockefeller, Jr., thought earnestly on the subject of aid to the South and talked it over with his father, Gates, and Wallace Buttrick, chairman of the Baptist Home Mission Society's Committee on Education, who knew southern problems at first hand. From his talks with Baldwin, Peabody, and others, he had become convinced that it was important to give assistance to the whites no less than the colored people of the southern states.

On January 15, 1902, six men—Ogden, Curry, Peabody, Baldwin, Buttrick, and John D. Rockefeller, Jr.—met at the home of the venerable banker-philanthropist Morris K. Jesup. They decided to form an organization for the promotion of education, thus taking the first step in what was to prove one of the most far-reaching philanthropic enterprises of the century. On February 27, 1902, the same group, with the addition of Daniel Coit Gilman, Albert Shaw, Walter Hines Page, and Edward M. Shepard, acting as counsel, met at the younger Rockefeller's house on Fifty-fourth Street. They elected Baldwin president, read and signed a statement of purposes, and made plans for obtaining federal incorporation under the name of the General Education Board. The elder Rockefeller, through his son, then promised that he would give $1,000,000 to be used during the next ten years for education without distinction of sex, race, or creed.

Shepard drew up a perpetual charter granting the Board authority to hold limitless capital and to engage in any activities whatever that could be construed as educational in any part of the nation. Congress alone could confer such broad powers. Nelson W. Aldrich, at that time the most influential figure in the Senate, carried the bill through Congress without delay, and incorporation became effective January 12, 1903. Thus was established an organization which shortly became the most powerful educational foundation in the world—one to which within the next decade Rockefeller was to give more than $50,-000,000 and before his death, almost $150,000,000.

The four men whose ideas dominated the early work of the General Education Board were Baldwin, Buttrick, Gates, and John D. Rockefeller, Jr. The influence of Wallace Buttrick, the secretary can hardly be overestimated. He was a born executive, of sturdy common sense, keen comprehension of human nature, and winning geniality; not a scholar, but a practical man of the world. Abraham Flexner has said, "He was the most unselfish worker I have ever known." A minister once asked him, "Dr. Buttrick, what is your idea of Heaven?" and Buttrick replied:

"My office!" His qualities complemented those of Gates to the great advantage of the Board. The two men strongly admired each other and worked in the utmost harmony: the daring, provocative initiator, Gates, who formed the Board, and the balanced, tolerant, tactful administrator, Buttrick, who molded it.

After a rapid examination of the field, the Board decided to use the whole million dollars for building and improving schools in selected southern counties, which would serve as object lessons to the whole section. But the leaders quickly saw that private philanthropy alone would be inadequate and would deaden the spirit of self-help. The best way to improve education in the South was to induce the South itself to better the quality of the teaching. The Board therefore invited each state university in the South to appoint to its faculty a professor of secondary education whose salary and expenses would be paid by the Board. The professors were to study their states thoroughly to discover the best places for the establishment of good new high schools, to hold public meetings in the selected localities, to explain the facts and appeal to community spirit, and to show how the money to build and maintain the high schools could be raised. This plan embodied real inspiration.

Buttrick, going himself into the South, supervised a long and searching inquiry into rural educational conditions. With the aid of field workers, he furnished detailed reports on school organization, supervision, finance, Negro education, number and pay of teachers, normal school education, and allied topics. At first these reports were confidential, given only to members of the General Education Board. Later, after the educational situation in the South materially improved, information gathered from some communities was published to assist others in solving their problems. The Board stoutly maintained its policy of never trying to impose an educational program upon the South, but of coöperating with the local spokesmen in working out a joint program.

Naturally, it was not long before the Board realized that improvement of the economic position of the rural South was basic to improvement of southern education. The poverty of the section was appalling, especially in areas bound by the one-crop system and filled with tenant farmers of meager resources. While at the beginning of the century the average annual earnings of farmers in Iowa were upwards of $1000, in some Southern states they were often as low as $150. The Board sought advice in many quarters and considered various possibilities. As the most immediately useful plan, the officers undertook a broad program for the agricultural education of the existing generation of farmers. Buttrick spent a year in the study of methods of teaching adult farmers, visiting agricultural schools from Canada to Texas and as far west as Iowa. At the Texas State Agricultural College he found just the leader required—the agent of the federal Department of Agriculture, Dr. Seaman A. Knapp, a man of boundless energy, great enthusiasm, and firm will.

Knapp, in his long life as farmer, editor, professor of agriculture, president of Iowa State College, head of a large colonization project in Louisiana, president of the Rice Association of America, and apostle of new farming methods, had done as much for the cause of scientific farming as any other man in American history. Among other accomplishments, he had helped to draft the law for federal experiment stations in agriculture, and had played a leading role in the fight against the boll weevil when it first threatened to devastate the cotton fields of Texas. His point of view coincided with Rockefeller's principle that stimulation of self-help is the best form of help, and that a vitally-rooted and self-continuing work is the proper goal of any well-planned philanthropy.

Conferences between Knapp and Buttrick quickly led to the entrance of the Board into the farm demonstration field. Knapp, while still serving the Department of Agriculture, agreed to direct the Board's activities in otherwise neglected areas of the South. In 1906 the Department and the Board made an alliance by which the Board was to promote demonstrations of efficient agriculture in coöperation with farmers in territories where the Department was not at work, the Department exercising supervision and appointing and controlling all the special agents engaged in the task. Rockefeller, kept informed by his son and Gates about the Board's early undertakings, took a keen and critical interest in all its work. He approved of generous appropriations for the activities in agricultural education, rising from $37,500 in 1905–06 to $252,000 in 1913.

The area covered by the farm demonstration program rapidly expanded. In 1907 the federal government supported it in Texas, Louisiana, and Arkansas, the boll weevil states; the General Education Board supported it in Mississippi, Alabama, and Virginia. In 1908 the government added Oklahoma to its list, and the Board added Georgia and the two Carolinas. As the boll weevil moved eastward, the government took over Mississippi, Tennessee, and other states. By 1913 the government was responsible for eight and a half southern states, while the Board had five and a half. Turning northward, the Board was also conducting similar work in Maine and New Hampshire. The hope of a number of people was that the South would be so strongly impressed by the demonstration program that it would coöperate in supporting it proved to be justified.

State after state began making appropriations. Between 1906 and 1915, the Board gave just over one million dollars to bring demonstration work to the southern farms; the federal government gave just short of two millions; and the states themselves contributed slightly over one million. Seldom has money been better invested. The Department of Agriculture's reports showed an impressive increase in the value of the crops and livestock of the ten principal cotton-producing states during those years.

The younger generation was not neglected in the program. Knapp took up the idea of corn clubs for the boys and canning clubs for the girls of the rural areas, and by 1913 more than 90,-000 boys and 30,000 girls had been enrolled in these highly useful organizations.

In all the Board's work, no race lines were drawn. Colored tenant farmers were selected as demonstrators through the region, and graduates of Hampton and Tuskegee soon joined the staff of agents and demonstrators. All over the South the colored race no less than the white farmers felt the general impulse toward more intelligent agriculture.

With the death of Knapp in 1911 and that of Ogden in 1913 (he had succeeded Baldwin as president of the Board in 1905), the first phase in the history of the General Education Board ended. During this period great additions had been made to its funds, and the Board had entered upon new paths.

One new undertaking holds special interest. In 1905, Gates suggested to Rockefeller the allocation of a large fund to be held and administered by able trustees—possibly a newly-organized board, though he inclined toward the General Education Board —to bear Rockefeller's name in perpetuity, the income to be applied from year to year to selected colleges and universities "as their need and worth shall be apparent." In his years of busy travel about the country for the Baptist Education Society and for Rockefeller, Gates had been becoming acquainted with many of the hundreds upon hundreds of so-called colleges and universities, "scattered haphazard over the landscape like wind-carried seeds," he wrote later. He and Starr Murphy believed that a great work of development and reformation could be carried out.

Accordingly, on June 30, 1905, Rockefeller gave $10,000,000 to the General Education Board, the income "to be distributed to, or used for the benefit of, such institutions of learning . . . as the Board may deem best adapted to promote a comprehensive system of higher education in the United States." To strengthen the Board in the field of university administration, William Rainey Harper and E. Benjamin Andrews were added to it. Early in 1907, when Gates became chairman of the Board, Rockefeller gave $32,000,000 more, of which one-third was to be added to the permanent endowment of the Board and two-thirds "to be applied to such specific objects within the corporate purposes of the Board" as Rockefeller or his son might direct. On July 7, 1909, Rockefeller increased his benefactions by another $10,000,-000, and authorized the Board, in its discretion, to distribute its entire principal or any part of it.

By 1924 it was evident that the purposes for which the Board had made grants to state departments of education in the South had been substantially achieved. The principal officers—Buttrick, chairman since 1917; Wickliffe Rose, president; and Abraham Flexner, the highly efficient secretary—could look with satisfaction at the great advances made in southern education since the Board had begun its work, and especially at the awakening of the southern states to their responsibility for good secondary education. The federal government had taken over all of the farm demonstration work.

The Board thereupon turned to new labors. While continuing certain remnants of its southern activities, it expanded in three directions: improvement of the work of colleges and universities, elevation of the standards of American medical schools, and the conduct of surveys to discover other needs in education. In the first two spheres, its activities were soon arousing vigorous criticism as well as praise.

The primary task in higher education was to examine the field. In its first dozen years of existence the Board had scrutinized all the higher institutions in the country—their number, orgins, purposes, location, resources, potential strength, relations to their communities. Plainly the nation had too many weak, ill-nourished schools: some 700, exclusive of technological institutions, called themselves colleges or universities. Only a few were articulated with the secondary schools of their states, and most of them were dangerously over-extended in their activities.

On a highly selective basis, the Board gave assistance to the institutions it thought the most deserving. By 1924 it had contributed more than $20,300,000 to 134 colleges and universities on condition that they raise nearly $76,500,000 more. The broad principles underlying the action of the Board were: to give only to schools of proved stability, with the stipulation that others give liberally; to regard centers of wealth and population as the natural capitals of higher education in America; to ask that effort be concentrated on the strengthening of endowments; and to coöperate with all religious denominations, as was natural in an organization partly an outgrowth of the Baptist Education Society. The formulation of these principles reflected the ideas of Rockefeller and Gates, and the counsel of such Board members as Charles W. Eliot, Walter Hines Page, Edwin A. Alderman, Albert Shaw, Anson Phelps Stokes, George E. Vincent, and the younger Rockefeller.

The Board never "required" any institution to raise a certain sum. On the contrary, the college always took the initiative, notifying the Board that it meant to collect certain amounts for specified purposes and asking for a contribution. Sometimes the Board gave half the total, sometimes a third or fourth. The plan worked wonders, often arousing strenuous effort in a community that had been thought hopelessly inert, and stimulating a continued interest shown in gifts and bequests.

With the gifts went an insistence on better financial administration, a policy that gave peculiar satisfaction to Rockefeller. Always requiring a financial statement from an institution requesting help, the Board officers often encountered amazing incompetence on the part of academic authorities—acceptance of gifts that were actually liabilities, lack of proper bookkeeping systems, "borrowing" from endowments in time of financial stress, and the like. To safeguard its gifts, the Board had in such instances to call for drastic reforms. For the guidance of college and university administrative officers, it published and widely distributed Trevor Arnett's incisive book on *College and University Finance.*

One especially noteworthy grant was Rockefeller's gift, made in 1919 largely at the instance of George E. Vincent, of securities worth approximately $50,000,000, to be used—both principal and interest—primarily in coöperation with institutions which were trying to increase the salaries of their teachers. Within five years, nearly four-fifths of the grant had been distributed among about 170 colleges and universities as additions to endowment; meanwhile, these institutions succeeded in raising some $83,-000,000 more. What this meant to a host of teachers and their families, struggling against the sharp increase in living costs following the first world war, can hardly be overestimated.

In the field of medical education the Board undertook a truly monumental program, which meant nothing less than a regeneration. Gates and Abraham Flexner, who, with Buttrick, dominated the work of the able Board during these years of tremendous expansion, were both inflexibly interested in better standards of medicine. Both men were intensely distressed by the defects of American medical teaching, which had made virtually no advance in recent decades. They discussed the problem again and again, and drew the hard-working, single-minded, unselfish Buttrick into their parleys. The program of reorganization which they envisaged was enormous: Flexner estimated that $50,-000,000 was the lowest amount with which it would be desirable to begin—and he, Gates, and Buttrick knew that the initial gifts would only start the ball rolling. They obtained the approval of both the Rockefellers, and set to work.

The plan was to create, at key points where they might serve as models, strong medical schools, operated in conjunction with well-equipped hospitals and clinics, and abreast of the finest European institutions. Existing colleges were to be utilized and other givers were to be enlisted. By the summer of 1919, more than $5,000,000 had been distributed in large grants to the medical departments of various universities, notably Johns Hopkins, Yale, and Washington in St. Louis. The war had emphasized the medical weaknesses of the nation, for the government had met difficulty in finding competent personnel for its base hospitals and medical corps. In September, 1919, Rockefeller gave more than $20,000,000 for the advancement of medical education in the United States and followed this grant with other large donations.

The Board then assisted in the establishment of one great medical center at the University of Chicago, and two in New York City in conjunction with Columbia and Cornell Universities; it gave Vanderbilt University sufficient sums to place its medical school on its feet and raise standards of medical education in the South; it enabled the University of Rochester to launch a medical school which was vigorously assisted by the generosity of George Eastman; and it helped the University of Iowa to erect an admirable school. The full story of its achievements, best told in Abraham Flexner's autobiography, is as fascinating as it is impressive.

One of the most salient innovations launched with the Board's aid was the establishment of full-time chairs of certain clinical subjects in leading medical schools. In 1913, the Johns Hopkins University asked for and received a grant of $1,500,000 to provide full-time staffs in the departments of medicine, surgery, and pediatrics. No more of teachers wrapped up in their private practice! Yale and Washington Universities followed with similar plans. The new departure aroused bitter and to the layman incomprehensible opposition on the part of the medical profession. Instruction in the laboratory branches of medicine had been on a full-time basis for some three decades in this country, with no objection on the part of practicing physicians, who contentedly benefited from research carried on in endowed laboratories. The placing of the clinical branches of medical teaching on the same undiluted, unhampered basis had been successfully put into effect by the Rockefeller Institute for Medical Research before Johns Hopkins and Yale followed suit. Yet it was met by an outcry that has not yet subsided, even though the plan has been adopted by more and more schools. As the officers of the General Education Board emphasized, only well-endowed and highly-developed institutions can afford to attempt it.

The General Education Board encountered heavy criticism of some of its labors. Southern politicians long remained suspicious of its rural program. Though most colleges and universities welcomed its aid, a few resented its stipulations, and many weak institutions indulged in petulant flings when they failed to receive aid. Even some able and sincere educators believed that colleges exposed themselves to grave perils, such as a paralyzing interference, in accepting the bounty of this richly-endowed institution. But the work as a whole was manifestly beneficial, and much of it paid magnificent returns upon the sums invested. The basis for most criticism was demolished when the founder and officers, in 1920, removed from grants made in the past all limitations to specific purposes, and abandoned the policy of making educational grants conditional upon various "reforms." Thereafter donations were frequently made to colleges and universities in contemplation of certain aims, but never upon a rigid requirement of them. This change of policy showed a wise development in Rockefeller's point of view, and the resultant freedom benefited education and the Board alike.

In 1928, with its programs in aid of the South, in medical education, and in the broad improvement of higher education virtually accomplished, the General Education Board began to merge its activities with those of other Rockefeller agencies.

But in carrying the educational story forward, we have passed over one of the most picturesque and interesting labors carried out under the aegis of the Board—the battle against the hookworm.

In 1908 President Theodore Roosevelt's Commission on Country Life traveled through the South gathering material for its report on the social, economic, and sanitary conditions of the farmers. Dr. Charles W. Stiles, a zoologist of the United States Public Health Service, accompanying the group, pointed out to Walter Hines Page a human wreck lounging on a railroad station platform: scrawny, yellow-skinned, pot-bellied, misshapen, apathetic—a typical hookworm victim. "He can be cured by fifty cents' worth of drugs, and in a few weeks' time be turned into a useful man," Stiles said. He spoke of the great benefits the rural South would derive from a campaign for the eradication of hookworm disease, for which he had been unable to find support.

Page was astonished and excited, for the regeneration of the South and the elevation of its people had long been his greatest passion. Associated with Rockefeller's work, he knew where to turn for aid. Shortly afterwards, he introduced Stiles to Wallace Buttrick, then secretary of the General Education Board; and at once Stiles was brought from Washington for conferences with Simon Flexner, Gates, Starr J. Murphy, and others.

The result was the formation of the Rockefeller Sanitary Commission, composed of Stiles, William H. Welch, and Simon Flexner as the medical members and nine laymen, who in 1909 set to work with a gift of $1,000,000 from Rockefeller for a ten years' war on hookworm. Wickliffe Rose, a Tennessean of broad culture and fine personality, who after a distinguished academic career had become general agent of the Peabody Fund, was appointed administrative secretary, and Stiles scientific secretary. With headquarters in Washington, the Commission undertook a plan of coöperation with the health authorities of the southern states, so tactfully managed that it overcame the resentment and prejudice of the citizens of that region. By 1913, approximately 900,000 people had been examined, and 500,000 infected persons had been treated. Whole communities were being restored to health. Charles W. Eliot called the Commission's work "the most effective campaign against a wide-spreading disease which medical science and philanthropy have ever combined to conduct." Page regarded it as effecting a veritable social revolution. "The hookworm," he wrote, "has probably played a larger part in our Southern history than slavery or wars or any political dogma or economic creed"—and now it was being abolished. In addition, the Commission was promoting general sanitation in the South, lessening the ravages of typhoid fever and other diseases, and stimulating a spirit of neighborliness and courage.

In October, 1914, the Rockefeller Sanitary Commission went out of existence. It had been absorbed by the International Health Commission (later Board), created the year before by the Rockefeller Foundation. The dramatic story of the creation of the Foundation, which was destined to overshadow all the other philanthropies, we must reserve to a later chapter.

# CHAPTER XIV

# THE TRUST SLAIN AND REBORN

O N A COLD February day in 1888, Chairman Frank B. Arnold of the New York Senate committee for investigating trusts rapped for order in the crowded room of the Superior Court in New York City, and announced: "Mr. John D. Rockefeller will now take the stand." Necks were craned as Rockefeller rose from a row of seats occupied by Standard officials and attorneys. Already the committee had inquired into alleged monopolies in sugar, rubber, and other commodities. Prominent business leaders (for example, Henry O. Havemeyer, supported by Elihu Root as counsel) had appeared. The public, however, evinced a special interest in Rockefeller—"the father of trusts, the king of monopolists, the czar of the oil business," to quote the *World;* the man "who stands head and shoulders above all businessmen in the country," as the *Herald* put it.

The taciturn Rockefeller told the committee little that it had not known before. He named the trustees, who since Oliver H. Payne's retirement were only eight. He disclosed the fact that the Trust now had about 700 shareholders. He stated that the trustees, who held quarterly meetings in New York, kept a record book; but this book, when produced, proved barren of interest. With only brief hesitation, Rockefeller also furnished the text of the Trust agreement of 1882. Joseph H. Choate, as attorney for the Standard, at first asked that its details should not be published, but soon withdrew this objection, another attorney then reading the tiresome document in full. In the course of his testimony, Rockefeller spoke feelingly of the strong Russian competition, remarking that the Rothschilds, Nobels, and other capitalists threatened to flood the world market; while at the close he placed in the record a list of 111 competing domestic refineries as evidence that the Standard fell short of an absolute monopoly.

He was followed by Archbold, who made a much less favorable impression, for he was evasive, insolent, and hot-tempered. Archbold partially explained the workings of the executive committee, and admitted that the proxy committee controlled the choice of the officers and directors of the component companies. But the records of the proxy committee were in Flagler's hands, and Flagler was in Florida. The investigation also brought out a list of the forty-one companies and firms bound up in the Trust, the first ever published.

The New York investigation, a loose, hasty, inconsequential affair, proved a disappointment to the public. Early in May the committee published an inconclusive report, both majority and minority agreeing that no new legislation should be passed until it became clear that the existing laws were inadequate.

Before the New York committee had finished its work, a federal agency had moved into action. The House Committee on Manufactures, after an exhaustive investigation of the Sugar Trust, proving conclusively that it was a greedy monopoly, turned its guns early in April, 1888, on the Standard. Its chairman was Henry Bacon of New York; its counsel and chief questioner was Franklin B. Gowen, famous for his stormy presidency of the Philadelphia & Reading. Handsome of face and figure, richly dressed, energetic and quick-witted as ever, Gowen was making his last great public appearance before his tragic suicide. A long list of interesting witnesses was called: railroad men like A. J. Cassatt, who had been vice-president of the Pennsylvania, the principal Standard executives, and such enemies of the Standard as George Rice and Lewis Emery, Jr. Various episodes of the Standard's history were more fully explored than ever before; the war with the Empire Transportation Company, O'Day's drawback arrangement on Rice's shipments over the Marietta railroad, the Buffalo conspiracy case, and the defeat of the Billingsley Bill. Much valuable documentary evidence was introduced.

Flagler's testimony, offered with characteristic grace of manner, gave the public a fuller view of the financial arrangements of the Trust and of its high profits. He described the increase of the capitalization to $90,000,000; he estimated the actual market value of the shares in March, 1888, at about $154,000,000; and he stated that since its formation, the Trust had averaged earnings of approximately 13 per cent a year—about 7 per cent being paid the stockholders in cash, 3 per cent distributed in stock dividends, and 3 per cent held in the treasury.

Rockefeller, called to the stand on April 30, was treated with great respect. Once more he was blandly uncommunicative. While he emphasized the benevolent intentions of the Trust, on one specific point after another he was totally vague. He could not tell what part of its export oil the Standard sold at seaboard, and what part it carried overseas. He could not hazard a statement as to the price of Scottish shale oil. He could not say whether the Trust controlled any natural gas properties in Indiana. When one Representative burst out indignantly at his "shortness of memory," Rockefeller gazed pityingly at him, and pointed out that the business was too vast and complex for him to master all its details. After remarking that the Trust had no books, each company keeping its own accounts, he did admit that the treasurer, Benjamin Brewster, kept an accounting of receipts; but he did not think he had ever seen it. He could not even tell from memory how many shares the Trust had issued in exchange for each share of the Standard Oil of Ohio.

Nobody could have been more gently evasive. All the Standard witnesses furnished as little information as they could, and Daniel O Day contributed actual misinformation. If they had wished to excuse their taciturnity, they would have said that the investigation was thoroughly hostile; that little effort was made to explore the economic situation which had forced a great part of American (and European) business to organize pools, trusts, and other restraints on competition; that every charge against them, no matter how distorted or exaggerated, was accepted at face value; and that no inquiry whatever was made into malpractices on the part of independents.

Altogether, the House Committee presented the Standard in as unfavorable a light as the Sugar Trust. The complaints of producers, independent refiners, and small distributors were thoroughly reviewed. Their testimony as to rebating and price-cutting offered little that was really novel; but evidence was given which strongly indicated that the pipe-line charges had been excessive. The large profits of the Standard were once more exhibited, the coercive power which it had exercised over trunk-line railroads was defined in detail, and the secrecy which had surrounded many of its operations was reëmphasized. Although the committee, in reporting to Congress on July 30, 1888, did not offer recommendations for any new law, to most readers the testimony spoke for itself.

The winter of 1888–89 found the subject of trusts heatedly discussed in half of the state capitols of the land. Numerous states already had constitutional or statutory provisions prohibiting any combination in restraint of trade. Between 1888 and 1896 these were greatly strengthened, or strict new statutes were passed. Michigan, Kansas, Tennessee, and Idaho acted as early as 1889, and a larger group of states in 1890; New York finally passed a drastic law in 1892.

In the Cleveland-Harrison campaign of 1888 both major parties denounced trusts and other monopolistic combinations, though the Democrats attacked them only in connection with the tariff. Public sentiment rendered it certain that the next Congress would move vigorously. On December 4, 1889, John Sherman submitted as Senate Bill No. 1 an earlier measure of his, entitled "A bill to declare unlawful, trusts and combinations in restraint of trade and production." As a result of much floor debate and committee work, a measure, to which Sherman of Ohio, Hoar of Massachusetts, George of Mississippi, and Edmunds of Vermont all contributed, was hammered into shape. Passed by an almost unanimous vote, it was signed by President Harrison in the early summer of 1890. This Sherman Anti-Trust Act was brief. Its two essential articles declared that every contract, combination, or conspiracy in restraint of interstate or foreign trade was illegal, and that every violator should be punished by a fine not exceeding $5000, or a year's imprisonment, or both. At the time of the passage of this act the country had fully fifty trusts. In discussions of the bill inside and outside Congress the Standard was naturally treated as one of the principal culprits.

Even before Congress passed the Sherman Act, the first effective prosecutions of the great trusts had begun in the states. Early in 1889 a decision against the Sugar Trust was handed down in the New York Supreme Court, and that fall it was affirmed, dissolving one of the amalgamated companies for violation of charter. In the following spring the attorney-general of Ohio,

David E. Watson, resolved to launch a suit against Standard Oil. Coming out of the capitol in Columbus one day, he picked up in a bookstore a copy of William W. Cook's small volume, *Trusts: the Recent Combinations in Trade.* This book, primarily a legal treatise, contained the trust deeds of the Standard and the Sugar Trust. It challenged public prosecutors to do their duty, and predicted that the states would soon forfeit or repeal the corporate charters which had been so misused and perverted. Watson, reading the Standard's trust agreement, saw at once a good chance to prove that the Standard of Ohio had for seven years been violating its charter by placing its affairs in the hands of trustees who were nearly all non-residents. He began searching the reports of the New York and Federal investigations for evidence; and on May 8, 1890, he filed a *quo warranto* petition against the Standard in the Ohio Supreme Court.

The Supreme Court of Ohio took no testimony in the case. It made its decision on the pleadings of the attorney-general and the Standard alone, assuming that all the basic facts were clear. Watson's amended petition pointed out that the stock of the Standard of Ohio had been transferred to trustees; that these trustees had thereafter chosen the directors of the Standard and controlled its management; and that the company had willingly acquiesced in this. He also declared that the company had assisted in carrying out a monopolistic agreement inimical to the public interest. For the defense, Choate, Dodd, and Kline denied that the Standard of Ohio had ever been a party to the Trust agreement. On the contrary, they asserted, the transfer of its stock had been merely an act of its *stockholders.* They denied, too, that its business was conducted by the Trust. On the contrary, it was conducted solely by the board of directors, who were chosen not by the trustees but by the holders of a majority of the stock. They contended that no relationship existed between the Standard of Ohio and the trustees; there was merely a relationship between the individual stockholders and the trustees. Finally, they held that the statute of limitations barred this belated suit.

Rockefeller doubtless expected, like everybody else, that the decision would go against the Standard of Ohio. Its arguments were so specious that nobody was astonished when on March 2, 1892, the court ruled in favor of the state. An able opinion by Judge T. A. Minshall held that the company was actually controlled and managed, indirectly but none the less effectually, by the Trust. It held also that the Trust had violated the common law, for its object was to establish a virtual monopoly and to control prices. Because of the statute of limitations, the charter of the Standard of Ohio was not annulled. But the company was forbidden to maintain the Trust agreement, to recognize further the transfer of stock, or to permit the trustees to control its affairs. It had also to pay the costs of the suit. With the road wide open for similar action in other states against various component elements in the Trust, the anti-monopoly press of the country was jubilant in its comments.

That the chieftains of the Standard were prepared for this blow is evident from the speed with which they took a series of far-reaching steps. The Trust could not stand; very well, the Standard Oil of New Jersey, chartered by a state notably liberal in its grant of privileges to corporations, the Standard of New York, and other major companies would consolidate certain holdings, and their officers would exercise the old consolidated power from 26 Broadway.

Two days after the Ohio decision, on March 4, 1892, the directors of the Standard of New Jersey voted to increase the capital stock from $3,000,000 to $10,000,000, issuing an additional 70,000 shares of $100 par value each. Stockholders owning more than two-thirds of the stock assented to this: Paul Babcock, J. H. Alexander, Thomas C. Bushnell, and the trustees of the Standard Oil Trust, with the two Rockefellers and Flagler at their head. Next day, March 5, President Paul Babcock took the chair at a meeting of stockholders in the Bayonne offices. They resolved to expand the scope of the company's business by adding to the statement of its objects in the incorporation papers the following words: "Also the purchasing, selling, and dealing in crude petroleum and all the products thereof, and all the products obtained by the mixture of petroleum with other products, and all the machinery and materials used in the manufacture of petroleum and any of its products . . . ; and the purchasing, selling, and dealing in the cars, pipes, ships, and packages in which petroleum and its products are transported and marketed, and in the materials and machinery used in the manufacture of such packages."

In short, the Standard of New Jersey was now prepared to do anything whatever in the wide realm of petroleum.

Then on March 17, 1892, after the directors had changed the

name of the corporation from the Standard Oil of New Jersey to the Standard Oil (New Jersey), a sweeping program of acquisitions was carried through. The company purchased *all the property* of the Baltimore United Oil Company, the Camden Consolidated Oil Company, the New Jersey Oil Company, the Bergenport Chemical Company, and the Gilbert & Barker Manufacturing Company. It also bought from the trustees of the Standard Oil Trust large blocks of stock in twenty corporations—the Vacuum Oil Company; the Waters Pierce Oil Company; the Galena Oil Works, Ltd.; Bush & Denslow, and so on—to be paid for with shares of its own stock. A few days later a special meeting of the directors ordered an issue of 60,000 shares, based on $6,000,000 of new capital, to pay for the properties and stocks just acquired. That spring the board of directors was reorganized; Flagler was made president, and Paul Babcock, Jr., the first vice-president; and the internal committees were dropped from the books. Early in 1893, with Rockefeller among the directors, blocks of stock in five more companies were purchased from the trustees. It was the Standard of New Jersey which was now becoming Leviathan.

Alongside it the Standard Oil of New York was also expanded to far greater size. The directors late in March, 1892, took steps to purchase the whole property of the Sone & Fleming Manufacturing Company; Thompson & Bedford Company, Ltd.; the Devoe Manufacturing Company; the Pratt Manufacturing Company; the Acme Oil Company; the American Wick Company; the Atlas Refining Company; and three smaller concerns—paying for them in capital stock. A special stockholders' meeting almost simultaneously increased the stock from $5,000,000 to $7,500,000. The Standard Oil (New Jersey) and the Standard Oil of New York had largely identical boards of directors. In 1893 both included John D. Rockefeller, William Rockefeller (president of the Standard of New York), Flagler, Archbold, H. H. Rogers, Paul Babcock, Jr., and W. H. Tilford. The New Jersey board also numbered J. H. Alexander and C. C. Burke; the New York board the able Charles M. Pratt and the redoubtable Ambrose McGregor. It need not be said that the two great companies, along with those in Pennsylvania, Ohio, and Indiana, acted as a practical unit. The Trust was dead, but the unitary control continued.

And what, meanwhile, of the Trust? The Ohio decision of

course affected merely one of its units; but all were open to attack, and Rockefeller and his associates at once announced through Dodd (March 10, 1892) that the entire Trust would be dissolved. They had no real choice; the Trust itself was illegal under the new Sherman Act, while the attorney-general at Albany had prepared papers and was ready to file them against the New York companies. The trustees asked only for leisure to carry out the dissolution in an orderly manner. They at once notified all holders of trust certificates by mail and by advertisements that a meeting would be held at 26 Broadway on March 21 to vote upon the termination of the Trust agreement, and to take what further action might be necessary.

On the appointed day a fateful air hung about the corridors of 26 Broadway. When some three hundred certificate-holders and spectators had squeezed into a room built for two hundred, Rockefeller rapped for attention—Archbold serving as secretary. The rotund S. C. T. Dodd made a long speech of explanation and defense. Then by unanimous vote of the certificate-holders present, 808,504 shares out of a total of 972,500 were registered in favor of dissolution. It was understood that Rockefeller and the seven other trustees would begin the work of division at once. "It will take about four months," the *Tribune* reporter optimistically predicted.

But was a complete distribution really possible? Dodd hastened to announce that each certificate-holder would get a proportionate share in each of the twenty component companies. (Though forty concerns had originally joined in the Trust agreement, since the recent consolidations only half that many were now controlled by the trustees.) Any other mode of distribution would be impracticable; each man now would necessarily get a part of the omelette into which the original eggs had been merged. The eight trustees therefore issued to each certificate-holder an assignment of legal title in the stock of all twenty companies. The document given to Rockefeller was typical. It recited that he was "the owner of 256,854/972,500 of the amount of corporate stocks held by the trustees of the Standard Oil Trust in each of the several corporations whose stocks were held by such trust on the 1st day of July, 1892," that he was therefore assigned "the legal title to the aforesaid amount of the said stocks," and that the officers of the said corporations would "issue corporate certificates for the required amount of their capital

*From a photograph by Ira Hill*

Rockefeller at Pocantico. With Mr. and Mrs. John D. Rockefeller, Jr. and four of their children: (Left to right: John D. Rockefeller, Jr., Mrs. Rockefeller (the former Abby Aldrich), Laurance S. Rockefeller, John D. Rockefeller, Sr., Winthrop Rockefeller, Mrs. David M. Milton (the former Abby Rockefeller), and Nelson A. Rockefeller.)

Raymond B. Fosdick and George E. Vincent:
Two later leaders in planning the benefactions.

stocks." Dodd assured the stockholders that their interests would remain unchanged. "The various corporations will continue to do the same business as heretofore, and your proportion of the earnings will not be changed."

A simple and natural result ensued. The large holders of Trust certificates presented them and obtained a pro rata portion of the stocks of the component companies. Rockefeller and the seven other trustees all did this. But the little fellows refused to take any such action. Nearly 1600 men and women held comparatively small amounts, and most of them declined to act. As Joseph H. Choate said in 1894: "There is no power that this company can exercise to compel me and other indifferent certificate-holders, if you please, to come forward and convert our trust certificates."

These hundreds of lesser investors continued to hold their Trust certificates, or liquidation certificates, or assignments of legal interest. They did not and would not take stocks. At the end of the first year after the dissolution of the Trust, 477,881 shares remained uncancelled. At the close of the second, third, and fourth years the figure was precisely the same—477,881. As Dodd says in his *Memoirs,* the stockholders bitterly disliked the idea of dissolution. Holding the three kinds of paper listed above, all of which were briskly traded in, they received their dividends from the liquidating trustees just as prior to the dissolution they had received them from the trustees. In fact, the small investor had the best of reasons for refusing to surrender his one piece of paper and take twenty instead. His one piece was readily saleable, but no immediate market existed for the stock of the twenty separate companies. Their shares simply did not pass current. Between 1892 and 1899, writes Taylor, "there was not a share of stock (leaving out of account directors' qualifying shares) in any of the twenty companies transferred from one holder to another except as part of the equivalent in stocks of the twenty companies in one or more Standard Oil Trust certificates."

In effect, the Trust still stood intact! Its management was as well centralized as ever by the interlocking directorates, and by the fact that the presidents (John D. Rockefeller of the Standard of Ohio, James A. Moffett of the Standard of Indiana, William Rockefeller of the Standard of New York, Flagler of the Standard of New Jersey) and other chief officers met so regularly at 26 Broadway. The revenues were distributed not by the eight or nine trustees, but by the same men acting as liquidation trustees. In a technical legal sense, the Trust agreement was dead; in every other sense it remained alive.

Whether because of the Ohio prosecution, or for more fundamental reasons, Rockefeller and his associates by the beginning of 1899 had resolved to alter the form of the great Standard Oil reorganization completely. Rockefeller and Archbold could never consent to a complete disruption of their powerful organization. Yet their practical position since the Ohio decree of 1892 was insecure, for it depended upon continued ownership of a majority of the stock of the twenty companies by a very small group willing to act as a unit. Moreover, it did not fall within any recognized form of legal organization, and therefore invited attack. A change was really overdue.

The use of holding companies on a broad scale was made possible by a New Jersey law of 1888, clarified and broadened in 1889, 1893, and 1896. Until this time the states had generally refused to let one corporation hold the stock of another, save by special enactment. Shrewd executives were quick to see the possibilities which the New Jersey law offered for business reorganization. Nevertheless, for a number of years the holding company remained a little-tried agency, which few attorneys were bold enough to urge upon their clients; and Rockefeller and S. C. T. Dodd rightly regarded it with caution. Between 1889 and 1898, only one of the ten major monopolistic combinations then formed or reorganized took the holding-company shape—the American Cotton Oil Company. The others (though often reincorporating under New Jersey law) tended to resort to outright fusion. The Standard Oil combination assumed a waiting attitude while its heads pondered all aspects of the question.

Such patient study was characteristic of Rockefeller's group, and so was the shrewdness of the decision at which they arrived. They saw that the holding company offered definite advantages over any other form of organization. It was both simpler and less expensive for one central corporation to acquire stock control (that is, mere majority ownership) in other companies than to buy the property of these companies by direct fusion. The operation could be accomplished by gradual steps, without publicity, and without arousing antagonism. It required no action by the stockholders of the companies acquired, and it did not affect the position of bondholders in the least. Rockefeller and Archbold probably also believed that a combination based on holding-company control might be less exposed to anti-trust attacks than a consolidation. Time soon proved that the holding company made possible a far more rapid development of gigantic business organizations than any other method. Only through use of it, or some kindred legal device, would it have been feasible to create such great enterprises, their capital ultimately running into the billions, as the American Telephone and Telegraph Company and the United States Steel Corporation.

The result was that in June, 1899, a great holding company emerged to take charge of the Standard Oil aggregation. The charter of the Standard Oil (New Jersey) was amended; its capital was increased from $10,000,000 to $110,000,000; and it was given 1,000,000 shares of common and 100,000 of preferred. On June 19 the directors authorized the company to exchange this stock for the outstanding certificates of the defunct Standard Oil Trust, and for the stock of the twenty constituent companies. This was done at the rate of one share of the New Jersey common stock for a designated fractional share of New Jersey preferred stock and designated fractional shares of each of the other twenty companies. The fractional share in every instance was the fractional share to which the holder of a Standard Oil Trust certificate became entitled on the distribution of stocks by the Standard Oil Trustees in 1892. The total amount of common stock of the Standard Oil (New Jersey) to be issued under the resolution was 972,500 shares; that is to say, one share for every share of trust certificates outstanding in 1892. The greater part of the stock of the twenty companies was immediately turned in for common stock of the holding company.

This reorganization of course had no effect whatever upon the continuity of the Standard Oil management. The same men remained in the same control, carrying out the same policies in the same way. There had in fact been no break in the continuity of the Standard's management since it became dominant in Cleveland in 1872 and reached out to conquer other fields; and there was to be none until 1911. The president of the Standard was John D. Rockefeller, the vice-president John D. Archbold.

This holding company immediately took its place as one of the richest and most powerful corporations on the globe. Made up at the outset of twenty companies, it soon began purchasing control of others, adding to its list year by year. In 1900 the total net assets of the Standard organization were $205,480,000, and the net profits more than $55,500,000. By 1906 the total net assets were just short of $360,000,000 and the total net earning exceeded $83,120,000. The corporation was a colossus of such size and wealth as nobody—save perhaps Rockefeller—would have dreamed possible twenty-five years before.

With all the properties of the Standard Oil being transferred to the New Jersey holding company, and the nation on the highroad of prosperity again, no reason existed why Rockefeller should not complete his retirement from business. In 1899 he was sixty years of age. His health was impaired. The constant struggles he had waged from 1865 to 1895 had left a deep mark, and his letters after 1890 complain of digestive ailments and nervous fatigue. In 1893 he was stricken with a nervous disease, generalized alopecia, which caused the loss of all his hair and was accompanied by a good deal of physical distress. At the same time he began to grow corpulent. Photographs of 1890 present a man still spare and erect, with abundant brown hair and mustache; those of a half dozen years later show him portly and stooped, his face deeply lined, his head crowned by a black skull-cap which he soon replaced by a wig.

By 1896, he was able to cease going to 26 Broadway every weekday, and thereafter he gradually sloughed off his responsibilities for the Standard Oil. In his *Reminiscences* he gives 1894–95 as the date when he gave up "association with the actual management of the company's affairs." But for several years he occasionally put his hand to the tiller. In 1907 he stated that he had rendered no substantial services for a decade, and had not entered the Standard offices for eight years, so that we may accept 1896 as the date when he relinquished his guidance, and 1897 as the date of final severance.

A younger, more physically vigorous head was really needed, for just after Rockefeller's retirement conditions in the oil industry underwent a momentous set of changes. After 1900 the development of new trans-Mississippi fields went forward at a pace which gave the industry an entirely new aspect. The total yield of crude oil shot up with tremendous rapidity, more than doubling in the first five years of the century. And as the industry adapted itself to this enlargement of the sources of supply, it had also to make the most of the urgent new demands created by the automobile. The horseless carriage of 1895 was a curiosity; by the turn of the century it was a plaything of the rich; a few years more and Henry Ford and others made it a general utility. The cars which grew from eight thousand in 1900 to two and a half million in 1915 in America alone ran largely upon Standard oil fuel and lubricants. Refineries had to be remodeled to give emphasis to gasoline as against kerosene. Instead of depots for tank-wagons, the company had to erect service-stations as ports of call for cars. And Rockefeller and Archbold did not read of what the Wright brothers accomplished at Kitty Hawk without realizing that there, too, lay a new field for applying gasoline power.

As the oil industry thus entered upon a transformation, the place of monopoly within it took on a new character. Rockefeller had built up his great trust primarily to stop the chaotic price-slashing by a multitude of small refineries. For decades, while a few tens of thousands of dollars sufficed to build an effective kerosene-manufactory, he and his associates felt they had to be ruthless in dealing with most newcomers; open the door to a few, and anarchy would overtake the industry again. But now that great new oil fields had been discovered, that the automobile was fast making gasoline the principal product, that oil-refining involved far more complicated processes and expensive machinery than before, and that business was being organized in huger units in every field, no place existed for the small refinery. It was impossible to carry on effective competition without a large capital, and such competition was less likely to be irresponsible and savagely destructive than in the old days. In a word, much of the partial oldtime excuse for monopoly was gone.

It was highly unfortunate for Rockefeller's reputation that he failed to make public his retirement, which was announced neither to the press nor to business associates. Even in the oil industry men were slow to realize that Archbold was the real head of the Standard. Rockefeller should have compelled Archbold to assume the title of president, and seen that his own abandonment of active responsibility was blazoned to the country. It is easy to comprehend his reasons for retaining the empty title of president. The Standard was under heavy fire, and resignation might be construed as retreat. His titular leadership seemed important to the unity and enthusiasm of the personnel. "No name," his associates told him, "can hold this able organization together as yours can." Archbold, who disliked prominence, was especially insistent that he remain. It seemed as difficult for the Standard to do without his fame as for Rome of the early imperial era to do without Cæsar's.

Yet his course was a mistake, for it led to a gross popular misconception of his preëminence which continued down to 1911. This was fostered by editors, cartoonists, financial men, and politicians. They identified Rockefeller with all the Standard's acts long after he ceased to have any responsibility for them. His name provided the obvious label for the Trust, and it was easier to stick to the stereotype than to tell the discriminating truth. Writers clung so tenaciously to it that muckraking magazines of 1900–10 without exception pictured the old man who was merely playing golf, looking after his investments, and supervising his benefactions as the controlling head of the Standard. The London *Economist* remarked in 1911: "Every performance of the Trust is attributed to the sinister figure of Mr. John D. Rockefeller—a figure so subtle and a career so delusive that his critics are forced to find a parallel in romance." Romance indeed! He had then been completely out of the oil business for more than a dozen years.

A double injustice was done Rockefeller by this fiction. Archbold no sooner took charge than he gave Standard a more aggressive direction in almost every department. As the Bureau of Corporations later showed, he raised prices and widened the margin between the cost of crude oil and the charge for refined. He indulged in harsher competitive practices to wipe out marketing rivals at home. He sold oil at low cost abroad and made up for the loss by higher rates in non-competitive domestic areas. At the same time, Archbold meddled with politics much more actively and indiscreetly than the Standard had ever done under Rockefeller. As nominal president, Rockefeller was inevitably held responsible for these acts.

*CHAPTER XV*

# ASSAILANTS AND
# DEFENDERS

B Y THE time that Charles H. Van Hise, president of the University of Wisconsin, published his *Concentration and Control* in 1912, most educated Americans had begun to take a more enlightened view of great industrial aggregations. The reasons for the rise of monopolies were better understood. Brandeis had publicly declared: "Unrestrained competition will lead necessarily to monopoly." Samuel Untermyer, asserting that "the logical outcome of unrestrained competition is legalized monopoly," had added: "Requiring the enforcement of unrestricted competition calls upon people either to make criminals of themselves or to ruin themselves in obeying the law." And Van Hise approvingly quoted Aldace F. Walker: "Unrestrained competition as an economic principle is too destructive to be permitted to exist."

The fact was, pointed out Van Hise, that while combination brought great evils, it also brought great benefits. The problem was to prohibit the abuses, but to see that the public shared in the profits from magnitude, efficiency, and coöperation. But before the detached scientific attitude of Van Hise was possible, an emotional abuse of Rockefeller and the Standard had risen in a wild crescendo, had evoked a series of answers, and had finally inspired his son and the heads of the Standard to undertake a belated use of publicity to present him and the corporation in a fairer light.

The assault on Rockefeller had four main phases: as the architect of the first powerful trust, a monopoly which came into intimate daily relations with the consuming public; as the associate of such men as Daniel O'Day, Henry C. Pierce, F. D. Carley, and Charles Everest, accused (often with convincing evidence) of ruthless and illegal acts; as the builder of perhaps the greatest fortune in history, a socially pernicious concentration of wealth; and as the alleged perpetrator of a number of specially mean offenses, notably the despoliation of the poor Widow Backus. On the first three heads a luxuriant growth of myth and legend came to flourish alongside verifiable charges. The fourth set of accusations, though completely unfounded, did Rockefeller more harm than all the others combined.

In any long-term view of Rockefeller or American economics, the importance to be assigned to Henry Demarest Lloyd's *Wealth Against Commonwealth* is slight. This book, which appeared in 1894, thirteen years after his article "The Story of a Great Monopoly," was based on voluminous new materials, but showed the same distortions and downright errors of his earlier writing. As a piece of business history (which it purports to be) it is ludicrous; as a contribution to biographical data upon Rockefeller it is at best misleading, at worst maliciously false. Its significance lies in the distorted stereotype of Rockefeller which it helped fasten upon the public mind. To be sure, it never mentioned him by name; but it pretended to be a record of the worst misdeeds of the Standard Oil, and he figures on many pages as the head of that colossus. Lloyd, a practiced journalist, brought out his book at the precise moment when it was certain to seize the public imagination. The country was suffering from panic and depression; the Populist movement was rising to its climax; the Pullman strike, marked by Cleveland's use of troops, filled the breasts of laboring men with bitterness; millions of mortgage-ridden farmers and unemployed workingmen were convinced that plutocratic forces were strangling democracy. Using the evidence gathered in the Hepburn investigation, the New York State Senate inquiry into trusts, the investigation of monopoly by the federal House committee, and other materials, Lloyd rehearsed in detail all the charges against the Standard. The very prejudice and distortion of his book added to its effectiveness.

What here concerns us is not an appraisal of the mixture of fact and fiction in *Wealth Against Commonwealth;* it is its effect upon the reputation of Rockefeller. Most people in 1894 were in no mood to read it critically. They found in it the first full, coherent story of the Standard Oil in print; they noted that a great part of it was built on government reports and court documents; they saw that the Standard made no effort to reply to it. As it harmonized with the mood of the moment, they accepted it as a truthful indictment.

Rockefeller and his associates erred, as they had thirteen years before, in not meeting Lloyd's attack with an emphatic defense. They had it in their power, had they supplied the evidence to some careful writer, to confute many of Lloyd's pages. But to do this now as in 1881 would involve making injurious admissions at various points, and for that they were not prepared. It would have dragged the Standard leaders into controversy, and stimulated anew the well-justified attack on their railroad arrangements and marketing practices. Rockefeller, believing a dignified silence the best policy, did not comprehend until too late that it was construed as an admission of guilt all along the line.

Oil Regions critics, hostile journals like the New York *World*, and men like Lloyd succeeded in fixing an ugly stereotype of Rockefeller and the Trust upon the public mind. It was deepened by the growing anti-monopoly feeling of the 1890's, and the widespread and warranted exasperation when Attorney General Richard Olney's case against the Sugar Trust broke down in 1895. A fear was arising that monopoly might prove too strong for the government to overthrow.

It was while the healthy antagonism to monopoly was growing more intense, moreover, that the Standard Oil conducted a long, stubborn-tempered, and happily unsuccessful fight against the competitive organization which ultimately took the name of the Pure Oil Company. And then occurred a dramatic event. The gifted Ida M. Tarbell published in *McClure's Magazine* the first installment of her *History of the Standard Oil Company* (November, 1902). The time, the magazine, and the writer combined to make this serialized book the most spectacular success of the muckraking school of journalism, and its most enduring achievement. Theodore Roosevelt had now been in power for a year; he had begun his trust-busting by ordering a suit against the Morgan-Hill-Harriman creation, the Northern Securities Company; and his annual message in December called for new weapons against industrial monopoly. S. S. McClure and John S. Phillips had given their monthly a circulation and prestige such as no magazine of equal solidity and literary quality had ever enjoyed. Directly or indirectly, it reached nearly the whole lit-

erate public of America. As for Miss Tarbell, she was a daughter
of the Oil Regions, where her father had been a prominent if
unprosperous producer. Growing up amid the tumult and shouting of the wars between Producers' Association men and Standard men, the girl felt a fervent sympathy for the independents.
A graduate of Allegheny College, a staff member first of the
*Chautauquan* and then of *McClure's,* the author of brilliantly
successful articles and of a path-breaking book on Lincoln, she
had achieved by 1901 a well-earned reputation as a writer. Now
she rose to her greatest opportunity.

Into her work on the Standard she threw all her industry,
earnestness, and skill. She went through the mountainous testimony of the various investigations and law-suits; she searched
the press; she traveled back to the Regions to interview people.
When H. H. Rogers sent word through Mark Twain that he
would talk with her, she held a number of conferences with him
at 26 Broadway. Rogers's ostensible motive was to help make
the story fair and complete, but he also wished to protect himself. Still other members of the Standard organization, with the
approval of the directors, assisted Miss Tarbell with information
until they became convinced that she had no intention of doing
the combination justice. Then her facilities were cut off. In every
respect but one her labors were as searching as four years of toil
and ample expense funds could make them. The principal de-
ficiency of her work was that she sought out comparatively few
of the hundreds of veterans of the oil industry, both supporters
and opponents of the Standard, whom she might have seen. Historians must always regret that she did not make a wider search
for evidence, and deal less frequently in half truths.

Although readers today are likely to find her sober, factual
history difficult to read, in 1902–04 the public had a background
of knowledge which lent the articles a stirring interest. Men
now forgotten were then vivid public figures; legal battles now
dimmed by time were then excitingly real. Before McClure,
Phillips published the two volumes in 1904 it had made a deep
impression on the public mind; the deeper because Miss Tarbell
avoided the hysterical emotion of Lloyd and strove to document
every part of her story. The gravamen of her indictment was
simple. Rockefeller and his associates, she argued, had built up a
combination which was admirable in its organized efficiency and
power; but nearly every step in the construction of this vast in-

dustrial machine had been attended by fraud, coercion, or special privilege, which had debased the whole standard of American business morality.

Her book was received with an explosion of applause from press, pulpit, and political leaders. Reissued in 1925, the work stands beside Lincoln Steffens's *The Shame of the Cities,* John Spargo's *The Bitter Cry of the Children,* and Ray Stannard Baker's *Following the Color Line* as an enduring product of the early progressive movement.

The first decade of the century found the dynamic, versatile, endlessly fascinating Theodore Roosevelt establishing the firmest and the most healthful ascendency over the American people gained by any political leader since Lincoln. He was an astonishingly forceful moral teacher, all the more effective for his superficial tendency to see the world in blacks and whites; he loved to teach by example; and in his crusade against monopoly, the Standard and John D. Rockefeller inevitably became as striking examples as were E. H. Harriman and the Union Pacific in his crusade against railroad malpractice. In his public utterance and private letters he repeatedly fulminated against Rockefeller, whom he regarded as still active director—nay, dictator—of the Standard's policies and acts. Quite properly, Roosevelt called for a moral regeneration of business. One result of such a moral regeneration, he told Congress in a special message of January 31, 1908, would be to prevent "a repetition of the successful effort by the Standard Oil people to crush out every competitor, to overawe the common carriers, and to establish a monopoly which treats the public with a contempt which the public deserves so long as it permits men of such principles and such sentiments to avow and act on them with impunity."

A not unnatural sequel of Ida M. Tarbell's book and articles, and of Roosevelt's denunciations, was the curious "tainted money" controversy which enlivened the American scene in the spring and summer of 1905. It flared up when a number of Congregational ministers, notably Washington Gladden, protested against the acceptance by the Congregational Board of Foreign Missions of $100,000 from Rockefeller. A three months' wonder, it died away when the most excited participants found, to their chagrin, that the Board had actually solicited the money! While the debate raged, it was announced on June 28, 1904, that Rockefeller had given a million dollars to Yale, and two days later that he had granted ten millions to the General Education Board; and nobody proposed that these sums be rejected! "Gifts of ten millions," wittily remarked the New York *Sun*, "deodorize themselves."

The phrase "tainted money" was telling even if absurd, and the whole press took it up. From the time of this tainted-money battle the Standard ceased to accept passively all the attacks rained upon its head; it struck back. The *Nation's* review of Miss Tarbell's *Standard Oil*, indicting the book as sensational, misleading, and ill-informed, was reprinted and scattered broadcast. Articles friendly to the combination and to Rockefeller blossomed out more frequently in important periodicals. The *Cosmopolitan*, the *Woman's Home Companion*, and the *Outlook* all published articles favorable to Rockefeller and the Standard. In 1907 Gates made a public statement, perfectly accurate, though it met with much jesting and incredulity, that Rockefeller's fortune was less than $300,000,000—"only three hundred, poor man!" said people. And in 1909 wide publicity was given to a list of his larger public benefactions, amounting to more than $112,000,000.

The shrill abuse of Rockefeller which reached a climax in the years 1900–10 had features which would repay study by a social psychologist. Men love to nurse any prejudice which gives them a sense of ethical superiority; from the day of Titus Oates people have rejoiced in personifications of evil; a prominent target always attracts missiles. In this very period Theodore Roosevelt was as harshly attacked by conservative periodicals as Rockefeller was denounced by the muckraking press. Some of the best of Americans, from Jefferson to Franklin D. Roosevelt, have suffered from a spate of foul abuse, from whispering campaigns, from libels too gross to print; and rich men are always found guilty before they are tried. It would be a mistake to take seriously the scum of libel which always floats on the stream of public discussion.

In this instance, however, four special circumstances contributed to the avalanche of obloquy that fell on Rockefeller's head. In the first place, the personal attacks on Rockefeller as an oppressor of the weak—the attacks based on the Widow Backus fable, and so on—were as effective as they were false. Rockefeller felt it beneath his dignity to refute them as Theodore Roosevelt refuted the charge of habitual drunkenness; hence they were believed. In the second place, the Standard as the first Trust, and as a marketing agency in touch with the masses, was singled out for a special attention that blinded men to certain historical facts. Most of the great combinations of the time were guilty of grave derelictions. It would have been wrong to palliate or excuse these offenses, but it was important to recognize that they were general. In the third place, Rockefeller was pictured as a despotic head of his organization, responsible for its every act, when he was simply the chief of a group of powerful men, each largely supreme in his own sphere. And in the fourth place, many critics assumed that Rockefeller's philanthropies were taken out of a Standard slush-fund and were used to wash away the sins of both. They did not know that his gifts stretched back to a poor lad's first earnings and had grown steadily with his income.

With his son and Gates urging him forward, Rockefeller after 1905 began to appear more frequently in the public view. He gave out occasional interviews, and allowed his few and modest speeches to be widely republished. It was observed that he never spoke querulously, never publicly alluded to any assailant, and never engaged in controversy. Norman Hapgood in *Harper's Weekly* noted to his credit that he had never, during all the muckraking period, made an impatient comment, and never in any public appearance betrayed the slightest irritation. He was satisfied to leave his reputation to history.

In the years 1906–09 the Standard underwent a veritable drumfire of government exposures and prosecutions. Federal bureaus assailed it. Legal representatives of the government brought actions. Rockefeller and others were pursued by subpoena-servers, haled to the witness stand, and threatened with dire punishment. By midsummer of 1907 the national government had seven suits pending against the Standard and its various subsidiaries, while others were being pushed by state officers in Texas, Minnesota, Missouri, Tennessee, Ohio, and Mississippi.

The federal government's attack on the Standard began in 1906. In May the Bureau of Corporations, which Theodore Roosevelt had induced Congress to establish, filed a report on the transportation of petroleum which had been apprehensively awaited by Standard executives. The government published a crisp, readable summary in the newspapers, where it caught the attention of the whole country.

Specifically, the Bureau made two basic charges with respect to the Standard's position in the transportation field. The first was that it had habitually obtained, and was then receiving, *secret* rates and other unjust and illegal discriminations from the railroads. The second was that it also obtained unjust *open* discrimination in rates. Both charges were supported by detailed evidence. This report was a telling blow at the Standard, and a most effective stroke in favor of new railroad legislation.

The most cogent answer by the Standard—an elaborate and technical answer—was written by Charles M. Pratt by order of the directors, and sent to stockholders in the middle of May. This wordy war over the question whether the Standard had been accepting discriminatory favors involved intricate technicalities in rate-making. But it is clear that the main charges were valid. Most of the evidence, indeed, spoke for itself. Roosevelt shortly delivered a speech on the trust question full of fiery denunciation; and the report, as he had planned, helped to batter a path for the Hepburn Rate Bill that summer.

It is significant that the Standard and the railroads took action to cancel most of the rates which the Bureau had condemned. The New Haven, for example, began to pro-rate on oil, thus saving about eight cents a hundredweight to independent refiners of Pennsylvania and Ohio who were shipping into New England. The published rates on oil shipments from Whiting to points in Michigan and northern Indiana were advanced by two or three cents a hundredweight. In California secret rates were abolished, and discriminations adjusted. The Senate swiftly passed the Knox Bill giving the Interstate Commerce Commission jurisdiction over the pipe lines as common carriers, and these provisions shortly became part of the Hepburn Act. With the threat of indictments hanging over their heads, the Standard and the railroads continued to make fairer rate adjustments.

Meanwhile, the suit of Attorney-General Hadley in Missouri to prove that the Standard of Indiana, the Waters Pierce Company, and the Republic Oil Company were parts of one monopolistic combination, was filling a vast amount of newspaper space. Overwhelming testimony was brought out during 1905 that these companies had a close working arrangement.

New storms were bursting about the Standard throughout the summer and fall of 1906. On June 22 Attorney-General Moody announced that the government would prosecute the Standard

Oil with all its might, and that every possible case against it would be brought to trial. The subject had been discussed at a mysterious night meeting in the White House, when all the lawyers among the President's advisers conferred with him, and it was the principal subject again at a regular Cabinet meeting.

Of all these attacks, the suit to dissolve the Standard under the Sherman Act, filed November 18 in the Circuit Court of Missouri, was the most important. The defendants named were the Standard of New Jersey, the sixty-five or more corporations which it was alleged to control, and seven individuals—the two Rockefellers, Flagler, Payne, Archbold, Rogers, and Pratt. The charges had the broadest character. Rockefeller and his partners, they recited, had conspired at an early date to control the oil industry through restraints upon interstate commerce. The trust agreements of 1879 and 1882, the evasion for seven years of the Ohio dissolution decree of 1892, and the erection of the New Jersey holding company in 1899, had been successive milestones in that history of a brazen monopoly. The government charged that the Standard had gained its dominant position not by superior efficiency, but by unfair and immoral acts—rebate-taking, local price-cutting, operation of bogus "independents," improper control of pipe lines, and so on.

Thus opened one of the greatest anti-trust cases in American history. It was plain that the time was now at hand when it would be decided whether the Standard Oil combination or the Department of Justice was the stronger. Early in 1907, the Interstate Commerce Commission published a fierce indictment of Standard methods. The Roosevelt administration, the officials of a dozen states, and the great majority of the American people had decided that the combination was a pernicious monopoly and must be broken up. By evasion and obstruction, it might postpone the decision, but not for long. Beyond the act of dissolution the government did not look; it did not inquire whether it would be effective or ineffective, its results good or bad. But as once in their history the American people had said they were tired of kings, as later they said they were tired of slavery, so now they were tired of flagrant monopolies; they would suffer them no more.

The first of several heavy shocks which the Standard sustained in 1907 was the report of May 20 by the Bureau of Corporations upon the position of the company in the oil industry—a docu-

ment which arraigned the combination as a violator of federal
and state laws.

On the heels of this report came the decisions in the Missouri
and Texas cases against affiliates of the Standard Oil. On May 24,
the findings of the commissioner appointed to collect testimony
in the Missouri suit were presented to the court. He had compressed into a moderate-sized volume the principal facts gained
from more than 3000 printed pages of testimony. The commissioner found the three accused companies guilty of an illegal
agreement to lessen competition, control prices, and deceive the
public by posing as independents. He recommended that the
charter of the Waters Pierce Company be rescinded, that the
other two companies be forbidden to do business in Missouri, and
that each be fined $50,000.

The Waters Pierce Company was found guilty of violating
the anti-trust law every day since its re-establishment in 1900; and
on June 1, 1907, it was ejected from Texas and fined $1,623,000.
In vain did it appeal to the federal Supreme Court. The decision was confirmed, and in the spring of 1909 it paid its fine and
interest, amounting to more than $1,800,000—officers carrying
bills for that amount in a suitcase to the state capitol! Before
the year ended the property of the company was sold to a friend
of Pierce named Fordyce, and soon a new company, the Pierce
Fordyce Oil Association, was running the old Waters Pierce business in the state. The Southwest was grimly satisfied with this
victory over the Standard. At once Mississippi sued the Standard
for $1,480,000 in penalties under the state anti-trust laws.

But if the Texas case was spectacular, far more so was one which
immediately followed it, bringing Rockefeller himself to the witness stand; the Alton case under the Elkins Act, which Judge
Landis's fine made a *cause célèbre*. By this time it had been abun-
dantly proved that the federal laws against rebating really had
teeth. Despite the efforts of Joseph H. Choate, the New York
Central had recently been found guilty of giving rebates to the
Sugar Trust. It was therefore not a light charge which government prosecutors made in alleging that in 1903–05 the Standard
of Indiana had taken rebates on hundreds of carloads of oil
shipped from Whiting to East St. Louis over the Chicago & Alton.

Kenesaw Mountain Landis, presiding over the trial, had but
recently been appointed to the federal bench. On August 3,
1907, the country was startled to read that Judge Landis, fol-

lowing a verdict of guilty by the jury, had fined the Standard of Indiana $29,240,000—assessing the maximum penalty of $20,000 each for the 1462 counts based on as many carloads of oil. Landis's bizarre name, lank form, and Lincolnesque features instantly became famous. The text of his decision, delivered before another huge crowd, contained stinging reproaches and accusations, which the audience greeted with uproarious laughter.

The Standard immediately appealed, and in August, 1908, Judge Grosscup of the federal Circuit Court found that Landis had grossly erred, and ordered a retrial. Because Grosscup assailed Landis's procedure in fixing the fine as an "abuse of judicial discretion," the latter refused to sit in the case. When the retrial took place, Judge Anderson instructed the jury that "the Government has failed to prove its charge." After a verdict of "not guilty," the government paid the costs.

Two days after Landis's fine, the Bureau of Corporations brought out its last excoriation of the Standard in a report on prices and profits in the oil industry. It was evident that this report had a special interest to tens of millions of American consumers who used Standard Oil products. Were they paying more than they should? To this question the Bureau uttered an emphatic "yes." Commissioner Smith assured the nation that when the Standard boasted of its great services in reducing costs, it was deceiving the public. Of course, the price of oil had fallen; but the report ascribed the fall in the period 1866–74 to competitive conditions, and in more recent years to automatic factors like the building of pipe lines. It pointed out that the few independents which survived did a profitable business at rates much lower than the average Standard Oil prices.

Commissioner Smith conceded that the Standard possessed much greater efficiency than its rivals, but he added that the difference had been exaggerated. The total economies through superior efficiency perhaps reached about $1\frac{1}{2}$ cents on each gallon of oil processed. But Commissioner Smith objected that the Standard did not hand on this saving to the public.

The two federal reports of 1907 produced an immediate effect. Independent refiners were soon testifying that the revelations had brought about a substantial improvement in their business. In 1909 Congress practically repealed the retaliatory duty which had shut out imports of petroleum from abroad.

The sharp but brief panic of 1907 was now at hand. The financial storm, which blew itself out before the year ended, did nothing to check the progress of the government prosecutions. The summer of 1907 had found seven federal and six state actions pending against the Standard or its subsidiaries. One suit loomed high above all others in importance: that begun in the federal Circuit Court of Eastern Missouri in the fall of 1906 to dissolve the entire combination as a conspiracy in restraint of trade. Seventy-nine corporations and individuals were named as defendants. The center of attack, however, was the New Jersey holding company, with its stock in nine Standard Oil companies and sixty-two other corporations. Roosevelt was determined to break up this combination once and forever. Frank B. Kellogg, as special prosecutor, spent most of 1907 in accumulating evidence before a federal examiner; and the second chapter of the suit began in May, 1908, when the Standard opened the presentation of its case.

As one witness after another testified before the federal examiner, an imposing amount of evidence was piled up. Counsel for the government succeeded in obtaining admissions, for the first time, of (1) the ownership by the Standard of New Jersey of recognized subcompanies; (2) the use of these subcompanies in managing the oil business by areas; (3) the Standard's monopoly of the export trade; (4) the fact that ten men, or their estates, owned far more than a majority of the holding company's stock; and (5) that the Standard's net earnings within eight years had been nearly one-half billion, and within a quarter century almost a billion dollars. The records of the trustees in liquidation after the Ohio decree of 1892 were procured, and the means by which the trust had been maintained virtually intact for seven years elucidated. Facts to prove actual restraint of trade were elicited.

Rockefeller appeared on the witness stand in the new Custom House in New York on November 18, 1908, to begin his three days' testimony. He had been carefully coached. Day after day early that month passers on lower Broadway stared as they saw him, wearing mittens and a paper waistcoat, enter No. 26. Reporters inferred that he was "attending to business again," but actually he was being drilled by Standard attorneys.

Questioned by his own lawyers on the first two days, Rockefeller gave a historical account of the Standard Oil combination. He spoke with a blandly reminiscent air, like a country gentleman regaling friends with some tale of the good old times. In a soothing discourse, he undertook to show that the Standard Oil empire had been built up by benevolent assimilation. The *World* listed the new definitions he had given business. *"Railroad Rebate:* A voluntary compensation paid by the railroads for ample services rendered at a great disadvantage to the beneficiary of the rebate." *"Trust:* A philanthropic institution created by the benevolent absorption of competitors to save them from ruin, combined with the humane conservation and ingenious utilization of natural resources for the benefit of the people." *"Riches:* Results of incessant borrowing from friends and uniform kindness to competitors."

This recital finished, Rockefeller was questioned closely for five hours by Kellogg. His swift change to taciturnity amused the press:

John D. Rockefeller's memory was bright as a coin from the mint while his own lawyer was interrogating him. During the two days on the witness stand there was scarcely the minutest detail that he could not recall for forty years back. But on the third day, when the government counsel began a cross-examination, he hadn't a memory as long as a shoestring. His mind was as opaque as an oyster-shell. Just think of it; in a single night that bright, clean mind vanished! Oh, the pity of it!

Taft had not been in the White House nine months when, on November 20, 1909, the Circuit Court gave a decision which entirely upheld the government. The Standard of New Jersey was ordered to divest itself of all subsidiaries within thirty days. Taft publicly congratulated Kellogg on his "complete victory." The Standard immediately appealed the case to the Supreme Court, where it was first argued in March, 1910, and reargued in January, 1911.

The final decision was handed down, after Taft had become irritable over the delay, on May 15, 1911. Chief Justice White, heavy of body and mind, mounted the bench. As he began reading his 20,000-word opinion, all his colleagues seemed in good humor save Justice Harlan, who alone dissented. White stated the case and pointed out the irreconcilable conflicts of law and fact in the briefs. He went on to say that all parties agreed that the controversy was controlled by a correct conception of the first two sections of the Sherman Act. His own interpretation was that the "standard of reason" of the English common law in monopoly cases should be the legal standard; that the Sherman

Act meant "to prevent undue restraints of every kind and nature." Harlan vehemently objected to reading "standard of reason" and "undue" into the law. Its prohibitions, he declared, were absolute. All the judges agreed that the Standard had violated the Sherman Act. No one could survey the history of the combination, asserted White, without concluding that "the very genius for commercial development and organization" which created the Trust had soon begotten an intent to set up a monopoly. The object of the Standard had been "to drive others from the field and exclude them from their right to trade."

Within six months, declared the court, the Standard must divest itself of all its subsidiaries. It should do this by transferring back to the stockholders of the original companies all the stock they had exchanged for shares in the New Jersey corporation. The companies and their officers were enjoined from doing anything to reëstablish the combination. The decree was aimed not against offensive trade practices, which were never really proved, but against the limitations which the huge holding company had laid upon freedom of competition in the market place.

Forty years earlier, in the fall of 1871, Rockefeller had begun to build his edifice. It had risen with amazing speed, expanded with prodigious vigor, awed the whole industrial world, and taught business a hundred memorable lessons. Now the courts had decreed not its destruction, but its separation into thirty-odd component parts—many of them giant in size.

And what were the results of the dissolution?

Even enemies of the Standard could not but feel admiration for the strength to which it had attained. In 1906 its plants, scattered from sea to sea, had consumed more than 68,200,000 barrels of crude oil. Its 88,000 miles of pipe lines netted the country, and it pumped oil direct from Oklahoma to Bayonne. Its tank farms contained 75,000,000 or 80,000,000 barrels of stored oil. On an average day it poured nearly 35,000 barrels of illuminants and gasoline into the markets of the world. It sold nearly 4,000,000 barrels of lubricants annually. It turned out enormous quantities of by-products, such as 300,000,000 candles of 700 different kinds every year. Its fleet of tankers numbered 78 steamers and 19 sailing vessels.

Now the empire had to be divided. Before 1911 ended the combination was separated into thirty-eight companies, which had no common officers or directors, the stocks of thirty-three subsidiaries being distributed to share holders in the New Jersey Company on December 1. This act involved the use of some complicated fractions. The denominator in each instance was 983,383, the number of outstanding shares in the Standard of New Jersey; the numerator was the number of shares it held in each subsidiary. Thus every share in the Standard of New Jersey entitled its owner to 994/983383 of a share in Swan & Finch, and 599994/983383 of a share in the Ohio Oil Company, these being the two extremes! At once several firms specializing in Standard Oil securities sprang up in Wall Street.

While the dissolution meant an enhanced initiative, for some time it carried little or no increase in competition. The various companies had divided their fields either territorially or functionally. They continued for years to respect the eleven old territorial divisions, though functional lines were less easily maintained. The Standard of Indiana long took pains not to cut into areas held by the Standard of Ohio, and vice versa. The Standard of New York, which had been the great exporting agency of the combination, now increased its distributing business in New York State; but it and the Standard of New Jersey tried not to trespass on each other's limits. The shares of the thirty-odd companies were so largely owned by the same small group that, in theory at least, the old chieftains could control the directorates and hence the policies. Rockefeller himself, despite his large benefactions, was credited at the time of the dissolution with 244,500 of the 983,383 shares of stock in the Standard of New Jersey.

No less a person than Theodore Roosevelt, the oldtime apostle of "trust-busting," was quick to acknowledge that the dissolution had in large part been a failure, and that the policy of the government in dealing with great combinations required a drastic modification. Control, not attack, should be its objective. Quite correctly, Roosevelt declared that the people of the United States had but one instrument which they could efficiently use against the colossal combinations of business—the Federal Government. Quite correctly, he declared that the decrees of the courts against the Northern Securities Company, the Standard Oil, and the Tobacco Trust were a vital affirmation of the power of the government to destroy monopoly. That "pure competition" was an anachronism, however, that the causes producing combination were natural and irresistible, and that the government must make a studied effort to preserve the good elements in big business while destroying the vicious, he and others by 1912 had come to recognize.

As the years passed, the units of the great Standard flotilla inevitably drifted apart. Stock ownership became widely diffused; old leaders gave way to new. As fields were opened in fresh areas, more capital came in. Automobiles were sold in tens of millions, the world market expanded, and the industry became more competitive. The principal companies engaged in refining and marketing began to "integrate backward" and obtain direct control over crude oil; the production and transportation companies combated this by integrating forward to control their own markets. In short, economic developments brought about a breakdown of the old Standard Oil monopoly which laws and courts had been unable to attain. But it should be noted that the competition which resulted has been primarily a service-competition, not a price-competition. Reduction of charges, all factors considered, has been illusory. Any motorist who finds at his crossroads four service stations of four different companies, selling substantially the same gasoline at precisely the same prices, and battling for trade by variations in washroom facilities, has reason to ponder upon the proper limits of competition.

Beyond question, the vindication of the Sherman Act by the 1911 decision was indispensable. The American people are committed to the theory that, in industries not natural monopolies, and not subject to strict government regulation, a reasonable competition must at all costs be preserved. The breakup of the oil and tobacco combinations under Taft establishes an invaluable principle. But it is certain that the mere passage of laws will not solve difficult problems of industrial organizations, and that, as the history of the Clayton Act, the Federal Trade Commission, the trade association movement under Hoover, and the N. R. A. all shows, the working out of a proper adjustment between competition and combination must be a long, slow, and painful process. The dissolution was in one sense a condemnation of what Rockefeller had accomplished. But some values of the great experiment in industrial organization which he had conducted, some uses of that huge object-lesson in efficient consolidation, were permanent.

The World War came on; the tumult and shouting over the trust problem died away as far more exigent tasks demanded attention. When the guns were silent again and the country entered on its post-war boom, the Sherman Act was for a time almost forgotten. Few suits were pressed to a conclusion. Adverse reports by the Federal Trade Commission on the Aluminum Trust and Sugar Institute were ignored, while the courts took a changed view. Said William E. Humphrey of the Trade Commission: "It is not that the courts flout statutory law, but that they interpret it in harmony with economic law. They are changing with the people and the times." The concentration of business control increased until in 1933 more than half the corporate wealth of the nation was owned by 594 companies. This was an unhealthy situation, and the New Deal days brought a much-needed reaction; but the fresh anti-monopoly campaign was never marked by the heat, impatience, and denunciation of the time of Theodore Roosevelt. The American people had learned much. They looked more tolerantly upon Rockefeller's objective of a completely controlled and efficiently integrated industry. What they chiefly condemned, in retrospect, was not the aim, but the unfair and unsocial practices which had accompanied the achievement and maintenance of that aim.

# CHAPTER XVI

# "THE WELL-BEING OF MANKIND"

THE first benefactions established by Rockefeller—the University of Chicago, the Institute for Medical Research, and the General Education Board—were primarily national in scope. But Americans were learning to look far beyond national horizons. Since Rockefeller had entered business, the United States had become one of the leading world powers; the plane of thought, science, and general culture on which Americans moved was increasingly international; poverty, disease, and social backwardness in far-off lands affected American welfare as well as sensibilities. Rockefeller realized, moreover, that as he had made his fortune in the world marketplace, he owed a debt to mankind as a whole. As the fortune grew, rising above the five hundred million mark toward a billion, it became imperative for him to find some powerful new agency of disbursement; and it was inevitable that he and his advisers, thinking upon the problem in the years 1905-10, should explore the idea of an institution of international scope. The result was the Rockefeller Foundation, the first strong agency of global philanthropy and stimulation erected in any land.

Rockefeller's first ten years of experience with the Institute and the General Education Board not only proved that great results could be achieved by placing large funds at the absolutely independent disposal of boards of expert and statesmanlike men; they also brought him into touch with three administrators who gained his confidence almost as fully as did his son and Frederick T. Gates—Dr. Wallace Buttrick, Dr. Simon Flexner, and Dr.

Wickliffe Rose. With this triumvirate at his command, Rockefeller felt safe in devoting an extraordinary sum of money (nearly a quarter of a billion dollars in the end) to an extraordinarily broad object, "the well-being of mankind." These men could find others of a vision and skill as great as their own. They did find such men: Abraham Flexner, George E. Vincent, Jerome D. Greens, and Richard M. Pearce, among others. An organization was established which, royally endowed and imaginatively directed, did a pioneering work of brilliant originality, enthusiasm, and vigor. It was the Columbus, the Sir Francis Drake, of foundations. As great funds rise and decay, its early years will always hold a special place, a pristine lustre, in the history of such bodies.

The origin of the Rockefeller Foundation doubtless lies in unrecorded talks among Rockefeller, his son, and the fertile-minded Gates early in the century. These men chatted freely with each other; they talked of American and foreign needs; with a lively belief in progress, they drew up numerous plans, revising, discarding, combining, perfecting. Gates was always the boldest thinker. A germ of the Foundation may perhaps be found in the letter which he addressed to Rockefeller on June 3, 1905:

I have lived with this great fortune of yours daily for fifteen years. To it, and especially its uses, I have given every thought. It has been impossible for me to ignore the great question of what is to be the end of all this wealth. . . .

Two courses seem to me open. One is that you and your children, while living, should make final disposition of this great fortune in the form of permanent corporate philanthropies for the good of mankind. . . .

The things to be done become obvious, though by no means easy. They are to ascertain:

First, what are the prominent lines of human need and human progress? It is a well studied but difficult field of inquiry.

Second, what men can be found competent to administer these trusts now and in successive generations?

Third, what elements of human progress suggest themselves as of sufficient practical importance and promise to invite specific legal endowment?

Gates went on to suggest that Rockefeller might well create a fund for the promotion of medical research throughout the world, and a fund for the promotion of Christian ethics and civilization on a global basis, as well as purely national funds for stimulating higher education, enriching rural life, and promoting intelligent citizenship. "It is true," he wrote, "that no historic personage has made benefactions so vast or so broad in scope as those here contemplated, but nothing less would befit the vastness of your fortune and the universality of its sources."

We may be sure that the ideas thus put on paper were frequently discussed in Rockefeller's presence, and with the son. In 1906 John D. Rockefeller, Jr. wrote his father about a recent conversation in which they had mulled over the idea of "a large trust fund to which you would turn over considerable sums of money to be devoted to philanthropy, education, science, and religion." Although troubled by the manifest difficulty of collecting a single compact body of men who would unite expertness in such diverse fields with the requisite working traits, the younger Rockefeller was anxious to develop the project. Conference followed conference. It was Rockefeller's wont to ponder such large matters slowly and cautiously. But when he reached a conclusion it was also his wont to act decisively. On June 19, 1909, he signed over to three trustees (his son, Gates, and Harold McCormick) $50,000,000 in Standard Oil securities, "to promote the well-being and to advance the civilization" of the people of the United States and foreign lands. The breadth of this statement harmonized with the letter of Gates just quoted. But Rockefeller made it plain that a federal charter should be obtained before the Foundation began its work. In March, 1910, Senator Aldrich introduced an appropriate bill in Congress.

This bill might well have been passed forthwith. Instead, it met a sudden surge of opposition. In part this came from editors and politicians who found anything connected with Rockefeller anathema, and who, as the Chicago *Inter-Ocean* remarked, would have denounced even a bill enabling him to give all his money to the government. In part it came from more responsible observers, who were disturbed by the vagueness of the objects proposed, the magnitude of the anticipated resources, and the implied perpetuity of the grant. Rumor predicted that a half billion might soon pass to the foundation, and suspicious men feared that so powerful an organization might indulge in wild destructive orgies. Stubbornly opposed by President Taft and Attorney-General George Wickersham among others (Taft actually spoke of it as a bill "to incorporate Mr. Rockefeller"), the measure failed of passage. Even when amended to set various limits upon the powers granted, it was halted short of vote in the Senate. A western editor remarked that the measure was represented by "the most powerful lobby ever seen in Washington"—though that lobby actually consisted solely of Mr. Jerome D. Greene, recently secretary of the Harvard Corporation!

The futile struggle to get the measure through Congress lasted three years. Meanwhile Rockefeller had revoked his initial gift. Finally, he and his associates turned to the New York legislature, which without the slightest difficulty, and without attracting any public notice, in May, 1913, chartered the Foundation. All the restrictions to which the Rockefeller group had consented in an effort to placate Congress were now happily omitted, and the purpose of the Foundation was summed up in a single crisp clause: "To promote the well-being of mankind throughout the world." During that first year Rockefeller endowed the Foundation with slightly more than $34,430,000 and the next year he added nearly $65,570,000 more.

At the initial meeting of the trustees in May, 1913, John D. Rockefeller, Jr., was elected president and Jerome D. Greene secretary, the latter post being that of direct administrative responsibility. Temporarily Greene might have been pardoned for thinking himself almost the whole Foundation: "There was a brief time in my little room at 26 Broadway," he remarked later, "when one secretary with a four-drawer file constituted the staff and equipment of the Rockefeller Foundation." The son of a missionary to Japan, a graduate of Harvard, secretary first to the president and then to the corporation of that university, and in 1910–12 general manager of the Rockefeller Institute, he possessed many qualifications for his post—an alert mind, wide reading, tact, and a creative instinct. Presiding over the Foundation was a board of nine trustees. They comprehended, in addition to the two Rockefellers, Gates, and Greene, President Harry Pratt Judson of the University of Chicago, Dr. Simon Flexner, Starr J. Murphy, Charles O. Heydt, and Wickliffe Rose. President Charles W. Eliot of Harvard and A. Barton Hepburn of the Chase National Bank—the man who had helped direct the famous Hepburn investigation!—were soon added. It was not an ornamental board; these trustees really worked. Most of all did Gates, Greene, and the younger Rockefeller work like devoted slaves.

"The well-being of mankind throughout the world"—just how was it to be promoted? Several years earlier Rockefeller had spoken of the importance of ultimates, of "finalities." The best philanthropy, he had remarked, "involves a search for cause, an attempt to cure evils at their source." To Greene was entrusted the task of preparing a report on principles and policies. On October 21, 1913, he laid before the trustees a memorandum which, based on the long experience of Rockefeller as a giver and on the practices of the General Education Board, established, as Raymond B. Fosdick remarks, "a rough framework within which the Foundation operated, with relatively few deviations, during subsequent years." Put into succinct language, his principles were: (1) that the Foundation should avoid individual charities; (2) that it should exclude purely local enterprises except those of a pilot nature; (3) that it should make its grants to any community or group in such fashion as to evoke community coöperation and generosity; (4) that it should assume no permanent share in the expenses of any institution or undertaking which it did not control; (5) that it should make no gifts hampered by narrow, long-term limitations; and (6) that it should give preference to objects which "go to the root of individual or social ill-being and misery."

Above all, of course, the Foundation was to be an agency for exploration and research, for guidance and advice, for stimulation and fertilization. It was to be a ferment in the world mass, not a pabulum. One fundamental fact regarding the use of Rockefeller's wealth must be as firmly grasped as he always grasped it. Huge as his fortune seemed, it was tiny in relation to the world's needs, especially in the decades of crisis following 1914. George E. Vincent, who shortly became president of the Foundation, pointed out in 1917 that although its endowment then had a book value of $120,000,000, its annual income would pay the correct expenses of the national government for only seven hours, and its principal for only five days. Had the Foundation tried to meet the whole bill for private charity in the United States, he estimated that its annual revenue would have carried the budget for but twelve and a half days. Obviously, the Foundation had in the main to be an institution of indirect assistance in meeting the world's problems; an agency of inquiry, inspiration, and leadership.

The first great grants were in the field of global health and medicine. As the General Education Board had pointed the way to the Southern States in this field, enabling them to carry forward an enduring work, so the Foundation would point the way to certain foreign lands. Dr. Rose's magnificent work for the elimination of the hookworm below the Potomac led the trustees at their first meeting to ask him to prepare a plan for similar activity abroad. The International Health Commission, under his directorship, was formed a month later. (In 1916 the "Commission" was changed to a "Board," and in 1927 to a "Division" of the Rockefeller Foundation.) It was to attack the hookworm in other lands, and to follow this campaign by the establishment of agencies to promote public sanitation and the knowledge of scientific medicine.

Because of their many friendships with missionaries, the Rockefellers had taken a keen interest in China. Jerome Greene and President Judson were equally interested, and at the first meeting of the directors both brought up the subject. Out of this grew an investigation of Chinese conditions, a conference in New York (1914) where medical missionaries were prominent, a plan by Gates for the development of a comprehensive system of medicine in China, and finally the establishment of the China Medical Board and the building of the Peking Union Medical College, which became the supreme beacon light of medical knowledge in the Orient. Both the battle against the hookworm and the activities of the Peking College were valuable not only in themselves, but as demonstrations of the possibilities of disease control in all retarded lands.

Other early grants were made to pioneering institutions in the United States and abroad—to the Bureau of Municipal Research, the Institute for Government Research, Wellesley College, the Palisades Interstate Park, and the American Academy in Rome, for example. The Foundation played a vigorous part in war-relief work in 1914–16. It explored the possibilities of pilot activity in the social and economic fields, finding by sad experience that some areas were too controversial to be touched. In 1914 Rockefeller and his son became involved in the labor troubles of the Colorado Fuel & Iron Company, an unprofitable company in which they held a forty per cent interest. Since Rockefeller, then almost seventy-five, had no active concern with the company, this story belongs to the biography of his son. In an effort to reach a just solution for the intricate labor problems which had resulted in the "Ludlow massacre" and other deplorable incidents, the trustees employed W. L. Mackenzie King, former Labor Minister of Canada, to become head (October 1, 1914) of a department of the Foundation to study industrial relations, Colorado being his first assignment. Nothing could have been better in intention. But much of the press and public proved suspicious of the Foundation's motives; the United States Commission on Industrial Relations, a body then studying labor problems under Senator Frank P. Walsh, began public hearings; and with some justice, honest citizens asked whether a proper line divided the Rockefellers' personal interests from those of the Rockefeller Foundation.

In the end, the motives and objects of the Foundation were vindicated. The elder Rockefeller, summoned before the Industrial Relations Commission, made an emphatic denial that the Foundation could or would abuse its wealth and powers. Let it go forward, he pleaded. "I have such confidence in democracy that I believe it can better be left to the people and their representatives to remedy the evils when there is some tangible reason for believing they are impending, rather than to restrict the power for service in anticipation of purely hypothetical dangers." But as the historian of the Foundation states, it learned from this episode that in all controversial fields it must step carefully. In general, in areas so explosive as labor relations it must act not by itself, but through outside agencies, properly staffed, which might use its funds, but would themselves accept all responsibility. Only in this way could it escape criticism and the projects which it undertook be lifted above suspicion.

The initial period of experiment and exploration in the Foundation's history ended in 1917, when the appointment of George E. Vincent as president opened a new era. Brilliant, magnetic, spirited, eloquent—"a genial and alert eagle"—Vincent had the true scholar's passion for quality and hatred of the second-rate; while his experience as university president had given him an ingrained love of system and harmony. Already Gates had fulminated against "the policy of scatteration." Vincent, with his support, saw to the adoption and prosecution of a more concentrated program, effort being focused in the main upon the advancement of public health and medical education throughout the world. Most of the Foundation's income in this second period was spent upon the International Health Commission and China

Medical Board, with a third agency created in 1919, the Division of Medical Education, renamed a decade later the Division of Medical Sciences. This period of concentrated global activity in medicine and health lasted until 1928. The constant aim of Vincent and the trustees was not to assume governmental or community functions in any of the lands entered, but to show that certain gains were possible, and then to turn the work over to the country or locality concerned.

In this period the Foundation built the Peking Union Medical College into what Dr. Abraham Flexner called "the Johns Hopkins of China," an institution which furnished Oriental leaders truly expert training in medicine and nursing. By 1952 the Foundation, indeed, had spent approximately $45,000,000 on medicine in China—the Communists then writing Finis. Meanwhile, in coöperation with the General Education Board, the Foundation carried forward Dr. Flexner's magnificent work in the elevation of American medical schools to a new plane of efficiency. One incident of this, the decision to help the University of Iowa establish a strong medical center at Iowa City, brought about a sharp disagreement between Flexner and Gates, who did not understand the propriety of helping state universities; and Gates in 1923, when he reached his seventy-first year, resigned as trustee. In a strict sense he was irreplaceable—but he had well trained his associates, and a new era needed new men.

Entering the foreign field, the Foundation made large grants for the improvement of medical instruction and research at the University College in London, to which it gave five millions in one sum, and in Edinburgh, Cardiff, Strasbourg, Lyon, Brussels, São Paulo, Beirut, and other places. Rockefeller was specially interested in a program of assistance to Canadian medical schools all the way from Dalhousie University in Halifax to the University of British Columbia. The Canadian people, he wrote in 1919, "are closely bound to us by ties of race, language, and international friendship, and they have without stint sacrificed themselves—their youth and their resources—to the end that democracy might be saved and extended." In this world-wide activity Drs. Richard M. Pearce, Alan Gregg, and William S. Carter were indefatigably busy, while Dr. Abraham Flexner constantly lent his wisdom and insight. A London newspaper

Rockefeller Memorial Chapel, University of Chicago,
dedicated in 1928.

Rockefeller Center in New York.

hailed the gift to University College in 1920 as "the finest moment we have known since the Armistice."

One undertaking in this era, the work of the International
Health Commission to stamp out yellow fever all over the globe,
had the stirring qualities of an epopee. Walter Reed and his
associates had demonstrated at the time of the Spanish War that
yellow fever was transmitted by mosquitoes, and General W. C.
Gorgas had substantially destroyed the disease in the Panama
Canal Zone. The Orient feared that after the opening of the
Panama Canal vessels from South America would spread the
fever all over the Far East. At the prompting of Dr. Wickliffe
Rose, the Foundation therefore established a yellow fever com
mission under Gorgas which, after an investigation of infected
areas in Latin-America, undertook a campaign of extermination.
In the midst of the battle, in 1920, Gorgas died while heading
an expedition to West Africa. For some years the work made
such impressive progress that complete success appeared at hand.
"The disease seems almost banished from the Western world,"
wrote President Vincent in 1927. Then a recurrence of South
American epidemics proved that the complexity of the problem
had been underestimated, and more laboratories, scientists, and
field workers had to be mobilized. Finally the New York laboratories of the Foundation developed an effective vaccine—and if
yellow fever has not been utterly conquered, it has been made a
controllable malady. Another little epic was written in the
Foundation's eradication of malaria from wide tropical areas.

With 1928 came a vigorous reorganization of the Rockefeller
boards. In this year Dr. Vincent and Dr. Rose retired from the
Foundation and the General Education Board; Dr. Buttrick,
the very heart and soul of the General Education Board, had
died in 1926; Gates was in retirement and would die in 1929.
The old personalities who had made the benefactions so impressive were passing from the scene. Apprehensions of troublesome
overlapping had developed. The Laura Spelman Rockefeller
Memorial Foundation, established in 1918 and endowed with
nearly $74,000,000, had under the direction of the fertile-minded
Beardsley Ruml done a remarkable work in supporting research
in the social studies, but was plainly ready for absorption into
the Foundation. Rockefeller, his thinking still shaped by his
business years, believed in consolidation as a means toward effi-

ciency. Looking back over his benefactions, he had written his son on May 4, 1926: "If the whole thing were to be done today, you have rightly understood me as feeling that it should be done and doubtless could be done through a single organization."

For a time a complete merger was brought under study. This proved impracticable for certain technical reasons. It was decided, however, that those activities of all four Rockefeller boards which bore upon *the advancement of human knowledge* should be centered in the Foundation. The Spelman Memorial was consolidated with the Foundation; the International Education Board was dissolved; and while the General Education Board still remained active in a few fields, the Foundation after 1928 annexed many of its provinces. It thus took responsibility for a greatly enlarged range of undertakings, large and small, national and international.

The question whether this consolidation was not carried too far has remained a point of debate. Defenders of the change assert that the Foundation thereafter enjoyed a better coördination of activities, a firmer handling of policy, and the ability to make quicker shifts in strategy. A small number of conscientious critics, however, declare that it was a mistake to deprive the General Educational Board of its ability to treat medical education and college and university development as wholes, that flexibility was replaced by rigidity, and that in the course of the changes "a tradition which can never be restored or mended was entirely destroyed." For good or ill, since 1928 the process of unification has been carried forward step by step. The Foundation and the General Education Board, possessing the same higher executives and trustees, have long been managed almost as one. The scope of the Foundation's activities and the extent of its influence have steadily increased.

Rockefeller's last gift to the Foundation was made in 1927. He had then granted it a total of $182,851,480.90; and the absorption of the Spelman Memorial brought the total endowment to $244,608,359.74. Wise investment policies not only conserved but augmented these resources. But it had long been Rockefeller's intention that the whole sum, principal and interest, should be spent within a few generations at the utmost. He had no sympathy with those who created foundations for perpetuity; "perpetuity is a long time," he had sagely remarked.

Like the General Education Board, the Foundation was fortunate (with some conspicuous exceptions) in its principal officers. It enlisted a number of men of high organizing and administrative ability. In the roster must always be placed John D. Rockefeller, Jr., who as chairman of the trustees labored indefatigably, and with sagacity, conscientiousness, and public spirit, until his retirement in 1940. He immersed himself in the work of this and the other agencies, always keeping in touch with their activities; other officers came and went, but his experience and self-sacrificing zeal gave continuity and steady direction to the labors of the Foundation throughout its first quarter-century. Wickliffe Rose deserves to be remembered among the true statesmen of philanthropy in America. This cultivated, courtly Southerner, versed in the Latin and Greek classics as in modern literature, deeply read in philosophy, gentle of spirit, tenacious in purpose, had depth as well as breadth of mind. He was nothing if not original. He saw far beneath the surface of contemporaneous trends; his ideas had often a touch of profundity. Among the early trustees Gates, Buttrick, and Simon Flexner possessed qualities to which no brief history can do justice. Jerome D. Greene did a valuable work in the Foundation's first years by able speeches in various parts of the country which helped to dissipate the prejudice against it; and his brother Roger was also valuable as resident director of the China Medical Board. George E. Vincent gave sagacious guidance to the Foundation for more than a decade. His ripe cultivation, breadth of view, unfailing tact and charm, witty vigor as a public speaker, and administrative experience, combined to make him an ideal head.

In any full history of the Rockefeller benefactions, a place of special distinction will be reserved for Raymond B. Fosdick. An attorney who first achieved notice as commissioner of accounts (an investigative post) in New York City, he spent 1913 in Europe studying police organization as a representative of the Rockefeller Bureau of Social Hygiene. Varied service in important public posts followed. For a time he was Under Secretary-General of the League of Nations. He became a trustee, one of the most active and resourceful, of all the important Rockefeller philanthropies—the Institute for Medical Research, the General Education Board, the Spelman Fund, and the Rockefeller Foundation. When Max Mason resigned in 1936, he was the logical choice for president of the Foundation. Under his energetic guidance the General Education Board moved toward the termination of its activities, while the Foundation carried forward its many-sided work.

For many years the Rockefeller offices, the Institute for Medical Research, the General Education Board, and to some extent the Johns Hopkins Medical School and Hospital, constituted one great family, bound together by the congeniality and common purpose of their heads. In a sense Raymond Fosdick became chief liaison officer, for he had leisure to move from office to office, the confidence not only of the Rockefellers but of such other philanthropists as Julius Rosenwald and George Eastman, and a remarkable faculty for taking ideas from any source and developing them to usefulness. Gates was an indefatigable energizer; Jerome Greene supplied numerous fruitful suggestions— his memoranda on the necessity for raising college teachers' salaries, and on the humanities as a proper field for philanthropy were specially notable; Murphy worked in perfect harmony with such different men as Rose and Vincent. It was Buttrick, however, whose versatility most impressed his associates. "Of all the unconventional things that Mr. Gates did," declares Abraham Flexner, "the most daring was the selection of Dr. Buttrick as first head of the General Education Board. He was equal to any demand, however, no matter how complex and how remote from his previous experience. There has been no other Dr. Buttrick in philanthropy since he passed from the stage." The elder Rockefeller, always ready to encourage, never interfered. Dr. Simon Flexner, for example, often visited him in Florida and the northern homes; but Rockefeller never talked with him about the problems of the Institute, for he wished Flexner to feel perfect freedom.

The comradeship of the various agencies and their officers contributed to the effectiveness as well as the happiness of their activities. Buttrick wrote Gates on April 1, 1902, on the twentieth anniversary of the founding of the General Education Board: "What a good time we have had working together all these years." And, writing to Buttrick on October 23, 1923, Gates remarked: "For 45 years you and I have been close friends—for over 30 years most intimate, confidential friends—engaged together in exacting, stupendous enterprise pregnant with measureless destinies, and there has never been a break between us. . . . We were built to work together just as we have, and surely it was a divine Providence that placed us side by side."

Looking back over the history of both the Foundation and the Board, students can see some changes of direction which might be interpreted as virtual admission of error in judgment. Money has now and then been wasted. A few unwise appointments to office have been made; friction has occasionally developed in internal management. All foundations have been criticized, and often with justice, for a tendency toward the development of inertia, insulation, and conservatism, so that they become stiffly bureaucratic and timidly cautious; criticized, too, for spending too much on "surveys" and too little on active work. The organizations created by Rockefeller have shared in this criticism, though little in their history thus far justifies it. They have also been brought to question, with more justice, for an excessive dispersion and fragmentation of activities and for a relative neglect of the humanities.

One reproach long leveled against the Rockefeller Foundation was that "potentially if not actually" it was dominated by the founder and his son. At first there was ground for this criticism; when the Walsh investigation took place only two of the trustees were not either on the Rockefeller payroll or in the "official family." But the elder Rockefeller and Gates resigned from the board in 1923; death and resignation had previously removed three others closely associated with the donor. There then remained but a few, like Buttrick, Rose, and Simon Flexner, who had long been entirely devoted to Rockefeller organizations. Mr. Fosdick has said emphatically that even if that group, of which he was one, had ever voted as a bloc (which on controversial matters it did not) it would have been outnumbered by the nine other trustees, among whom were such notably independent men as Charles Evans Hughes, John G. Agar, Martin Ryerson, and Ray Lyman Wilbur. Perhaps the existence of a group of "Rockefeller men" on the executive committee gave rise to doubt whether that powerful body was not, like the finance committee, dominated by the official family; but Mr. Fosdick points out that the frequent difficulties of getting a quorum were responsible for any occasional appearance of official domination of the committee.

Yet even if valid, the criticism had little weight. For if the younger Rockefeller had the power to dominate, he never exercised it. "Time and again," writes one observer, "Mr. Rockefeller, Jr., has been outvoted on the boards of his father's donations." His colleagues give striking instances of this; for he always insisted that they treat him precisely as they treated each other, and some of them took President Harper's pride in dissent. Moreover, as a sharp critic of foundations remarks, the younger Rockefeller was "a man of such catholic and impersonal interests and of such statesmanlike qualities" that his influence always proved strongly beneficial.

Upon this subject Mr. Rockefeller, Jr., has made a frank statement to the author. "The philanthropic boards which my father established," he writes, "usually began in a small way and developed gradually. Since they were the immediate outgrowth of his own personal philanthropies it was only natural that, generally speaking, they should have been manned at the outset by members of our 'official family' and those with whom we had been working along similar lines. However, as rapidly as capable and interested men were found outside this group they were added to the boards, in which members of the 'official family' gradually and properly became a minority." He adds that this principle has also pertained to the committees of the boards, except that he has been chairman of several of the Finance Committees. This was largely because he had means of knowing more than other trustees about the companies in the securities of which the original gifts had been made. "As my father's son, and his representative most closely related to the development of these boards; as a trustee for the longest period of time, I have naturally and properly felt a peculiar responsibility to the founder for the wise use of the large sums of money he gave to the boards. It is significant that with at least some of the officers and directors my interest in a project has been more apt to prejudice its favorable consideration than to forward it, so wholly independent of the founder and his so-called 'official family' have they been."

Another early criticism of some Rockefeller gifts, as of other foundations, was that the conditions imposed were unduly rigid. This, too, had some validity. But the trust instrument of the Rockefeller Foundation itself was so liberal that many attacked it for excessive breadth, and Rockefeller's letters of 1920 did much to nullify restrictions that experience had proved to be unwise. The Rockefeller funds have a really impressive record for work on what John Dewey calls "the growing edge of things." The Medical Institute has kept a pioneering spirit. The General

Education Board has exercised a highly progressive influence on primary and secondary education, and has made grants for experimental college programs: to Sarah Lawrence, Bennington, Swarthmore, the General College of the University of Minnesota, and so on. It has helped to broaden legal education as well as to raise the standard of medical education. All around the world the Rockefeller Foundation has been a great pioneering agency in health and medicine.

No doubt foundations are in many respects "status quo" agencies. Beyond question their heads prefer to avoid controversy—though the Laura Spelman Rockefeller Memorial in 1924 laid down twelve principles to guide foundations in controversial fields, and they have been used by all the Rockefeller trusts and many other foundations. Holes may be picked in foundation programs, and fault found, as Harold J. Laski and E. C. Lindeman have shown, with trustees and officers. But the Rockefeller agencies have amply justified themselves. They have undertaken much-needed labors in fields which no existing agency, governmental or private, would have entered. They have blazed trails in many directions; they have set on their feet projects which others have then carried forward; they have added immeasurably to the resources of health, economic well-being, and culture in an ill-ordered world.

And few critics, no matter how much they dislike the principle of the private funding of wealth for the general welfare, have ever denied that the Rockefeller benefactions have been created in an enlightened spirit. Setting aside the debate on the principle, it must be admitted that the distribution of the fortune has been admirably accomplished. Rockefeller always dealt with his wealth in humility, not in arrogance. He never used it to minister to his vanity or power. Regarding it objectively, he never let personal predilections impair the wisdom of its employment. He applied careful planning to the principles that should guide his giving; but once the money was given, he took the view that it was no longer his own. Unlike Carnegie, he did not appoint personal favorites to trusteeships. Unlike Leland Stanford, Jonas Clark, and many another, he never meddled with the men in control. Unlike James B. Duke, he never for a moment mingled private commercial interests with philanthropic acts. His attitude was ideal, and it permitted the placing of his philanthropies on the highest plane. The American people, as we have said, felt little if any gratitude to Rockefeller for the distribution of a fortune which was largely an historical accident. But reflecting citizens have properly felt a warm gratitude to him and his son for the care, wisdom, unselfishness, and public spirit with which the distribution has been made.

For the purse was opened wide. During his lifetime Rockefeller devoted to public uses approximately five hundred and fifty million dollars, while most of the remainder was made over to the son for a continuance of the work. The fortune has long since ceased to be one of the greatest American accumulations. Though information as to its size is withheld, it is still shrinking. According to Gates, Rockefeller took a warm and constant pleasure in his philanthropic activities. It delighted him to give, and delighted him still more to hear about the results of his giving. He was entitled to take a deep satisfaction in the thought that he was an agent in doing so much good: in helping to heal the sick, to raise the standard of life, to enlarge the frontiers of science, and to enrich the human mind.

# CHAPTER XVII

# TRIAL BALANCE

O N THE whole, Rockefeller's long years of retirement were placid and happy. While keeping healthfully busy, he never allowed himself to become overburdened. He cultivated the equanimity and serenity which he had inherited from his mother; and he tried to plan his life as he had once planned an industry and later his benefactions. The inevitable bereavements of old age—the death of Mrs. Rockefeller in 1915, and the passing of Flagler in 1913, of William Rockefeller in 1922, and of Gates in 1929—he accepted with manifest grief, but with resignation. He was a living contradiction of Cato's remark: "All want to attain old age, and all grumble when they get it."

Early in the century stories had been widely circulated that he lived in constant apprehension of attack. The fact was that Rockefeller never showed any apprehension of violence and often made his friends uneasy by his constant disregard of that possibility. He never had a bodyguard. While in earlier days he had kept a revolver at his Euclid Avenue house, he never fired it once. At church in New York and Cleveland the ushers took care to place anybody who acted like a crank where they could watch him, but no other precautions were taken. The idea that Rockefeller lived in fear was absurd.

And equally absurd were the stories about his digestion. Except for a time in the early eighteen-nineties, it remained excellent. If he ate bread and milk, it was because he had always been fond of that dish. He never lost his teeth. To the end of his life they, like his eyes and his hearing, were excellent, and in his last year, at ninety-eight, he was allowed a varied menu, including poultry of all kinds, fish, lamb, and a variety of vegetables. Intellectually he showed few tokens of senility; his memory was acute, he told humorous stories with his oldtime gusto, and he retained his interest in public affairs.

Rockefeller was never quite a billionaire. Shortly after the dissolution, one of the year-end inventories of his fortune showed that it amounted to $815,647,796.89. Probably when the stock market was highest before the recession of 1913 it would have totaled about $900,000,000. As he had believed in constant expansion in business, so now he believed in an ever-expanding philanthropy; there must be no halt, no suspension of effort and enterprise, until most of his wealth was gone.

The investment of the fortune was given circumspect care. Rockefeller had organized a small group which managed it under his direction somewhat as the best investment-trusts are managed today. The executive expenses were never as high as are those of investment-trusts of similar magnitude, and the results compared favorably with the efforts of these bodies. Most of the fortune remained in Standard Oil securities. A part of the fortune, particularly after the issuance of the Liberty Loans, was always in United States bonds. Another small part Rockefeller kept in cash and liquid Wall Street loans, using it to seize investment opportunities when the stock market was low, and to assist financial institutions in time of national distress. The remainder of his estate was placed in widely diversified investments. No attempt was ever made to dominate any one investment field; Rockefeller remained to the last essentially an industrialist, and refused to become a manipulator.

Throughout the final decades his pride and confidence in his son were the principal element in his contentment. Relations between some of the personal agents employed by the two men were not devoid of jealousy and friction; one of Rockefeller's secretaries became a sharp critic of several of the son's aides. But never the slightest shadow marred the mutual trust and affection of the two men. Whenever Rockefeller spoke of "Mr. John," a note of happiness came into his voice.

It pleased Rockefeller to see his grandchildren carefully reared, and he often emphasized the importance of this in his letters. For example, in 1909 he wrote his son: "I know that you and Abby will be careful to educate the children in financial matters as we sought to educate you, that they may understand the value of money and make the very best use of it." The younger Rockefeller and his wife brought up their five boys and one girl in exemplary fashion. "I say to them with perfect frankness," Mr. Rockefeller, Jr., once remarked, "that wealth will go only to those of them who show fitness and ability to handle it wisely; that neither their father nor grandfather will leave them money unless they give evidence that they know how to lead decent, useful lives and that they will make good use of any property." Alta's children were trained with equal circumspection. Edith was the temperamental and erratic member of the family. Though Rockefeller disapproved strongly of some of her acts and wrote her several sorrowfully reproachful letters, he was very fond of her, her husband and her children. Harold McCormick, gay, hearty, and spontaneous, swept all barriers away whenever he came to pay a visit, and was a great favorite with every one. It is recorded that he was the only man who could march into Mrs. Rockefeller's room and unconcernedly light and puff a cigarette there—for she disliked smoking. The son Fowler McCormick became an equal favorite, and when he passed through stormy waters Rockefeller made his loyal affection for the young man extremely plain.

But it was "Mr. John" upon whom Rockefeller always leaned most strongly, and who was the special stay and comfort of his declining years. "What a providence," he wrote the son in 1918, "that your life should have been spared to take up the responsibilities as I lay them down! I could not have anticipated in the earlier years that they would have been so great, nor could I have dreamed that you would have come so promptly and satisfactorily to meet them, and to go beyond, in the contemplation of our right attitude to the world in the discharge of these obligations." And he continued, with a display of feeling rare in either his letters or speech: "I appreciate, I am grateful, beyond all I can tell you. There is much for you to accomplish in the future. Do not allow yourself to be overburdened with details. Others must look to these. We will plan and work together. I want to stay a long time to help do my part. I hope you will take good care of your health. This is a religious duty, and you can accomplish so much more for the world if you keep well and strong."

In all the varied activities of his son after the First World War Rockefeller took the keenest interest; but it was an entirely passive interest except when his help was especially requested. He did lend active assistance when his son espoused the cause of the liberal element in the Baptist Church, as against the Fundamentalists. Dr. Woelfkin and both Raymond B. and Harry Emerson Fosdick were, of course, highly liberal in outlook. They grew alarmed in 1920–21 lest the Fundamentalists, who, as Raymond B. Fosdick wrote, "are thinking in terms of the Middle Ages," should gain control. When the Northern Baptist Convention in 1921 voted in favor of accepting a gift of about one and a half millions which had been offered with a proviso that it should be used only for ministers and missionaries holding the Fundamentalist creed, the younger Rockefeller protested vigorously. He thought it deplorable that the church should eagerly grasp a donation which thus limited freedom of faith and of thought within its ranks. The elder Rockefeller agreed with him, and at once took steps to make sure that if the Fundamentalists did gain an ascendancy, they could not lay hands on any of the Rockefeller donations. This attitude contributed to the maintenance of the liberal tradition of the Baptist Church. In these same years Rockefeller abetted the leading part his son took in the Interchurch World Movement, and followed with interest his speeches during the campaign of 1920 to raise $330,000,000 for all the Protestant denominations.

The aged magnate also supported his son in the heated contest of 1928–29 to eject Colonel Robert W. Stewart from the chairmanship of the board of the Standard of Indiana. This was a sequel to the shocking oil scandals of the Harding Administration which had involved Albert B. Fall, E. L. Doheny, and Harry Sinclair. It appeared that a sum of $300,000 which Sinclair had paid to Secretary Fall had been derived from the receipts of a mysterious Canadian company called the Continental Trading Corporation. Sinclair and Stewart, who had been connected with it, declined to explain its funds. Sinclair was sent to jail for contempt. Senator Nye sent the record of Stewart's testimony before the Senate investigative committee to the younger Rockefeller, and, with strong press support, appealed to him to take some action. On May 9, 1928, after an investigation of his own, Mr. Rockefeller, Jr., made public a letter requesting the resignation of Colonel Stewart. But Stewart prepared to fight for his place; and the following January he formally announced his candidacy, while President Seubert and various directors of the company gave him their support. A fierce fight for proxies was already raging.

To strengthen his son's committee, Rockefeller on January 30, 1929, publicly commended his fight against Stewart and called on the colonel to resign. Despite the fact that the family had only a small interest in the company, the younger Rockefeller, with the aid of his counsel Thomas M. Debevoise, the banker Winthrop W. Aldrich, and others, obtained a two-thirds majority of the proxies. In this process the prestige of the elder Rockefeller was all-important. Charles M. Higgins, for example, one of the largest stockholders, had long been a warm friend of Stewart; but because of his loyalty to Rockefeller he unhesitatingly placed his large block of stock at the son's disposal. On March 7, 1929, Stewart was ignominiously ousted—a notable victory for sound ethics in business.

From 1920 onwards Rockefeller was an appreciative watcher of the long list of benevolent activities which made his son one of the most useful citizens of the country. The principal items in this roster are widely familiar. The gift of two millions to the Cité Universitaire in France; the restoration of Rheims Cathedral, and the repair of the palaces at Versailles and Fontainebleau; the grant of $500,000 for the Shakespeare Memorial Theatre at Stratford-on-Avon; the gift of $4,000,000, including land, to the United States for Acadia National Park; the donation of $500,000 for Jewish farm development in Russia; special aids to Lincoln School, the Ethical Culture School, and a long list of colleges; the expenditure of $2,360,000 for building and maintaining International House at Columbia; the building of similar houses at California and Chicago; the grant of $600,000 for the improvement of Rockefeller Hall at Brown University with the stipulation that it be renamed W. H. P. Faunce Hall; the conveyance of fifty-four acres of land to New York City in 1930 for one of its most beautiful parks, with additional gifts later; the offer to the nation of 30,000 acres in the Jackson's Hole area in Wyoming; the assistance given to the creation of Palisades Interstate Park, with its beautiful cliff scenery; the transfer to public ownership of The Cloisters and George Gray Barnard's collections therein; gifts of $3,500,000 to the New York Public Library and $2,500,000 to the Hampton and Tuskegee Institutes; a donation of $1,540,000 toward restoring the Imperial University of Tokyo, ruined by fire; the establishment with an endowment of $21,000,000 of the International Education Board, devoted especially to all forms of science; and that splendid historical enterprise, the restoration of Williamsburg, at a cost of about $50,000,000, to its appearance in old colonial days—these are but the principal benefactions.

Nor should we omit mention of an enterprise partly commercial in character, though it had its inception in a desire to aid the Metropolitan Opera—the building of Rockefeller Center in midtown Manhattan on the neglected site of the Elgin Gardens, given generations earlier by Dr. David Hosack to Columbia University. Twelve acres in area, this "city within a city" represents an investment of more than $100,000,000; and it has benefited alike the university, the municipal treasury, and the city's appearance.

The benefactions have been invariably credited to the older Rockefeller by his son. The son laid the plans and made the decisions; the father's accumulations supplied the money. These labors represented a remarkable association, the spirit of which was finely expressed by the son in the letter which he wrote his father on July 7, 1933, just before the latter's ninety-fourth birthday:

I have tried to do what I thought you would have me do. I have striven to follow in your footsteps. I have endeavored to use wisely and unselfishly the means that you have so unselfishly placed at my disposal. . . . In all these years of effort and striving, your own life and example have ever been to me the most powerful and stimulating influence. What you have done for humanity and business on a vast scale has impressed me profoundly. To have been a silent partner with you in carrying out these great constructive purposes and benefactions has been the supreme delight of my life.

On Sunday morning, May 23, 1937, at 4:05 o'clock, Rockefeller died at "The Casements," his Florida estate near Ormond. The cause of death was sclerotic myocarditis, or hardening of the heart muscles. His health had been good to the last, though he tired easily and had to be given constant attendance. Just before he died he was displaying a keen interest in plans for some remodeling at "The Casements."

He left a net estate of $26,410,837, of which $16,630,000 was taken by federal and state taxes. About two-thirds of the estate was in United States Treasury notes. At death he owned only one share in a Standard Oil Company—a share of Standard of California common, which he had retained for sentimental reasons because it was Certificate No. 1. Most of the property which he had not given to the various philanthropies had passed to his son and to other heirs long before his death. It may be noted that his probated estate exceeded very slightly that of $23,247,161 left by his rival in wealth and philanthropy, Andrew Carnegie.

Rockefeller was at peace, his hand stilled. But on May 26, the day of his burial at Pocantico, thousands of students poured into the classrooms and libraries of the University of Chicago. Scores of scientists toiled in the finely-equipped laboratories of the Medical Institute above the East River, peering through microscopes or busy with test-tubes. Throughout China graduates of the Peking Union Medical College were struggling to give health and life to areas where disease had walked unchecked. Over vast districts of Africa, Asia, and South America experts were trying to stamp out the last vestiges of yellow fever, and to imprison the dread forces of malaria. In our Southern States men were busy building on the firm basis laid by the General Education Board when it had helped to revitalize agriculture, and by the Rockefeller Foundation when it had led in destroying hookworm disease. Hundreds of thousands of students that day were using facilities provided by the Board or the Foundation. Around the globe, Rockefeller's benefactions were training physicians, stimulating research in psychiatry, ameliorating the hardships of persecuted men in totalitarian lands, aiding field work in archaeology, astronomy, and biology, and helping to support economic institutions. Through a thousand channels the beneficent activities which his money had helped to create were pushing forward and widening the boundaries of civilization. The work he had done lived after him.

It was a massive and stirring chapter of American history which was written by McCormick, Carnegie, Morgan, Duke, Armour, James J. Hill, Harriman, and the other towering figures of industry and commerce in the late nineteenth century; and reasons exist for placing Rockefeller, the richest, the longest-lived, the most attacked, and the most famous, at the head of the group. No other, not even Carnegie, gained such a double preeminence: foremost in business, foremost in philanthropy, in his era.

All observers must be struck, in studying his career, by his single-mindedness; his sharpness of insight; his cool disdain of emotional factors; his instinct for the future—that ability to "see around the corner" which Archbold lauded; his breadth of ambition; and his skill (which to opponents sometimes seemed merciless) in finding novel weapons to attain his ends—his strategic ingenuity, in short.

In the omnipresent business warfare Rockefeller fought after his own fashion, which was that of a cool, subtle strategist, relentlessly intent on his goals. Deeply shocked by his early experience with the chaos of the oil industry, disillusioned by his contacts with the irrepressibly speculative producers, convinced that much law-making on industry fitted only a bygone age, he resolved to organize the refining industry to furnish stability, economy, solvency, and if possible high profits. He would form an alliance of the chief companies, who would impose a centralized control. When the trial failed, young Rockefeller turned to the building of a refiners' combination so complete that it would possess a virtual monopoly, and to the creation of a central direction so trusted and efficient that he could be sure of compliance with his and his associates' policies.

Monopoly was and is a hateful thing. Rockefeller's aim, when pushed to almost complete monopoly, was and is repugnant to believers in social and economic freedom and was certain to involve him in opprobrium. We must be sufficiently objective, however, to keep in mind a basic fact: that in industry after industry at this time the chaos and cruelty of over-competition bred a resort to monopoly as the natural cure. To every element in the oil industry by 1870—transport interests, producing interests, refining interests, marketing interests—the excesses of competition seemed absolutely insufferable; they caused constant confusion, turmoil, loss, and bankruptcy; the little men and the big alike were harried by anxiety, tortured by peril, and not infrequently crushed. His Trust, and dozens of the other trusts which sprang up between 1870 and 1900, were not primarily an expression of Lawless Mammonism. They were primarily a spasmodic, inevitable response to the uncertainties, wastes, and cruelties of unbridled competition.

Rockefeller had perfectly understood that demand must be continuously maintained at high level if the refineries were to operate continuously at anything like capacity. He had therefore taken efficient steps to construct a complex marketing organization, and to maintain customer demand by recognized trade names and high standards of service.

The oil business was thus vertically integrated from the well-head to the consumers of the multiple oil products; mass production of raw materials, mass manufacturing, and mass distribution were meshed in a mechanism of unexampled power and efficiency. Under Rockefeller, integration had taken place downward from manufacturing and marketing to crude oil production; later, when powerful new oil companies arose, it was usually to take place upward from production to distribution. But the vital fact is that Rockefeller and his group saw the importance of vertical integration when it was still a novelty in business; they set a pattern which was quickly followed by Duke in tobacco, and by other leaders, and which in time became a norm for much of American industry. This was constructive pioneering of a high quality.

It is obvious that a great part of Rockefeller's success first in business and then in philanthropy is to be credited not to his personal efforts, but to the extraordinarily able and devoted groups of associates who labored with him. In business, Flagler, Harkness, Payne, H. H. Rogers, Charles and Charles M. Pratt, Archbold, Warden, Lockhart, the Bedfords, McGregor, Folger, and by no means least, William Rockefeller, were but the more outstanding men in a staff which, we may repeat, was perhaps the most brilliant that American business has yet known. Yet strong as it was, it was not more remarkable than the group which helped Rockefeller disburse his fortune in ways beneficial to mankind: Frederick T. Gates, Simon and Abraham Flexner, Wallace Buttrick, Drs. Herter, Prudden, and Biggs, Seaman A. Knapp, William H. Baldwin, George E. Vincent, Jerome Greene, Raymond B. Fosdick, and perhaps above all his son, John D. Rockefeller, Jr., who in time became one of the most respected of all Americans. In the history of philanthropic planning and administration that group, too, would be difficult indeed to match. Writing in the *Random Reminiscences* of the Standard Oil combination, Rockefeller remarked that its starting-point was "not so much the consolidation of the firms in which we had a personal interest, but the coming together of the men who had the combined brainpower to do the work." Much that was credited to him individually was really the result of "combined brainpower."

In giving full credit to the talents and energies of these two groups, however, we little diminish the stature of Rockefeller himself. Men of preëminent capacity do not place themselves under the guidance of a bungler or weakling; strength is attracted to strength, and when we find a full-panoplied staff harmoniously at work, we may be sure that in the background stands some powerful figure. It is significant that, ruggedly powerful as Rockefeller's chief associates in business were, they never challenged his primacy; that, quarrelsome as some of them were, nobody ever quarreled with *him*. It is significant also that his associates in philanthropy, men far better educated than he was, never once complained of a major decision of his, and never once had to reproach him for meddlesomeness after a grant was made.

That the debit side of the ledger has a heavy account is undeniable. The combination of which Rockefeller was captain was one of the most hard-hitting entities in a hard-hitting business world. Its methods were often as questionable as its central aim of monopoly. It made small competitors, as we have noted, "sick," it forced them to "sweat," it stifled them without compunction. It used, like nearly every other concern that could do so, the rebate. For a time it took not merely rebates but a drawback payment secretly exacted from competitors by the railroads, as cruel a device as business history records. Though the period in which this drawback was pocketed was short, it left an ineffaceable stain on the history of the Trust. Like various competitors in the oil business, but more systematically and effectively, the Standard resorted to espionage. With a duplicity that all must find repugnant, it sometimes employed dummy companies. It often "cut to kill," as Miss Tarbell wrote, reducing prices in a given locality until competition was destroyed, and then restoring high charges. That it drew excessive profits from the oil consumers is proved by the size of the fortunes which its heads accumulated. All this, and the long battle with state and Federal opponents of monopoly, entailed forty years of obloquy, most of it visited on Rockefeller's head.

All the while Rockefeller remained a fervent Christian, unhesitant in his devotion to the church and its ethical principles. How, some critics asked, could he play such a double role? The answer is that to him it did not appear a double role. From a chaotic industry he was building an efficient industrial empire for what seemed to him the good not only of its heads but of the general public. If he relaxed his general methods of warfare (he was not blamable for some extreme acts of Carley, Pierce, and O'Day) a multitude of small competitors would smash his empire and plunge the oil business back to chaos. He always believed in what William McKinley called "benevolent assimilation"; he preferred to buy out rivals on decent terms, and to employ the ablest competitors as helpers. It was when his terms were refused that he ruthlessly crushed the "outsiders." And he did so because, as John T. Flynn writes, "he had that quality of the great commander engaged on large enterprises of surveying the necessities of his task with high intelligence, and appraising the suffering of his victims in its proper proportion to the scene." It seemed to him better that a limited number of small businesses should die than that the whole industry should go through a constant process of half-dying, reviving, and again half-dying.

Obviously, any comprehensive judgment on Rockefeller's business career must be subjective and dependent on the economic assumptions brought to the judgment-bar. Did the deadweight the Standard Oil hung upon business ethics (for though it would be hard to prove that it depressed the current code, it certainly did nothing to raise it) outweigh the great constructive innovations of the combination, and the example set by its efficiency and order? Were the exterminative ravages of the Standard among its rivals greater than the exterminative ravages of over-competition before it rose to power? These are but two of the many questions whose answer depends upon variable assumptions. One fact, however, is certain: that the oldtime black-and-white antithesis between monopoly and "perfect competition" is as dead as the view that industrial concentration can or should be destroyed. Imperfect competition is the rule in modern industrialized nations; the best competition is that which Joseph A. Schumpeter called the Process of Creative Destruction, an industrial mutation which "incessantly revolutionizes the industrial structure from within, incessantly destroying the old one and incessantly creating a new one." Both the Standard's type of monopoly, and the types of oligopoly exposed by the Temporary National Economic Commission inquiry, are in the long run intolerable; but they are not so intolerable as the "perfect competition" contemplated by the makers of the Sherman Act would be.

Once the fortune was acquired, Rockefeller's use of it was in most respects exemplary; he was as great an innovator and organizer in philanthropy as he had been in business. The unexampled scale of his gifts, running to some $550,000,000, was not their most striking feature. What made them arresting was the skill with which he and his experts planned them. The various foundations which he, his son, and their aides set up, governed by able men working in almost complete independence, became models for large-scale philanthropy in America and other lands. Their objects, administrative mechanisms, methods, and spirit, have been widely copied. Foundations had existed long before, but not any like these. Some of their principles, moreover, had stamped his thoughtful, conscientious giving from the days when he was comparatively poor. His emphasis on ameliorative work at the sources of misery or evil, his use of money to stimulate self-help and giving by others, and his desire to establish continuing activities, remained fundamental in his distribution of the fortune.

The size of that fortune, as we have said, was an historical accident. In no true sense of the word did he, Carnegie, and Henry Ford earn the huge accumulations which came to them. Only the special economic, legal, and fiscal situation of the United States 1865–1917 rendered it possible to make and keep so much money. Recognizing this fact, Rockefeller always regarded himself as a trustee rather than an owner. His statement at the University of Chicago that "God gave me money," sometimes quoted as a piece of sanctimonious arrogance, was actually uttered in a spirit of complete humility. He devoutly believed that Providence had made him a trustee for these hundreds of millions, not to be kept but to be wisely disbursed. He meant to see that the gold was used to do the utmost possible good. It is for the meticulous care, the administrative ability, and the general sagacity which he and his staff applied to the laborious work of distribution that gratitude is really due them.

And though the United States has resolved that such aggregations of wealth shall henceforth be regarded as unjust, antisocial, and dangerous, in this instance fate did not serve the nation ill. The fortune fell into the hands of a man who even as a youth earning a few dollars a week, his necessities poorly met, had given a substantial part of his meagre wage to charity. Few indeed are those who make the sacrifices recorded in Ledger A. He had given from the outset without regard to religion, race, party, or section; he had increased his giving as his means grew.

We may well decide, in our final view, that the extremes of

praise and blame heaped upon Rockefeller were both unwarranted. His enemies during his years of power abused him as one of the arch-criminals of the age; his admirers during his later years of philanthropy lauded him as one of the world's chief benefactors. Neither estimate possessed historical truth. We may well decide also that, viewed critically, he was not a very attractive personage. Much as his intimates admired him, to the world at large he seemed—and seems—deficient in humanly likable qualities. But that he was one of the most powerful leaders of his time there can be no doubt. Innovator, thinker, planner, bold entrepreneur, he was above all an organizer—one of the master organizers of the era. Taking the most confused, muddled, and anarchic of American industries, he organized it with a completeness, efficiency, and constructive talent that amazed beholders and affected all business activities. Turning to the vague field of philanthropy, he organized a series of undertakings that became models for all givers who followed him. By virtue of this organizing power, backed by keenness of mind, tenacity of purpose, and firmness of character, he looms up as one of the most impressive figures of the century which his lifetime spanned.

# INDEX